D1526845

Gentleman of the Press

Julian Ralph, taken about 1893

Gentleman of the Press

The Life and Times of an Early Reporter, Julian Ralph of the *Sun*

Paul Lancaster

Syracuse University Press

Portions of Chapter 9 appeared in substantially the same form in an
article by the author in the October/November 1982 issue of *American
Heritage*.

The paper used in this publication meets the minimum requirements of
American National Standard for Information Sciences—Permanence of
Paper for Printed Library Materials, ANSI Z39.48-1984. ∞

Library of Congress Cataloging-in-Publication Data
Lancaster, Paul.
    Gentleman of the press : the life and times of an early reporter,
Julian Ralph, of the Sun / Paul Lancaster. — 1st ed.
        p.   cm.
    Includes bibliographical references and index.
    ISBN 0-8156-2552-9
    1. Ralph, Julian, 1853–1903—Biography.   2. Authors,
American—19th century—Biography.   3. Journalists—United
States—Biography.   I. Title.
PS2673.R15Z75   1992
070'.92—dc 20
    [B]   91-17818

Manufactured in the United States of America

"To write news in its perfection requires such a combination of qualities, that a man completely fitted for the task is not always to be found."

Samuel Johnson, *The Idler*, 1758

For Susan

Paul Lancaster spent sixteen years with the *Wall Street Journal* as a reporter and editor, including several as front-page editor. He has written historical articles on journalism and other subjects for *American Heritage*. He lives in Old Greenwich, Connecticut.

Contents

Illustrations

Preface

I spent four years as a newspaper reporter. I found the work hard—days filled with rebuffs and unreturned telephone calls—and, despite the occasional small reporting triumphs, I was relieved when I became an editor. I had always suspected it was easier to be an editor than a reporter, and it was. In less than a minute an editor can dream up an assignment that will keep a reporter scrambling for days on end—and then it may turn out that the assignment was a dumb idea and impossible to fulfill. An editor's lot is more comfortable than a reporter's in other ways, too. One day during the Vietnam war a full-fledged riot broke out on the street below the newsroom where I worked as an editor. Construction workers wielding clubs rampaged through a gathering of antiwar protesters. A fellow editor summoned two reporters and told them to hurry down to the street and find out what was happening. I was happy I could stay at my desk.

Reporters' contributions and tribulations notwithstanding, journalism histories seldom focus on them. I set out to remedy that lack, at least in part, by telling the story of the life of a reporter back in the days when the profession was new and its practitioners were far more anonymous and faceless than now. Conventional sources were limited. Then as now reporters had no secretaries to file their papers, and in any case their papers would have consisted of little more than indecipherable notes. Consequently, the principal source of information had to be the news stories they wrote. The catch is that hardly any of these stories bore bylines—in the case of Julian Ralph, apparently none of those he wrote for the newspaper that employed him during most of his career, the New York *Sun*. There were enough clues, however, to make a search for Ralph's work feasible, and that search has filled much of my time for the past few years. Often, as I spun through issue after issue of a newspaper on microfilm or turned yellowed pages that crumbled in my hand, I felt that I was looking for needles in haystacks, but more than once I found a needle. The newspaper collections where I carried on this hunt included those of the New York

Public Library, the Library of Congress, the British Library in London, the Monmouth County Historical Society in Freehold, New Jersey, and the Webster, Massachusetts, Public Library.

I am grateful to my family for putting up with my monomania and encouraging me through the years. I am also grateful to Russell Galen of the Scott Meredith agency, who was the first person in the publishing world to think that there might be a book in Julian Ralph's life, and to the editors at Syracuse University Press who agreed with him.

Gentleman of the Press

1. A Summons from Mr. Dana

Newspaper reporters toiled anonymously through most of the nineteenth century, so the public would have had no way of knowing who was writing the descriptions of the adultery trial of the Reverend Henry Ward Beecher that began appearing in the New York *Daily Graphic* when the case opened in Brooklyn in January 1875. But regular readers surely must have noticed something special about the reports. In contrast to the fussy, ponderous style of much of the journalism of the day, these were direct and colorful. Somebody on the *Graphic's* staff had a particularly sharp eye and sure feel for human behavior. The *Graphic's* man—in the 1870s readers could be almost certain that the reporter was not a woman—often sorted out confusing scenes with a single bold turn of phrase. Rival reporters tried for similar effects but generally lacked his flair and dash. The *Daily Graphic,* an afternoon tabloid that claimed to be "the only illustrated daily newspaper in the world" (it performed the remarkable feat of reproducing sketches overnight), crowed over his work. "We aim to give the spirit and life of the trial and not its dry bones," it declared.

What the *Graphic* had done was to assign the reporter to capture the atmosphere in the Brooklyn City Court—the mood of the throng that sought admittance to the courtroom every day, the conscious and the off-guard demeanor of the principals and the witnesses, the reactions of the jury, the byplay of opposing lawyers. These observations, sometimes written with a latitude denied reporters after objectivity became a larger goal, set the stage for the columns of verbatim testimony that the *Graphic,* like other newspapers, was carrying. Since each day's *Graphic* began emerging from the pressroom in the basement of its offices on Park Place in lower Manhattan even as witnesses testified and lawyers clashed, the work demanded speed and fluency. The *Graphic* reporter arrived at the domed, porticoed Brooklyn courthouse around ten o'clock each morning. In the courtroom he watched the spectators and the players in the drama take their places and then focused on the proceedings when the judge mounted the bench at eleven. At intervals he dashed off snatches of copy with a pencil and handed them to messenger boys who hurried to the Fulton Street ferry and then to the *Graphic* building. The earliest edition carrying news of the day's developments went to press at 2 P.M. and another was printed at 4 P.M. There was no time to revise or polish. It was as if the *Graphic* reporter sat down at his assigned table in the courtroom and wrote a letter about what was going on around him, pausing frequently to glance up and keep abreast of events.

The raw material presented by the trial was rich beyond belief; a novel making use of it would be derided as overripe. Henry Ward Beecher, the best-known preacher in the United States, a member of one of the country's most prominent families, was the defendant in a suit brought by Theodore Tilton, an editor who was a public figure in his own right. Beecher, the suit charged, had seduced Tilton's wife, Elizabeth, and had thereby "wholly alienated and destroyed" her affection for her husband. The Tiltons, two decades younger than Beecher, who would turn sixty-two before the end of the trial, had been members of Beecher's Plymouth Church, a fashionable, prosperous Congregational body in Brooklyn Heights. Beecher's wife, Eunice, was weary, gray, and forbidding; Elizabeth Tilton was dark-haired, petite, and vulnerable. Tales of a liaison between Beecher and Mrs. Tilton had spread in widening circles, then spilled into print in lavish detail. There were stories of other Beecher affairs as well. The cast of the scandal abounded with titillating minor characters, including servants who had witnessed indiscretions and Victoria Woodhull, the champion of free love. Melodrama ran rampant: anguished confessions, floods of tears, over-wrought letters, suicide talk, charged late-night confrontations.

Tilton's suit against Beecher gripped the nation. The legions of Americans who continued to admire the clergyman and disbelieve the charges against him looked on with dismay, seeing the moral underpinnings of their world under assault. Undoubtedly, there were also more than a few people who followed the proceedings with the shudder of guilty pleasure produced by the fall of the mighty. But for most Victorians—particularly the expanding, striving middle class—the great fascination of the case lay in its glimpses into the forbidden. A suffocating propriety often enveloped nineteenth-century American life, above all where sex was concerned. Earthly passions were habitually cloaked in heavy silks and broadcloth and in elevated language. Here was a legitimate opportunity to feed the prurient curiosity that normally went unsatisfied.

Newspapers labored heroically to slake this vast public appetite. No other domestic scandal has ever inspired such elaborate coverage. Day after day during the six months that the trial lasted newspapers across the country devoted many columns to the case. The big morning papers in New York printed every word of testimony, filling entire pages with unbroken expanses of small gray type. Newspapers in Boston, Philadelphia, and Chicago were not far behind, and even a continent away in San Francisco the Beecher story regularly made page one of the *Chronicle*.

The millions of words about the trial were produced by scores of reporters—"more reporters than ever gathered within the walls of a court-room before," according to the Boston *Globe*. The nine tables provided for the press in the courtroom were occupied by sixty or so men, most fairly young and most sporting beards or luxuriant mustaches. Each morning they deposited their top hats and derbies and an occasional walking stick on their tables and scribbled notes with little respite till late in the afternoon. "When counsel paused for rhetorical effect in speaking and the audience sat breathless," the *Daily Graphic* reporter commented early in the trial, "the intermittent rustling of pencils gliding over paper was oppressively audible."

The *Daily Graphic* had been assigned seats at a table at the front of the courtroom, a few feet to the left of the bench. Besides the reporter, the *Graphic* had sent stenographers who worked in relays to jam as much testimony as possible into each day's editions. The courtroom descriptions and the testimony frequently ran under the headline "The Great Scandal Trial." The *Graphic* contingent also included an artist who sketched courtroom scenes and portraits of the leading participants, and, said the *Graphic*, all those in court marveled at the speed and accuracy with which the tabloid illustrated its trial coverage. One day the judge was seen studying with obvious satisfaction a portrait of himself that filled the *Graphic's* front page that day.

If the *Graphic* reporter sat with his back to the front wall of the courtroom, he had a panoramic view. Close by to his left was the judge, and almost in front of the reporter was the witness stand. Tables of lawyers and reporters filled the center of the courtroom. Glancing a little to his right, the *Graphic* reporter could look down the two rows of jurors in their box. Theodore Tilton usually sat at the table designated for his lawyers. Most days the Beechers sat in the front row of a group of chairs placed inside the bar for participants and well-connected members of the audience, and outside the bar and in the gallery sat the other spectators.

The crush of spectators was newsworthy in itself. From the day early in January when jury selection began, hundreds more people than the courtroom could hold sought to attend the trial. A system of tickets was set up, with preference given to those who could establish some link to the contending parties or their lawyers or who simply impressed those in charge as sufficiently important to warrant special treatment. But this failed to diminish the pressure for admittance significantly, and spectators filled every open space, standing along the walls and behind the jury and even edging into chairs on the raised platform where the judge sat. Eventually, the judge, concerned for the decorum of his court, barred standees, but this added little breathing room because many spectators set up camp stools in the aisles. Another of the judge's orders that had scant effect was a ban on women in the audience because of his fear, in the words of the *Daily Graphic,* that the trial "would abound in indelicacies." Mrs. Beecher and Mrs. Tilton, now estranged from her husband and siding with Henry Ward Beecher, were present much of the time from the beginning, and other women attended in increasing numbers. All told, almost eight hundred people regularly crowded into a room designed to hold half that number. The closely packed bodies, along with the smell of the damp wool brought inside from the chill, wet winter weather, so fouled the air that perfume-spraying machines were installed in the courtroom.

Bad weather did not deter the crowds from arriving well before court time each morning by horsecar or foot from around Brooklyn and by ferry across the East River from Manhattan—which was then, along with part of the Bronx, the separate city of New York. "The ferry-boats that left New York for Brooklyn bristled with umbrellas, and when the boats landed in their slips the umbrellas, moving off them, formed two glistening lines, black and dripping, from the river to the Court House," reported the *Daily Graphic* one miserable day in January. In the courtroom, lit by a circle of gas jets hanging from the ceiling, many of the ordinary run of spectators were shunted to the gallery. "The gallery is all attention," wrote the *Graphic* reporter. "It has prominent eyes and a sharp nose. . . . It frequently improvises an ear trumpet by curving its hands and placing them behind its two ears. . . . Its head is often very heavy, and then it leans its chin on both hands and looks over the railing at its ease. . . . Sometimes it sits with its hands in its pockets, sometimes it rubs its beard and sometimes it picks its nose. . . ."

On the main floor, the most privileged spectators were a dozen or so pillars of Beecher's Plymouth Church. They showed up each day, seemingly wrapped in a mantle of moral superiority intended to convey to all that the charges against their pastor were absurd on their face; no leader of their number could be guilty of such conduct. Chairs close by the Beechers had been reserved for the Plymouth members, and a Mr. Caldwell, aided by an assistant minister named Halliday, took charge. Caldwell "keeps intruders from the chairs by arriving early, placing Pastor Halliday at the furthermost one and posting himself at the other extreme end of the row. Then as the members enter the room he ushers them to their places." It was almost as if they were in church, and Plymouth members frequently furthered this illusion by placing a cut-glass vase of flowers on the table used by Beecher's lawyers.

Henry Ward Beecher and Eunice Beecher usually arrived just before the trial began at eleven. Henry, his waist thickening and his long, lank hair gray, looked like an aging actor, but the magnetism that had long filled churches and lecture halls seemed undiminished. As he took his seat, the Plymouth delegation pressed around to shake his hand. Sometimes he stood a moment surveying the audience, nodding at acquaintances, "smiling pleasantly upon them as in a prayer meeting." Early in the trial the *Graphic* reporter was struck repeatedly by Beecher's magnificent aplomb—his "look of unconcern over a matter that must be at the least of some slight importance to him." When one of Tilton's lawyers launched into an opening speech denouncing Beecher as a seducer and home-wrecker, the clergyman "crossed his legs and leaned back in his chair with the air of a man who had nothing to do but sit there and wait—just the expression one sees on the faces of passengers in the cars or ferry-boats." The reporter saw that Beecher was almost always on stage, as on the February morning when he "walked in slowly from the anteroom to his chair with his head bowed as if in meditation. He held a letter deeply edged with black in his hand."

Eunice Beecher was also playing a role—the loyal wife utterly incredulous of the awful tales told about her husband. But it was a difficult part, requiring that she cast loving looks at Henry even as the testimony seemed to make it unmistakably clear that he had gone elsewhere to satisfy sexual needs unfulfilled at home. Eunice lacked entirely Henry's presence and outgoing nature, and it was with a "hard, cold face" that she attempted to smile at him early in the trial. Gradually, however, as the trial dragged on and her fortitude in a humiliating situation became increasingly apparent, the *Graphic* reporter's attitude toward Eunice would soften.

The *Graphic* reporter also observed the other participants closely. Theodore Tilton, tall, handsome, talented as a writer and lecturer as well as an editor, proved too clever for his own good on the stand; as the trial progressed he evolved from aggrieved husband to something of a libertine

One of the *Graphic*'s many sketches of the Beecher trial. Beecher is the beardless man to the left of the woman—Eunice, his wife—at center right. *Newspaper Collection, The New York Public Library, Astor, Lenox, and Tilden Foundations*

whose own personal life did not bear up well under scrutiny. Elizabeth Tilton, the reporter noted ungallantly, looked "girlish"—until she raised her veil.

The jury and the lawyers were focal points of interest. The twelve jurymen, mostly Brooklyn merchants, initially made a great show of rapt attention and conscientiousness. "The jury looked like a small Sunday-school class this morning," said the *Graphic* in mid-January. "It had the appearance of being washed and combed and having been told not to talk nor to misbehave in any way."

Three lawyers presented Tilton's charges and six defended Beecher, the opposing counsel "deferring to each other only as much as the coldest politeness required." The most formidable among them was Beecher's chief counsel, William M. Evarts, who had defended President Andrew Johnson in his impeachment trial seven years earlier and who "never surrenders a step without a struggle." Gauging the disposition of the lawyers as they arrived gave clues to the likely tenor of the proceedings. Thus, one contentious day "Mr. Sherman came in late and snappish. General Pryor was especially defiant in his manner. Mr. Evarts looked stern and uncompromising. Mr. Beach . . . was taciturn and moody." As the legal arguments grew tangled and precedents were resorted to more often, in the eyes of the *Graphic* reporter the tables of rival lawyers suddenly took on a new appearance: "The two larger tables used by the counsel are piled high with law books since the opening of the argument over the admissibility of Mr. Tilton's evidence. The tables seem to frown at each other, as if they were fortresses and their books had been brought in range, like pieces of heavy ordnance, ready to do serious damage when the engagement begins."

Theodore Tilton's suit against Henry Ward Beecher, which demanded $100,000 in restitution, rested largely on statements and letters emanating from Henry and Elizabeth over a period of several years that seemed to point inescapably to an adulterous relationship. Concluding the opening statement for the plaintiff, a Tilton lawyer addressed the jury: "Oh, gentlemen, you have homes, you have children! You know what it is to return from the day's labor to the bosom of a happy family, and you can appreciate the wrong and the suffering my unhappy client has experienced. . . . I call upon you in the name of morality, in the name of Christianity, by the Saviour, by the teachings of the Sermon on the Mount, by the teachings that were thundered from Sinai, by every consideration that is near and dear to you, to brand the seducer as his crime deserves to be branded." "He seemed," said the *Daily Graphic* reporter, "to tear the burning words from his hoarse throat."

The defense devised by Beecher's lawyers relied in part on blackening Tilton's character, implying that he had strayed from his own marriage bed so often that he was not fit to challenge the conduct of others. But the centerpiece of Beecher's case was to be the appearance of Beecher himself on the stand, explaining away the incriminating letters and statements and overpowering the charges against him by the sheer weight of his presence.

The *Graphic* reporter had a close view of the witnesses. Tilton did not come off well as his lawyers guided him through his evidence. "There is a forced calmness in his manner that is more suggestive than any demonstration of feeling could possibly be. When his hands loose their grasp from the arms of the chair to make gestures in miniature they move with rigidity and precision. The blue veins are filled to correspond with the flush on his cheeks and forehead." Evarts was intimidating during cross-examination. "He puts his questions severely and with threatening accompaniments of his forefinger. When such a question was delivered Mr. Evarts would throw his head back, compress his lips and stare confidently at the jury."

But Francis Moulton was another story. Moulton was a businessman who had acted as an intermediary in an attempt to reconcile Tilton and Beecher, and as such he had been a repository for Beecher's confidences and for the letters that were such an important part of the case. Now he was testifying for Tilton, and he was a cool, devastating witness who "measured out each sentence in convenient packages" for the stenographers. His wife, Emma, also testified powerfully against Beecher. She wore a dress of heavy black silk and a dark purple hat with feathers and streamers, and she had glossy nut-brown hair and fair skin. "When Mrs. Moulton left her seat and walked to the witness chair she moved with the ease and assurance of a lady hostess in her own parlor who was about to make a recitation for the entertainment of her friends in the room."

There were days filled with tedious legal arguments or with testimony going over material already printed in every newspaper in the land. Then readers could fall back on stories about the Whiskey Ring, the Carlist uprising in Spain, Boss Tweed's life in jail, or the Charity Ball. (The trial reporter definitely did not cover the ball. The *Daily Graphic* account began:

"Charity has always considered it rather meritorious than otherwise to cozen what she can from her more pretentious rivals, Fashion and Terpsichore. Her attempts on the wallets of the two last evening at the Academy of Music must have been gratifying because of success. The little absent beneficiaries of the Nursery and Child's Hospital will doubtless put away their rattles and take up the report of the Financial Committee to-day with a great deal of satisfaction." Then followed almost five columns describing the decorations and the toilettes of the ladies in attendance.)

When the trial proceedings yielded little of interest—or when the juicy testimony came too late in the day to make the afternoon papers—the *Graphic* reporter looked elsewhere. He studied the eating habits of the spectators, most of whom remained in the courtroom at the one o'clock recess lest they lose their places. The "rich young man with the timid side whiskers and the bold stare" lunched on "snow-white bread and a bit of fowl—done up in a napkin and taken from a little hand-satchel, which also contains a small flask of claret or of water." The young man gazed with "wondering awe at the rustic next to him" who ate a sandwich that "he seems to have bought . . . on his way to court and to have thrust . . . into his pocket without wrapping it up." On a January day when the weather was nasty a peddler brought a basket of steaming mutton pies wrapped in white paper into the courtroom, and the dignified Evarts and a rival lawyer joined the messenger boys crowding around him.

The presence of persons of note in the audience was recorded: the Earl of Rosebery, President McCosh of Princeton, and Robert Todd Lincoln, son of the late President. There were frequent rumors about the arrival of Bessie Turner, a young woman who had lived for a time in the Tilton household and was said to have shocking tales to tell about Theodore. "Bessie Turner came into court this morning in another of her protean shapes," said the *Graphic* in mid-February. "This time she was little and pale and retiring." Once a "veiled lady" rumored to be Bessie turned out to be Mrs. Beecher's maid come to fetch the pantry key. The Plymouth members continued to show up, but after a while assistant pastor Halliday no longer helped Mr. Caldwell seat them. Caldwell had explained, as the *Graphic* reporter put it, that "the duty requires suavity and imperturbability, and these are not Halliday's strong points."

The defense began its case on February 24. Some days the weather was mild enough to allow the tall windows of the courtroom to be opened. The air grew more healthful, although periodically the proceedings still had to be interrupted when one of the key participants was struck by an attack of vertigo or a fainting spell. The merchants in the jury box had begun "to look more and more at home in their chairs, and now they stare about the court-room at times in a perfectly natural way, and lean back in their chairs as much at ease as if they were listening to a discussion of the scandal, tipped back against their own counters." For amusement they had divided themselves into three four-man marching units, and at lunchtime they paraded to and from Park's Restaurant nearby, three court officers acting as drillmasters.

Preliminary defense witnesses contributed to the darkening picture of Tilton. Bessie Turner herself finally showed up and testified that Tilton had tried to insinuate himself into her bed one night. Three servants of Victoria Woodhull told of seeing Tilton and their mistress embrace like lovers, and a coachman said the pair went bathing in the sea together at Coney Island. Another minor witness against Tilton, a Miss Oakley, was less convincing. The *Graphic* reporter commented: "She is very clear in her replies, and utters them with helpful gesticulations of her hands. But it is marvellous how persistently she makes wrong answers to the most simple interrogations."

Henry Ward Beecher took the stand for the first time on April 1 at 11:45— early enough for the *Graphic* to describe his initial appearance in its 2 P.M. edition. So great was the pressure for admittance to the courtroom that camp stools for spectators were set up even on the platform where the witness sat. Most members of the Beecher family were present, though not Henry's sister Harriet Beecher Stowe, the author of *Uncle Tom's Cabin*. Henry wore his customary black broadcloth. "The Rev. Henry Ward Beecher was as fresh in his appearance as if the last few days had been spent in the country, and during this time he had erased every trouble from his mind. His face was ruddy, his eye clear and bright, and his manner brisk and cheerful." The courtroom fell silent when his name was called. "Mr. Beecher arose, laid his overcoat in his chair, and walked to the stand. He held four or five violets, drooping and lifeless, in his right hand. His hat was folded into an oblong shape in his left hand. He placed it at the back of the chair, and, standing profile to the audience, waited a moment in hesitation."

"The turning point of the scandal trial is reached," summed up the *Graphic* man. "The verdict of the jury even is of secondary importance. The public . . . will render its decision before Mr. Beecher leaves the witness chair. . . . Thousands of persons who are strongly impressed by the manner in which the charges against Mr. Beecher have been maintained withhold their final decision until Mr. Beecher has had a hearing. Thousands of others who believe the great pastor clean of stain proudly await the safe deliverance offered him upon the stand."

Under carefully prepared questioning by his own principal counsel, William Evarts, things went fairly well. Beecher denied the charge of adultery, insisted that he had never conceded guilt in the past, and suggested that at worst he might have unwittingly allowed the childlike Elizabeth to entwine her pastor in "the tendrils of her affection." Beecher's rationalizations for behavior that seemed to point in other directions were tortuous. Great preacher that he was, however, "there was a mesmerism in his tones, and his words tuned the emotions of his auditors according to their import, just as a master sets his copy and the pupils follow." He continued to carry a nosegay to the stand each day, and when he stepped down women in the audience asked for it. Sometimes as he testified his eyes filled with tears.

But now the audience awaited the cross-examination by William Fullerton, one of Tilton's lawyers, and after it began Beecher's defense went downhill rapidly. Fullerton was withering. Time and again Beecher's explanations of why his words and actions did not mean what they plainly seemed to mean were shattered. Contradictions multiplied, and often he was reduced to pleading failure of memory. A *Graphic* tally showed that Beecher evaded answers 875 times. He stammered and perspired, and his face sometimes flushed deep red. As the cross-examination drew to a close, Fullerton "stood between two tables, and held himself in that position, with his head thrown forward, his teeth set, and his firm gray eyes fastened on Mr. Beecher, as though he had to hold himself back lest his feelings prompted him to pounce physically upon him. Mr. Beecher was at bay."

Other witnesses and rebuttals are still to be heard when Beecher leaves the stand for the last time on April 21, but interest tapers now. A reporter for a German-language newspaper in Buffalo attempts suicide by poison but survives. "He is said to have grown weary of the scandal trial, and, seeing no end to it, thought to escape his duty of reporting it by suicide." The *Graphic* reporter holds an inconsequential interview with the judge, and the judge asks "any gentlemen of the press" who have not signed his autograph book to please do so. One day the court adjourns at noon, and the Plymouth members hurry off for lemonade, cake, and ice cream at an affair at the church.

The crowds swell again when the summations begin toward the end of

May. Evarts speaks eight days for Beecher, and a lawyer named William A. Beach reviews Tilton's case for ten. Both are masterful orators. Beach "gives the impression of brushing aside all immaterial circumstances as if they were cobwebs." Evarts "speaks as a clock ticks—slowly, regularly, distinctly, and so smoothly that he seems able to continue an indefinite length of time." Evarts's arguments boil down to one main point: It is inconceivable that a man of Henry Ward Beecher's lofty character and standing could be guilty of adultery.

The judge charges the jury on June 24. The *Daily Graphic* has outdone its afternoon competitors by installing a three-mile wire from the court-house to its editorial rooms so it can rush into print with extra editions covering up-to-the-minute developments. The *Graphic* reporter says that "the general impression for the last week has been that the jury would disagree." Hours pass and the reporters grow edgy. Two come to blows. They are arrested and taken to the judge's chambers, where they refuse his request to shake hands. But one says, "He hit me and I hit him; that satisfies me," and the judge discharges the men. Back in the courtroom reporters hurl wads of paper at each other until the battle becomes so boisterous that the police must restore order.

The hours of waiting turn into days. The reporters speculate on the jury balloting, and the *Daily Graphic* reporter somehow lays his hands on discarded ballots that point to a majority favoring Beecher. The weather has turned brutally hot. "Imagine eight hundred people in a close, badly ventilated room, the thermometer at 90 and expectation at 200 degrees." To stay on the shady side of the building, the weary, drained jurors change rooms at noon, "looking like the pale ghosts in 'Richard III' " as they cross the hall. On June 30 the *Graphic* reporter finds, however, that the jurors' appetites are unaffected: for dinner they order four servings of roast lamb, four of roast beef, two of porterhouse steak, and two of lamb chops, plus twelve pieces of pie and twelve dishes of ice cream.

Henry Ward Beecher has been passing much of the time at his country home on the Hudson, near Peekskill, where he often retreats to write his sermons. Eunice Beecher continues to sit in the courtroom, and "there is a depth of pity felt by the throng for this woman now, that approaches tenderness. . . . When she is left to her own thoughts she sits with her eyes held to the floor, and sometimes with her white thin hand before her face."

Her husband is still not by her side when the jury gives up and returns to the courtroom on July 2. The foreman, whose name is Carpenter, an-nounces that the jury is hopelessly divided. Apparently a majority of these twelve solid citizens of Brooklyn have agreed with William Evarts that Henry Ward Beecher could not possibly have committed adultery. Carpenter announces the jury's disagreement at 11:31 A.M., according to the *Daily Graphic,* and an edition carrying the news is selling on the streets of lower Manhattan fourteen minutes later. "This is, we believe, the quickest newspaper work ever done in this country," boasts the *Graphic.*

Foreman Carpenter had not immediately disclosed the number of jurors on each side, but after the judge dismisses the jury word quickly circulates that Carpenter, violating a secrecy agreement, has let slip to John Hill, one of Beecher's half dozen lawyers, that the vote was nine for Beecher, three for Tilton. Carpenter dodges the reporters, and, leaping over tables, they pounce on other jurors for confirmation. The *Daily Graphic* man corners a juror named Hull:

Reporter—Mr. Hull, have you any objection to stating how you jurors stood when you were discharged?
Mr. Hull—I am pledged to keep the matter secret.
R.—But Mr. Carpenter has already told John L. Hill that you stood nine to three.
Mr. H.—I can't help what he has done.
R.—But you can say whether he spoke truly.
Mr. H.—He did. We stood nine for acquittal.
R.—Is that how you stood when the first ballot was cast?
Mr. H.—No; there was a change of one vote.
R.—In what direction?
Mr. H.—(testily, and making an impatient attempt to push out of the room)—We stood eight to four when the first ballot was cast, and one man has gone over to the majority since.

Having obtained what he wanted, the *Daily Graphic* man hurries off. In the early afternoon crowds still linger outside the courthouse, but inside the building the corridors that have been packed daily with hundreds of people hoping for a glimpse of the trial are deserted—"dull as a cloister."

Beecher rode out the storm almost unscathed, even after Elizabeth Tilton in 1878 confessed publicly that she had indeed committed adultery with her pastor. Beecher remained at Plymouth Church, which appropriated $100,000 for his legal expenses, and retained his popularity on the lecture platform as well as in the pulpit until his death in 1887.

The reporters went on to other stories, and very soon the *Daily Graphic* reporter went on to a new job with the New York *Sun*—by general agreement the leading newspaper of the day. His trial reports had caught the eye of the *Sun's* brilliant editor, Charles A. Dana, and by inquiry or from word of mouth among New York journalists, Dana had learned the identity of the *Graphic* writer. His name was Julian Ralph and he was twenty-two years old. Eventually newspapermen who knew and worked with him over the next quarter century would call him the greatest reporter of his time. One colleague would speak of "the prince of reporters, Julian Ralph, Ralph of the *Sun.*"

2. The Item Gatherers

The handful of known likenesses of Julian Ralph show him between his mid-thirties and late forties, long after the Beecher trial. But among them are two portraits taken in photographers' studios in which he has a look that must have marked him from his youth and that must have proved useful through the countless difficult passages that filled his life—riots and wars, great disasters and small human tragedies, encounters with pompous officials, imperious tycoons, and assorted scoundrels. It is a bold, confident look. He appears to have been fairly tall, perhaps six feet, and sturdily built—a man of Victorian solidity, with thick chest and shoulders. He had a wide, strong nose, a firm chin, and the sweeping handlebar mustache of the time. By the age of forty his dark hair had receded considerably, giving him a high, broad brow. Going about his work for the *Sun,* he wore a derby, a wing collar and four-in-hand tie with a bulky knot, a waistcoat, and a high-buttoned cutaway suit jacket. He must have been a commanding figure, but his physical advantages went beyond appearances. "If I have done anything uncommon in newspaper work," he reflected toward the end of his life, "it has been in the way of covering the main stem of important events completely, and at great lengths, unaided and alone." His "physique," he said, contributed to this ability.

Ralph's physical toughness and endurance mattered in a day when reporters did not gather news by telephone and travel was often arduous. Coupled with the talent for fast, colorful, informative writing he had displayed at the Beecher trial, they made him a natural for journalism. But Julian Ralph was also lucky. He entered the field at a time when it was expanding and flourishing. Between 1870 and 1900, the number of general-circulation daily newspapers in the United States rose from 489 to 1,967. In 1875, the year Ralph started at the *Sun,* newsboys in New York hawked thirteen dailies. Philadelphia had fourteen, Boston had eight, and Chicago, St. Louis, and San Francisco each had six. Cincinnati had five dailies, and Cleveland and Indianapolis each had four.

The quadrupling of dailies between 1870 and 1900 compared with a doubling of the U.S. population over the same thirty years. Despite fierce competition for readers, however, circulations were climbing. Cities, where the dailies had their market, were growing much faster than the nation as a whole, and urban residents were becoming better educated and increasingly curious about what was happening in the world around them.

This mounting appetite for news was also Julian Ralph's good fortune. He came along as it was changing the content of newspapers and making the reporter's work more important. The change had emerged as a dominant trend during the Civil War. Readers had displayed an eagerness for the telegraphed news from the battlefront far greater than they had ever shown for the political argument and literary miscellany that had previously filled many papers. For the first time, the reporter had begun to supplant the editorial writer at the center of journalism, and that shift had accelerated in the years after the war. If publishers and editors wanted to attract readers, they needed good reporters. Writing in the *North American Review* in 1866, James Parton, a prominent observer of the journalistic scene, declared:

> The prestige of the editorial is gone. . . . There are journalists who think the time is at hand for the abolition of editorials, and the concentration of the whole force of journalism upon presenting to the public the history and picture of the day. The time for this has not come, and may never come; but our journalists already know that editorials neither make nor mar a daily paper, that they do not much influence the public mind, nor change many votes, and that the power and success of a newspaper depend wholly and absolutely upon its success in getting and its skill in exhibiting the news. . . . The news is the point of rivalry; it is that for which nineteen-twentieths of the people buy newspapers; it is that which constitutes the power and value of the daily press.

And a writer in *Lippincott's Monthly Magazine* commented in 1871: "For the majority of readers it is the reporter, and not the editor, who is the ruling genius of the newspaper."

It is true that the number of youthful would-be reporters eager to take up the mantle of ruling genius exceeded the number of decent jobs, and that many reporters were poorly paid and shabbily treated by their employers. But for those with exceptional talent, like Julian Ralph, the job held possibilities that had never existed before.

On June 30, 1704, six pirates were hanged on the banks of the Charles River in Boston. An onlooker described the executions in the Boston *News-*

Letter, founded only two months earlier and the first regularly published American newspaper. The account included the "exhortations to the male-factors" and a prayer intoned by one of the clergymen present while the pirates waited on the scaffold, "as nearly as it could be taken in writing in the great crowd." According to a nineteenth-century history of American journalism, this represented "the first effort at reporting in this country."

An early-twentieth-century history of journalism told a different tale. It called Harry Ingraham Blake of the *New-England Palladium,* founded in Boston in 1793, "the Father of American reporting."

> He was the first to go after news without waiting for items to come to the newspaper office. Though he occasionally reported local matters in and around the city, he made his reputation as a gatherer of ship news. . . . Instead of going to the coffee-houses to get the news retold there by sea captains, he would go down to the wharves, get into a boat, and often go out alone to meet the incoming vessels without regard to what the weather was or to what time of day the vessel would dock. After getting the news from the captain or some member of the crew, he would rush back to the office of *The Palladium* and there, with the help of his wonderful memory and by a few notes on his cuffs or on his finger nails, he would put the matter into type as he sang to himself in a monotone.

Frank Luther Mott's *American Journalism,* a standard reference originally published in 1941, locates the "first professional reporters" in America in Philadelphia. Mott was referring to a handful of men who covered the activities of the new Federal government for Philadelphia newspapers between 1790 and 1800, when Philadelphia was temporarily the capital of the United States. Their work assumed national importance because newspapers around the country freely copied from the Philadelphia papers under a system by which editors exchanged newspapers to obtain reports of events outside their own communities. Almost from the start reporters had at least some access to congressional proceedings, although there was occasional squabbling over such matters as where they should sit. When the House was meeting in Philadelphia reporters were assigned "four seats on the window sill."

It is as risky to single out "firsts" in journalism as in any other field. The safest conclusion is that as long as newspapers have been around, so has reporting. The colonial editor who composed a few lines about an accident observed on his way to work or passed on in print a snatch of gossip brought into his office was reporting. But it is also safe to say that the examples of reporting "firsts" cited by journalism historians are exceptions to the rule where early American newspapers are concerned. The exploits of the journalists involved caught the historians' eye because they were so rare. The truth is that from colonial times until well into the nineteenth century most American newspapers were not greatly interested in news—certainly not enough to go in search of it.

Eighteenth-century American newspapers were usually published by printers as sidelines, something to keep their presses busy and supplement their income from the official printing, legal forms, and handbills that made up the bulk of their business. Often the printer-editors simply filled their little four-page weeklies with whatever material came easiest to hand. A mainstay was royal proclamations, court gossip, and parliamentary addresses to the king lifted from newspapers brought over by ship captains from England, which was still viewed as "home" by the colonists. Editors also printed sermons, colonial government documents, and essays on social, political, and moral topics by local contributors.

If there was little sense of urgency about any of this, part of the explanation lay in the slowness of communications—as long as two months from England by ship, up to two weeks in the winter between Boston and New York by postrider. Concern about printing timely news would frequently have been futile. But even when newsworthy happenings occurred right outside the office door, colonial newspapers often did not bother to inform their readers. In many issues the only items that might be classed as news were ship arrivals and sailings, a matter of great moment to the colonists. Other scraps of news—deaths, weddings, fires, crimes—crept into print sporadically, but eighteenth-century newspapers generally scorned events in the lives of ordinary citizens as insignificant. In the summer of 1755, for example, only two weeks after General Edward Braddock's defeat at Fort Duquesne by the French and Indians, the *Pennsylvania Gazette,* published by Benjamin Franklin in Philadelphia, carried a graphic account of the event. The *Gazette* also found space to report that in April "the Post-Chaise His Majesty went in broke down near the Sign of the Three Pigeons just beyond Stratford, into which House His Majesty went till the Chaise was put in order." But over a five-week period that included these reports Franklin's paper printed not a word about the doings of any citizen of Philadelphia.

As the Revolution approached, political matters dominated the press increasingly. Newspapers in Boston, New York, Philadelphia, and elsewhere lined up on the Patriot or Royalist side, and the editors' overriding interest lay in promoting causes, not in reporting the news. Political partisanship, its expression unleashed by a degree of press freedom found nowhere else in the world, continued to shape most newspapers after the Revolution. In the early years of the republic, major newspapers, many edited by men known primarily for their skills in political debate rather than by old-style printer-editors, served as organs of the Federalists or the followers of Jefferson. Newspapers later proclaimed themselves champions of the Whigs or Democrats and, still later, of the Democrats or the Republicans.

News was hit or miss. There was no systematic coverage of the Revolution, and such reports of the struggle as did appear were often warped and inaccurate. By and large, according to Mott, the historian, "the papers of the Revolutionary period took their news as it drifted in." The constitutional convention went unmentioned in the press, and the coverage of the War of 1812 was almost as sketchy and haphazard as that of the Revolution. Local news was still deemed scarcely worthy of notice, and accounts of crimes and other sensational occurrences were sometimes criticized as injurious to morals. William Duane of Philadelphia, a prominent Jeffersonian editor, declared: "I never admit into my paper accounts of murders, robberies, crimes and despertitions, because . . . familiarity with tales of crimes will blunt the faculties and form habits of indifference to crime."

Isaiah Thomas, editor of the *Massachusetts Spy,* a leading Revolutionary-era newspaper and author of an early history of American journalism, observed in 1810 that "gazettes and journals are now chiefly filled with political essays; news does not appear to be always the first object of editors." Writing of the first three decades of the nineteenth century, Mott noted that "even on the largest papers, the editor was commonly his own reporter; if the paper was prosperous, he might have an assistant who shared the work of reporting with him, but with the prevailing disregard for local news, reporting had as yet no standing."

Though editorial columns were fairly common by the early 1800s, in reality the entire newspaper of the period was a blend of the editor's opinions and stray bits of fact, the latter often distorted by the editor's views. These years were the "dark ages" of American journalism, the era of "black journalism." Scurrilous assaults on the breeding, morals, and ideas of opposition politicians and rival editors were standard fare. One leading Federalist editor who directed a relentless drumfire of insult and invective against the Jeffersonians has been described as almost without peer in his talent for "sustained vituperation." The notable journalists of the late eighteenth and early nineteenth centuries were polemicists and propagandists, not reporters of the news.

And yet, as in the decades before the conflict between the colonies and England developed, some news did find its way into print. Protests against the Stamp Act, which hit editors in the purse, were widely reported, and Isaiah Thomas wrote a detailed eyewitness account of the battles of Lexington and Concord for his *Massachusetts Spy*. (On the other hand, the Boston *Evening-Post,* published almost within sound of the musket fire, disposed of Lexington and Concord with the observation that "the unhappy Transactions of last week are so variously related that we shall not at present undertake to give any particular account thereof.") After Washington died at Mount Vernon on December 14, 1799, the news spread to newspaper readers in New York on December 21, in Boston on December 25, in Cincinnati on January 7.

The gathering of some sorts of news was becoming regularized. Congressional reporters were using shorthand to make accurate reports of debates in Philadelphia before 1800, and they continued to do so when the government moved to Washington in that year. By the mid-1820s a few out-of-town newspapers had their own correspondents in Washington. There was also a rising sense of urgency about some news. Perhaps unknowingly following the lead of Harry Blake and the *New-England Palladium,* editors in New York by the 1820s were sending out fast little sailing craft to pick up newspapers from ships inbound from Europe and thereby speed foreign news into print. In 1829 express riders carried President Andrew Jackson's annual message to Congress from Washington to New York in twenty hours. Even before 1800, daily newspapers—in themselves a recognition of the importance of timeliness in the news business—began appearing. Philadelphia had six dailies by 1800, New York five, Baltimore three. These dailies, most of which had *Advertiser* in their names, sought readers among merchants, stressing ship arrivals and descriptions of goods newly landed on the docks.

The various *Commercial Advertisers* and *Daily Advertisers* combined their mercantile news with the rabid political partisanship of the day, generally sharing the conservative attitudes of their audience, and they were soon joined in the daily field by primarily political newspapers representing more diverse viewpoints. Whatever their political bent, however, daily newspapers of the early 1800s reached mainly well-to-do readers. They were sold chiefly by subscription, and they were expensive—eight to ten dollars a year, a week's wages for a skilled craftsman. Individual copies were available at the newspaper office for the considerable sum of six cents—the cost of a pint of whiskey—but the papers were not sold on the street. Not surprisingly, circulations were low. In the 1820s most dailies printed 1,500 to 2,500 copies and the largest New York newspapers no more than 4,000.

Unimpressive as these figures appear, the United States was becoming a newspaper-reading nation. By 1850, when the population would reach 23 million, American newspapers would print well over 400 million copies annually, almost five times the number printed in Great Britain, a country with only two million fewer people. Even so, in the earlier decades of the nineteenth century there remained a largely untapped market among rank-and-file city dwellers in America: bricklayers, clerks, carpenters, bar-keeps, draymen, housewives. And in the 1830s, while the party organs and the equally partisan mercantile newspapers continued to hold sway, another sort of newspaper was taking shape. It aimed at readers whose tastes were ignored by the political and mercantile journals, and to serve those readers it would eventually have to go out and look for news.

The New York *Sun* appeared in 1833. It marked the first successful attempt to publish a newspaper for the great mass of American city dwellers, citizens who, in the words of one journalism history, were "more interested in *news* than in *views*." The *Sun* cost a penny, and newsboys sold it on Manhattan street corners. Initially, like so many early papers, it was merely the sideline of a printer, in this case a young man named Benjamin Day. But it was totally unlike the past efforts of printers, nor did it bear any resemblance to the *Sun* that Julian Ralph would go to work for four decades later, except perhaps in its eschewing of pomposity and dullness.

Its menu of news was insubstantial: accounts of crime and violence and domestic tragedy, sentimental tales, heavy-handed humor. Much of the news fell under the heading of what would later be decried as sensationalism, and much of it was trash. But the formula, borrowed from cheap London newspapers, worked. Six months after its founding the *Sun* was selling 8,000 papers a day. By 1837, with the help of a new steam-powered cylinder press, it had achieved a circulation of 30,000—more than the combined circulation of all New York dailies when the *Sun* first appeared. Advertisers liked the *Sun* and quickly filled almost half of its four small pages with ads.

Except for a printer who stopped off at the police court each morning on his way to the shop, located on William Street in lower Manhattan, and jotted down notes on titillating cases, the *Sun* initially got along without reporters. Editor Day copied entertaining items from out-of-town news-papers, rewrote the few snippets of local news he could find in his six-cent New York competition, and perhaps now and then tried his hand at fiction to fill the odd corner. But in demonstrating the existence of a large audience for a cheap, readable daily, he had opened the way for the man who was to play the leading role in the development of true *news*papers—James Gordon Bennett.

Bennett was a different sort of man from the editors who had come before him. A Scottish immigrant who had arrived in the United States in 1819, he was neither a printer nor a politician. True, he had strong partisan views—generally of a Democratic hue—that colored what he wrote, as did other editors of his time, but he was not linked to any party and he was not the tool of any political faction. Rather, he was interested in news, and in using news to sell newspapers.

As a young man, he displayed the characteristics of an instinctive reporter. He had a broad, insatiable curiosity, and he spent endless hours roaming the streets of Boston, the first American city he settled in, fascinated by everything he saw. He was an easy questioner of all those he encountered, driven to learn about matters as varied as tariffs and theology, prostitution and schools. And he was also driven to try to capture what he saw and heard on paper—sometimes in bad poetry. So in 1823, at a time when the job scarcely existed, Bennett began working as a reporter. He worked for newspapers in Charleston and New York and served as a correspondent in Washington. He wrote not only of political developments and the sober doings of important men, but also of lighter matters such as social customs and fashions.

In 1835, with five hundred dollars of capital, Bennett launched his own penny newspaper, the New York *Herald*. He contracted with a printing firm to handle the mechanical side, but otherwise he was the entire staff, filling the news columns and selling advertising. Each day he somehow found time to go out from his basement office on Wall Street and work as a reporter. He visited "the Stock Exchange, the coffee houses, the city hall, piers, shops, and the police courts, in search of news," according to a biographer. Bennett's "money articles" gave the public a rare glimpse into the financial maneuvers on Wall Street, and his extensive coverage of the hatchet murder of a prostitute in 1836 represented one of the first all-out efforts at journalistic exploitation of a crime.

The detailed accounts of the gamy murder case helped drive the *Herald's* circulation to 20,000, and it was soon challenging the *Sun*. A rise in price to two cents in 1836 did not slow growth, and in the next few years Bennett made good on a promise to use the extra revenues to expand the *Herald's* news coverage. He had already hired a reporter to follow police court cases, and soon he was assigning others to write about society, the churches and—most novel of all—sports. In 1838 he left the *Herald* in charge of an assistant and took the sidewheeler *Sirius,* the first ship to cross the Atlantic entirely under steam, to Europe, where he arranged for six correspondents to contribute articles. In 1841 he opened a news bureau in Washington. When major developments occurred, such as the Mexican War or the California gold rush, he deployed correspondents to cover them. Along the way, he took advantage of every improvement in transportation and com- munications to speed the movement of news, capitalizing on the telegraph when it came into use in the 1840s and hiring a locomotive to speed a reporter on a mission as casually as others might engage a hackney. By 1860 the *Herald,* with a circulation of 77,000, had far outstripped all rivals, including the *Sun.* Although Bennett's paper looks antique to modern eyes, with its florid prose, its lead paragraphs that leave no doubt where the writer of a news story stands in any controversy, and its offhand use of loaded language, the *Herald* represented a magnificent leap—from newspapers that simply printed such bits of news as drifted into the office to an organization that systematically set out to tell its readers what was going on in the world.

There was no sudden rush to follow Bennett's lead. But beginning in the 1840s other signs of change did appear in New York, which was also the base of two other major figures in the transformation of the press: Horace Greeley of the New York *Tribune* and Henry Raymond of the New York *Times.*

To some extent, Greeley, who founded the *Tribune* in 1841, and Ray- mond, who started the *Times* a decade later, resembled the political-organ editors. Both were deeply involved in Whig and, later, Republican politics, and Greeley, an eccentric man who had been trained as a printer, also promoted a variety of other causes, ranging from vegetarianism and tem- perance to abolition. Both on occasion sought political office, Raymond with more success than Greeley; he served terms as lieutenant governor of the state of New York and as a congressman. Both, in common with other editors of the period, regularly allowed opinion to blend with news. But both also advanced the cause of reporting, hiring reporters to seek out the news and presenting it in a more balanced, accurate way than Bennett's *Herald*. Although they did not ignore murders and other lurid events, they did not base the appeal of their papers on sensationalism.

In 1854, when full-time reporters were still scarce at most newspapers, Greeley employed fourteen on the *Tribune*. Editors were not above doing reporting themselves in those days, and Greeley has been credited with conducting the first formal newspaper interview with a public figure, though it might be more accurate to say it was the first such interview to be widely noticed. It took place in 1859 and the subject was Brigham Young, whom Greeley called on when the stage dropped him off in Salt Lake City while he was on a cross-country trip. Greeley asked the Mormon leader straightforward questions about many aspects of Mormonism, including polygamy, and Young gave straightforward replies (he said he had fifteen wives). It seems strange that before this newspapers had not routinely resorted to such a commonsense approach to gathering the news, but that appears to have been the case. As the practice spread after Greeley's feat attracted attention, it drew criticism from people who insisted that interviews amounted to unwarranted invasions of privacy.

Henry Raymond was a college man, a graduate of the University of Vermont, at a time when there was considerable debate over whether that sort of man was wanted in journalism. (And, on the other hand, whether a college man should have anything to do with journalism; "I fear," a scholarly acquaintance wrote Raymond when he entered the field, "you are in a way to injure your constitution irreparably, and what is at your time of life an equally deplorable evil, that your present occupation is one which to say the least is unfavorable to intellectual development.") For a time Raymond worked as Greeley's chief assistant at the *Tribune*, and later he joined a paper called the New York *Courier and Enquirer*.

At both papers he served as an editor but did stints of reporting as well. He covered almost every kind of story—murders, scientific lectures, politics—and he traveled to Washington and Chicago to write articles. One spring evening in 1849 he witnessed a riot in Astor Place in Manhattan in which nineteen men were killed and hurried to the *Courier* office to write a detailed account. He learned of the rough-and-tumble of reportorial competition. On one of his first out-of-town assignments for the *Tribune*, a murder case in upstate New York, a rival reporter barred him from a special train back to New York City and thereby got his story into print a day before Raymond.

He also experienced the endurance tests that were routine in a nineteenth-century reporter's life, as when he was sent to cover a speech by Daniel Webster at Andover, Massachusetts, one afternoon in 1843. Hurrying from the outdoor gathering, Raymond boarded a train for Boston, switched to one for Norwich, Connecticut, and there boarded a steamer that took him down Long Island Sound in time to make the evening edition of the next day's *Courier* with a story written en route. All the while, he sharpened his reporting techniques, devising his own system of shorthand and honing his style down from a florid, moralistic one to fairly direct prose.

In his planning for the *Times,* Raymond envisioned coverage of all aspects of life. On the local side, he promised reports on public meetings and dinners, sermons, ship news, Wall Street, and crime. He would assign two correspondents to cover Congress in Washington, and he would also have correspondents in Albany to cover the state legislature and in Boston, Philadelphia, Charleston, New Orleans, and Montreal. Correspondents would be retained in Europe. But perhaps even more significant than the breadth of the news coverage Raymond offered in the *Times* was its tone. "Raymond's contribution was the development of reasonable decency in public reporting," observed a journalism history. The *Times* "was invariably fair in tone, if not in content, and no rival equaled it in developing the technique of careful reporting. It substituted accuracy for wishful thinking, even when Raymond was deep in politics." Bennett had replaced windy polemics with accounts of what was happening down the street and across the ocean; Raymond introduced a note of civility and a concern with precision into news reports.

The first issue of the New York *Times,* dated September 18, 1851, and turned out by editors and reporters working by the light of guttering candles in a garret in lower Manhattan, contained a variety of local news. Two men convicted of the murder of "two fellow beings" were to be hanged by the sheriff in the City Prison yard that afternoon. Two rival groups of blacksmiths had engaged in a bloody battle at the corner of Seventh Avenue and Twenty-second Street. The fountain at Washington Square was nearing completion, four women wearing "Bloomers" had been spotted on Manhattan streets the previous day, and a bricklayer, "in consequence of missing his footing" while at work high on a new building, "was precipitated to the ground and instantly killed."

Generations later, none of this is especially noteworthy, save perhaps the bloomers story as an early example of journalism's fascination with fads, but one other minor paragraph is significant, at least from the point of view of journalism history. Along with several reports of fires, the front page of the first issue of the *Times* remarked that there had been a false alarm: a fire bell had rung at nine o'clock the evening before, but "our item gatherer failed to discover the first spark of a fire." The note is interesting on two counts. It was one of the few contemporary acknowledgments of the existence of the person who spent his days gathering the news—the reporter. And the term "item gatherer" suggests, correctly, that the position was not viewed as a particularly substantial or demanding one. In the 1850s reporters were still a rare breed, and their calling was not much more highly esteemed than it had been in 1842 when John Quincy Adams wrote disdainfully of James Gordon Bennett's "hired reporters."

Partisan political organs set the tone for journalism in this period, and news was still a secondary interest for them. The handful of reporters beginning to practice their craft faced difficult obstacles. In 1892 Murat Halstead, who had served as editor of the Cincinnati *Commercial,* recalled journalism in the Cincinnati area before the Civil War. Henry Clay of neighboring Kentucky typified the attitudes of most public men toward the press, which was that its only use lay in giving them unqualified editorial support and printing their pronouncements in the form they chose. Not long before his death in 1852, Clay, then a senator, rose to speak at Lexington when he spotted a reporter for the fledgling Associated Press poised to take notes. The reporter "was compelled not only to drop his pencil, but to leave the ground," said Halstead. "The impertinence of sitting right before an orator addressing his constituents, and taking down his words, was resented and had to be abandoned."

Despite the efforts of Bennett, Greeley, and Raymond, pre–Civil War journalism was by and large a sleepy business. In Cincinnati, according to Halstead, "there was mingled with feeble editorial matter beautiful poetry by lovely women, inspired by a dollar per verse." Tales about bears and Indians also appeared regularly. The advent of telegraphed dispatches was actually resented by some editors, partly because they cost more than mailed articles but also because they injected an unwelcome note of bustle and agitation into what had been a leisurely profession. "These were conservative times, days of delightful communion, no unseemly competition, no strife for 'scoops.' "

The Civil War changed all this. From Sumter to Appomattox, reporters, mainly from the North, roamed battlefields, wrote about what they saw and heard, and schemed to get their stories back to their offices by telegraph or train. Along with Associated Press reporters, more than 150 "special correspondents"—representatives of individual newspapers—covered the war for Northern papers. The New York *Herald* alone had forty, and the New York *Tribune* and the New York *Times* each had a score. Boston, Philadelphia, Cincinnati, and Chicago newspapers also had "specials" with Union armies. Far from being meandering "item gatherers," the Civil War reporters operated aggressively to get the news of large events and to get it into print.

Their accounts had an immediacy that has seldom been matched in war reporting. The correspondents brought the fighting to readers unfiltered by military "spokesmen," and the public eagerly snapped up the papers containing their stories. A few months after the war began in 1861 Oliver Wendell Holmes wrote: "Bread and the Newspaper—this is the new version of the *Panem et Circenses* of the Roman populace. . . . We must have something to eat, and the papers to read. Everything else we can give up." The *Herald* became the first daily newspaper to cross the 100,000 mark in circulation, and many other urban dailies also had huge gains.

When the shooting ended, readership tapered off, and it was obvious that the papers would have to redeploy their reporters and seek out news of other kinds. They did, and circulations soon resumed their climb. As newspapers proliferated and vied for ever larger stakes, the field of daily journalism churned with excitement. At its center was the reporter.

3. Country Journalist

Julian Ralph was born on May 27, 1853, in New York City. His family was living three blocks south of Washington Square in lower Manhattan, on Houston Street. Ralph was to spend part of his boyhood away from New York, and reporting would eventually take him to almost every corner of North America and to Europe, Asia, and Africa. But the city molded him, in the view of his close friend Frederic Remington, the artist, and he never stopped looking at the world through a New Yorker's eyes. New York is "where I belong," he wrote Remington from Cape Town in 1900. He had just been badly hurt when hurled headlong from a horse into a wire fence while accompanying British troops during the Boer War, and he was thinking fondly of the day he would return to New York.

Six years earlier Remington had said of Ralph that he "is very worldly, as befits a metropolitan bringing up, and is easily and quickly at home in the most unheard-of places." But his "geographical centre of gravity" always remained "a point between Park Row and Madison Square." Park Row, angling northeast from Broadway just above the financial district, was, by the time Ralph went to work as a New York reporter in the 1870s, the focus of the daily newspaper business in Manhattan. Madison Square, at the intersection of Fifth Avenue, Broadway, and Twenty-third Street, was on the upper edge of the built-up part of the city when Ralph was born in 1853, and two decades later it was still the northern limit of most business and commerce.

Lower Manhattan was a lighter, airier place in the mid-1800s than in the twentieth century, with few structures rising more than three or four stories, but the atmosphere was thoroughly urban. In 1860 the city of New York, then coterminous with Manhattan, had more than 800,000 residents, and most were squeezed into the southern tip of the island. Broadway, the principal thoroughfare, swarmed with New Yorkers of high and low estate bent on business or pleasure. Horsecars, omnibuses, carriages, and delivery wagons battled the pedestrians and each other for right of way. "Traffic jams lasted hours on Broadway and the other main arteries, while the air was blue with the oaths of cursing, quarreling drivers," said a *Sun* colleague of Ralph's describing New York of the 1860s.

Life was less hectic in the backwater of Greenwich Village, where Julian Ralph spent his earliest years, though it was not a setting in which boys learned rustic pursuits like hunting or riding a horse. "I still hate and fear a horse as a woman does a mouse," Ralph remarked to Frederic Remington in the letter from Cape Town. But an adventuresome boy of ten or eleven must often have wandered amid the noise and bustle of nearby Broadway, and such excursions would have offered compensations for someone who was to spend many of his days seeking information from strangers who had no particular reason to part with it. Being a youngster in the city, encountering street toughs in one block, elegantly turned-out men of affairs in the next, surely contributed to Ralph's talent for coping with the infinite variety of human nature he was thrown up against in his work and for falling easily into conversation with almost anyone he met.

When Ralph was at the pinnacle of his career in the 1890s, Remington, who had traveled extensively with him, marveled: "He drops into a Canadian forest, a Mississippi steamboat, or the private depths of the inner office of the greatest men in America, and the Indians, the negroes, and the great men warm up instinctively and tell him the secrets of their lives. It is possible for Mr. Ralph to go right to a total stranger and become engrossed in the man's own private, personal, or business affairs in twenty minutes, and when others would be unceremoniously kicked out of the place, his strangers like it, and unburden their cares."

Julian Ralph's work was his life. When he finally left the *Sun* in 1895 to take a job with William Randolph Hearst—a move he was to regret—he found himself with a free week, and it struck him that this was his first week of complete idleness since he had been a schoolboy. The record of his career as a reporter can be pieced together from the recollections of others and from clues he left in a slapdash autobiography he compiled near the end of his life, at a time when he was ill and living abroad. Most important, there are the news stories he wrote. The experiences of his contemporaries help round out the picture of what it was like to be a reporter in Ralph's day.

Following his upbringing and other personal matters is more difficult. Published accounts vary on numerous points, and Ralph himself is of little help. His autobiography touches only glancingly on personal history. His entry in the 1901–2 edition of *Who's Who in America,* for which Ralph presumably supplied the material, has the year of his marriage wrong. The man who wrote millions of words about others apparently had little interest in recording anything about himself that did not relate to his work. He kept no diary. His relations appear to have shared his lack of concern with archival matters, and no family Bibles or packets of letters have been handed down to later generations. Their only links with Julian have been a few stories circulated in the family over the years and a memento or two.

All the same, from the scattered scraps of information there does emerge a picture of young Julian growing up and launching himself into journalism. His childhood circumstances were a curious mixture. They were partly those of the genteel middle class, partly those of a family in financial straits. Julian attended the best public school in New York City and for a time even went to boarding school in Europe. Books, music, and familiarity with foreign languages, all suggesting a degree of leisure and comfort, characterized the Ralph household. But in important ways Julian's youth seems more like that of a boy from a working-class background. His schooling ended for good when he was only thirteen. Soon thereafter he went to work, and he earned his own way from then on.

In point of fact, Julian was the son not of a workingman but of a physician. His name was Joseph Ralph, and he had been born in England and brought to America by his parents as a boy. Julian's mother, Selina, had also emigrated from England when young. She married Joseph Ralph when she was only fifteen and he was in his late twenties and already practicing medicine. There were four children in the family, three boys and a girl. Julian was the youngest.

Medicine did not automatically confer prosperity on its practitioners in the mid-1800s, and having a doctor as a parent did not guarantee a privileged childhood. A handful of physicians who had studied in Europe or who had useful social connections acquired affluence and prestige, but in economic standing the great majority of American doctors ranked closer to skilled tradesmen than to successful businessmen throughout much of the nineteenth century.

One reason was the ease of entry into the field. Licenses were rarely required. Most physicians had not attended medical school, and for those who did the course of study consisted of two terms of three to four months, which were seldom preceded by much general education. Many other doctors had served brief apprenticeships, and still others had simply pronounced themselves physicians and commenced practicing with no training. The lack of standards produced a surplus of physicians and intense competition for patients. The doctors' plight was aggravated by the public's well-founded suspicion that the professional treatments of the time—even bloodletting still had its advocates in the 1850s—were often no more effective than home remedies.

In these circumstances many physicians had to struggle to maintain a facade of middle-class respectability. A study of the hierarchy of incomes in the United States in 1860 placed doctors at the lower end of the middle class, with earnings of around $800 a year (to be classed as "rich" required an income of at least $5,000 a year). Most doctors did not even own their own homes.

Julian Ralph's father would seem to have had some advantages over the competition. Dr. Joseph Ralph's father not only was a physician himself but also was one of the select few trained abroad, having graduated from the University of Edinburgh and qualified for membership in the Royal College of Surgeons in London. In all probability, Julian's father acquired his medical knowledge at *his* father's elbow and thus would have been better prepared than most American doctors.

Nevertheless, he seems to have been one of the strugglers. He appears to have moved from one rented house to another, sticking mainly to Greenwich Village; after Houston Street, there were houses on Bleecker, East Ninth, and Stuyvesant streets, among others. Sometimes he maintained his office in his home; other times he announced office hours in separate quarters. The inescapable impression is that he never built a practice profitable enough to hold him in any one place for long and that he kept moving on in hopes of finding greener pastures. To judge from the character of the succession of neighborhoods he settled in, however, he made little headway. The block on Houston Street where the Ralphs were living when Julian was born consisted mainly of single-family homes occupied by professional men and small merchants. But some years later a New York city directory listed Dr. Ralph as living on a stretch of Stuyvesant Street where most of the houses took in lodgers and his neighbors would have included a saloonkeeper, a butcher, and a tailor.

Julian's early departure from the classroom was not at all unusual for the period, even for children from relatively prosperous families. Most youngsters had finished with formal instruction by the time they reached thirteen, the age at which Julian left school. Public high schools were still rare; in the 1869–70 school year only 2 percent of the country's high-school-age population was enrolled in high schools. But in Julian's case one is nevertheless left wondering. How did he manage to acquire the breadth of knowledge and the skills as a writer that he displayed as a young newspaperman? From where came the knowledge of the ways of the world evident in even his earliest stories, the easy acquaintance with literature that seems to bubble to the surface in his copy of its own accord?

Part of the answer lay in his family. Joseph Ralph may not have prospered as a physician, but there is a hint that he had some aspirations to learning in the classical names of two of his sons, Julian and Justus, which he must at least have approved. (Joseph and Selina had another mild eccentricity in names: All the males in the family had the initials "J. E." The doctor was Joseph Edward and the eldest son was Joseph Emile. Justus's middle name was Edward and Julian's was either Elbert or Egbert; he never used it, no one remembers it with certainty, and no records show it.) Selina Ralph, however, was the dominant parental influence on Julian. She was known as a cultivated woman, well-read and capable of supplementing the family income on occasion by taking pupils for instruction in French and German.

According to Ralph family legend, the marriage of Selina and the doctor was troubled almost from the outset, and this appears to have affected Julian in ways not altogether harmful to his education. Apparently on more than one occasion, Selina somehow scraped together the money to pack herself and the children off to Europe. They stayed for lengthy periods in Germany and France, and the children attended boarding schools. Julian very likely studied in France. It must have been from such schooling and from Selina that he picked up at least some lasting knowledge of French— enough so that during the Greco-Turkish war of 1897, while sprawled on the dirt floor of a tent in Thessaly, he could compose a dispatch in French when the Turkish censor insisted on the use of that language.

Julian read both deeply and widely, a habit that Selina undoubtedly helped shape. Near the turn of the century he compiled a list of favorite books that included the novels of Thackeray, Scott, Balzac, and Hugo (but, surprisingly, not Dickens), plus Grant's *Memoirs* and the essays of Emerson. An aspiring writer, he said, should steep himself in Shakespeare, but he added that if he could have only two books they would be the *Bible* and *Robinson Crusoe*. The story of the castaway sailor is an interesting choice. Its author, Daniel Defoe, one of the outstanding journalists of the eighteenth century as well as a novelist, was a master of clear, forceful narrative, with an eye for the detail that makes a scene leap to life. So, in his own way, was Julian Ralph in his reporting of events from the 1870s through the turn of the century.

Julian's love for *Robinson Crusoe* was almost certainly inspired by the principal of the public school he attended in Manhattan. Along with Selina Ralph, Thomas Hunter of Public School No. 35 on West Thirteenth Street was a central influence on the boy, and one of Hunter's favorite books was *Robinson Crusoe.* An intense, dark-haired, bearded young Irish immigrant, Hunter had arrived in New York in 1850 at the age of eighteen possessing little more than a box of books and a rigorous education. He had been forced to flee Ireland because he had written newspaper articles that the British authorities viewed as treasonable, and in New York he first sought work as a journalist. Failing in that effort, he joined the faculty of P.S. 35, whose students were limited to boys. In 1857 he became principal, and under his sway the school quickly attained such a reputation for excellence that well-to-do parents outside its district paid special fees to enroll their sons. Hunter later founded the Manhattan college that bears his name.

Hunter mixed kindliness—as principal he did away with the rattan—with stern demands on staff and students. He once dismissed a teacher who had written a note containing two spelling errors and a double negative. He pressed the boys to read, and a regular drill was to have them retell stories in their own words, useful training for grasping the plot lines of confused real-life dramas. To open young eyes to the world beyond the schoolyard, he invited notables to speak, and among those who came were Horace Greeley and Henry Raymond. Hunter recalled that Greeley "warned the boys against two things—free trade and indulgence in alcoholic liquors."

When Hunter founded the Normal College, later Hunter College, in 1869, its purpose was to train young women as teachers. The curriculum ran heavily to ancient history, geography, mathematics, Latin, and the sciences, and he also insisted that the would-be teachers learn to write competently. After the college had been operating a year, Hunter noted these grave weaknesses in the written work of the students:

1. There was a general deficiency in clear, vigorous and legible penmanship.
2. A want of executive force in the arrangement of the subject-matter.
3. A curious indifference to capitals and periods, whole pages sometimes being found without the least attempt at punctuation, and without a capital letter.

Hunter might have graded the mature Julian Ralph severely in penmanship—though vigorous, it was sometimes barely legible—but he surely would not have faulted the "executive force" of some of the stories Ralph wrote at white heat years later.

What led Julian Ralph into journalism can only be speculated upon. As a boy on the streets of Manhattan, he must have been aware of the excitement of Civil War journalism, with newsboys crying headlines of battles as papers vied to be first on the street with the latest news. He must have wandered past the buildings emblazoned with the names of famous newspapers—the *Tribune,* the *Herald,* the *Times,* the *Sun,* the *Evening Post.*

In later years Ralph took a mystical, romantic view of the reasons why he and others entered journalism. In a swaggering mood, to which he was sometimes given when talking about his profession, he observed that newspaper work in the nineteenth century was rarely the route to comfortable old age. He went on:

> No man born of the press will deny the other side of the case—namely, that if the microbe is in your blood, facts and figures may go hang themselves, and hardship, exposure, danger will only serve to push you further in. . . . You might as well ask the coming Nelson if he has thought what a dog's life a sailor's is.

"Newspapermen are born and not made," Ralph said, and after more college men began entering the field in the 1890s, he was skeptical of the value of their education. He didn't think college hurt a reporter, but he was never convinced it did much good.

In Ralph's case, the New York *Times* said after his death, "he could not help being a newspaper man." Writing was as natural for him as breathing, and in a day when budding writers did not polish their skills in college seminars or angle for fellowships, newspaper work must have seemed the only course. When the vicissitudes of the Ralph family's existence brought Julian to Red Bank, New Jersey, probably soon after the Civil War, he entered a newspaper office for the first time. And soon he would experience for the first time the thrill of putting words down on paper and seeing them transmuted into print for all the world to read.

Red Bank perches on a bluff of red clay overlooking the broad waters of the Navesink River. It is on the south shore of the river. The Atlantic Ocean is five miles down the Navesink; New York City is thirty miles to the north. In 1844 the town was described this way: "The principal source of the prosperity of Red Bank is the trade with New York. Thirteen sloops and schooners sail from here with vegetables, wood and oysters for that market, and a steamboat plies regularly between here and the city. Vessels week after week have taken oysters to New York and returned with $600 or $700 for their cargoes."

In the late 1860s Red Bank was much the same sort of place, a country town but closely linked to the city. It had 2,000 residents. The sailing vessels still carried cargoes of produce and oysters to New York, and the only consistently industrious reporting the local weekly newspaper did was to collect the latest wholesale prices for vegetables and eggs in the city. Train service to New York, with a ferry link across the Hudson, would start in the 1870s, but in the 1860s the steamboats were the most pleasant and convenient way to travel between Red Bank and Manhattan. In the years after the Civil War, two white sidewheelers with single tall black stacks, the *Sea Bird* and the *Helen,* made the round trip daily. The steamboat wharf at the base of the bluff was the focus of village life. Partway up the road leading from the wharf was a hotel and tavern. Farther up were a cluster of houses, some with backyards stretching down to the river, and a few blocks of commercial structures. One two-story building was occupied by the weekly paper, the *New Jersey Standard.*

It was the final breakup of his parents' marriage that brought Julian to Red Bank. Probably in 1866, the year Julian turned thirteen, the continuing friction between Selina and her husband led to a divorce, a step so rare at the time that the marriage must indeed have been a mismatch. Dr. Ralph remained in Manhattan, and Selina and the four children boarded one of the white sidewheelers at a pier on the Hudson River and sailed for Red Bank. How they chose to settle in Red Bank is not known, but over the next few years Selina and her offspring carved out roles for themselves in the community. In 1870 the *New Jersey Standard* carried an advertisement stating that "Mrs. Ralph desires to announce that she is now forming classes for instruction in the French and German languages." Julian's sister, whose first name was Lucy but who was known as "Bram" from her strange middle name of Brambilla (the last name of a famed Italian surgeon), had grown up knowledgeable enough about music to open a music store, and in 1870 Miss Ralph's Music Room was advertising a new shipment of pianos. One of Julian's brothers, Justus, was working as a railroad ticket agent in Red Bank.

By most accounts Julian went to work at the *New Jersey Standard* when he was thirteen, soon after he arrived in Red Bank, although some sources say fifteen. In any case, when he was still a boy, he joined the *Standard.*

Despite the *New Jersey* in its name, the *Standard* was a small local weekly. Founded in 1852, it was the only paper in Red Bank. In 1870 it had eight hundred subscribers, each of whom paid $1.50 a year. From all appearances, its two proprietors were more concerned with promoting their job-printing business and selling advertising than with informing the public about what was going on in Red Bank and the rest of Monmouth County. Consisting of four full-sized pages, the *Standard* devoted almost two-thirds of its space to ads—a dry goods store, painless dentists, a flour and feed dealer, a clothing store, a maker of "round and flat top" coffins, freight service to New York via sloop, a plea for the return of a lost heifer. Most of the rest of the space was filled with articles reprinted from other newspapers received under the exchange system or from magazines. Such articles could be almost anything—treacly romances, ghost stories, the tale of a missing ocean liner, an attack on the deplorably low salaries paid the clergy.

Except for the wholesale produce prices on page 3, the only real news consisted of two columns on page 2 headed "Local & State Items." These contained a score or more paragraphs cursorily covering—in no particular order of importance—such varied matters as an attempt to rob the First National Bank of Red Bank that was foiled by a new vault door with "the most approved combination locks"; the approaching visit of President Grant to the nearby seaside resort of Long Branch; a parade of volunteer firemen; an accident involving a runaway horse and buggy; and announcements of a piano concert by Miss Adelaide Manzocchi, a temperance society meeting, and lectures on "Travel in Oriental & *Bible* Lands."

Julian began at the *Standard* as a printer's devil, an apprentice printer. Sometimes youths were installed in such jobs by their fathers. Addressing the Wisconsin Press Association in 1862, C. W. Fitch, editor of the weekly Manitowoc *Herald,* said:

> Men who appreciate the value of thorough mental culture are placing their sons in the printing office for the benefit of one or two years' practical experience. This is done because it has been demonstrated that the knowledge there attained is not uncertain or superficial, but makes its recipient the equal of those who attain a more easy notoriety for education and intelligence. Take the bundle of exchanges that are placed upon the table of every country printing office, and each day's depository is an abridged encyclopedia of knowledge; and to this ample and unfailing supply, every printer has constant access.

Since Julian's father was thirty miles away in Manhattan, it is more likely that the boy took the job on his own initiative. Perhaps he stood in the doorway of the *Standard* office and watched as a printer translated scrawled copy into type and observed him working at the flatbed press, pulling the stout wooden lever that pressed the sheets of newsprint against the inked type. Perhaps then he got the first glimmering that the microbe was in his blood.

Printing was still the most common route for entering journalism in the post–Civil War years. Many older editors scorned aspirants who had not dirtied their fingers with type. "School masters, book keepers, daguerreotypists, dentists, hair dressers—in short, the whole catalogue of employments—have become ambitious of newspaper fame, as reporters or editors," complained Mr. Fitch of the Manitowoc *Herald* in 1862. "They carry a superabundance of stationery—you might even mistake them for members of the Legislature—write voluminous correspondences, which printers finally make over for him, as a milliner does last year's bonnet." As for Fitch:

> For my own part, I stand committed to the belief that the editorial profession is the proper and legitimate calling of the printer—that the printing office is the college in which the editor should finally graduate—that, while the ordinary institutions of learning have furnished statesmen and patriots—men skilled in diplomacy and legal lore—they have never produced a class of editors equal to those who have been bred to the types; but, on the other hand, the printing office has furnished the legal profession with some of its most brilliant stars, and the country with its most renowned philosophers, patriots and statesmen. All the employments and influences of the printing office are calculated to cultivate and strengthen those qualifications which are indispensable to the accomplished editor.

And, Fitch would undoubtedly have agreed, to the accomplished reporter.

Such views were not merely the quirks of small-town editors. Horace Greeley of the New York *Tribune,* trained in the composing room himself, loudly declared his preference for printers, even though in practice he tolerated others as employees; Henry Raymond, for example, was a college man. Julius Chambers told of calling on Greeley in 1870 to ask for a job and announcing that he had just graduated from Cornell. "I'd a damned sight rather you had graduated at a printer's case!" Greeley barked before turning back to the chaos of copy and clippings on his desk. Chambers, who would eventually achieve prominence in the newspaper world, never had a chance to inform Greeley that he had earned his way through Cornell by working as a printer.

When Julian Ralph joined the *Sun* in 1875, Charles Dana, the editor, was one of the few nonprinters among the principal staff members. "The idea prevailed in those days that printers were familiar with the way to prepare copy, with condensation, and were wise to the value of news," said Chester Lord, who joined the *Sun* as a reporter in 1872 and served as its managing editor from 1880 to 1913. Lord was not a printer, having attended Hamilton College for a few semesters and then gone directly into newspaper work. But long after he entered the field ex-printers still dominated the staffs of some newspapers. Ray Stannard Baker, later to win fame as a muckraker, found when he joined the Chicago *News Record* in 1892 that most of his fellow reporters were "of the old-fashioned up-from-the-composing-room type." Baker remembered unrolling his diploma from Michigan Agricultural College to show to the *News Record* city editor when he applied for a job. "I cringe yet when I recall the look in his eye and the slight disdainful wave of his hand. I was to understand later how inconsequential in those days was a college diploma in a newspaper office."

Nineteenth-century printers were known as profane, hard-drinking men who could not stick at one job for long, a stigma that often clung to those who forsook setting the news in type for writing it. But many printers also had reputations as highly literate and as founts of knowledge. If the standards for apprenticeship set down in *The American Printer,* a manual for the trade published in 1866, were applied even minimally, such reputations had some basis in fact. Suggesting requirements for youthful apprentices, Thomas MacKellar, author of the manual, asked: "Has he had a fair common-school education? Is he a perfect speller? Has he a turn for reading?" So that they could do their own proofreading, MacKellar continued, a printer "should understand clearly the grammar and idiomatic structure of his mother-tongue, and have, as it were, an encyclopediac knowledge of the names, times, and productions of its writers, as well as an entire familiarity with the *Bible* especially, and with Shakespeare. He should be, in fact, a living orthographical, biographical, bibliographical, geographical, historical and scientific dictionary, with some smattering of Hebrew, Greek, Latin, French, Spanish, Italian, and German."

At the age of thirteen—or even fifteen—Julian did not possess all these qualifications. But he had enough, coupled with a forceful personality, to persuade the proprietors of the *New Jersey Standard* to take him on as an apprentice printer. Typically, an apprentice spent a year at such menial tasks as running errands, sweeping the floor, and sorting the pi. In returning this spilled, jumbled type to the proper boxes in the type cases, the apprentice learned the positions of the letters—the upper case for capitals, the lower case for small letters. He also learned to distinguish "u" from "n," "b" from "q" and "d" from "p."

Then it was time for "going to the case." The apprentice stood before the banks of type. In his left hand he held a "stick," a small tray with room for ten lines or so of type. With his right hand he plucked letters from their boxes and placed them in the stick, setting the lines backwards, the mirror image of a printed page. The stress was on accuracy; speed would follow naturally. The techniques to be learned were precise and various. The left hand, with the stick, followed the right as it darted from box to box. The letters had to be kept tight and straight in the stick, and, said Thomas MacKellar's manual, when the apprentice "essays to empty the stick he must be taught to lift the entire mass in one square solid body, and to place it squarely and vertically on the galley." He must also be taught to distribute the type in the cases after use by taking a word or two of type between the thumb and forefinger of his right hand and easing the pressure just enough to drop the individual letters back into their boxes one by one.

The job of setting type by hand had its special rhythm. "Pick and click/Goes the type in the stick" began a poem called "The Song of the Printer." Apprentices were admonished not to add extra movements and flourishes, "such as swinging the body as the types are picked up, nicking the type against the stick several times before placing it in line, standing on one leg, & c."

Charles Congdon, a leading editorialist on the New York *Tribune* in the 1860s and 1870s and before that a reporter, was among those convinced that printers made superior writers. Congdon was a graduate of Brown, but he also had learned the printing trade at his father's weekly newspaper in New Bedford, Massachusetts, and he maintained that such training resulted in an economical writing style useful in newspaper work. He offered no explanation, but it might be theorized that the stress on avoiding wasteful motions in setting type carried over into avoiding unnecessary words in writing—or it may simply be that anyone who had set a column of type letter by letter instinctively eliminated superfluous words. C. W. Fitch, the Wisconsin editor, suggested further that the printer had an edge because "his mind is constantly directed to definite objects." Fuzzy abstractions yielded to concrete details—gestures, tones, smells, looks—that put life into stories.

A less conjectural explanation of why printers often developed into excellent writers is that they got a lot of practice, particularly if they started at small weeklies like the *New Jersey Standard*. At such papers a printer of necessity had to write some of the matter he set in type. Sometimes, like Harry Blake, the *New-England Palladium* printer who gathered news from ships, he composed directly in type. For young Julian, writing the news quickly took on more appeal than the mechanical side of the business. "The handling of types in the country office in which he was early employed set his fingers tingling to 'make copy' for other compositors," said the New York *Times*.

As Ralph himself recalled it: "I became a newspaper writer in a day by describing the antics of a mad bull in the streets of a village." Beyond this, not much is known about Ralph's writing at the *Standard*, but presumably he henceforth mixed reporting with setting type. In the yellowed copies of the *Standard* that survive, it is impossible to single out definitely which of the short, matter-of-fact news items Julian might have written. But now and then in an issue from 1868, 1869, or 1870, years when he is known to have been on the staff, there appears a brief story that evidences more effort than might be expected from an older editor mainly concerned with selling advertising and printing—an item that is not just a smattering of facts but offers a coherent explanation of a swindle, a strange accident, or some other local happening. One such item, reporting the suicide of a Red Bank man in 1870, almost certainly was the work of a wide-eyed seventeen-year-old determined to bring home to his readers the full horror of the event. The man had rigged a shotgun so that he could place the barrel in his mouth and then discharge the gun by pulling on a rope. "When found, his brains had run out of his mouth, down upon his clothing," reported the *Standard*.

Julian's first years in journalism were marked by a number of comings and goings. At some point as a youth he went to Toms River, a fishing community thirty miles south of Red Bank, and took a job with the weekly Toms River *Courier*. The job lasted one day. His employer had printed the ballots for an election to be held the next day, but, as an active participant in local politics, he had neglected to include on the ballot the candidates put forward by his political foes. Ralph had been left in charge of the office when members of the slighted faction showed up to protest. Julian agreed with them that a mistake had been made and obligingly printed up new ballots listing all the candidates. When the editor returned and discovered what Julian had done, he was discharged.

Another short-lived venture took place in the fall of 1871. Julian and a friend launched their own weekly, the Red Bank *Leader*. It lasted nine weeks and no copies survive. Sometime soon after that Julian traveled to Webster, Massachusetts, a small cotton-mill town in the south-central part of the state, just above the Connecticut border, where he had somehow obtained a position as "acting editor" of the Webster *Times*. He stayed about a year, but since the proprietor's tastes seem to have run heavily to reprints of temperance tracts and gossipy items from amateur correspondents, Julian had little chance to display his talents. In any case, his stint as an editor in Webster, like his attempt to start a new paper in Red Bank, led nowhere, and it may be that Julian began to realize that his true bent was for reporting and writing.

After the year in Webster, probably late in 1872, Ralph returned to Red Bank and rejoined the *Standard* briefly as the "local editor." One tale remains from this period. In the village on the Navesink River lived an eminently detestable man—a loudmouth, drunk, and scandalmonger, according to Ralph—and one week the *Standard* minced no words in relating some of his activities. At a time when Ralph happened to be running the office, the lout climbed the steep stairs to the second-floor office and demanded an apology. A mature Ralph recounted his youthful reaction, complete with Victorian bombast:

> At that I exclaimed: "Confound you, you old reprobate! Leave this instant or I'll throw you out of the window and more than that—I'll thrash you every time I see you in the street." "You shall sweat for this," said he. "You shall go bankrupt for this." Without another warning I lifted the man in my arms and threw him down the stairs. . . . Never was threat of a libel suit met in that fashion before.

One consideration that would have drawn Julian back to Red Bank was that he had fallen in love with a girl from the hamlet of Chapel Hill, two miles north of the Navesink. Her name was Isabella Mount, but everybody called her Belle. Perhaps it was dawning on Julian that a small-town weekly offered little scope for advancement and that if he wanted to marry Belle, a member of a family prominent in the area for generations, he would have to seek a larger arena in which to try his skills. The New York newspapers delivered each day to the *Standard* office were a reminder that only two hours away in Manhattan lay a world rich with new possibilities. And so sometime in the early months of 1873 Julian Ralph returned to the city whose streets he had known as a child to look for a job as a reporter. He was nineteen years old.

4. 'I Have Pictured It as I Saw It'

I n 1873 the daily newspapers of New York clustered in a few blocks of lower Manhattan. They did so largely out of habit, but the location was also handy to nerve centers of city life—City Hall, police headquarters, Wall Street, the Broadway hotels. This was particularly important in a day when most news was gathered in face-to-face encounters.

Park Row, destined in time to become synonymous with the newspaper industry in New York, was the axis of the district. Overlooking City Hall Park to the west, it ran from Broadway and Ann Street to Printing House Square, an open space formed where Park Row and Nassau Street converged and adorned by a statue of Benjamin Franklin. On the two blocks of Park Row were the *Express,* the *Evening Mail,* and the *World.* At Broadway and Ann, just south of Park Row, were the *Herald* and its offshoot, the *Evening Telegram.* At the other end of Park Row, on Printing House Square, were the *Times,* the *Tribune,* and the *Sun.* Just to the north of the *Sun,* on Chatham Street, in a block that would be mostly obliterated as the Manhattan approach to the Brooklyn Bridge took shape over the next several years, were the *Star* and the *Daily News.* Back to the south again, on Nassau, were New York's two most venerable dailies, the *Commercial Advertiser* and the *Evening Post.* And a hundred yards west of Broadway, on Park Place, the city's newest daily, the *Daily Graphic,* was just starting up in the spring of 1873.

Many newspapers, many possibilities—so it must have seemed to Julian Ralph and other would-be reporters. But, in truth, getting a job was anything but a simple matter of knocking on an editor's door and announcing that one's services were available. Often it was a struggle merely to be allowed to approach the editor's door. There were many applicants—too many—and their ranks would swell through the final decades of the nineteenth century as word spread of the reporter's expanding role and as an increasingly glamorous view of the field took hold. Along with the print-shop products still favored by some editors, there was, despite the lingering prejudice against them, a steadily increasing flow of college men eager to

Printing House Square in the late 1870s. From left, French's Hotel, the *Sun*, the *Tribune*, and the *Times*. *From* Memoirs of an Editor *by Edward Page Mitchell (Charles Scribner's Sons, an imprint of Macmillan Publishing Company, New York, 1924), p. 200.*

try a job that promised something out of the ordinary. There were also drifters from the professions, immigrants desperate for any way to make a living, and youths with literary ambitions who saw journalism as an outlet for their talents. In search of reporting work, all these sorts gravitated to big cities, where the ferment transforming journalism was centered. The largest group came to New York, home of the best-known newspapers and the best-known editors.

Julius Chambers, the Cornell graduate sent packing by Horace Greeley in 1870, had other discouraging moments as he sought a job. He was told that the *Herald* and the *Sun* never hired beginners and that it would be a waste of time even to apply. At the *Evening Post* he climbed "steep and dark" stairs to see the city editor, Charles Nordhoff. "Every time you walk up Broadway, every time you walk down Broadway," Nordhoff told him, "something occurs that never occurred before and never will recur. If you have the eye to see and the faculty to describe this phenomenal happening, your success as a reporter is assured." As Chambers puzzled over the proper response to this profundity, Nordhoff dismissed him with a wave of the hand. At the *World* the city editor had no use for "kid reporters."

But Chambers at least obtained audiences with editors. Later, when the number of applicants had risen to a flood, even that was often impossible.

Charles Russell had served as a jack of all trades—printer, reporter, editor—at three small dailies in the Midwest before coming to New York to seek a job as a reporter in the early 1880s. Still barely past twenty, he brought with him an imagination fired by accounts of the brilliant feats of New York reporters in solving crimes that had baffled the police. A Midwestern colleague accompanied him to New York. "We had pictured ourselves walking up to the city editor's desk, sitting down with him in cordial discourse, and impressing him with the advantages that we offered," Russell recalled many years later. Instead, they could not make it past the office boys. Their first stop was the *Herald*.

We climbed the three long flights of iron stairs to the city department and came face to face with a board partition, an iron gate apparently locked, and a push button with a small sign above it, reading "Ring."

So we rang and after a time there appeared a youth that regarded us with manifest contempt and then said, out of one side of his mouth, "Well, whadda youse want?" We said we wished to see the city editor. With his left hand he flung at us a small card thus worded:

Mr. ————
wishes to see the City Editor
about ————
———, 188—.

With which he vanished. One of us filled out the blank as best he could, stating that we were experienced newspaper men and had called to mention to the city editor our willingness to accept positions with the *Herald* if sufficient inducements were offered. This, the youth having returned, we intrusted to his care. After a long interval he reappeared and this was his remark:

"Hey, youse! City editor says he regrets t'say there's no vacancy on the *Herald* staff."

Whereupon he disappeared.

Much the same thing happened at the other morning papers—the *Sun*, the *Times*, the *Tribune*, and the *World*—except that at the *World* their way was barred by not one but two office boys. Russell and his friend then tried all the evening papers, with the same result. It seemed that city editors, the men who oversaw the local reporting staffs, had a uniform policy of not seeing applicants for reporting jobs—at least applicants unknown to them. "How on earth, then, did one secure a position in New York?" wondered Russell.

Persistence, sometimes mixed with a bit of luck, was the answer. On a second visit to the *Tribune*, Julius Chambers went behind Greeley's back and sought out the editor's chief lieutenant, Whitelaw Reid. Reid, a future editor of the *Tribune*, turned out to be not only a college man but also a fraternity brother, and he asked the city editor to make room for Chambers. Chambers would rise to the top of New York journalism, becoming managing editor of the *Herald* in 1886. Charles Russell also made repeated rounds of the newspaper offices. On his third try at the *Commercial Advertiser*, whose office at Fulton and Nassau streets was a "frightful barrack," the city editor paused long enough in the anteroom to tell Russell that he would give him a try as a reporter.

If anything, the way of the applicant was even more difficult in 1894, when Theodore Dreiser, then twenty-three years old, came to New York seeking a job as a reporter. He had two years' experience at newspapers in Chicago, St. Louis, and Pittsburgh, but on Park Row he met with one rebuff after another. "Whoja wanta see?" an office boy would ask.

"The city editor."
"Wha'ja wanta see him about?"
"A job."
"No vacancies. No; no vacancies today. He says to say no vacancies today, see? You can't go in there. He says no vacancies."
"But can't I even see him?"
"No; he don't wanta see anybody. No vacancies."
"Well, how about taking my name in to him?"
"Not if you're looking for a job. He says no vacancies."

At the *World* the unapproachable city editor was none other than Charles Russell, who had risen considerably in life from the time he landed a job as a *Commercial Advertiser* reporter. One day, finding Russell as inaccessible as on several previous visits, a desperate Dreiser pushed past two office boys and burst into the *World* city room. The first person he encountered there was a handsome, assured fellow in his early thirties who he later learned was an established journalistic star named Arthur Brisbane. Brisbane inquired what he wanted. A job, Dreiser replied.

"Where do you come from?" asked Brisbane.

"The West."

Brisbane approached Russell's desk and pointed to Dreiser. "This young man wants a job," said Brisbane. "I wish you would give him one." Russell did.

As Dreiser quickly learned, a job of the sort he held at the New York *World* did not guarantee a steady wage. He had been taken on as a "space reporter." Throughout the last three decades of the nineteenth century and into the twentieth century, many reporters—most, at times, in New York—worked "on space." It was a piecework system. They were paid according to how much space they filled, and depending on their ability and their luck, they either prospered or starved. Each reporter clipped everything he wrote that appeared in print and pasted all the items—minus the headlines—into a "string." At the end of the week he presented his string to the cashier. The cashier measured it with a ruler and paid the reporter at a set rate per column—between five and eight dollars a column in New York. Generally, but not always, there was also a "time" allowance of fifty cents an hour that was paid to a reporter sent out on an assignment that did not produce a story.

Many reporters in New York were working under the space system by the 1860s. In the latter part of that decade, each daily had a salaried staff—as many as thirty reporters at the larger papers—that was supplemented by an additional group of reporters who hung around the office waiting to be called on as needed and who were paid according to how much space they filled. Over the years the system evolved until New York newspapers relied on a handful of salaried reporters mainly for routine matter such as police court happenings and ship news but looked to space writers for the bulk of their material, particularly features and other out-of-the-ordinary stories.

The system had great advantages for editors. Like bench warmers on a football team chafing to be sent into the game, space reporters waited for the nod from the editor that would send them out on an assignment. An editor was assured of having plenty of help on hand should a tenement go up in flames or a flood of newsworthy visitors check in at the Astor House or the Fifth Avenue Hotel. He could send a reporter to look into the flimsiest tip, to handle an assignment so trivial that the resulting story would be needed only on the slackest of news days, or to see if anything could be made of a superior's most harebrained suggestion. "The *Tribune*, in particular," said Alexander Noyes, recalling his days as a new reporter there in 1883, " . . . manned its reporters' room on what appeared to be the theory that the way to 'cover' everything was to install in its office so many space reporters that the human machinery for assignments would much more than meet any conceivable requirement." But some other New York papers followed much the same practice.

For experienced, talented, and industrious reporters, the space system sometimes proved lucrative, yielding more income than they could have earned on salary. For beginners the effects of the system were mixed. On the negative side it meant a precarious financial existence. A newcomer to the city room usually drew marginal assignments—and not many of them. But the space system also meant that, despite the discouragements encountered initially by most aspirants, a beginner generally had a better chance to show what he could do than his counterpart a century later. It offered at least a glimmer of hope to "an applicant arriving without recognized credentials," said Alexander Noyes, who eventually became financial editor of the New York *Times*. As the space system became entrenched, once a would-be reporter had brazened his way past the office boys guarding the entrance to the newsroom, it was sometimes not terribly hard to persuade the city editor to add yet another novice space writer. Why not? If an aspiring reporter showed any spark, any hint of promise, it cost the newspaper next to nothing to give him a try, and he just might come in handy in a pinch. Merely making it past the boorish office boys signified a trait that the mature Julian Ralph would rate among the most essential for a reporter—"unconquerable persistence."

Ralph never said much about how he got his start in New York, but after he had achieved success he suggested that one way for a beginner to gain a foothold in the field was simply to hang around a newspaper office day after day, for weeks if necessary, until something newsworthy happened and no one else was available to cover it. That sounds like the way the space system often worked, and if Ralph's advice reflected his own experience, he presumably began his career in New York as a space writer. Office boys barring the way to city editors would not have daunted him much, given his persistence, his ability to strike up an easy relationship with almost anyone, and—just possibly—a hint of physical menace. Maybe the office boys sensed something in this job applicant that suggested he might throw *them* down the stairs if they tried his good nature too severely.

The first newspaper Ralph worked for in New York was the *World*. The *World* is usually associated with Joseph Pulitzer, but in 1873 it bore almost no resemblance to the sensational and enormously successful paper it would become after Pulitzer acquired it a decade later. After a shaky start as a religious daily in 1860, the *World* had soon been converted by new owners into a general newspaper, but it remained sober and straitlaced. Private scandals and lurid crimes received little space. A *World* reporter could never hope for an assignment as dramatic as the one Henry Morton Stanley had recently carried out for James Gordon Bennett, Jr., now in command at the *Herald*—to find David Livingstone in Africa. Stanley was one of young Julian Ralph's idols.

Indeed, in a day when many newspapers were declaring their independence from political parties, the chief distinguishing characteristic of the *World* was its strong allegiance to the Democrats. Its editor through most of the 1860s and 1870s, a man with the theatrical name of Manton Marble, is described as a scholarly, talented journalist, and in his lifetime he was sometimes spoken of in the same breath as Greeley, Raymond, and Dana. But his main interest was politics and editorial advocacy of the Democratic cause, not vigorous pursuit of a wide variety of news. Because Marble was out of step with the reading public's shift in interest from opinion to news, the *World's* circulation had been slipping steadily. In 1873 it was selling 20,000 papers a day, by far the lowest circulation of the five New York morning papers.

The *World's* relative poverty undoubtedly contributed to its lack of news-gathering enterprise, but on one occasion it displayed a sense of humor about its straitened circumstances. The newspaper's shabby Park Row headquarters were unusual in that its printing press did not rest on a solid basement floor but instead shared the fourth floor with the compositors and the reporters and editors. In 1875, at a time when the *Tribune* was moving into a lavish new building and printing letters of praise for the structure from prominent figures, part of the *World's* press crashed through a rotten section of the floor. After the floor was repaired, the *World* carried a paean to "Our New Composing Room Floor" and accompanied it with invented tributes to the floor, including one in Latin from the Pope.

Despite its shortcomings, the *World* could teach a beginning reporter a thing or two. Not all newspapers had copy desks to scrutinize stories in the early 1870s; at the *Herald* trusted men sent their copy directly to the composing room, complete with headlines. But the *World* had a copy desk, and it dealt mercilessly with novices. A young Amherst graduate named Selah Merrill Clarke, who later became an influential editor on the *Sun,* joined the *World* shortly before Ralph. As an old man he remembered his early days on the job.

Imagine a young fellow in the fury of late and hasty scribbling, his fingers and forehead all sweat and ink, yanked off the track by a perspiring, yelling apparition from the copy-desk, who thrust a sheet of his vernacular at him and cried aloud:
"Now, what would that mean in English?"
Need he have yelled it?

Clarke was sent to cover a murder. A man had brained his wife with a coal hod, then almost severed her head with a bread knife.

I thought I was warranted in beginning with "A most brutal murder was committed," and so on. The office-boy grabbed the first sheet and vanished with it. Then the copy-reader came galloping and brought it back.
"Do you think you're an editor?" he shouted. "Do you think the public needs your opinion whether it was brutal or not? You tell what happened and keep yourself out of it."

The copy desk's efforts to keep opinion out of the *World's* news columns were not entirely successful. A glance at issues of the *World* from 1873 shows that Clarke's editorializing was mild compared to what appeared in the paper many days. Political writers could not suppress their glee at developments favorable to the Democrats or unfavorable to the Republicans, though the savage tone of earlier newspaper partisanship was gone. Writers dealing with crime sometimes could not resist moralizing. An account of the hanging of a murderer in the Arizona Territory concluded: "It is thought that this exhibition of the majesty of the law will not be without its salutary effect upon the lawless character of the Territory." The *World* of 1873 also looks old-fashioned in other ways. Summary opening paragraphs were still not the rule, and many stories took forever to get to the point. Accounts of political meetings and other public occasions often sounded like a secretary's minutes; a reader could slog through two columns and still not be certain whether anything of significance had occurred. Even an account of a baseball game between the Philadelphia Athletics and the New York Mutuals forced the sports follower to thread his way through most of the story before discovering that, thanks to the "lively style" of the Athletics' batting and seventeen errors by the Mutuals, Philadelphia had won, 11–7. Nor had the *World* entirely escaped American

newspapers' old propensity for treating European news with excessive
deference. Every tremor in French or Spanish politics was spread over page
one, and thousands of words explained a German scientist's theory that
oysters caused insanity.

On the other hand, there were days when the *World* performed im-
pressively. In the spring of 1873 the editors became exercised over the filth
that clogged the old cobblestone streets in the poor neighborhoods of
Manhattan. Reporters described the garbage, sewage, manure, and uniden-
tifiable muck—"whatever rots and pollutes and poisons"—and gathered
warnings from doctors about the health peril. In September, when the
biggest story of the year occurred, the financial panic that was to mark the
start of a long depression, the *World* began in competent but obvious
fashion, relating the chain of events on Wall Street—the collapse of financial houses, the stock market plunge—that had brought the nation's economic troubles to a head. But within a few weeks, as the gravity of the
debacle sank in, the newspaper looked beyond Wall Street and explored its
impact on ordinary Americans. Reporters wrote about factory workers,
clerks, seamstresses, and servants suddenly dismissed from their jobs.
They told of the homeless and of the rising numbers of women driven to
walk the streets of Manhattan as prostitutes.

A new reporter like Julian Ralph could well have taken part in these
undertakings—picking his way through the garbage to document the foul
state of New York streets, mingling with the Wall Street crowds on Black
Friday, calling on the Superintendent of Outdoor Poor to inquire about the
destitute. Perhaps on occasion he took the Fulton Street ferry across the
East River to Brooklyn Heights to listen to Henry Ward Beecher; the *World*
reported on the Sunday morning services and Friday evening prayer meetings at Plymouth Church at considerable length, which meant they were a
profitable assignment for a space writer. Ralph also undoubtedly supplied
some of the brief paragraphs with which the eight-page *World* disposed of
most local happenings—a suicide, the robbery of a visiting Russian count,
a Sunday school convention, a lecture on a proposal for a canal across
Central America. Such items filled only an inch or two of a column and
probably yielded no more than fifty cents in space rates.

Long afterward, reminiscing about his career, Ralph mentioned only two
assignments from his brief stay at the *World*. One was a public flogging in
Delaware that took place soon after Ralph joined the newspaper.

Corporal punishment for crime had gradually fallen into disuse in the
United States in the nineteenth century with the notable exception of

Delaware, where the flogging of criminals remained a regular practice. The scene of many of the floggings was the old colonial town of Newcastle, county seat of the most populous of Delaware's three counties. A foot-square wooden whipping post stood in a courtyard behind a handsome red-brick Georgian courthouse.

New York newspapers regularly reported the floggings at Newcastle. Because the growing revulsion against corporal punishment was particularly strong when it was applied to women, they took special interest in May of 1873 when a young black woman named Mary Meeter, convicted of the murder of her seven-month-old child, was included among those to be whipped. She had also been sentenced to prison for life. Ralph was one of six reporters from New York who took the train to Newcastle to witness her whipping and that of two teen-aged boys convicted of theft. As events developed, Mary Meeter was not flogged; Ralph later suggested that the authorities held off because the press was focusing on the case. But the two youths were punished, and Ralph was horrified.

Apparently Ralph then left the courtyard, found a quiet corner, and proceeded to write a story that violated all the rules the *World* tried to hammer into young reporters. It seethed with revulsion, employed scathing irony, and did not even mention such details as the names of the boys flogged or their crimes or the names of the officials in charge of the proceedings. Ralph went to the telegraph office in Newcastle and dispatched his account of the day to the *World*. Then he boarded a train for New York.

When he looked at the *World* the next morning, his story was not there. Instead, the *World* disposed of the events in Newcastle with a brief item, bearing no dateline, that said the whippings had been carried out in perfunctory fashion and made no mention of Mary Meeter. The assumption must be that an editor or copy reader at the *World* had looked at the new reporter's story, decided it would not do, and concocted a substitute, perhaps drawing on an Associated Press account or cribbing from one of the evening papers. Very likely Julian Ralph exploded in fury when he saw what had been done. In any case, on May 27, Julian's twentieth birthday, the *World* printed his original story from Newcastle. It was prominently displayed on page 2 under the headline "The Whipping-Post—Scenes and Incidents at a Delaware Flogging."

Ralph began by noting that Delaware's penal code, revised hardly at all since colonial days, was refreshingly free of legal niceties and pussyfooting. The penalties for various crimes, he said, "are pleasantly relieved from the monotony of legal phraseology so common in other states by a cheerful reference to the pillory or a kindly allusion to the slave market." (Ten years after the Emancipation Proclamation, Delaware still had not gotten around to deleting a penal code provision ordering some convicted blacks to be auctioned off as slaves.) "Sometimes," Ralph continued, "the offenders receive sixty lashes, sometimes only thirty-nine, or twenty, or ten, according to the extent of their mischief."

Then this:

The Delaware people say that the whipping-post is a good thing. It promotes a healthy circulation of the blood; it frightens New Yorkers, Pennsylvanians, and Jerseyites away from the State, and then—and this seems most reasonable—it is the only circus they have. New York, New Jersey, and other pagan commonwealths are visited by Buffalo Bill, the "Black Crook," and other shows, but Delaware can't raise enough money to entice them within their borders. And Barnum—he's too big a gun for them, and Delaware would be lost under his mammoth tent. So they have the lash and the pillory, and every Saturday in May and November the citizens don their "best beshines," and taking their opera-glasses, children, and servants with them, proceed to the jails. (There are three jails—one in Newcastle, one in Georgetown, and one in Dover.) Then the gates are thrown open and the crowd rushes in and fills the courtyard, and the Sheriff and warden, with Sunday suits on and cigars in their mouths, stand beside the great post spitting tobacco-juice on the children and serenely eyeing the crowd, and by and by a delicate, fair-haired youngster of fourteen or fifteen, with great tears streaming from his blue eyes, and his white shoulders and back bared to the delighted gaze of the audience, steps out from the inner court of the prison and the warden pinions his slender wrists to the post with iron bands, while the Sheriff swings his "cat-o'-nine-tails" over his head, and a murmur of pleasure comes from the appreciative crowd. The Sheriff bites his cigar a little harder, tips a meaning wink to a bystander, and then he raises the "cat," steps a little back and whizz! down it comes on the boy's back, and the thongs wind under his arm and bite great holes in his side and chest, while his back is striped red and white. "Two," says the warden, "Oh-h-h-h," from the boy, and crash, down comes the lash again and again and again, and the boy's back is all raw and bleeding, with great ridges across it. The little fellow in his agony asks once or twice "for God's sake" to be more mildly whipped, but his sobs choke him, and when the ten lashes have been dealt, he staggers, faint and exhausted, into his cell. "Ah! there's justice for you. Our sheriff's a man—no d———— chicken about him," says a representative citizen, and the crowd murmurs, "No, indeed."

The onlookers dispersed after the second youth had been whipped. The crowd had been unusually large, Ralph wrote, because word had spread that a woman was to be whipped. Ralph talked to Mary Meeter through the bars of her cell. She was "a fine-looking, neatly-attired young girl, betrayed by a white man, and through ignorance led to slaughter her offspring." Ralph gave her five cents.

The story from Newcastle ended:

I have pictured to you the performance as I saw it, and in very truth it seems to be popularly regarded as an amusement, as I have said.

The other *World* assignment Ralph reminisced about was to chase down Cornelius Vanderbilt when the seventy-nine-year-old magnate was maneuvering in 1873 for the acquisition that would make his New York Central railroad the first through line between New York and Chicago. Often a reporter of the period literally had to chase down a figure like Vanderbilt to put questions to him, and on this occasion Ralph had to content himself with interviewing Vanderbilt as he leaned out of his light carriage, "the fastest pair of horses in America" eager to be off. Vanderbilt's words as set down by Ralph long afterward do not have the ring of verisimilitude; like most other nineteenth-century reporters, he sometimes quoted people as they ought to have spoken rather than as they actually spoke. But Ralph's version undoubtedly reflected accurately Vanderbilt's honest puzzlement over why a bright, ambitious young man would want to be a reporter.

"You have mastered the intricacies of a very complex business matter," said he, "which has been the subject of thought and study with me for years. That you can do this and still remain in the newspaper business is very remarkable. Why do you do it? What do you gain by it? You are only just at the edge of manhood and are getting the wages of a clerk. Stay in this business and you may eventually make five times as much, but it will still be wages; you will still be working for others, and as you grow older you must work harder and harder. Take my earnest advice: leave newspapers alone and go into something that offers a better chance—something that will give you a solid reward—that will let you rest when you are tired."

By delivering this lecture, and then causing his team to step off smartly, Vanderbilt neatly deflected Ralph's questions, and the resulting story didn't amount to much. But he failed to deflect Ralph from the path he had chosen. He would remain a reporter.

Probably around mid-1874, but in any case sometime before the adultery trial of Henry Ward Beecher began in January of 1875, Julian Ralph moved from the *World* to the New York *Daily Graphic*. Although the morning newspapers continued to be the best-known, most powerful voices of the press in New York, the *Daily Graphic* and other evening newspapers were on the rise. They enabled the public to read about events the same day they happened, and they often beat the morning papers into print with important news. Workers and shoppers bought evening papers on the way home. Housewives picked them up off the doorstep late in the day, when they had leisure to read.

The *Daily Graphic* was to have a relatively brief existence, from 1873 to 1889. From the start it had financial troubles. As an early promotional stunt, it spent $50,000 to dispatch a balloonist, a Captain Wise, from Brooklyn across the Atlantic, but after notifying European governments to be on the lookout for the captain, the *Graphic* had to inform its readers that the balloon had made it only as far as Connecticut before coming down. Its managers proved inept and on occasion dishonest, and its processes for printing illustrations encountered patent and technical problems. The technical problems meant that the *Graphic* had to use relatively slow printing machinery fed with sheets of paper instead of the fast new presses that printed from a roll on both sides of the paper simultaneously. When other newspapers learned to print pictures on these high-speed presses in the 1880s, the *Graphic* lost its chief selling point and its days were numbered.

All the same, the *Daily Graphic* made its mark. In 1875, only two years after its founding, it boasted a circulation of 11,000 even though it sold for five cents a copy at a time when the trend was toward cheaper newspaper prices. It was the largest of the New York afternoon newspapers except for the New York *Daily News,* a sleazy one-cent paper that circulated in tenement districts and often exceeded the largest morning papers in circulation in the 1870s and 1880s.* The *Graphic* stressed its elevated tone. It billed itself as "A Model Journal of News, Society, Art, and Literature" and claimed to circulate "among families and people of refined taste who will not touch those papers which rely upon their attention to sensational incidents of criminal occurrences." The Beecher trial was a pretty sensational affair, of course, but no newspaper could have ignored it and stayed in business.

Some journalists deplored illustrations in newspapers, contending they engendered mental laziness in both writer and reader. Pictures were "childish," said Edwin Lawrence Godkin, founder of the *Nation* magazine and editor of the staid New York *Evening Post* in the 1880s and 1890s. But much of the *Graphic's* appeal undoubtedly lay in the novelty of its illustrations—"a mirror of the events and scenes of the day," the paper called them.

Although accurate reproduction of photographs in newspapers through the halftone process was still two decades off in the mid-1870s, the *Graphic's* photolithographic methods permitted it to print not only drawings but also detailed etchings closely derived from photographs. The top two floors

---

*No connection with the tabloid New York *Daily News* founded in 1919.

of its white-marble building on Park Place were taken up by the departments that produced the illustrations, and the eight-page tabloid abounded in pictures of statesmen, actors, ship launchings, shipwrecks, train wrecks, fashions, monuments, battles, and street scenes. Often the pictures did not bear the remotest connection to the news; the art department simply tossed into the paper whatever came to hand—a cricket match in England, a lugubrious painting of the death of William of Orange, the Cambodian countryside. But sometimes the editors rushed into print illustrations of recent happenings. "An unparalleled feat in journalism," they proclaimed in May 1875 when the *Graphic* carried a drawing of the scene of an explosion that had occurred the previous day in Boston. During the Beecher trial the *Graphic's* coverage was regularly accompanied by drawings of witnesses testifying and other courtroom tableaux. Looking back on the *Graphic* long after its demise, a former editor maintained that it had left a legacy of "the most complete pictorial history of its period."

The illustrations took so much space that the *Daily Graphic* had limited room for news stories, but even so the paper touched at least briefly on most significant occurrences. In 1875 the *Graphic* had nine reporters in New York, plus twenty part-time correspondents in Washington, Albany, and other cities. The local reporters had small desks along one wall of a large room on the second floor of the *Graphic* building, but they often wrote their copy away from the office—at police headquarters, in courtrooms, at City Hall—and hurried it to the office by messenger or telegraph to make the deadlines for the three editions printed starting at noon. Being first with the news was all-important to a reporter for an evening paper, and the competition was intense. Julian Ralph learned just how intense when he was excused from his duties at the Beecher trial in Brooklyn one Friday in January 1875 and sent farther out on Long Island on a story.

The assignment brought another brush with the lingering brutality of nineteenth-century criminal justice. Two black men convicted of murder were to be hanged at the courthouse in Hempstead, just under twenty miles east of Manhattan. Hangings were commonplace—death was the usual penalty for murder—and judging from newspaper accounts, they were frequently bungled. Hanging was supposed to snap the condemned's neck with a violent jerk, bringing instant unconsciousness and a quick end. In practice, according to a doctor who pronounced death at many executions, in most cases the cause was strangulation.

The day of the double hanging was bitterly cold, and the roads and fields around the courthouse were covered with ice. Except for the weather, the atmosphere resembled that in Newcastle when the two boys had been flogged. A crowd of three hundred people showed up to watch. Laborers came on foot, farmers in sleighs. Not all could squeeze into the jail yard where the scaffold stood, two nooses dangling from the crossbeam, and some of those excluded cut peepholes in the wooden fence with jackknives or climbed trees. One man in a tree wrapped himself in a buffalo robe for warmth.

Shortly before noon the two black men were brought from their cells into the yard. Their arms had already been pinioned. Ralph was startled when one of the prisoners made a comical face at him as he passed on his way to the scaffold; then Ralph recognized him as an acquaintance from his childhood days in Greenwich Village. The condemned men mounted the scaffold. A minister prayed for them, the nooses were adjusted around their necks, and black hoods were drawn over their heads.

The usual method of hanging called for the rope to be slack and for a trap to fall away under the victim's feet, causing him to drop suddenly the full length of the rope. But at Hempstead that day a new "foolproof" method was to be used. There was no trap, and the hang-ropes were drawn taut. From the nooses they ran through pulleys on the crossbeam, and the other ends were attached to heavy suspended weights. When the hangman, concealed in a box at one corner of the platform, released the weights, their plunge would yank the condemned men skyward. This initial jerk would usually kill a man, but, according to an authority on the subject, "If the neck is not broken when the victim is originally yanked from the earth it is sure to be when he falls back again taking the slack out of the rope, the falling weight having pulled the rope up to such an extent as to make it impossible for the condemned person to touch the ground upon the return fall."

This bleak day on Long Island the latest in hanging methods failed. The sheriff released the weights, and both men bounded into the air. One fell back down and was clearly seen to be alive as he swung to and fro—his body, Ralph wrote, "writhing in agonizing contortions." The other man's rope broke and he crashed back onto the platform. "He stood there in a crouching position. A deputy sheriff and a policeman sprang upon the scaffold and held the suffering man on his feet. He did not speak." A boy mounted the crossbeam and threaded the hang-rope through its pulley again, while someone below secured the noose for a second time on the neck of the black who had fallen. Then, pulling on the rope, the sheriff and a helper raised him into the air. Both of the condemned slowly strangled. The spectacle unsettled even some of those who had been eager to watch, and "a spasm of horror ran through the crowd of spectators."

Ralph's story was unclear at some points, and the morning papers had details he missed. But as a young reporter witnessing what was probably his first execution he must have been shaken. Moreover, there was no time for fine writing. At the courthouse he dashed off his story; then, as he was leaving for the local telegraph office, located in a settlement some distance away across icy fields, he spotted a rival reporter running ahead of him. Ralph recognized him as an experienced man and knew that he hoped to reach the telegraph office first. Perhaps he might even "pay to keep the telegraph busy for hours, so that I would not be able to send in a word of my report."

A race began. Ralph soon pulled even, but then the field became a glare of ice that slowed both runners. Here the older man was holding his own, even gaining, when they came to a gully. Ralph plunged straight through. The other reporter tried to skirt it but slipped and tumbled "down the side of the gully to lie stunned and torn and bleeding at my feet."

"I am hurt," he cried; "will you help me to the village?"
"Will you give me first chance at the telegraph?" I asked.
"Yes, I am beaten; I acknowledge it," he answered.
So I helped him to the town and looked after him—but took care to send in my report ahead of his.

As the Beecher trial progressed, Ralph improved his mastery of his craft. Meeting the demand for a steady flow of copy from the courtroom to the *Daily Graphic* office, he wrote rapidly without sacrificing clarity or detail. The trial consumed most of his waking hours during the six months it ran. When he was not listening to the testimony in Brooklyn, he was seeking out key figures in the scandal for interviews. He later described cornering a "millionaire" involved in the case, probably Henry Bowen, the publisher of daily and weekly newspapers in Brooklyn that were edited by Theodore Tilton, Beecher's accuser. Bowen had been a prime mover in founding Plymouth Church in 1847 and in bringing Beecher from Indianapolis. He was a figure of great interest to followers of the trial because it was said that his first wife had confessed on her deathbed to adultery with Beecher and that he had prodded Tilton to act against Beecher. But he was avoiding the press. "I pursued my millionaire because I had it to do," said Ralph. "I sat on his doorstep till midnight. I was at his house before breakfast. I sent in my card wherever he called on business or social rounds. At last, at one o'clock in the night, he bade me come in."

And then the trial ended and the summons came from Charles Dana of the *Sun*.

5. Dana and the *Sun*

I n 1875 almost any ambitious young reporter in the country would have leaped at the chance to join the *Sun*. It had long since regained a wide circulation lead over its old rival, the *Herald,* and was once again the best-selling morning newspaper in the nation's largest city. Everybody was talking about the *Sun*. Sometimes it was because of one of the outrageous editorials that appeared regularly in the paper, but more often—and for most of the public—what stirred interest was the surprising things in the *Sun's* news columns. The *Sun* had a way of approaching conventional news from unconventional angles and of poking into odd corners of the news. The results sometimes shocked readers, sometimes delighted them, and sometimes both.

Journalists shared the public's fascination with the *Sun* of the 1870s. Its originality and imaginativeness were making it the newspaper that editors and reporters everywhere looked to for inspiration, "the newspaperman's newspaper." "In my opinion," said young Joseph Pulitzer in 1871, "it is the most piquant, entertaining, and, without exception, the best newspaper in the world."

Charles Anderson Dana, the man who lifted the *Sun* to its new prominence, had become its editor in 1868. He held absolute sway over the *Sun*. The editorials reflected his attitudes, the news stories his interests and stylistic judgments. "Dana was the *Sun,* and the *Sun* Dana," said his friend and biographer, General James H. Wilson, and everyone else who has written about the newspaper has echoed his words.

The world beyond the *Sun* office formed its picture of Dana largely through the paper's editorials, and the result was unflattering. Cruelty, vindictiveness, and cynicism were among the traits conveyed. When Dana selected a target, the *Sun* attacked mercilessly with sledgehammer and rapier—denouncing, ridiculing, mocking, belittling. Moreover, Dana seemed erratic and unpredictable; if a reader happened to find an opinion he could agree with one day, the *Sun* might well take the opposite tack the next. Dana was once quoted as saying: "No citizen in this town can go to bed at

night with the certainty that he can foresee the *Sun's* editorial course the
next morning on any given topic." The shifting positions meant that no
segment of the public was left for long without a reason to fume at a *Sun*
editorial. And that was fine with Dana, for he liked nothing better than to
cause a fuss. "Your articles have stirred up the animals, which you as well
as I recognize as one of the great ends of life," he wrote to an associate on
the *Sun*.

This cantankerous public figure bore no resemblance to the man the
members of the *Sun* staff knew. That Dana was a gentle-mannered scholar
who demanded much of his employees but to those who measured up
offered much in return. He encouraged writers with high pay and unstinted
praise for good work, backed them when outsiders complained about their
articles, and tolerated disagreement. Seemingly without exception, the
editors and reporters who labored for him during the almost three decades
that he directed the *Sun* expressed admiration for his brilliance as a journalist and unalloyed affection for him as a man. "I never knew a person in his
employ who quarrelled with him or bore him a grudge or did not like him,"
Julian Ralph once said.

As some newspapers prospered and became big businesses, they erected
elegant buildings. The *Times* built a showplace at the foot of Printing House
Square that was filled with marble and fine paneling. The *Herald* boasted a
colonnaded white marble palace on Broadway. The building completed by
the *Tribune* in 1875, at Nassau and Spruce, was a Victorian skyscraper—
nine heavily ornamented stories surmounted by a clock tower.

No such display for the *Sun*. Throughout Ralph's career with the newspaper, it was housed in a dowdy five-story red-brick building, capped by a
mansard roof, at the south corner of Nassau and Frankfort. The new
Tribune building, next door, loomed over the *Sun* building and underscored
its inconsequentiality. Facing Printing House Square and City Hall Park,
the *Sun's* headquarters dated from 1811 and had formerly been the home of
Tammany Hall. A promotional advertisement that the *Sun* ran in *Harper's
Monthly* in 1870 described the building as a "model newspaper office," but
most of those who set foot in the place described it as a slum.

The newsroom, reached by climbing two long, straight flights of stairs to
the third floor, had been renovated little since Tammany used the space for
meetings. A gate—guarded, of course, by office boys—led into the barn-
like room, which ran the whole depth of the building. Down the center were
two rows of desks for reporters. Near the five windows above Nassau Street

were the desks of the managing editor, the city editor, the night editor, and the copy readers. The two stories above the newsroom had been added after the building's original construction, and they rested on iron pillars here and there among the desks and on exposed foot-square timbers in the ceiling. The timbers were studded with rings and hooks for attaching the apparatus of a German Turners society that had formerly rented the room from Tammany for gymnastic exercises. The splintery floor was strewn with discarded newspapers and copy, and cockroaches scuttled about despite periodic efforts to eliminate them with a white arsenic paste. The walls were sooty and decaying. Once an office cat and her litter disappeared through a hole and were immured when a workman patched the wall. An awful stench permeated the newsroom until the wall was opened up some time later to repair a steam pipe and the remains were discovered.

The Nassau-Frankfort corner of the third floor was partitioned into three small rooms: a library, the editorial writers' room, and, in the very corner, Dana's office. A visitor to the editor's office saw that the entire *Sun* building mirrored his attitude toward his working environment—supreme indifference. "Surroundings were nothing to Dana," said Frank M. O'Brien, the editor of the *Sun* in a later era and a historian of the paper. "To him an office was a place to work, to convert ideas into readable form." He wrote and edited at a small black walnut desk in the middle of the room. Books and newspapers were piled on a table. Over the years there accumulated about Dana a variety of pictures and other objects that had drifted into the office for forgotten reasons and that remained simply because he had other things on his mind. A stuffed owl perched atop a revolving case of reference books on his desk, and an ugly little feather-haired totem figure from Alaska stood on the mantel. For a long time a chart showing the variations in divorce laws from state to state occupied much of one wall. Elsewhere was an advertisement from a textile company featuring a photograph of a New England mill girl.

As his recruitment of Julian Ralph showed, Dana was always on the alert for talented writers to add to the *Sun's* staff. The editors who read newspapers from around the country in search of material worth reprinting in the *Sun* were instructed to bring to his attention articles of unusual sparkle or pungency. When one appealed particularly to Dana, he often sought out the name of the author and dashed off a note suggesting there might be an opening at the *Sun*.

Edward P. Mitchell started at the *Sun* as an editorial writer about the same time in 1875 that Ralph began working there as a reporter. Mitchell,

The *Sun* building in the early 1870s. *From* Memoirs of an Editor *by Edward Page Mitchell (Charles Scribner's Sons, an imprint of Macmillan Publishing Company, New York, 1924), p. 200.*

who eventually became the editor of the *Sun,* had attracted Dana's notice when he submitted humorous articles to the *Sun's* editorial page while employed by a newspaper in Lewiston, Maine. When he visited the *Sun* at Dana's invitation, he was shown into the editor's office. Dana was then a vigorous fifty-five-year-old, his thinning brown hair and his luxuriant brown beard and mustache just beginning to gray. He pulled a rush-bottomed chair alongside his desk and invited Mitchell to sit. When Mitchell uttered "the usual commonplace about a busy man's time," Dana "smiled through his glasses with his pleasant and rather quizzical blue eyes, and said something about the Day of Judgment being yet far off, and went on to talk for nearly an hour. It was always thus with him. I never saw him in a hurry, or preoccupied, or impatient with anybody except fools at a distance." Dana offered Mitchell a salary of fifty dollars a week—a comfortable income in a day when Mitchell and his new wife could live respectably in a Manhattan boardinghouse for fifteen dollars a week.

Dana had not established himself in metropolitan journalism until his late twenties. After a straitened boyhood in New England and western New York state, he attended Harvard for two years, then lived for five years at Brook Farm, the attempt to create a model socialist community near Boston. Brook Farm failed, and in 1847 Dana, who had done some newspaper and periodical writing while at the farm, went to work for Horace Greeley at the New York *Tribune.* Except for eight months in Europe to report on the Revolution of 1848, he spent the next fifteen years as an editor of the *Tribune.* Most of the period he served as managing editor, the first American journalist to hold that title. Differences with Greeley led to Dana's departure in 1862. Later he said that he thought Greeley "always had a little grudge against me because I came up through a college" instead of having been a printer's apprentice who "slept on newspapers and ate ink." For the rest of the Civil War, Dana held high posts in the War Department. As an observer with the Union forces at Vicksburg in 1863, he became a strong advocate of Grant against those who were questioning his fitness for high command because of drinking.

After the war Dana returned to the newspaper business. For a year he edited a daily in Chicago, and then he was back in New York laying plans to start a new newspaper with the help of a group of wealthy backers, including, among others, William Evarts, Senator Roscoe Conkling, and Cyrus W. Field. Meanwhile, it turned out that the *Sun* was available. The founder, Benjamin Day, had dropped out of the picture in 1838, five years after the paper's launching, and since then the *Sun* had been owned by a family named Beach. The Beaches had made the *Sun* into a serious newspaper, but it was no longer flourishing. Unenterprising and unimaginative, it neither led in morning circulation among its traditional working-class following nor carried weight with the more prosperous residents of New York. With the newspaper business still in a lingering postwar slump, the 50,000 "mechanics and small merchants" who bought the *Sun* gave it the second-largest circulation in the morning field, but it trailed the *Herald* by 20,000. Dana thought he could make the *Sun* do better, and he persuaded his backers—whom he seems to have ignored ever after—to join him in purchasing the paper for $175,000. Dana also arranged to purchase the Tammany Hall building for $220,000 and to move the *Sun* there from the building at Nassau and Fulton that had housed it since 1842.

In January 1868 Dana took charge of the *Sun*. He kept founder Day's old slogan: "It Shines for All." He also kept the existing two-cent price, instituted when the Beaches finally abandoned the *Sun's* original penny price in 1864; the other morning papers charged four cents. And he kept the existing format of four full-sized pages, half the size of the other morning dailies. Little else would remain the same at the *Sun*.

As a young man Dana had been an idealist, a utopian socialist, but by the time he came to the *Sun* disillusionment had set in. Somewhere between Brook Farm and the corner office at Nassau and Frankfort, he had lost his faith in human nature and in the ability of men to cooperate unselfishly for the common good. "The realist slowly dispossessed the idealist and then the cynic swallowed up the realist," said Vernon L. Parrington in *Main Currents in American Thought*. "The last forty years of his life were spent undoing the work of his earlier years." In the *Sun* Dana and his editorial writers propounded the values of the Gilded Age, defending the pursuit of self-interest as exemplified by big business of the day. He opposed unions, curbs on monopolies, income taxes, pure-food legislation. He favored high tariffs to protect American manufacturers and grants of public lands to the railroads.

Such views set the teeth of Dana's old Brook Farm associates on edge. And yet so fluid were his politics and so varied his prejudices that, at one time or another, he offended most of his fellow supporters of big business and a host of other groups as well. Anti-vice crusaders, feminists, civil service reformers, animal lovers, prohibitionists, and West Pointers were among the butts of *Sun* editorials. Neither Republicans nor Democrats could rely on Dana. He started out in 1868 by making common cause with powerful Republican industrialists and financiers on behalf of Grant, but after the scandals erupted the *Sun* backed Greeley against Grant in 1872 and took up the cry "Turn the rascals out!" In the disputed presidential election of 1876 the *Sun* supported Tilden, the Democrat, and Dana was so angered when Hayes, the Republican, was declared the winner that the *Sun* thereafter referred to him as "the fraudulent President." In the 1880 election the *Sun* rejected the Republican, Garfield, as corrupt but then turned the Democrat, General Hancock, into a laughingstock by offhandedly describing him in an editorial as "a good man, weighing two hundred and fifty pounds." In 1884 the *Sun* had no use for either Cleveland, the Democrat, or Blaine, the Republican; out of sheer perversity it backed the hopeless cause of a badly tarnished third-party candidate, General Ben Butler.

In keeping with accepted practice at the time, *Sun* political reporters generally made their copy mesh with the editorial page, particularly during election campaigns. But for most *Sun* reporters the significant point about the newspaper's editorials was how little they mattered in the newsroom. In an earlier era James Watson Webb, a contemporary of James Gordon Bennett who edited the New York *Courier and Enquirer,* a Whig organ, had declared in an editorial: "We wish it to be distinctly understood, that whenever we shall have occasion to reduce the force in this office, *the reduction will be made from the ranks of those whose differ from us on questions of national importance!*" At the *Sun,* during the election campaign of 1884 many reporters wore large buttons bearing Cleveland's portrait, flaunting their disagreement with Dana. Jacob Riis, who carried out some of his landmark investigations of the evils of New York's slums while working for an evening edition of the *Sun* introduced in 1887, said that Dana never censored his reports even though it seemed "impossible for anybody to get farther apart in their views of most things on earth and off it than were my paper and I."

There were probably days when Julian Ralph didn't bother to read the *Sun's* editorials. Off and on in his career he wrote about political matters, but, said Frederic Remington, "That he ever himself developed a personal interest I could never discover." Although Ralph held Dana in high regard, he took a condescending view of editorial writers in general. In his autobiography he singled out "clearness of brain" and "indomitable perseverance" as essentials for rising to the top as a reporter and then added: "The only men on the press who can thrive without these qualities are the editorial and the descriptive writers."

Ralph to the contrary, Dana prized his clever editorial writers, but his willingness to tolerate dissent among his reporters showed that he also valued them highly and recognized their central role in the new journalistic climate that had emerged from the Civil War. Reporting was "a high art," he said, and the reporter was "the eye of the paper." While some editors continued to focus their attention largely on the editorial page, Dana took a strong hand in shaping the news columns of the *Sun*. The news sold papers. "The first thing which an editor must look for is news. If the newspaper has not the news, it may have everything else, yet it will be comparatively unsuccessful." The *Sun's* news, said Alexander Noyes, explained why "a good part of the thinking public, wholly out of sympathy with Dana's political vagaries, habitually read the *Sun*."

In the first issue of the *Sun* under his regime, the one for January 25, 1868, Dana promised:

> *The Sun* will always have All the News, foreign, domestic, political, social, literary, scientific, and commercial. It will use enterprise and money freely to make the best possible newspaper, *as well as the cheapest*.
>
> It will study condensation, clearness, point, and will endeavor to present its daily photograph of the whole world's doings in the most luminous and lively manner.
>
> It will not take as long to read *The Sun* as to read the *London Times* or *Webster's Dictionary;* but when you have read it, you will know about all that has happened in both hemispheres.

James Gordon Bennett had pioneered in widening the range of matters reported on in newspapers, but now Dana defined the news even more sweepingly. "To Dana," wrote *Sun* historian Frank O'Brien, "life was not a mere procession of elections, legislatures, theatrical performances, murders, and lectures."

> Life was everything—a new kind of apple, a crying child on the curb, a policeman's epigram, the exact weight of a candidate for President, the latest style in whiskers, the origin of a new slang expression, the idiosyncrasies of the City Hall clock, a strange four-master in the harbor, the head-dresses of Syrian girls, a new president or a new football coach at Yale, a vendetta in Mulberry Bend—everything was fish to the great net of Dana's mind.

Dana possessed, said Willis J. Abbot, who joined the *Tribune* as a young reporter in the 1880s and later edited the *Christian Science Monitor,* "a unique comprehension of the multifarious interests of the human mind."

He was not above catering to these interests on occasion with tales of crime and passion that offended some Victorian sensibilities. It was argued, said Dana in a lecture to the Wisconsin Editorial Association in Milwaukee in 1888, "that certain kinds of news ought not to be published. I do not know how that is. . . . I have always felt that whatever the Divine Providence permitted to occur I was not too proud to report."

Dana also broke new ground in the way the *Sun* presented the news. He sought, according to journalism historian Willard Grosvenor Bleyer, "to encourage originality in American newspaper writing and to discourage imitation of English journalistic style, long considered a model" despite what Dana saw as its tendency to be prolix and pedantic. All advice to newspaper writers could be boiled down to one essential, he told an audience at Cornell in 1894:

> The invariable law of the newspaper is to be interesting. Suppose you tell all the truths of science in a way that bores the reader; what is the good? The truths don't stay in the mind, and nobody thinks any better of you because you have told him the truth tediously.

To keep the *Sun* interesting—and to fit all the news into a four-page newspaper—required drastic condensation. Each day the *Sun* devoted several columns to the briefest of summaries of routine government business, run-of-the-mill crimes, accidents, obligatory notices of public events, minor cabled items from Europe. In his zeal for condensation, Dana often flouted conventional newspaper practice. He once approached Chester Lord, his managing editor at the time, with a sheaf of proofs containing the lengthy obituary of a political figure. "Mr. Lord," he said, "isn't this a lot of space to give to a dead man?" A dull Congressional hearing that filled a column in a morning rival might rate only a sentence or two in the *Sun*. Such treatment undoubtedly struck those with a deep interest in the subject as superficial but probably told most readers all they cared to know.

Moreover, condensation of routine news created space for exhaustive reports of momentous events and for *Sun* reporters to spin out at length stories that lent themselves to full-blown narrative. Many of the latter fell into the category of "human-interest stories," a term coined by the *Sun* for the accounts of comedies and tragedies in the lives of ordinary people that became a trademark of the paper. The *Sun's* feel for the right mixture of brevity and length was its most notable quality in the eyes of Willis Abbot. Looking back in 1933 on Dana's *Sun,* he wrote:

It was a model of rigid condensation throughout—yet when a good story came in, the lucky reporter could get columns in which to tell it if he had the true art of storytelling. . . . The real test of journalistic ability is to tell when to be profligate of space and when to throw brevity to the winds. We all do that now with a President's message; Dana was shrewd enough to do it with the story of a lost child, if he had a man who knew how to tell the tale.

The *Sun* of the 1870s looks like the antique that it is. Seven columns march across the front page, as uniform as fence pickets. The small, subdued headlines never exceed a column in width. Only on rare occasions is there an illustration—a map, cartoon, or portrait reproduced from a woodcut. The placement of stories on the front page seems odd; in the 1870s newspapers put the story judged most important in the lefthand column rather than on the right.

Despite the praise heaped on the *Sun,* its news columns yield dross as well as gold. The human-interest stories sometimes fall flat, and now and then readers learn more than anyone could possibly want to know about a recondite subject like bearded women (a woman who enters a male occupation "need not be surprised if after that she becomes hirsute," said one authority). Revoltingly graphic descriptions of death and decay—a Victorian fascination—disprove Dana's contention that whatever Providence allows is fit to print. There is an obsessive interest when lovers murder lovers and clergymen stray from rectitude. As at other newspapers, editorializing still warps political news; an insane man attempts to call on President Grant and the headline reads "Another Lunatic at the White House." The narrative approach is often used in stories where a crisp summary of important facts would seem preferable.

But a newspaper is by definition imperfect, and some of what now looks like flawed journalism would not have perturbed *Sun* readers in the nineteenth century. They were accustomed to opinion folded into political news, and the leisurely narratives suited their more leisurely age. With fewer distractions competing for their attention, they had time for stories that began at the beginning. In any case, the popularity of Dana's *Sun* is undeniable, and generations later its appeal is not hard to understand.

The arrival of each day's issue was like a favorite uncle showing up at the door bursting with tales to tell, his pockets overflowing with notes on everything from a raging theological dispute to a new fashion in men's hats. When great issues or events commanded the attention of all the New York papers, even rival newspapermen agreed that more often than not the *Sun* had the best story. The latest scandal in Washington, the opening of the

Centennial Exposition in Philadelphia, a Moody and Sankey revival, a six-day walking match at Gilmore's Garden in Brooklyn—the *Sun* turned up curious facts, illuminating details, and ironic asides that others missed. Moreover, day after day it offered news its competitors overlooked entirely—a social history of the toothpick, a bloody five-hour dogfight staged across the river in New Jersey for the delectation of well-dressed "sports," a day in the life of a cheerful, round-faced man named Dan Russell who drove a red and white wagon filled with coffins around New York picking up the dead of families too poor to pay for funerals.

Some *Sun* stories could be classed as sensationalism, but by and large it shunned the extreme sort of sensationalism that would become known as "yellow journalism" as Joseph Pulitzer and William Randolph Hearst battled for readers in the 1890s. Yellow journalism—the term derived from the rival versions of the "Yellow Kid" cartoons that appeared in Pulitzer's New York *World* and Hearst's New York *Journal*—manipulated readers with cheap sentiment, exaggeration, and outright lies. It showed contempt for readers. Dana and his writers were never guilty of such disdain. Although they sought popularity, they did not talk down to the public. On the contrary, they sometimes raised journalism to the level of art.

The warm response to the new *Sun* came not only from the working-class homes that had provided the bulk of *Sun* readers in the past, but also from the business and professional classes that had previously ignored it. Some members of the latter groups, it is said, felt compelled to indulge in the *Sun* in private when a spate of particularly outrageous editorials or shocking stories had made the paper unacceptable in polite society. For a time the *Sun* was barred altogether from the Century Association, a club whose membership included the city's leading literary men. Dana once said that he did not belong to a club because there was no club where he had not offended a member.

From the 50,000 of 1868, the *Sun's* circulation, according to its own figures, climbed to more than 100,000 by 1871 and to 131,000 by 1876. The gains in the mid-seventies came as the economic depression that had begun in 1873 was slowing the sales of most other newspapers. The *Herald,* which the *Sun* had passed in circulation in 1870, dropped from 88,000 in 1873 to 60,000 in 1876. Some of the *Sun's* sales undoubtedly reflected its low price of two cents, but before Dana took charge it had been losing ground in the morning field despite the same price edge. Moreover, even though nineteenth-century circulation figures are sometimes untrustworthy, the *Sun's* are generally regarded as honest. When the *Sun* had setbacks in circulation it acknowledged them.

Advertisers obviously believed the *Sun* was reaching a wide audience. Space for advertisements was usually limited to part of the back page, and most of the time the *Sun* seems to have tolerated rather than courted advertisers. Editors working late at night threw out ads if they needed the space for a good story. In the 1870s Dana toyed with the idea of doing away with advertising altogether and getting along with only circulation revenues. "Newspapers," said a *Sun* editorial, "if they are worth the taking, really resent the encroachment of advertisers on their space, which they could readily fill with reading matter of much more general interest than business announcements. . . . The four pages of the *Sun* are really needed by us for the presentation of the news of the day . . . and the time may come when we shall politely decline to have any of our space used by advertisers."

But that time never came. In fact, the pressure from advertisers was so great that in 1875, when Dana decided to join other editors in the move to Sunday editions, he found he had to shift at least for that day from his favored four-page format to eight pages to accommodate the demand. By most measures the *Sun* had become the most successful newspaper of the day.

The training young reporters received at the *Sun* carried cachet throughout the newspaper world. "To have worked at the *Sun* was a sort of certificate of journalistic ability," said Willis Abbot. Sometimes the certificate was fabricated by job-seekers. Eugene Field, the newspaperman-poet, wrote a ballad about a man who was hired by a Denver newspaper on the strength of his claim that he had "worked with Dana on the Noo York *Sun*" but who suddenly disappeared when Dana visited the paper.

People spoke of the *Sun's* "school of journalism," but there was nothing systematic or organized about it. Beginners learned by studying the work of the leading lights of the office and by noting well what parts of their own stories editors blue-penciled and what emerged unscathed. "It was mainly education by absorption," said Edward Mitchell. "It came to the aspiring by example rather than precept. They were taught by observation and the self-preservative instinct what to do and what to avoid."

But there were powerful personalities on the staff who impressed themselves more directly on young reporters. One was Amos J. Cummings. Cummings had worked as a printer at the *Tribune,* then as a reporter and editor. When Greeley fired him because he swore too much, Dana hired him. In the early 1870s he was the *Sun's* managing editor, in charge of gathering and editing the news. As such, Cummings, who had been the hero of a Civil War battle, was still hot-tempered. "This paper is for people who read English!" he bellowed at a new reporter who used a French phrase in a story. Chester Lord recalled bruising encounters with Cummings after coming to the *Sun* from the Oswego *Advertiser* in upstate New York in 1872:

> I started in New York as a news reporter, and in about a week Cummings warned me that if I wished to stay I must get over my country way of doing things. My composition was slovenly, he said; I was pushing my own opinions into news reports which should be free from opinion; I was wasting space on introductions and I had a lot of other faults.

Lord was sent to cover a convention of "freethinkers" who nominated Victoria Woodhull for the presidency in 1872. He returned to the office "full of the fun and absurdity of the thing" and wrote two columns about it, but a copy reader cut the story to half a column. The next day Cummings stormed into the office shouting, "Who wrote that Woodhull stuff?"

"I did, sir," volunteered Lord.

"Damn you, why didn't you write two columns?" thundered Cummings, adding an epithet.

Lord leaped up, swung his chair above his head and yelled: "You call me that name again and I'll knock your damned head off!"

Cummings looked startled, then grinned and said: "Oh, sit down, you little fool! No one has called you any names." Lord explained what had happened and Cummings went off to flay the copy reader.

Cummings was known for spotting the out-of-the-ordinary stories that Dana liked, and when he was managing editor he sometimes left his desk and reported them himself. In 1872 he abandoned his editor's desk altogether, and during Julian Ralph's first years on the *Sun* Cummings was one of its leading reporters, known for his prowess at every sort of story—murders, boxing matches, humorous sketches, interviews. For Ralph and other young reporters, he was a dominant influence even without an editor's title and his work was a model.

The *Sun's* city editor during most of Ralph's time with the newspaper was John B. Bogart. He was no less demanding an editor than Cummings had been, but his manner was gentle like Dana's. Bogart was the man who said: "When a dog bites a man, that is not news, because it happens so often. But if a man bites a dog, that is news." It may be a neat aphorism, but it does not fit some of the *Sun's* most celebrated stories, the masterful retellings of commonplace human tales.

As city editor, Bogart sorted through the possibilities for local stories each day, gave reporters their assignments, checked on their progress, prodded them to finish, and appraised the results at a glance. The job was taxing, and Bogart allowed himself just six minutes each noon for half a dozen oysters and a glass of milk at a lunch counter on Nassau. But in odd moments he found time to counsel new reporters. Frank O'Brien preserved a recollection of a soft rebuke by Bogart to a man who had covered a small fire:

"I notice," he said . . . , "that you begin your story with 'at an early hour yesterday morning,' and that you say also that 'smoke was seen issuing from an upper window.' "

"Isn't that good English?" asked the young man.

"It is excellent English," Bogart replied calmly, "and it has been indorsed by generations of reporters and copy-readers. If you look in the other papers you will find that some of them also discovered smoke issuing from an upper window at an early hour yesterday morning. We do not deny that it is good English; but it is not good *Sun* English."

Julian Ralph remembered John Bogart for his certainty that some mysterious force guided him to news. Bogart, who had started at the *Sun* as a reporter, told Ralph of walking up Broadway one day "when suddenly a current of news came up from a cellar and enveloped me." Bogart said he was irresistibly drawn down the stairs to the cellar, a basement oyster saloon. "I ran down the steps, and as I did so a pistol-shot sounded in my ears. One man had shot another, and I found myself at the scene upon the instant."

Ralph never quite claimed he could scent news on the breeze, but as his career progressed he became convinced that Bogart's tale was not absurd. He believed that some reporters, of whom he was fortunately one, possessed a preternatural alertness to news. He called it a "sixth sense" or a "news instinct." "None except newspapermen have it," he said, "unless detectives share it feebly with us, which I doubt, for detectives are distinctly a lower order of men, whose alleged feats of ratiocination and of judgment occur only in works of fiction."

A skeptic suggested that Ralph was merely describing a keen intuition sharpened further by wide experience, and O'Brien called Ralph's claimed clairvoyance "an exalted hunch." Ralph himself acknowledged that the news instinct might sometimes be indistinguishable from industriousness, a willingness to knock on one more door, ask one more question. But, he maintained, it was his conviction that he would find news, a conviction born of his inexplicable news instinct, that drove him to persevere in his reporting. Time and again, Ralph insisted, "this strange gift" led him to stories.

"Let every man write in his own style," said Dana. Yet he expected his editors to examine critically every line that made up the *Sun's* "daily photograph of the whole world's doings." Everything must be free of affectation, "perfectly clear, perfectly simple," and until a writer could meet these requirements on his own he must be helped. General Wilson said of Dana: "It was as natural for him to run his pencil through words and phrases, to substitute other words, and to transpose paragraphs and expressions in the contributions of others as in his own. His constant effort was to clarify, to strengthen, and to condense for the purpose of bringing out the meaning of the writer, saving the time, and finding the line of least resistance to the understanding of the reader."

In practice, Dana's personal editing was limited to editorials. Even if he had wanted to look over the news stories, he departed in the late afternoon before most were finished. But he made his influence felt in the newsroom after he read the paper the next morning. Sometimes there was gentle criticism. Indicating a passage that displeased him, he would say to the managing editor: "I think I would have killed that paragraph if I had been running the paper last night." Sometimes there was a stern reprimand—or worse—for a reporter who had disobeyed one of Dana's strictures on word usage. As a twenty-year-old reporter on the *Sun* in the 1880s, Charles Rosebault was shocked one day when John Bogart passed along a note from Dana. "Mr. Rosebault must be discharged," it began. Dana had enjoyed Rosebault's account of the flurry caused by the installation of the cook of a visiting maharajah in the kitchens of the Waldorf Hotel:

> But never could that atone for the unpardonable sin I had committed. I had used the word "balance" in the sense of remainder, a colloquialism which never should have passed the copy-reader. He undoubtedly got what was coming to him, too. To rub it in, that letter told me I had not only been discharged but I ought to realize that the discharge was fully justified.

Rosebault did not stay fired for long, which seems often to have been the case with reporters who stirred Dana's passing displeasure. And what those who worked under him remembered most vividly were the times he inspired reporters to new heights of achievement with praise.

One such looked up from his writing to see the chief looking down upon him with that warming smile in his blue eyes which transformed his usually dignified and somewhat aloof expression into one of intimate kindliness. In one hand he held a small clipping, which the reporter had no difficulty in recognizing as his own offspring, a vagrant paragraph but written in the *Sun's* peculiar vein and with a snap all its own.

"Very good, young man, very good," said Dana. "I wish I could write like that!"

Reporters also remembered a day when Dana stepped to the door of his office late in the afternoon, the time when the tempo begins to pick up at a morning newspaper, and called: "Mr. Bogart, who wrote the football story in today's paper?"

Bogart was deep in conversation with the night city editor, who was about to take over from him. He thought a moment, then called back: "Mr. Fairbanks."

"Reads like a page from Homer; another battle of Troy!" exclaimed Dana loudly enough so that all in the newsroom, including Charles M. Fairbanks, could hear.

The *Sun* had a night editor as well as a night city editor. To the night editor fell the responsibility for fitting the news into the limited space available, for deciding what material would survive and what would have to go. In the 1870s the night editor was a former printer named John B. Wood, known to the staff as "Doc" Wood and as "the Great American Condenser." Edward Mitchell described Wood as he attacked late copy under the blazing gaslights in the newsroom one night in 1875, pausing now and then "to project a violent stream of tobacco juice in the direction of a distant cuspidor":

His eyes were protected by a huge visor of green pasteboard. He was apparently over fifty, of spare frame but endowed with an energy little short of demoniac. Every few minutes boys came up to him on the run, bringing sheaves of yellow paper. These manuscripts he seized and scrutinized beneath his green blinder, and disposed of them with a speed nigh incredible. To one batch he would scarcely give a glance before tossing it contemptuously into the basket at his feet. Another batch he would submit to merciless mutilation, seemingly sparing neither the dignity of the stateliest paragraph nor the innocence of the most modest part of speech as his terrible blue pencil tore through the pages leaving havoc in its wake.

Wood's vision was so poor that he had to wear two pairs of thick glasses, and sometimes when his eyes tired he edited by ear. A colleague recalled hearing a reporter read to him from a story: "The application of Mrs. Jane Smith for divorce from her husband, John Smith—"

"Cut out 'her husband,' " snapped Wood.

When Doc Wood and his blue pencil have finished with the last of the copy, it ascends in a dumbwaiter to the fifth floor, where the printers set it in type—still by hand—in the garret-like composing room under the mansard roof.

An hour before midnight the night editor climbs the stairs to the composing room to lay out the pages of the paper. He must cut more words and kill some items altogether. "Rhetoric becomes an offense to him; circumlocution stirs his indignation." When type for a page is locked in place, stereotype plates curved to fit the press cylinders are cast and these descend by dumbwaiter to the pressroom in the basement.

Soon early-arriving newsboys—some are really old men and some are women—are crowding into the high-ceilinged business office on the first floor of the building. They buy metal checks that they will later exchange for stacks of papers. Some must wait outside, and on cold nights they warm themselves on the sidewalk grates where steam escapes from the boilers that run the presses and heat the building. In narrow Frankfort Street the delivery-wagon horses "stamp on the cobbles, impatient to be off." Then, in the small hours, the three presses clank into motion, rumble and roar, and another issue of the *Sun* is born.

6. Marching Through History

A bout the time Julian Ralph joined the *Sun* in 1875 he took one of the white sidewheel steamers back to Red Bank and married Isabella Mount, the girl he had come to know while growing up in Red Bank and working on the *New Jersey Standard*. Belle was twenty-one, a year younger than Julian.

In the first half-dozen years of marriage they moved from one Manhattan boardinghouse to another, never staying put for more than a year or so. For a time they lived in Greenwich Village, where Julian had spent his earliest years. At the start of the 1880s, after the new elevated trains had brought parts of Manhattan that were almost rural only a few years earlier within easy reach of downtown, they moved to a boardinghouse on Lexington Avenue between Fiftieth and Fifty-first Streets. Most young New York couples like Julian and Belle lived in boardinghouses in the late 1800s. The poorest residents of the city crowded into filthy tenements, but apartment buildings offering civilized accommodations were still an expensive novelty. For middle-class New Yorkers the choice was a single-family home or a boardinghouse.

Some boardinghouses catered to families, setting separate tables for them in the dining room, and Julian and Belle had their first child, a son, while boarding at an establishment on the south side of Washington Square. Eventually they would have five children, three boys and two girls. While Belle tended to the upbringing of the expanding family, Julian would go off to the *Sun*. When they lived in the Village, he took the horsecar that wound its way to Park Row. After they moved uptown he rode the Third Avenue elevated, its steam engine belching smoke and sparks.

From the limited evidence available, Julian was a loving husband and father, devoted to his family. Although there are hints that other women came to view him as a romantic, dashing figure as his journalistic reputation grew, he and Belle remained partners to the end of his life. He influenced at least two of his children powerfully: his eldest son would accompany him to two wars as an artist and another son would follow him into reporting.

But any suggestion that Julian Ralph led a conventional family life— leaving for the office at eight each morning, returning in time for dinner, playing with the children before bedtime—would be misleading. Indeed, his only references to home and family are to note that a successful reporter cannot expect to see much of them. Although he called Belle and the children his "treasures," he acknowledged that in times of high excitement they were the furthest thing from his mind. Where he rested between assignments concerned him little. He and Belle kept up the pattern of frequent moves through most of their married life, and they never owned a house, even though there were times when Julian should have been able to afford one easily. His work was the focus of his life, and being a reporter for the *Sun* was an all-consuming job.

The promotional advertisement that the *Sun* placed in *Harper's Monthly* in 1870 described the newspaper's reporters. They were

all young men, full of vitality and enthusiasm, who love their work and are proud of their paper. They shirk nothing, but are always ready to start for Coney Island or California, for Alaska or Australia; to take part in a railroad collision or a steamboat explosion; to go down in a diving-bell or up in a balloon. These young men contribute much to the vivacity and vitality of the *Sun,* and are to be estimated among the elements of its success.

This was the sort of romanticized picture of reporting that was drawing so many into the field in the post–Civil War years. The picture was not entirely fanciful. One of the lures of reporting has always been its variety and unpredictability, the knowledge that each day's work may bring something totally unexpected. A *Sun* reporter could suddenly find himself sent off on a great adventure that he had never dreamed of or plunged into the midst of chaotic and exciting events that he would remember the rest of his life. The *Sun* advertisement was also accurate in describing the reporters as young; probably few were much beyond thirty.

But the ad did not explain that youth was almost essential because the job was so grinding and exhausting. To maintain the pace required youth, or at least youthful energy. Twelve-hour days of reporting and writing were routine, and fifteen-hour days were not unusual. Although the staff supposedly worked six days a week, ambitious space writers sometimes skipped their days off. In part Julian Ralph's success as a reporter reflected his ability to keep going—scrambling for a story, sorting out a flood of confusing facts, scribbling page after page of copy—when others stumbled from fatique. He was, said *Sun* historian Frank O'Brien, "untiring in mind, legs, and fingers."

As with writers for other morning newspapers, *Sun* reporters' lives did not synchronize with those of stockbrokers and lawyers. Except for a few men with morning duties—a murder trial, a dignitary's funeral, or perhaps a standing assignment like Wall Street—they rose late and, having missed the customary boardinghouse breakfast fare of fishballs, hash, and griddle cakes, stopped to eat on the way to work. Over a dime's worth of rolls and coffee, they studied the *Sun* and its rivals, partly to see how their own work measured up against the competition and partly because steeping in the news gave a reporter a running start on the day's work. "By the time he reaches his desk in his office," the *Writer* magazine advised the would-be reporter, "he should be familiar with every item of news that has occurred during the night. His mind is in a wonderful state of activity . . . brim full of affairs."

Sun reporters usually showed up at the office shortly after noon. They did not waste time waiting for assignments. The *Sun* shunned the prevailing practice of allowing a flock of underemployed space writers to hang around the newsroom on the off chance they might prove useful, preferring instead to pile work on a small group of reporters that had emerged from the paper's constant effort to spot and recruit talented men. In the early 1870s the *Sun* probably employed no more than a dozen local reporters, less than half the number on call at other morning papers in New York and a surprisingly small staff even considering that the *Sun* then never exceeded four pages. Although the staff grew in subsequent years, it remained relatively small, and *Sun* reporters would pride themselves on singlehandedly covering stories to which other papers assigned two or three reporters.

On a typical day a *Sun* man could count on two assignments. By the time a reporter arrived at the office, John Bogart, the city editor, had prepared the afternoon assignment book, which listed the day's initial stories along with the names of the reporters responsible for each. The normal routine was for a reporter to don his derby, go off in search of the required information, then return to the office late in the afternoon to write the story.

After a reporter had finished his afternoon story, he consulted Bogart's evening assignment book and started over. Frequently the evening story was a public meeting of some sort—a lecture on science or a political gathering—and a reporter assigned to such an affair would stop for supper at one of the Park Row neighborhood restaurants favored by newspapermen and then head for the meeting hall. If all went smoothly, his day's work would be done by midnight—the second story turned in, the *Sun's* grubby premises exchanged for the convivial atmosphere of one of the spots where reporters and editors on morning papers gathered for a drink before departing for home.

But often things did not go smoothly. The news did not always follow convenient timetables or come in neat packages. The afternoon story might prove elusive or complex; sources might be unhelpful, trails might lead in many directions, and the reporter might still be gathering up loose ends well into the evening. An evening political meeting might erupt into controversy and drag on. Word of the death of a prominent citizen or of a theater ablaze might reach the office just as editors and reporters were laying aside their pencils for the night. On such occasions a reporter might be hard at work into the early morning hours, struggling to get a few facts down on paper for the early edition, expanding and polishing the story for subsequent pressruns.

Later generations of reporters would face similar pressures and aggravations. But the early days of reporting had their own special hardships. Most fundamental, the public was not accustomed to responding to the prying questions of this somewhat suspect new breed of journalist. As Ralph found when he had to chase down Commodore Vanderbilt's carriage as a young representative of the *World,* men who made news often felt little obligation to keep the public informed or to sit still for reporters. There were no established procedures for dealing with the press. The public relations apparatus of a later era had not begun to take shape, and although its absence may sometimes have benefited the search for unvarnished truth, it also meant that reporters had to scrabble for routine facts that their successors could simply crib from a press release.

There were also mechanical hindrances. Even if a speaker wanted to be helpful, he could not quickly run off copies of his remarks for distribution to the press. Thus, as longwinded Victorian orators droned on, reporters got little respite from note-taking. (Although some of the earliest reporters had been little more than stenographers able to record speeches accurately, by the 1870s and 1880s editors rated other talents more highly and shorthand was seldom mentioned as a reporting requirement.) The sheer physical effort of setting down in longhand a story of several thousand words was also daunting—particularly, one old-timer suggested, on a summer night when gaslights combined with the lingering heat of the day to make a newspaper office stifling. Julian Ralph would quickly develop a reputation as an iron man capable of reporting all day and then spending six hours or more turning out column after column of copy, his heavy shoulders hunched over his desk, his big fist enveloping a pencil.

But doing without a typewriter or a copy of a speech was trivial alongside reporting without telephones. The first New York telephone directory was issued in 1878. The single sheet listed fewer than three hundred sub-scribers, and not a newspaper was among them. In the 1880s newspapers, including the *Sun,* began installing telephones in their offices, and reporters sometimes called in stories from drugstores; reporters who worked this way came to be known as "legmen," and the men who took down their stories in the office were called "rewritemen." But not until well after the turn of the century would reporters routinely gather news by telephone. Before that, many of the people they needed to talk to did not have telephones; in the early 1890s there were 9,000 phones in New York for a population of more than 1,500,000.

Just as important, older reporters couldn't shake the feeling that they needed to look news sources in the eye. Charles Rosebault, whose report-ing career with the *Sun* began in the 1880s, observed long afterward that reporters of his era would have regarded using the telephone for interviews as "a rank evasion of duty." The person interviewed, said Rosebault, "had to be seen, studied, analyzed, cross-examined. The way a man looks or acts is often more significant than what he says, besides giving the reporter the opportunity to put the color of life into what he writes."

By and large, the only way to get even the most minor piece of news—or sometimes merely to check the spelling of a name—was to go somewhere. Reporters spent endless hours traveling about by horsecar, elevated and suburban train, ferry and hansom cab. Fortunately for its reporters, the *Sun,* unlike some newspapers, took a liberal view of expenses. A reporter who missed the last scheduled Staten Island ferry late one night and grandly chartered a ferry with himself as the sole passenger caused only a momen-tary stir when he submitted a bill for thirty dollars. "I was told to get the story and get back with it," he explained.

Reporters also walked a lot. A police reporter named Edward Weston built a reputation as a valued member of the *Sun* staff mainly on his speed afoot. "Whatever faults there may have been in his literary style, his knee action was a perfect poem," said O'Brien. "He could bring a story down from the Bellevue morgue faster than all the horse-cars."*

For those who could meet the challenge, the *Sun* offered not only the joy of working for a newspaper that they were convinced was the best but also an adequate income. Wages beyond the meanest subsistence were not always to be found in the newspaper field. "There is probably no industry of modern times in which the part played by labor is so large, and the share of the profits received by labor is so small," the *Nation* observed of journalism in 1873.

Twenty-five dollars a week—enough for a couple to live at a respectable boardinghouse and have just enough left over to keep up a semblance of middle-class appearances—was about the best most New York reporters could hope for in the late 1870s and early 1880s. And many space writers earned much less. At the New York *Tribune* in 1883 young reporters considered it a good week if they picked up six to ten dollars at the cashier's window. At the *Commercial Advertiser,* which paid a niggardly $4.32 a column, Charles Russell found in the early 1880s that some reporters made only five dollars many weeks—less than a laborer earned.

Instead of starting new reporters on space and allowing them to sink or swim, the *Sun* initially paid a salary—ten dollars a week in the early 1870s, fifteen after that. As soon as the reporter had shown that he could do the quality of work the *Sun* demanded, he went on space at eight dollars a column. With a small staff dividing assignments, fifty dollars a week— the starting pay Dana had offered Edward Mitchell, who had already contributed to the *Sun's* editorial page and who would quickly become one of the editor's key lieutenants—was a realistic target for a space writer. Some, including Julian Ralph, would eventually earn considerably more. Thus, at a time when many reporters scarcely matched the pay of manual workers, *Sun* writers earned livings comparable to those of businessmen and lawyers.

---

*In the end Weston decided his future lay in walking, not reporting. Endurance walking stunts developed into a fad in the late nineteenth century, and Weston became a professional walker. He competed in six-day walking races in Madison Square Garden and pulled off some prodigious long-distance hikes, including a 104-day trek from New York to San Francisco at the age of seventy. At his death in 1929 at the age of ninety, the New York *Times* called him "the greatest walker of his day."

Some reporters became specialists. The larger New York newspapers had Wall Street men, sportswriters (known as "sporting writers"), and reporters concentrating on the police, the courts, City Hall, and ship news. Washington correspondents were already a distinct breed. But in the 1870s the compartmentalization was not rigid, and in the course of a week or two a general reporter might cover a bank failure, a boxing match, and a political speech as well as a miscellany of stories that fit no category.

Although toward the end of his life Ralph would achieve something of a reputation as a war correspondent, he generally avoided being pigeonholed. He was thankful not to be a "department" man, stuck in a routine of covering police headquarters or City Hall. He preferred to plunge repeatedly into new fields, and he particularly relished the role of "special correspondent," rushing for trains at a moment's notice to pursue distant stories for the *Sun.*

Ralph would spend two decades as a reporter for the *Sun,* and in that time he would write thousands of stories. Because they were unsigned, only a small number can be identified with reasonable certainty. But in even this limited selection—as a handful of stories from the late 1870s, his first years with the *Sun,* demonstrate—Ralph had to cope with subjects as varied as life itself.

One of the stories Ralph recalled may have stayed in his mind because the assignment came directly from Dana, which was not the usual procedure. On a day in January 1877 Ralph had been filling in briefly for John Bogart, the city editor, who was absent from the office for some reason. First a messenger had delivered a "flimsy"—a carbon copy of a press association dispatch—reporting without elaboration the arrest of a clergyman in St. Johnsbury, Vermont, for stealing large sums of money. Shortly thereafter a visitor had called at the office and informed Ralph that he possessed a pair of boots made from the skin of a black man hanged for murder. Would the *Sun* be interested in a story?

Given the *Sun's* sometimes quirky tastes, there was always a chance it might be, and Ralph went into the corner office to ask Dana for a decision. He took the flimsy about the clergyman with him.

"Sir," said Ralph, "there is a man here who has a pair of boots of leather made from a negro's skin."

"How disgusting!" said Dana. "Put the man out of the office."

"Yes, sir. And here is news that a clergyman has been arrested in St. Johnsbury for—"

Dana cut him off. He never passed up stories about clergymen with feet of clay. "Go yourself, and telegraph us long accounts of it."

"He was arrested for—"

"It makes no sort of difference what he was arrested for," said Dana. "He is a clergyman, and he is arrested. Take the half past six o'clock train, and get all the facts."

Ralph later wondered if Dana had been remiss in not ordering someone to look into how the human skin had been obtained, but at the time he headed for northern Vermont without further question. There he gathered material for a story that appeared in the *Sun* on January 19, 1877, under the headline "From the Pulpit to Jail." It recounted the "fall from grace" of the Reverend Enos Hopkins, a Methodist minister who had heretofore been "an example for the pious and a beacon for the sinful." Hopkins—short, black-bearded, with a "well-fed look" and "small, bright, jet black eyes"—had left no stratagem untried in bilking the community. He had speculated crookedly in eggs and butter; he had welshed on notes endorsed by local businessmen; he had arranged bank loans for a struggling church, then pocketed the funds. Most brazen of all was an insurance agency scheme in which "the reverend agent" had somehow managed to steal both his clients' premiums for fire insurance and insurance company payments for fire losses.

It was an inconsequential but neatly done portrait of a scoundrel in clerical guise, and it showed Ralph doing well what a reporter who rises beyond the most routine work must do so often—drop into an unfamiliar setting, master the intricacies of a complex situation, absorb the atmosphere of the place, and then get it all down on paper so it is clear and vivid for others.

The front page of the *Sun* for April 20, 1879, an eight-page Sunday issue, carried this headline at the top of the third column:

The Story of a Foundling.

What Happened to the Child
Found in Wm. Heese's Hallway.

It introduced Ralph's step-by-step narrative of the mournful passage through the municipal bureaucracy of a baby abandoned at the entrance of a house on Sixth Avenue in midtown Manhattan. The account began with the discovery of the baby, which was dressed in clothes made of cheap material but with exquisite needlework, suggesting a mother who was loving but in such desperate circumstances that she could see no way to raise the child herself. A policeman carried the infant to the Fifty-first Street station, and from there another policeman, awkward but tender, took it downtown by horsecar to police headquarters on Mulberry Street.

There a matron fed the baby, judged to be about three months old, after which it was passed on to the office of a Mr. Blake, the Superintendent of Outdoor Poor, at Eleventh Street and Third Avenue. His responsibility was to name the baby. Formerly, said Ralph, Blake had followed Mr. Bumble's procedure in *Oliver Twist,* picking foundlings' names in alphabetical order, but now he selected names at random. So, from Blake's inspiration of the moment, the foundling discovered on Sixth Avenue became Mabel Jennings—until he noticed it was a boy, whereupon it became Martin Jennings.

Martin Jennings was then put aboard the boat that made the rounds of the welfare and penal institutions on the East River islands—in company with "pickpockets, thieves, drunkards, vagrants, paupers, and abandoned women." Deposited at the somber, turreted Infant Asylum on Randall's Island, Martin was dressed in the institution's standard baby clothes. "That his little garments were all sufficient made no difference; the routine permits no exercise of mind." Martin was next assigned to a foster mother, a nursing mother sent to Randall's Island by a police court for drunkenness or some other offense, and laid in an iron crib tagged with his name and the date of his abandonment.

One more step in the prescribed procedure for new foundlings remained. On the Sunday morning the story appeared Martin was to be baptized. For this foundlings were alternately delivered to a Protestant and a Catholic clergyman, and Martin had drawn the Protestant.

The fundamental flaw in the system was that the foster mothers, almost all impoverished and malnourished, could scarcely nurse their own offspring, let alone a second baby. A doctor at the asylum conceded that the mothers usually gave short shrift to the foundlings. The story ended:

> "What proportion of the foundlings die?" the Doctor was asked.
> "They nearly all die!" was the answer.

"The Story of a Foundling" exemplified the *Sun's* knack for spotting a column of readable copy in a trifle of news that other newspapers dismissed in a few lines. It was a moving human-interest story, and while it was playing on the emotions it was shedding light on the harshness of life at the bottom of Victorian society. It was the sort of story that could sometimes nudge those in positions of power to make changes for the better, which was one of the satisfactions of being a reporter.

Periodically New York had a murder that caused the city's newspapers, including the *Sun,* to lose all sense of proportion. One occurred in June 1879, not quite two months after the foundling story.

The victim was the wife of an allopathic physician named Alonzo Hull. Dr. and Mrs. Hull had lived in a brownstone on West Forty-second Street. On the morning of June 11, 1879, Mrs. Hull was found dead in her first-floor bedroom, smothered with the bedclothes. Jewelry and money were missing, pointing to a panicked burglar as the likely killer. But soon the Hulls' strange relationship began to come to light, and this suggested that the doctor might have wanted to do away with his wife. Mrs. Hull, fifty-eight, who had weighed three hundred pounds, had treated the meek, ineffectual seventy-four-year-old doctor contemptuously. She had slept in her first-floor chamber, relegating her husband to the attic. She had controlled the household money and had required her husband to pay rent, and she had led a lively social life from which the doctor was excluded. Perhaps, it was speculated, the pipsqueak husband had used chloroform or ether from his medical supplies to subdue his outsized wife and then killed her.

The gothic circumstances of the case dominated front pages for days, and Ralph may well have gathered some of the details for the *Sun.* But he definitely took command of the story when it was learned that the initial supposition that the murderer had been a burglar was correct. A black man who had done odd jobs in the Hulls' neighborhood was arrested in Boston after he pawned jewelry that matched a description of Mrs. Hull's jewelry circulated by the New York police. He immediately confessed to the murder.

Ralph credited his news instinct—the sixth sense that John Bogart had spoken of—with guiding his next step, but common sense would seem to be a sufficient explanation. Ralph surmised that the New York detective in charge of the case, a police captain known as "Clubber" Williams, would go to Boston to return the murderer, whose name was Cox, to New York. If Ralph accompanied Williams, he would be the first in the New York press to have access to Cox. So even though Bogart had given him another assignment and Captain Williams, who scorned reporters, objected vigorously to his presence, Ralph boarded the Boston train with the detective. "I disobeyed orders, and went with the police captain, trembling lest someone else should realize, as I did, the importance of coming back with the murderer and getting his story of the crime. No one else thought of it."

Because no one else thought of it, Ralph had Cox to himself through the whole of one June night. The prisoner was to be returned to New York by train to Fall River and from there by the Fall River Line night boat. On the train Ralph wedged himself into a parlor car compartment with Captain Williams, several other detectives, and Cox. When the policemen and their prisoner boarded the steamboat *Bristol* at Fall River, Ralph joined them in an upper-deck stateroom with red draperies on the windows. By this time Ralph was on easy terms with everybody, including Clubber Williams; he even joined a group including Williams for supper in the steamboat's dining saloon. Most important, Cox, who said he was resigned to dying for his crime and was indeed hanged a year later, talked freely. Ralph drew from him the details of his background and of the murder. A sympathetic and rounded picture of Cox emerged—a drifter who had eked out the barest of existences, turned in desperation to thievery, and then blundered into his terrible deed when his movements awakened Mrs. Hull. When Cox realized that in silencing Mrs. Hull he had smothered her, he had frantically tried to revive her by dousing her with cologne and ice water, as evidence at the scene confirmed. "The most imaginative person could not detect evil in Cox's face," Ralph observed.

After a three-hour delay caused by fog over the Sound, the *Bristol* tied up at its Murray Street pier on the Hudson River around ten o'clock in the morning. Ralph, who had left for Boston on the eight o'clock train the previous morning and spent much of the night listening and taking notes, followed in a hansom cab as the police saw Cox into a cell at police headquarters. Then he went to the *Sun* and wrote almost eight columns of copy for the next day's edition—June 26, 1879. More than five columns ran on the front page.

He had scored a "beat"—an exclusive piece of news—which, in his view, would always be "the chief aim and glory" of every reporter. "There was not a teaspoonful of news left in the case when I got through," he said.

Most of the crimes and scandals that *Sun* reporters wrote about were forgotten in a day. But now and then, even in his early years as a New York reporter, Julian Ralph dealt with matters of more enduring interest. His coverage for the *Daily Graphic* of the Beecher trial, which stands as a symbol for Victorian piety and hypocrisy, was one such assignment. There were two others within the span of a few weeks in 1877, when Ralph had been with the *Sun* two years. Both reflected the widening of the chasm between capital and labor in the United States as large, impersonal enterprises gained dominance in business, and both were bound up with the shattering economic depression of the 1870s.

The Molly Maguires were a secret, violent group of Irish immigrants in the anthracite coalfields of eastern Pennsylvania. The immigrants had powerful grievances. Their lot in Pennsylvania was proving little better than it had been under oppressive English landlords in Ireland. The miners' work was brutal and low-paying. They lived with their families in primitive company housing and were forced to deal with extortionate company stores. Their anger mounted, and beginning in the early 1860s there were sporadic murders of mine bosses in Schuylkill and Carbon counties that were attributed to the Molly Maguires.

The killings continued off and on for more than a decade with few arrests and no convictions. Then, after a long and unsuccessful strike by the miners against drastic wage cuts was followed by several murders in the depression year of 1875, the authorities struck. Ten Mollies were arrested for various murders, one dating back to 1871. They were brought to trial in 1876, and all were convicted, largely because of the testimony of a Pinkerton agent named James McParlan, who had infiltrated the organization at the behest of the largest mine operator, the Philadelphia and Reading Coal and Iron Company. Their appeals denied, they were sentenced to hang on June 21, 1877—six at Pottsville, the county seat of Schuylkill County, and four at Mauch Chunk (later renamed Jim Thorpe), the county seat of Carbon County. Ralph was dispatched to Mauch Chunk.

The train from New York took four hours and deposited its passengers right in front of the Mansion House, the leading hotel in Mauch Chunk, which was set in a valley hemmed in by mountains and liked to call itself "the Switzerland of America." Ralph arrived at least two days before the executions. He slipped up almost immediately. Though he was normally the soul of amiability, the grating manner of another reporter—very likely the representative of an evening paper in New York—vexed Ralph so much that he tried to send him off on a wild goose chase by concocting a rumor that the Mollies were planning to rescue their imprisoned fellows. The annoying reporter promptly telegraphed a story on the rescue plan to his paper, and soon all the other reporters in Mauch Chunk were manufacturing similar stories out of thin air to avert blistering messages from their editors asking why they had missed the news. The next day's *Sun* carried a story that began with a vague report, probably sent by Ralph, of "apprehension in Mauch Chunk of a possible Molly Maguire uprising for the rescue of the four murderers" and then set the scene for the hangings in a passage that was unmistakably his:

Under the shadow of Mount Pisgah, behind the picturesque village of Mauch Chunk, the four doomed men—Michael J. Doyle, Edward Kelly, John Donahue, and Alexander Campbell—lie, shackled and hopeless, in separate cells in the Carbon County Jail—a granite structure, solid as a fortress, and enclosed within a massive, towering wall of stone.

Public feeling against the Mollies was virulent, but once more Ralph showed sympathy for the cornered criminal. In this story he went on to tell of Kelly's wife fainting at the sight of the gallows when she visited her husband. The next day, shunning the moralizing still common in stories written on such occasions, he described how the prisoners were spending their last hours in their cells. Kelly knelt before a crucifix and "greeted his visitors absent mindedly, and talked in a low, boyish voice, as though his attention was not upon what he said." Donahue, who would leave eight children, "sat as he always does, in a corner by the bed, reading the book on death which Father Bunce gave him."

The front-page account of the hangings showed that Ralph was able to do what many reporters of the time could not or would not do—summarize clearly at the start what had happened without sacrificing all drama and suspense.

MAUCH CHUNK, June 21.—The four Molly Maguires who have been confined in the Carbon County jail, in this place, twenty-one months, were hanged at six minutes before 11 o'clock this morning. The town was quiet. Many families, expecting a conflict between the troops and the Mollies, had fled from their homes. The militia guarded the neighborhood of the prison, and the Coal and Iron police were stationed in the jail.

In the jail, where the gallows with its four dangling nooses had been erected in a corridor between two tiers of cells, the chilling and the incongruous had blended. One hundred and fifty men pressed inside to watch, "swearing, joking and laughing." "Four handsome coffins" were stacked before the scaffold, and the sheriff neatly piled caps of white linen, handcuffs, and leg shackles in the four corners of the gallows. "Somebody brought in two floral crosses for Doyle's and Kelly's coffins; a man below asked the men above not to spit through the perforated gallery." The prisoners, variously cocky, dazed, and trembling but in the end all in control of themselves, were brought in.

Sheriff Raudenbush and his assistants fitted the leg irons and the handcuffs on each of the victims, the priests in tremulous voices gave them absolution, and then the nooses were adjusted. The Sheriff personally saw that each noose was properly adjusted, and then the great, baggy white caps were drawn over the men's heads and all except the condemned left the platform. . . . While all four men stood stolidly under the gallows beams, the Sheriff and his men pulled the rope that drew the bolt from under the trap. There was a loud crash as the platform fell, and the four men were swinging and circling round and round, their feet a few inches from the floor.

This time the condemned died quickly of broken necks. The bodies were placed in the waiting coffins, and as the coffins, "in rude wagons, passed down the village main street, relatives and friends followed in the middle of the road."

The next day Ralph, along with other reporters, attended a wake in a tavern that had been owned by Alexander Campbell, one of the men executed, and that had been the scene of planning for one of the 1875 murders. Campbell's body lay on view, and near it forty women, cloaked and hooded, keened and cursed the informer, McParlan. A hush fell when the presence of reporters was discovered. Armed Mollies were about, and the reporters were warned that they risked their lives if they stayed. They left, but the incident was one of the last gasps of the Molly Maguires. The hangings had marked the end of the Mollies as a force to be reckoned with in the anthracite fields.

Reminiscing about Ralph in *Harper's Weekly* in 1894, Frederic Remington mentioned that his friend had covered "the riots." He did not amplify and Ralph's own recollections offer no enlightenment, but logic and evidence indicate that Remington was referring to the railroad strike of 1877.

The strike began after the nation's major railroads, their traffic reduced by the depression, peremptorily cut wages 10 percent. Railroad employees, already in desperate straits because of shortened working hours, struck, blocking tracks and halting freight between the East and the Midwest. Other workers and jobless men, plus troublemakers looking for excitement, joined their ranks, and in half a dozen cities the assemblages turned into rampaging mobs that fought with troops. Scores died—no one seems ever to have added up the precise total—and much property was destroyed.

The riots erupted in mid-July and were largely over by the end of the month, with the defeated strikers returning to work at the reduced pay levels. But for a time the country appeared on the verge of insurrection, and many Americans were left shaken. "The action of the mob . . . seemed to threaten the chief strongholds of society and came like a thunderbolt out of a clear sky, startling us rudely," said a historian with memories of the period, James Ford Rhodes. Previously, said Rhodes, Americans "had hugged the delusion that such social uprisings belonged to Europe and had no reason of being in a free republic where there was plenty of room and an equal chance for all."

The episode taxed the *Sun's* small staff. For a week riot stories filled the front page and spilled over to the inside of the paper. Many came from the Associated Press (although the *Sun,* like most other newspapers of the period, did not give the news service credit), some may have been written by part-time local correspondents of the *Sun* around the country, and some were produced by the *Sun's* own reporters. The first mob violence took place on the Baltimore and Ohio line at Martinsburg, West Virginia, on Tuesday, July 17, and it is known that the *Sun* sent its own man there because a story said he had arrived in town on a train carrying federal troops. The *Sun* also probably had its own reporter in Baltimore, where, on Friday, July 20, the first deaths occurred. And in Pittsburgh, which on the weekend of July 21–22 was the scene of the bloodiest fighting and the greatest property destruction of the strike, Julian Ralph was almost certainly present.

The target of the mob in Pittsburgh was the Pennsylvania Railroad, which had already imposed one 10 percent wage cut at the start of the depression. The railroad's workers, along with other laboring men and the usual admixture of toughs, had stopped freight trains. Local militiamen having proved useless—many simply melted into the crowds they were supposedly controlling—other state militia units were brought from Philadelphia, arriving at the Union Depot at midafternoon on Saturday.

The 650 Philadelphia militiamen promptly marched from the depot to a point a mile to the east where the mob had blocked the Pennsylvania tracks. That was the start of twenty-four hours of chaos. The mob numbered some 8,000 by one estimate, and around five o'clock it clashed with the troops. The soldiers used bayonets and rifles, and the rioters threw rocks and fired revolvers. At least sixteen of the rioters were killed and many wounded, but at dusk the troops withdrew to a roundhouse. There they were besieged by the mob, which had obtained more firearms by breaking into gun shops and had even acquired a cannon. When the troops fired at the men manning the cannon, more rioters were killed.

In the night the rioters took up the torch. They set fire to railroad shops and began burning rolling stock, eventually destroying 1,600 passenger and freight cars and 126 locomotives. Again and again they sent open cars filled with flaming oil-soaked coke against the roundhouse where the soldiers had taken refuge, and by seven-thirty Sunday morning it was burning so fiercely that the soldiers had to flee to avoid being roasted. They fought their way through the streets of Pittsburgh, suffering three or four deaths in their own ranks and killing at least nineteen more members of the mob. Eventually the troops reached safety across the Allegheny River, and the mob again focused its energies on burning. The climax of the orgy of arson came in the afternoon, when the rioters pushed railroad cars filled with blazing coke against the Union Depot and set it and adjacent buildings afire.

New York reporters traveled in packs on big stories, and most of those assigned to Pittsburgh, including Ralph, probably reached the city on a train that arrived early Sunday. An armed mob had delayed the train at Johnstown until it ascertained that no troops were aboard. As the train neared Pittsburgh shortly after 1 A.M., the passengers could see fires burning in the city, and to avoid encountering rioters along the Pennsylvania tracks they got off and walked the last three miles.

Picture Ralph setting out—the big-city reporter, imposing in size, dapper at the start, his derby perhaps exchanged for a summer straw boater. As he makes his way through the streets toward the heart of the violence, he takes in the layout of the city, the fires, the crowds, the troops' situation. Through the night and all day Sunday he watches, listens, and questions rioters, officials, and onlookers. Now and then he jots down a reminder to include something in his story, but mostly he doesn't bother with notes; everything he sees and hears prints itself indelibly on his mind.

As the day progresses he is no longer dapper; his clothes are rumpled and stained with sweat and with soot from the fires. Whenever he has a chance he ducks out of the way to write a few paragraphs. The telegraph is uncertain—service was interrupted for a time in the night—and to make sure his copy gets to New York he sends snatches at every opportunity. As a result the story that will run on the front page of the *Sun* the next morning reads like a running account of the day. It begins:

PITTSBURGH, July 22.—The sun dawned this morning on one of the most terrible scenes ever witnessed except in the carnage of war. The fire raged with unabated fury, and the flames kept creeping steadily toward the depot. . . .

The burning of the Union Depot in Pittsburgh as depicted in *Harper's Weekly* for August 11,

Later passages describe the soldiers' "desperate sally" to escape from the roundhouse and their begging for food and water as they retreat; their commanders had neglected to provision them, and they had eaten almost nothing since leaving Philadelphia. Looters empty freight cars of hams, sewing machines, boots, and tobacco; they roll away barrels of flour too heavy to lift. At 1:30 P.M. the burning cars start "thundering down" toward the Union Depot, and at 3:30 P.M. it ignites. As evening comes on, the rioters' energies flag; and as the thousands of citizens who have spent the day watching from a distance begin to make their way home, Ralph sends a paragraph remarking on their strange detachment, on the way they "looked upon the riots, the bloodshed, and the burning of millions of property as they would look at a sensational drama." And at 10:17 P.M. he telegraphs a final description of the fires still raging:

> There are fifty miles of hot rails, ten tracks side by side, with as many miles of ties turned into glowing coals, and tons on tons of iron car skeletons and wheels almost at white heat. Hundreds of coal and coke cars are still at full blast; two hotels, an elevator, and many dwellings are burning furiously, and hundreds of smaller buildings along the line are still in a blaze. . . .

There were other stories to be written from Pittsburgh in the next couple of days as order returned, but these were easy compared with what Ralph had done this Sunday. He had spent the day attempting to sort out chaos from the midst of the chaos, trying to make instant sense of a rush of confusing, noisy happenings. He did not succeed completely; his story had awkward spots, and his casualty figures turned out to be wildly inflated. But he had performed well for a young reporter who had been without sleep for one night, perhaps two, and who had been going full tilt for many hours. Despite his reputation for indefatigability, he must have been exhausted by the time he sent his last copy Sunday night.

He had been doing what he would prove best at: "covering the main stem of important events . . . unaided and alone." And as he dashed off his story amid the tumult and flame he was experiencing one of the many occasions when, from the perspective of a later generation, he would seem to be marching through the history of his time.

7. 'Get What You're Sent For'

Once reporting had become an established occupation, all sorts of people—both journalists and laymen—came forward with ideas on how reporters should go about their work. Much of the advice, dealing with such matters as interviewing, political writing, sermon reporting, proper style, cultivation of sources, and journalistic ethics, appeared in the *Writer* and other periodicals. But perhaps the most comprehensive guidance for beginners was contained in a slim 1889 book entitled *The Ladder of Journalism: How to Climb It.*

Its author, Thomas Campbell-Copeland, described himself as a "practical newspaper man," and he sprinkled his book with practical suggestions. "A gentlemanly address and a courteous recognition of individual sensibilities," said Campbell-Copeland, would elicit more information than brashness and browbeating—sometimes referred to as reportorial "cheek" in the late nineteenth century. A reporter who donned his official fire badge and hurried off to a fire, *The Ladder of Journalism* warned at another point, had to guard against being so carried away by the excitement—flames, billowing smoke, shouting firemen—that he turned in three-quarters of a column of vivid description when his editor wanted three lines of unadorned fact. At a wedding the reporter should describe the presents (noting who gave what), the bride's gown, her complexion, and "her bearing as she enters the church."

It would seem that a reporter would have to witness at least the start of the wedding ceremony to describe the bride's bearing as she entered the church. But Campbell-Copeland advised that in reporting most events—bazaars, dinners, reunions, dedications, and funerals as well as weddings—it was a waste of time to hang around for more of the actual proceedings than absolutely necessary. At a funeral, for example, only on rare occasions "does a reporter need to stop until the body has been consigned to its last resting place." For an ambitious young reporter, the whole idea was to cover as many events as possible, and to do this he must quickly corner some knowledgeable person at each, pump the source for the necessary details, and then hurry on. He should, in Campbell-Copeland's words, spend his days "flitting about from place to place, something in the same way as the industrious butterfly passes from flower to flower, or taking a better illustration, like the proverbial busy bee, which does not stay long at any one place, but never fails to carry something back to the hive, represented in the case of the reporter, by the City Editor's desk."

Now and then a general reporter might find himself called upon to fill in for the regular music or drama critic. A reporter substituting for a music critic should be circumspect. "In writing up notices of concerts, vocal or instrumental, it will be of advantage to the reporter to possess a knowledge of music, and if he does not possess this, it is better for him to obtain the points from some expert than to risk betraying his ignorance by using terms with the meaning of which he is unacquainted."

Reviewing a play, on the other hand, was a breeze; nor, as in the case of funerals and weddings, was there any need to sit through the whole thing. "A very little effort on the part of a reporter will enable him to gain all the necessary information concerning dramatic performances from the regular attachés of the theatre, who, having no interest in individual performers or companies, are likely to give fair and trustworthy hints as to the merits of any particular evening's representation." Presumably this meant that the reporter should ask the ushers what they thought of the play.

Campbell-Copeland also had special words of advice for reporters assigned to "district work"—covering a section of a city for a large metropolitan newspaper. Such a reporter should make it a point to know the police in his territory, as well as such potential founts of local gossip as barbers and saloonkeepers. But he must not waste time loafing in saloons and must deport himself so as to maintain a creditable reputation among the people in his district.

> Neatness in dress, cleanliness in habit and propriety in general conduct never fail to gain respect. There can be no apology for dirt under any circumstances. There is very little excuse for carelessness in dress. Vulgar language creates disgust and more or less contempt in the mind of every respectable citizen who hears it. A reporter who carries out an interview with his mouth half full of chewing tobacco carries a strong smell with him and leaves an impression not at all favorable or pleasing.

Dana, who was sometimes called upon to lecture to students and editors after he had led the *Sun* to new prominence, offered advice on a somewhat loftier plane. Even though circumstances had forced him to leave Harvard after only two years, he was an immensely learned, cultivated man, and he was pleased when he discovered reporters who shared his scholarly interests. He recognized that some men lacking in formal education—like Julian Ralph—could perform brilliantly as reporters, but at the same time he disagreed with many of his fellow editors that there could be such a thing as an overeducated newspaperman. "I had rather take a young fellow," he once said, "who knows the Ajax of Sophocles, and who has read Tacitus, and can scan every ode of Horace—I would rather take him to report a prize fight or a spelling match, for instance, than to take one who has never had those advantages."

Latin and Greek instilled rigor and precision in the use of language; the *Bible* and Shakespeare and Milton lent a richness and flow to a writer's style. Broad, varied knowledge of the world also benefited a reporter. As every issue of the *Sun* demonstrated, Dana's own interests were catholic. "Dana was interested in everything, read everything, saw almost everybody," said Frank O'Brien, and the best newspapermen, in Dana's view, possessed similarly wide ranges of interest. The education of a newspaperman "must be universal," he said on one occasion. "He must know a great many things, and the better he knows them the better he will be in his profession. There is no chance for an ignoramus in that trade." And on another occasion: "I never saw a newspaperman who knew too much, except those who knew too many things that were not so."

In the course of acquiring knowledge, Dana told students at Union College in upstate New York in 1893, the would-be reporter must also acquire the habit of accuracy. "There is no question that accuracy, the faculty of seeing a thing as it is, of knowing, for instance, that it is two and one quarter and not two and three eighths, and saying so—that is one of the first and most precious ends of a good education."

A reporter must also possess common sense, good judgment, keen intuition—by whatever name, the ability to recognize instantly whether a suggested chain of events was plausible, a proffered explanation reasonable. In Dana's words, this was

the critical faculty, the judgment which, when a proposition is stated to you or a fact is reported, looks at it calmly and says, "That is true," or else, "That is false"; the judgment, the instinct, the developed and cultivated instinct which knows the truth when it is presented and detects error when it comes masquerading before you, without the necessity of any long examination to ascertain whether it is truth or error.

Get the facts, "state them exactly as they are" and "with a little degree of life," add touches of eloquence, feeling, perhaps humor—if a reporter could do this with a story, "why you have got a literary product that no one need be ashamed of," Dana told the Union College students. "Thus we see this department of the newspaper is really a high art, and it may be carried to an extraordinary degree of perfection."

Ralph had his own ideas on what made a good reporter. Predictably, having left school at thirteen himself, he stressed formal education less than innate talent. Education, he said, "or the lack of it, should not either rejoice or deter any earnest youth who is going to join the press, for service there is in itself an education, and to get its benefits the main requirement is to be naturally gifted or fitted for it."

It was true that every newspaper, including the *Sun,* had reporters who could scarcely spell their own names or string together three grammatical sentences—men who despite their ineptness at writing were so good at laying their hands on news that it was worth an editor's time to puzzle out their copy. Other things being equal, however, it was infinitely better to be able to write. As might be expected of someone who on occasion was called upon to fill an entire page of the *Sun* by himself, Ralph placed a high value on fluency as a writer. He offered a simple criterion of such ability: "Whoever cannot freely and easily write a good, readable, informing or amusing letter cannot write at all; whoever does write good letters *may* be able to write for the press."

May because a facile pen alone was not enough to assure success as a reporter. Clairvoyance—the "news instinct" or "sixth sense" that Ralph claimed guided him to news—was handy, of course. And an attribute that Ralph usually labeled "news sense" was absolutely essential. In part, news sense, which marked good editors as well as good reporters, was an eye for a story that would interest the public. Henry W. Grady, the brilliant managing editor of the Atlanta *Constitution* in the 1880s and a legendary reporter as well, was said to have "perceived instantly the multitudinous interesting things of life." That was another way of saying he possessed this sort of news sense.

But news sense also embraced skill in putting a story together once you had the raw material. Ralph described this as "the light or intuition by which you know what to write and what to leave out, what to make the most of, what is worth a paragraph, and what is worth a whole page of a newspaper." In this usage news sense was knowing how to tell a story— what the point of the story was, where to begin, what details were essential for clarity and vividness, what were minor or irrelevant.

Early reporters could get by without this storytelling ability when they stuck to droning chronological accounts of events and verbatim reports of speeches. But by the time Ralph was hitting his stride reporters were expected to sort out confused, undifferentiated reality and to shape stories so that their significance became clearer. The change made the reporter's role more important. By emphasizing an indiscreet offhand remark by a politician in an interview, for example, he could—intentionally or not—influence public attitudes more subtly and powerfully than the old-fashioned blatant editorializing in news columns.

Important as were storytelling ability and other journalistic skills, it helped if they were accompanied by a resilient spirit and an easy way with people. Writing in *Scribner's Magazine* in 1893, Ralph described the ideal special correspondent, that elite breed of reporter constantly called on to charge off into unfamiliar situations:

> He must have such a temperament as to be new-born every morning, and to look on all that he is to write about with new eyes and fresh interest. He must have a made-to-order sort of soul, that will suffer itself to be thrown into whatever he does as a boy's soul enters into what games he plays at college. . . . He must be as sanguine as a song-bird, and as strong and willing as a race-horse. . . . He must have a personality all vigor to keep on past every hindrance, and with much candor and sweetness to win and keep men's confidence, so that they will admit him everywhere and talk to him unrestrainedly.

Ralph would have ranked "vigor to keep on past every hindrance" high among the essential qualifications for a reporter. "Unconquerable persistance," "indomitable perseverance"—phrases he used at other times—counted heavily. No matter how well a reporter wrote, no matter how thoroughly he charmed those he encountered in the course of his work, if he did not bring back the story he had failed.

> "Follow the copy if it blows out the window," is the order printers always give to their apprentices. "Get what you're sent for, if you have to go through fire and water," is the corresponding injunction of the old hands to the new ones in journalism.

And:

> If a reporter gets what he is told to, he is a good reporter; if not he is no good. There is no half-way in that course of schooling.

Reporters would go to almost any lengths to get what they were sent for. If a reporter could not carry out his assignments, there was always someone else eager to take his place from among the throng clawing for a foothold in the field. Excuses for failure were seldom accepted. "Let me tell you, sir, that reporters upon this paper never miss trains," Ralph recalled being admonished by an editor when as a young reporter he had botched an assignment by missing a train.

Sometimes the gentlemanly approach commended to beginners by *The Ladder of Journalism* did not work, and resort had to be made to more aggressive tactics. Ralph told of an occasion on which an architect's shoddy design had led to the collapse of a heavily trafficked building in New York. One of the local newspapers—Ralph does not say which—sent a "slender young gentleman" to ask the architect for an explanation.

The architect listened to the young reporter's request for an interview, and then replied that if he did not leave his presence at once he would throw him out of the window. Thirty minutes later the architect once again heard a rap at his door and called out "Come in." In strode the biggest reporter in New York, who was also one of the largest men in the country. He weighed three hundred pounds. . . .

"What do you wish?" the architect inquired.

"I am another reporter," said the gigantic scribe, "sent to ask you to throw me out of the window instead of the man we sent here half an hour ago. He was too small to be worth your while, but I am different. And now, sir, you will either throw me out of the window or I will throw you out—or you will, more wisely, sit down and explain how you came to do such bungling work on that building."

The architect decided to grant the interview.

Ralph did not record the fate of the slender young reporter, but given prevailing standards of newsroom justice, he was probably discharged. Physical risk sometimes went with the job.

Indeed, for much of Jacob Riis's reporting career, it was an everyday affair. From 1877 to 1899 Riis was a police reporter in Manhattan, first with the *Tribune,* then with the *Evening Sun.* Many of his working hours during these twenty-two years were spent in Lower East Side neighborhoods where gangs ruled the streets and murder and robbery were commonplace. Gathering material that eventually emerged in *How the Other Half Lives* as well as in his newspaper stories, he "went poking about among the foul alleys and fouler tenements" of the notorious slum known as Mulberry Bend. His favorite time was 3 A.M. because then "the veneering is off and you see the true grain of a thing."

He insisted that such excursions involved little danger for someone who exercised prudence—who, for example, "will take the other side of the street when he sees a gang ahead spoiling for a fight." He also suggested that hostility against him was dampened because he wore the slouch hat and spectacles that the slum dwellers associated with doctors, and he had, in fact, sometimes aided persons injured in the endemic violence. But Riis's equanimity amid such fearsome surroundings implies an unusually high tolerance for danger. By most people's standards he had chosen a rather frightening line of work, and even he acknowledged that on a couple of occasions he had feared for his life.

> One was when a cry of murder had lured me down Crosby Street into a saloon on the corner of Jersey Street, where the gang of the neighborhood had just stabbed the saloon-keeper in a drunken brawl. He was lying in a chair surrounded by shrieking women when I ran in. On the instant the doors were slammed and barred behind me, and I found myself on the battlefield with the battle raging unabated. Bottles were flying thick and fast, and the bar was going to smash. As I bent over the wounded man, I saw that he was done for. The knife was even then sticking in his neck, its point driven into the backbone. The instinct of the reporter came uppermost, and as I pulled it out and held it up in a pause of the fray, I asked incautiously:—
> "Whose knife is this?"
> A whiskey-bottle that shaved within an inch of my head, followed by an angry oath, at once recalled me to myself and showed me my role.

His role for the moment was to play doctor, and he tended to the saloonkeeper, trying to stanch the bleeding, as the fighting swirled about him. He listened anxiously for the tramp of policemen coming down the street from a nearby stationhouse. Once he thought help had arrived, but when he heard "the wail of men being beaten in the street" he realized that a contingent of his fellow reporters had shown up and been set upon by gang members gathered outside the saloon. Riis was something of a pariah among police reporters because he operated independently instead of going along with the prevailing practice of exchanging news and thereby lightening everybody's work, and he conceded that he "smiled wickedly in the midst of my own troubles" at the yelps of his rivals. Moments later, just as "an empty keg knocked my patient from his chair," the police burst through the door and Riis was safe.

Most reporters did not jeopardize life and limb in a normal day's work, but most now and then found themselves in the sort of circumstances never encountered by men who went each morning to banking or insurance offices. Thus in March 1886 a young New York *Times* reporter named Thomas B. Fielders was sent to report on the sinking of a Cunard ocean liner, the *Oregon,* in the Atlantic off Long Island. For Ralph, Fielders' exploit in getting the *Oregon* story back to his office was a shining example of a reporter's reckless disregard of his person to get what he was sent for.

Just before daylight on a Sunday, the *Oregon,* a swift new steamship, had been rammed by a heavy-laden three-masted schooner about ten miles offshore. The schooner sank quickly with all hands. The *Oregon,* a hole big enough to drive a horse and wagon through piercing her port side, went down slowly, and all 896 of her passengers and crew had time to get into lifeboats. Two small vessels, a pilot boat and a coastal schooner, had happened on the scene, and during the morning the *Oregon* survivors jammed aboard these. Toward noon they transferred to a passing inbound German liner, the *Fulda.* Late in the afternoon the *Fulda* signaled news of what had happened to shore with code flags, and the report was telegraphed to Manhattan.

Word reached the *Times* about 6 P.M. Sunday. The customary base for reporters assigned to meet incoming ships—usually to interview notables aboard—was the Quarantine Station on Staten Island, and the *Times* already had representatives there. But it was known that all through the evening and till about 1 A.M. tide conditions would keep the *Fulda* anchored off Sandy Hook, outside New York Harbor. She would not reach Quarantine until it was too late for reporters to get the full story of the *Oregon* in time for the morning newspapers. So Fielders and two other *Times* men were instructed to hire a tug to take them out to the *Fulda* at Sandy Hook. They found one on the Brooklyn waterfront, anxiously endured a lengthy wait while the crew assembled, and then steamed for the *Fulda.*

Around midnight they reached her at her Sandy Hook anchorage— brilliantly lighted, decks aswarm. Not entirely sure how they would be received, they had the tug's captain sound a few imperious toots on his whistle, hoping to convey the impression that there was something official about their mission. The toots apparently had the desired effect. A line was made fast from the tug to the liner, and the two were linked by a swaying ladder. The three reporters clambered up.

Once on the *Fulda's* main deck, they quickly realized that the ship's officers had mistaken them for the party of the port health officer. "Being in a hurry, however," the *Times*—then in a period of eclipse and in need of something to crow about—said in a gleeful column of self-congratulation, the reporters "decided to defer explanations." Before the *Fulda's* officers could grasp the situation, the reporters began collecting accounts of the day's events from the *Oregon's* passengers, who were still dressed in whatever clothes they had been able to fling on before entering the lifeboats. In the smoking cabin one of the reporters found the *Oregon's* captain, who spoke freely about the collision and rescue.

All went smoothly until the *Times* men reunited on the main deck, ready to depart. It was after 1 A.M. The *Fulda* was under way again, and they noticed that their tug's line had been cast off. Not suspecting anything was amiss, they signaled it to pick them up, but as the tug approached, the *Fulda's* captain rushed up to where they waited by the rail. He knew who they were, and he was not pleased. "Nobody can leave this vessel," he commanded, and crew members stood by to enforce his edict. The reporters were dismayed; they had a gripping tale all to themselves, but now it looked as if they would be prevented from returning to their office with it.

The tug was alongside, far down the *Fulda's* towering hull. For a moment Fielders studied the distance to the tug's heaving deck. Then, in a flash, he swung his legs over the rail. The captain grabbed his coat collar. Fielders slipped free—by one account he flung up his arms and slid out of the unbuttoned coat—and leaped for the tug. He landed safely, snatching the tug's forestay to steady himself as he hit the deck. Crew members seized the other two *Times* men, but they somehow managed to toss wads of their copy down to Fielders on the tug. "He caught them, and felt a great calm," said the *Times*.

Fielders reached the *Times* building on Printing House Square just before 3 A.M. A few hours later, over their breakfast tables, *Times* subscribers were reading a dramatic front-page account of the *Oregon* sinking that was as lucid and detailed as if the whole episode were unfolding before their eyes in slow motion.

The other morning newspapers had workmanlike stories but did not match the *Times*. Their reporters may have chartered tugs, too, but only the reporters from the *Times* boarded the *Fulda* that night. Their rivals apparently had to rely largely on snippets of information shouted from the deck of the *Fulda* and from secondhand material passed on by the real health officer after he eventually did visit the ship. Fielders had beaten the *Sun*, among others. But Ralph, who had probably known Fielders since both covered the Molly Maguires and who would later serve as a correspondent in London when Fielders was there, had nothing but ungrudging admiration for the *Times* man and his magnificent leap.

Even before he began traveling in remote places and writing about wars, Ralph faced his share of uneasy moments. At a shipboard dinner in New York Harbor in 1876, a drunken Southerner menaced him with a pistol when he balked at singing a Confederate war song. Covering one of the coal-mine disasters that occurred with dreadful regularity in the nineteenth century—in this instance it was probably an explosion at Pocahontas, Virginia, that killed 154 men in 1884—Ralph foolishly ignored the superintendent's warning of continuing danger from the volatile firedamp and paid a miner to guide him through the mine. Only when the miner, a Welshman who had seemed a colorful, quotable fellow, began poking his open-flame lamp into crevices to show where the firedamp lurked did Ralph realize that his guide did not have all his senses about him. Ralph grabbed the lamp and retreated as the miner conceded that, yes, "mebbe she might blow up again." Ralph also recalled a chilling experience that took place when he was dispatched across the Hudson to New Jersey just before Thanksgiving in 1883 to look into the murder of a seventeen-year-old girl.

The girl, whose name was Phoebe Paullin, had lived in a crossroads settlement consisting of a dozen unpainted shacks and two general stores. It was on the side of a hill less than fifteen miles from Manhattan, and from the top of the hill you could see the city and the towers of the new Brooklyn Bridge. But the hamlet could just as easily have been set in the mountains of West Virginia. The residents were poor, superstitious, and wary of outsiders, and they were even known as mountaineers. Phoebe's three brothers, sturdy, full-grown men, were impatient to take justice into their own hands.

Ralph arrived on the scene two or three days after the murder, before Phoebe's funeral. The bare facts of the crime had been told: a lonely, rutted country road, the victim "outraged," her throat cut. Ralph sought to flesh out the story. Phoebe was a wholesome country girl, and "Nobody yet found breathes a whisper against her character." She had been killed late on a Saturday afternoon while walking home from an excursion to Orange, three miles distant, to buy quilt batting for her mother. When found, Ralph would report in the *Sun* with an explicitness that undoubtedly offended many readers, she lay on her back with her dress pulled up: "Her heels were four feet apart. There was shoeblacking on her stockings." Several men from the neighborhood had been seen walking on the road the afternoon of the murder.

None of the men had been seen with Phoebe, however, and in the end none of the details Ralph turned up shed any particular light on who the murderer might have been. (The case, in fact, was never solved.) Meanwhile, Phoebe's brothers had come up with ideas of their own on the crime. They were convinced that a stranger had done the deed and that he would be irresistibly drawn back to the vicinity. For some unfathomable reason, they were further convinced that even though other strangers were about—

several newspapers had sent reporters—the guilty one was Ralph. Early in the course of his reporting Ralph had stopped at Phoebe's house, its door marked by a black and white rosette with streamers, and when he passed by again he was invited to view her body as it lay in the bare front room.

As I could not judge what manner of girl she had been without seeing her, I went in. Her three grown-up brothers were there, and as I stood beside the coffin one returned to the door of the room, closed it, and put his back against it. The others then attempted to carry out a project they had cherished but concealed, which was to have me touch the body in order that they might see whether blood flowed from the wounds, according to an age-old superstition which holds that such dumb mouths will accuse a murderer. At the moment I would not have done as they wished for a fortune.

"Put your hand on her," said one.

"I will not."

"Touch her with your hand. You must, I tell you," said another.

"You cannot get away. Touch her." They were terribly in earnest.

"I will do nothing of the sort," I said, and then I made a very short but very earnest speech, in which I explained who I was and how easily they could satisfy themselves about me. "And now," said I, advancing to the fellow who had his back against the door, "stand aside and end this folly—quick!"

He obeyed, and in an instant the air of out-doors tasted almost as sweet as anything that I ever drew down my throat.

Ralph must have been shaken. Robust as he was, the brothers could have forced him to touch the body, and if they had, there was no telling what their wrought-up states might have led them to imagine they were seeing. But he was not too shaken to have the wit to use the incident to give the beginning of his story on the front page of the next day's *Sun* a twist that none of the other reporters had.

More often than they faced danger, reporters faced daunting demands on their stamina and endurance. A tolerance for grinding travel and bursts of round-the-clock labor would always be a requirement for moving to the forefront of the field, but the demands were greater in the nineteenth century. Consider experiences of two of Ralph's journalistic contemporaries in New York, William J. C. Meighan and Charles Russell.

Meighan had a long career with the New York *Herald*. He joined its staff in 1867. He was only seventeen years old then, and James Gordon Bennett, Jr., was taking over the management of the *Herald* from his father. The senior Bennett had once unflinchingly paid the bill when one of his correspondents ordered a telegraph operator to start transmitting the *Bible* to keep the wire out of the hands of rival reporters, and Meighan appreciated the younger Bennett's adherence to this tradition of free spending in pursuit of news. Otherwise James Gordon Bennett, Jr., was a terror to work for— demanding, arrogant, utterly unconcerned with the difficulties his men might confront in fulfilling his instructions. When he offhandedly sent Stanley to find Livingstone in Africa, an errand that took a year and a half, he was acting completely in character.

Meighan never achieved the fame of a Stanley, but he was one of the *Herald's* stalwarts. When still in his teens he was ordered on a lonely trek through the South to investigate the nascent Ku Klux Klan, and there were undoubtedly many other taxing missions as the years went by. But a political assignment in the fall of 1871 stuck in Meighan's memory as one of the most arduous of all.

Pressure was building to end the reign of Boss Tweed and Tammany Hall in New York City and Albany. The *Herald* had never opposed Tweed very forcefully, but now, with the full details of the Tweed Ring's thefts disclosed by the *Times,* Bennett sided with the reform movement fighting the boss. A key test would be whether the reformers could triumph over the Tweed forces at the New York state Democratic convention, to be held in Rochester in the first week of October. The reformers would be strengthened, Bennett reasoned two weeks before the convention, if the *Herald* could marshal in its pages an impressive display of the anti-Tweed opinion known to prevail among Democratic leaders in outlying parts of the state. All that was needed was for a reporter to race from one end of the state to the other interviewing these leaders. Young Meighan was just the man.

Late one night Bennett handed Meighan a list of the Democrats he was to call on. Meighan was an uncomplaining sort, but even he was taken aback as he studied the list. The party leaders were scattered all over the state, many in hard-to-reach backwaters. "The prospect of covering in two weeks the total distance in search of them, to say nothing, if I found them, of having time to write out in full the views that would be required from each man, appalled me," Meighan recalled two decades later.

Bennett read the dismay on his reporter's face. "I had better send somebody else," he said. "I see you cannot cover the ground in time."

That was all it took to stiffen Meighan's spine. "If I cannot do this, no one else can," he responded.

"Well, go," said Bennett. "Those interviews must be published before the convention meets."

Go I did; I didn't even go home for a grip-sack; and half an hour later I was whirling on my way on the Central Railroad. It so happened that it rained nearly every day after I had started, and, as much of my travelling had to be done on horseback, or in ramshackle wagons over rough country roads, in order to make time between out-of-the-way places where teams were not seen frequently, I had little rest. From the time I left New York till I reached Albany on my return I did not take off my clothes once. Indeed, I did not go to bed at all. A dash of cold water in my face and a hasty rub of a brush over my head was my daily and nightly toilet. An hour or two on a sofa, stretched weary, worn, and generally wet from head to foot, afforded me a little doze. It was travel, Travel, TRAVEL, then write, Write, WRITE, and after writing till the "wee hours of morn" in a dingy country inn and at times in a fine city hotel, my only exercise, off a horse's back, a buggy's stretch-board, or a seat in a car, was the dash I made for the main post-office to catch the earliest mail. Very often I had to bunch my points of search in my interview campaign so as to capture two or three men on the same day who were miles apart. When this bunching became four or five I had to call a halt at some inn or hotel, and, instead of resting, go to work with the knowledge that I was not only three or four columns behind, but had many miles yet to cover, and many men yet to find.

Meighan crossed the state to Buffalo, then zigzagged his way back east conducting interviews. At each stop he sent in his card announcing himself as a representative of the *Herald,* was ushered into a parlor or an office, pressed for answers to his questions, and hurried on.

Two days before the convention he reached Albany, his assignment finished. He checked into a hotel to recover. He slept, ate a decent meal, and treated himself to some new clothes. Thus restored, Meighan, who had not heard from his office during his travels, located a file of the *Herald* and settled down to the exquisite pleasure of perusing his own words in print.

He could not find a single one. Short of death or dismemberment, nothing worse could have happened. He had given his all for the *Herald* and it had thrown his work in the wastebasket. He remembered later that he almost fainted.

Sunk in despair, Meighan returned to his hotel. There he found a terse message directing him to proceed to Rochester, the site of the convention. Still the good soldier, he obeyed and arrived on the eve of the convention, just as the delegates were picking up that day's newspapers from New York. And then he saw that everybody was reading the *Herald* and that what they were reading was his report—more than a dozen columns recounting, as his opening paragraph put it, his "conversational intercourse with the leaders of the country democracy." Said Meighan: "Talk of a man dreaming that he had lost all his family in a railroad collision and suddenly waking up to find his wife and little ones playing tag around the parlor table,—such a man's joy was something like mine."

Despite the initial flurry of interest, Meighan's rather dry, ponderous effort had little immediate impact. Although he had predicted that the anti-Tammany forces would dominate the convention, Tweed clung to control and pushed through his own slate of candidates for state offices. It was his last gasp as a political power, however, and Meighan's demonstration of the breadth of opposition to Tweed may have helped inspire the last-minute alliance of reformers and Republicans that crushed the ring in the state and city elections in November.

In any case, within a few days after the Rochester convention William Meighan's mind was on other things. He had gone west to cover the Chicago fire.

Like Meighan, Charles Russell was put to the test as a reporter for the *Herald,* though James Gordon Bennett, Jr., was not involved. Russell was the Midwestern journalist whose expectations of instant success in New York had been frustrated by office boys barring his way to city editors, eventually reducing him to such despair that he was glad to settle for a starvation-wage reporting job at the *Commercial Advertiser.* Russell had talent, and his situation soon brightened. In the mid-1880s he became a reporter for the *World,* now flourishing under its new proprietor, Joseph Pulitzer. Toward the end of the decade, he moved to the reporting staff of the *Herald,* where he remained till he returned to the *World* as city editor in 1894. Soon after joining the *Herald* he covered the Johnstown flood.

The flood occurred on May 31, 1889. Johnstown lies in a valley of the Allegheny Mountains in western Pennsylvania. At midafternoon of May 31, after heavy rains, a dam impounding a reservoir above the city burst. A mass of water cascaded down the valley, destroyed Johnstown, and took more than two thousand lives. It was, David McCullough has written, "about like turning Niagara Falls into the valley for thirty-six minutes."

The dam gave way at midafternoon on a Friday. At ten o'clock that night, just as Russell was finishing a story about a parade of New York City policemen, the night editor showed him a bulletin from Latrobe, Pennsylvania. "It was to the effect that a dam had burst at Johnstown, a few miles above Latrobe, and at least twelve persons had lost their lives." Later bulletins increased the dead to twenty, then forty. But Russell suspected that, as sometimes happened, the "country correspondent" might be exaggerating—"Such things as forty fatalities in a dam-burst do not happen"—and he was dubious that the story would prove to be of major significance when fact was sorted out from speculation. Nevertheless, the night editor wanted him to depart for Johnstown. Russell drew a hundred dollars for expenses, borrowed a colleague's overcoat of robin's-egg blue with watered-silk lapel facings, picked up his own silver-handled umbrella, and set out from the *Herald's* white-marble building at Broadway and Ann. He saw the assignment, he recalled years afterward, as "a night of rest in my lower berth, a column story filed early, and back to-morrow night."

Russell crossed to Jersey City on the Cortlandt Street ferry to catch the 12:15 A.M. Pennsylvania train to Johnstown. He quickly linked up with three other reporters bound for Johnstown on the same train—men from the *Times,* the *Tribune,* and the *World.* He remembered that one was wearing a frock coat and gleaming patent-leather shoes.

When they boarded the train at Jersey City Russell and the others got their first inkling that the trip might not go quite as planned. There was no sleeper to Johnstown. In fact, the twelve-fifteen would terminate at Philadelphia; flooding had disrupted travel west. But the outlook was still not too bad. Someone had arranged a special one-coach train to carry newspaper reporters on to Johnstown, and when Russell and his fellow reporters reached Philadelphia at 3 A.M. they switched to this train and rolled toward Johnstown.

Approaching Harrisburg, 130 miles short of Johnstown, at eight o'clock Saturday morning, their special ploughed through a vast lake over invisible tracks, the engine's firebox almost touching the water. Russell now began to understand the situation. Downpours surpassing all records had soaked the mountains of western Pennsylvania, and the runoff had overflowed watercourses in the mountains and the surrounding region. "Every creek had become a river and every river a flood. . . . Miles upon miles of track had been washed away, cuttings filled, bridges and trestles smashed to pieces and swept down." No trains would move west from Harrisburg for days.

Then began a period of circling first one way, then the other, trying to find a way to approach Johnstown. A hundred miles south of Harrisburg was a line of the Baltimore and Ohio that paralleled the Pennsylvania and had a branch to Johnstown. The B&O line passed through Martinsburg, West Virginia, and a small railroad, the Cumberland Valley, ran from Harrisburg to Martinsburg. There was a train in five minutes. Russell and the others jumped aboard.

At Hagerstown, Maryland, eighteen miles from Martinsburg, the Cumberland Valley train halted. Up ahead the Potomac River was a raging torrent, and the railroad bridge to Martinsburg was tottering. The reporters wangled a ride to the bridge on a wrecking car, a derrick on a platform. On foot they crossed the shaky planks of the bridge; soon after it dissolved into the yellow flood.

They were making progress. Down the road a farmer fed them corn pone, salt pork, and potatoes—it was now 2 P.M. Saturday—and then hitched up his team and drove them to Martinsburg.

When they reached there at six in the evening, they learned that the B&O tracks to the west were under water. There were no trains.

For a time it appeared that the only possible solution might be to hire a team to drive them forty miles south, into Virginia, where they could take a train still farther south to Richmond, then make an even wider circle west and north to try yet another approach to Johnstown. They had started from New York for Johnstown, 370 miles west, Russell was thinking; if they went to Richmond, they would be 400 miles south of New York. Russell was ready to give up. "We seem to be cast away on an island," he said to the train dispatcher at Martinsburg. "I will wire the *Herald* that I have made a hash of this thing and they must send someone else to cover the flood."

"You can't do that either," said the dispatcher. "The last wire went down more than an hour ago. You can't telegraph from here in any direction."

A B&O superintendent offered a glimmer of hope. He would obtain an engine and return the reporters to Hagerstown in Maryland over a route where the bridge crossing the Potomac was still intact. They slept that night in chairs in the lobby of a Martinsburg hotel, and by eleven Sunday morning the superintendent had them back in Hagerstown. Briefly they thought of returning to Harrisburg and circling to the northwest in hopes of reaching Johnstown that way. The helpful B&O man had a better scheme. Take the train to Chambersburg, in southern Pennsylvania, he suggested, and proceed northwest from there to Johnstown by road, a journey of some ninety miles. The telegraph was working at Hagerstown, and he would even help them wire ahead for teams and carriages along the way.

The reporters agreed to the plan. They reached Chambersburg at two o'clock Sunday afternoon and climbed into an open carriage waiting at the station. Through the rest of Sunday they jounced along mountain roads, switching to a new team and carriage at a town called McConnellsburg at 7 P.M. and fording a swollen stream a few miles farther on. At 2 A.M., at a point where the road had become impassable for a carriage, they roused a farmer's household. The farmer and his two sons greeted them with guns, but after it was determined that the reporters were harmless, the women of the family served them pie and cheese and coffee and the sons agreed to act as guides. Carrying lanterns, the youths shepherded the reporters along a washed-out road to the Juniata River, halfway between Chambersburg and Johnstown. At 3:30 A.M. they filed across the river on the planks of a crumbling bridge, one of their guides in front with a lantern, the other behind.

The telegraphed requests for transport were working out marvelously, and a new rig awaited the reporters on the other side of the river. Dawn was breaking as they started off. Sometime before nine Monday morning they changed teams and carriages yet again. It began to rain, and the road became so muddy that at intervals they had to climb down and walk. By now Russell had lost his silver-handled umbrella and his borrowed robin's-egg blue overcoat was smeared with mud. Presumably the patent-leather shoes worn by his colleague had long since lost their sheen.

The last stretch to Johnstown was down a mountain along a rough, steep loggers' track. They walked most of this, through the mud and over jagged rocks. Shortly before two o'clock Monday afternoon their goal lay in sight below them—in Russell's words, a "bare swept plain at the junction of two rivers where once had stood the greater part of Johnstown." For the first time they began to grasp the enormity of what had happened. A little distance on they came to a house on a hillside in which a temporary seat of government had been established. They learned that they were the first reporters from outside western Pennsylvania to reach Johnstown. Then they went to work.

8. Rules of the Game

S candals and domestic dramas, political squabbles, sermons and science lectures, interviews with visiting actresses, murders, fires, strikes— such was the life of a *Sun* reporter in the late 1800s. Stories blurred together, a new one taken up before the notes from the last had been cleared away. But in Ralph's case there were a few assignments that stood out in his memory or in the memories of others recalling his career. In 1885 and 1886 he went to Albany to cover the thoroughly corrupt New York state legislature. In 1885 he also described one of the principal ceremonial occasions of the age, the funeral of Ulysses S. Grant in New York City. In 1888 he wrote the *Sun's* account of the great blizzard, and in 1889 he covered the Thanksgiving Day football game between Princeton and Yale with aplomb even though his understanding of what was happening on the field was obviously sketchy.

He was exercising his talents on the national scene as well, reporting the Presidential nominating conventions in 1888 and 1892 and the Presidential inaugurations in 1885, 1889, and 1893. As early as 1882, in fact, Ralph was writing about Presidential activities, although not very important ones.

The occasion was a fishing trip to the St. Lawrence River and the Thousand Islands by President Chester A. Arthur in the fall of 1882. Arthur, a Republican machine politician who had ascended from the vice presidency a year earlier after the assassination of Garfield, had served as collector of customs in New York City, and Ralph almost certainly had encountered him before traveling to the upstate New York resort village of Alexandria Bay by train and steamboat to write about the President's vacation. Other newspapers did not pay much attention to the vacation, but ever since the days of Grant's long summer sojourns on the New Jersey shore Dana had been grumbling about such displays of idleness and frivolity on the part of the nation's chief executives. "The pernicious and costly example of Gen. Grant in abandoning the seat of Government, and in turning over the great public business to irresponsible clerks for months, has been adopted by Gen. Arthur as worthy of imitation," fumed a *Sun* editorial as Arthur began his fishing trip. Arthur was not earning his $50,000 a year, and Congress should pass a law docking a President's pay whenever he went on vacation, declared the *Sun*.

Dana's pique may have inspired Ralph's assignment, but if the editor hoped that his reporter would portray the President in a bad light, he must have been disappointed. Although Arthur, like other chief executives of the period, usually kept the press at arm's length in Washington, he and Ralph apparently got along pleasantly enough at Alexandria Bay, and in Ralph's stories the President came across as a generally unassuming fellow whom most readers would be unlikely to begrudge a few days' sport.

The tourist season was over, the nights were chilly, and the cavernous resort hotel was almost empty when Arthur, who was a widower, checked in. He was accompanied by his black valet and a businessman friend—not, from all evidence, by even a single guard. Aside from the President's small party, there were only a half-dozen other guests, including Ralph and three or four other reporters. The other reporters didn't write much. One filed a dispatch whose main news was that one evening "At half-past 9 o'clock the President was sleeping soundly." But although Arthur would not discuss anything remotely political—he was not even bothering to look at the newspapers—Ralph found enough material to make a gossipy story in the *Sun* daily for a week.

The President ate most of his meals in the hotel's main dining room, where at one breakfast he chatted with Ralph about a muskellunge he had caught. Sometimes he sat on a piling at the hotel wharf and talked to the boatmen. One day a patent medicine peddler presented the President with a bottle of "the Great Dutch Respiratory Remedy," and another day the President set out on a solitary walk and Ralph caught up and tagged along. In the evening Arthur smoked a cigar on the veranda overlooking the St. Lawrence, and later he read in his room. One night as Ralph walked along a corridor he passed the open door of the President's sitting room and glimpsed him reading before a crackling log fire.

But Arthur's main pastime was fishing for bass, pickerel, and muskie, and each day he ventured onto the river and among the Thousand Islands in a sixty-foot steam yacht, the *Minnie*. Much of the time Ralph seems to have been aboard. At first there was some question whether it was proper for the President to cross into Canadian waters—it was said that no sitting President had ever left the United States—but this concern was soon forgotten and the *Minnie* steamed wherever the fishing looked best. A constant presence was a local photographer named McIntyre, who had his own steam yacht "with which he pursues the President like a man after a consulship." While Arthur "submitted with the resignation of a man in the hands of a barber," he was careful to keep his minnow bucket out of the pictures because he did not wish to mar his considerable reputation as a fly fisherman.

Arthur was a large man with a large appetite, and food was a major preoccupation. Breakfast might feature duck and muskie. Before each excursion on the *Minnie* waiters from the hotel paraded aboard with hampers of beefsteaks, lamb chops, and pastries. When the party disembarked at an island for a picnic, a table was spread with a white cloth and "from among the dishes and glasses there rose the gilded neck of a champagne bottle." Nothing approached, however, the feast a group of prominent local men laid on for the President. Ralph was not invited, but he peeked in the dining room beforehand and saw that each place was set with six wine glasses. He also recorded the endless procession of food—oysters, three soups, two kinds of fish, roast turkey, beef, and lamb, quail on toast, jugged squirrel, ten vegetables, a choice of seventeen desserts. The dinner began just after 4 P.M., and not till 8:30 did the participants push back from the table and light cigars.

Each night after the day's activities were finished Ralph wrote up his account and took it to the local telegraph office. One night he and two other reporters returned to the riverfront hotel at 2 A.M.—they had found a tavern open along the way—and discovered the doors locked. The only lights were those in the President's rooms. Ralph and his companions pounded on a side door, hoping to arouse a member of the hotel staff. No one responded. And then the door opened and there was President Arthur, come to let them in. They apologized. "Why, that's all right," said the President. "You wouldn't have got in till morning if I had not come. No one is up in the house but me."

The Presidential fishing trip was an easy assignment for Ralph, as it would have been for any reporter with an eye for detail and a sense of the absurd. The stories were there for the taking, and the competition was scant. Even a terribly arduous assignment could sometimes be a relatively uncomplicated reporting job. Although Charles Russell had to struggle for three days to reach Johnstown, and had to sleep in a barn and forage for food during the two weeks he spent there, the flood survivors were eager to pour out their tales of heartbreak and terror to anyone who would listen.

But for all reporters there were assignments where laying their hands on the story was not so straightforward a business. Sometimes people were simply disinclined to talk to reporters and other times they had good reason to conceal information. Sometimes reporters could not bring off stories without talking to persons certain to appear in print as fools or knaves. A touch of brass might solve the problem. More often, some measure of deception, dissembling, or subterfuge was required. But how much of this kind of thing was acceptable? How far could you go to get a story?

In part, the answer depended on what newspaper you worked for. Among the major New York newspapers, at the *Herald* under James Gordon Bennett, Jr., at the *World* after Joseph Pulitzer took over in 1883, and at the *Journal* after William Randolph Hearst acquired it in 1895 and began vying with Pulitzer in sensationalism, anything went. Misrepresentation was fine with Hearst; he instructed his *Journal* reporters to pose as law enforcement officers whenever it would help get a story. At the *World* the Washington bureau chief obtained derogatory financial information about a Cabinet member by bribing a bookkeeper, and on another occasion he informed Pulitzer that he planned to pay a clerk in a government agency to spy for him. The *World's* Nellie Bly, one of the first women reporters to break out of the society and literary columns, assumed one pose after another in pursuit of stories. When she was not circling the globe in less than eighty days, she raved until she got herself locked up in an insane asylum, schemed to get inside a jail as a prisoner, donned a Salvation Army uniform, and worked as a factory girl. "Stunt" reporting was the name given to such exploits.

Julius Chambers, the Cornell man who joined the New York *Tribune* as a reporter in 1870, moved to the *Herald* in 1873, and his recollections of a dozen years as a reporter there show the latitude existing under the younger Bennett. To expose an extortion ring involving the health officer at the Quarantine Station on Staten Island—ships were prevented from entering New York Harbor until they had greased the right palms—Chambers greased a palm himself, paying someone two hundred dollars for a look at incriminating records. Investigating theft on East River piers, he bought a sailor's outfit from Brooks Brothers and hung around the waterfront until he was so well accepted that he was invited to meet with the thieves in a room over a saloon on South Street. At a political convention he hired a deaf woman who could read lips to observe the private chats of political leaders in the meeting hall and pass along to him whatever she learned. As part of an investigation of corruption in the Pennsylvania legislature, Chambers posed as a businessman and parceled out $1,900 among three influential state senators to buy their support for a charter for a bogus new gas company. Chambers's superiors at the *Herald* obviously knew of his strat-agems, since he was not buying sailors' outfits or paying bribes out of his own pocket.

No newspaper reporter could afford to be totally candid or guileless as he made his rounds, but compared with their counterparts on the *Herald,* the *World,* and the *Journal,* reporters for the *Times* and the *Tribune* were relative innocents. They were not above eavesdropping and misrepresenta-tion on occasion, but their editors did not stress the sex and scandal stories that spawned some of the most devious reporting. As for the *Sun,* it occupied something of an ethical middle ground.

On the one hand, in mining the vein of "human interest" the *Sun* sometimes descended to voyeuristic exploitation of the personal troubles of ordinary citizens. A reporter assigned to such a story had to penetrate the distraught household, and this usually required him to feign deep sympathy or use some other deception. On the other hand, Dana sometimes professed a lofty moral approach to journalism. In his speech to Wisconsin editors in Milwaukee in 1888, he declared that a newspaper should "never print an interview without the knowledge and consent of the party interviewed," nor should it ever ridicule "the weak or the defenseless . . . unless there is some absolute public necessity for so doing."

Dana's first injunction perhaps made sense in connection with formal interviews with public figures about great issues, but it had little relevance to a *Sun* man's day-to-day reporting of mankind's stumbles and mishaps. When someone indiscreetly blurted out the truth about a delicate situation, the *Sun* reporter who asked his source to pause and consider whether quotation was in order probably would not get far in the business. And Dana's warning against ridiculing the defenseless was hypocritical in light of the cruelty of some of the *Sun's* human-interest stories.

All the same, perhaps by his gentlemanly ways in the office, Dana seems to have engendered a sense that there were limits to acceptable reportorial enterprise. The reminiscences of *Sun* reporters yield no tales of payoffs to bookkeepers in return for news, and in a field in which honor and honesty were often expendable if they stood in the way of a story, Dana's subordi-nate editors stuck to some principles. As managing editor, Chester Lord once praised a reporter for refusing to betray a confidence, even though his refusal had caused the *Sun* to be beaten on an important story. Shortly after the turn of the century, a reporter informed the city editor at the time, George Mallon, that he had been given a clear opportunity to steal a secret

report of an official investigation into a gigantic insurance fraud. What
should he do? "A *Sun* man who would do that would lose his job," said
Mallon.

The fact of the matter, of course, was that the editors of the *Sun,* like the
editors of other newspapers, did not always know what their reporters were
up to. Indeed, Irvin S. Cobb, a celebrated reporter for the *Evening Sun* in
the early 1900s, said that "the wise city editor is the one who never asks
how his men attain their results." In any case, reporters had their own ideas
about propriety and decency.

Theodore Dreiser, over the course of his reporting at the New York *World*
and other newspapers, became increasingly perturbed by "the methods and
the effrontery and the callousness necessary at times for the gathering of
news." Deception was an inherent part of the job, he decided.

> For instance, one of the problems that troubled me most . . . was how to get the
> facts from a man or woman suspected of some misdeed or error without letting him
> know that you were so doing. In the main, if you wanted facts of any kind,
> especially in connection with the suspected, you did not dare tell them that you
> came as an enemy or were bent on exposing them. One had to approach all, even
> the worst and most degraded, as a friend and pretend an interest, perhaps even a
> sympathy one did not feel, to apply the oil of flattery to the soul. . . . To appear
> wise when you were ignorant, dull when you were not, disinterested when you
> were interested, brutal or severe when you might be just the reverse—these were
> the essential tricks of the trade.

Dreiser took a jaundiced view of his colleagues' ethics. "The counsel of
all these men was to get the news in any way possible, by hook or by crook,
and to lose no time in theorizing about it." The rationalization for dealing
deviously with people, or for appropriating a document lying on an official's desk, was that it was essential for survival. "Cheat and win and you
were all right; be honest and lose and you were fired."

Like Dreiser's fellow reporters, Julian Ralph did not brood much about
ethics, but his work inevitably required him to make decisions about ethical
questions. Contrary to Dana's insistence that persons interviewed be put on
notice that their remarks were for publication, Ralph often avoided taking
notes for the very reason that it reminded people that their words might
appear in print. "Note-books and pencils frequently alarm and put upon
guard a man who would talk freely in ordinary conversation," he said. He
probably would have agreed with Dreiser that deception went with the job,

but he would not have been unduly bothered. A reporter must be an actor who masks his own attitudes as he goes about his work, he said.

Writing about his career, Ralph mentioned two occasions when he used blatant misrepresentation to get stories. Both probably occurred during the first decade of his reporting career, though he does not date them.

One involved a fast new train. The mile-a-minute speeds passenger trains were achieving in the late 1800s thrilled Victorians, and Ralph was ordered to report on a demonstration run of the new train. But officials of the railroad, possibly nursing a grievance against the *Sun* because of one of Dana's unpredictable editorials, passed the word that Ralph was not welcome. Further, they let it be known that a reporter for a rival newspaper was to have the exclusive privilege of covering the demonstration. Ralph was stymied only briefly. Surmising that the train would stop en route to pick up the mayor of an outlying community, he hurried there and persuaded the mayor to let him pose as a secretary and go along. Thus, said Ralph, "I was able to report my sensations during the bullet-like journey."

The other assignment on which Ralph recalled misrepresenting himself was more significant. In December 1876 three hundred people died when the Brooklyn Theater burned. The fire had started when one of the gaslights bordering the stage ignited a piece of scenery. It spread across the stage, and when someone opened the stage entrances a rush of air drove flames and black smoke throughout the auditorium. In the pandemonium some people were trampled to death and others were suffocated or incinerated. Over the next several years a succession of fires at other local theaters came within a whisker of duplicating the Brooklyn tragedy, and at some point Ralph was instructed to look into the whole question of fire hazards in theaters.

Many of the theaters were poorly built and had inadequate exits, but it was obvious that the great source of concern lay on stage and behind the scenes. Painted canvas, curtains, and gauzy scrims fluttered close to gaslights, and there was a general clutter of flammable material. When Ralph sought to look backstage, however, one theater manager after another barred his way. Ralph's solution was to go to a friendly fire department official and borrow a fireman's uniform. The theaters were accustomed to having firemen show up to act as watchmen (and very likely to paying the firemen a dollar to cause as little bother as possible). Dressed in the uniform, Ralph inspected backstage areas and gathered information for a series of articles on the fire dangers posed by theaters. The managers of the theaters, he said, never knew how the detailed descriptions of backstage conditions had been obtained.

Ralph apparently never had any doubts about his actions in posing as a mayoral secretary or a fireman. But later in his life he acknowledged that there was room for debate over reportorial ruses and stratagems. Theft was wrong, he decided, and disguise and misrepresentation sometimes raised questions. In his autobiography he told of two incidents that occurred when he was working in London after leaving the *Sun*. In one a reporter had posed as a mechanic to talk to Rudyard Kipling, an obsessively private person. (Ralph and Kipling had become friends when both were in South Africa during the Boer War.) The other incident involved an eminent Chinese passing through London on his way to the United States who chatted with a reporter under the mistaken impression that the reporter was a member of a committee planning his U.S. visit. In both cases, said Ralph, it could be argued that the reportorial tactics were improper.

That rather inconclusive conclusion was indicative of Ralph's thinking on such matters. By and large, he appears to have been a pragmatist whose judgments about the acceptability of reporting tactics varied from assignment to assignment. When, as an older reporter, he made a halfhearted attempt to sort out his views, he did so in unsystematic fashion, and for the most part it is necessary to read between the lines to discern his attitudes. At one point, for example, he seems to imply that if a news source is laboring under a misapprehension of his own making when he unwittingly talks to a reporter—well, that isn't the reporter's fault. Reading between the lines further suggests that if pressed, Ralph would have agreed that a central criterion in determining how much deception is justified is the worthiness of the reporter's goal. If the purpose is to expose unsafe conditions in theaters and possibly save lives, almost any means of getting at the truth short of mayhem would be acceptable. In lesser causes the answer is less clear-cut.

When President Grover Cleveland became engaged to Frances Folsom in August 1885, he decided that his marriage was strictly a private matter. He said nothing publicly until May 28, 1886, when he authorized a brief announcement that he was to be married on June 2 in the White House. The wedding was to be a small affair, and no representatives of the press would be present. No honeymoon plans were disclosed.

The marriage of a beautiful young woman to a prominent middle-aged bachelor would stir at least passing interest even in normal circumstances. When the groom was the President of the United States, the curiosity was overwhelming. Despite Cleveland's preference for privacy, the nation's newspapers had begun pursuing the story well before the official announcement.

Rumors of the impending marriage first appeared in print a month and a half before the wedding. The President and his inner circle would clarify nothing, and Frances Folsom and her widowed mother had left their home in Buffalo and were discreetly traveling in Europe. Reporters sought out second- and thirdhand sources—among others, a Boston flour merchant who said he was an uncle of Frances and a Buffalo informant who was "but two persons from Col. Folsom," Frances's grandfather. Speculation and misinformation flourished. Was the President going to marry Frances or her mother? Was her name really Frances or was it Frank, as some said, and was she twenty-two or twenty-three? The wedding was scheduled for early June, or perhaps toward the end of the summer. It would take place in Washington, in Baltimore, or in Buffalo. A woman society reporter who tried to question the President directly "got a severe wigging for her impertinence."

When the White House finally broke its silence about the wedding less than a week before the event, the floodgates opened. Frances Folsom had landed in New York the day before the announcement, and her every word and gesture were chronicled. So were President Cleveland's when he called on her at her hotel in the course of a visit to New York to review a Decoration Day parade.

On the wedding day reporters clustered at the foot of the steps of the North Portico of the White House. They studied the drawn blinds, noted the delivery of four red, white, and blue floral shields, and watched the arrival of the guests' carriages. As the ceremony began at 7 P.M., they listened to the sounds of the wedding march, played by "Professor" John Philip Sousa and his Marine Band, drifting from inside the White House.

Later, as the likely time for the couple's departure on their honeymoon neared, the reporters took up stations at the White House gates and at key points beyond the grounds. Carriages and saddle horses were ready for instant pursuit. Despite these elaborate precautions, the President and his bride almost eluded the press by departing through a little-used gate, but two reporters spotted the Presidential carriage and followed in their own. They saw the pair onto a special Baltimore and Ohio train waiting at an out-of-the-way yard and decided that earlier conjecture about the honeymoon had been corrrect—the site would be a resort owned by the B&O at Deer Park in western Maryland. Less than an hour later six reporters were aboard a regular train following the route of the special. At stations along the way they checked on its progress and wired bulletins. When they reached Deer Park about dawn, they spotted the special on a siding and gave a cheer.

At Deer Park there were a number of cottages scattered around a hotel, and the Clevelands were staying in one of these set in a grove of tall oaks. To keep intruders away, railroad detectives were posted about the grounds. Nevertheless, the President received a start the first day of his honeymoon. As one reporter described the scene:

> When President Cleveland rose at ten o'clock this morning and looked from the front windows of his cheerful little domicile upon the handsome vista of glade and green that stretched before him, among the objects which met his astounded gaze was a small pavilion standing in the midst of a handsome cluster of tall trees, and in and around this pavilion lounged the flower of Washington journalism, somewhat battered by lack of sleep and midnight wrestle with country telegraph operators, but still experiencing a lively interest in the Chief Executive and his whereabouts.

Their ranks swollen to a dozen, the reporters spent the six days of the honeymoon observing everything that went on at the cottage as best they could over the 150-yard separation enforced by the detectives. They recorded the time the President strolled out onto the porch with his morning cigar, noted when Frances changed from her blue tulle morning gown to her gray traveling dress for a drive, and concluded that a nap was in progress when quiet descended on the cottage at midafternoon. Some said they lifted the napkins on the trays sent from the hotel kitchen so they could see what the President and his wife were eating. They questioned a visitor about the President's luck on a trout-fishing outing, and when he attended church on Sunday morning they were allowed close enough to see that he put a five-dollar bill in the collection plate. Every detail was front-page news.

After it was over, one of those who had been a member of the band of reporters at Deer Park said: "All in all, they were a self-respecting set of men, who had gone to Deer Park in the line of their business in response to a good natured, unobtrusive popular demand, and they found means through callers and in ways perfectly legitimate and inoffensive to get enough information for truthful and entertaining reading."

Many outside the press disagreed. The coverage of Cleveland's marriage brought to a head a controversy over journalistic invasion of privacy that had been growing ever since newspapers began building up their reporting staffs. It was true that early editors had savaged the characters of their political foes, but such attacks could generally be dismissed as political bombast. In the 1880s reporters were doing something different, poking into private lives in ways seldom seen before.

Cleveland was particularly sensitive to such probing. He bore scars from the 1884 presidential campaign—a Buffalo newspaper had initiated the story that he had an illegimate son—and even before his marriage his relations with reporters were distant. As the wedding day approached, he grew almost paranoid about the press. In a letter to a sister he bemoaned the prospect that the families involved would be subjected to the "impudent inquisition" of the "dirty gang" of reporters. He felt no mellower toward them on his honeymoon. The detectives around the cottage, he wrote his secretary back in Washington, were "charged with the duty of protecting us from newspaper nuisances." There were "certain limits within which such animals are not allowed to enter, and these limits are to be watched and guarded night and day. There are a number of newspaper men here and I can see a group of them sitting on a bridge which marks one of the limits, waiting for some move to be made which will furnish an incident."

Cleveland's contempt for the press was widely shared. "Nobody has a right to know everything about anybody on any occasion in life, except the police about a man convicted of a crime," declared the *Nation*. If the press would go to any lengths to increase sales of newspapers, it was "the lowest occupation, not absolutely criminal, known to modern society—in some respects, worse than keeping a brothel or gambling house." Even the *Journalist,* the profession's own periodical, called the Deer Park affair "an impertinent intrusion into private life." And a contributor to the *Forum* said of the behavior of the reporters at Deer Park:

Suppose that these acts had been committed by a private person instead of by newspapers, what would have been the verdict? Why every man and woman of ordinary good breeding in the land would say that a man who would do things of this kind was not a respectable person. The most natural epithet to apply to him would be that of blackguard. No other people, in private life, pry about their neighbors' houses, peer into their windows, listen at their keyholes, and try in other ways to penetrate the sanctities of their homes. If we call by so harsh a name the person who does such things for his own malicious delight or for that of a few gossiping friends, what shall we say of the espionage when it is made fairly terrible with all the resources and power of a modern newspaper, and when all its discoveries are published to the world?

In time Cleveland's secretiveness about his marriage would seem unrealistic. It would be acknowledged that those who seek the presidency must expect the public to be interested in everything about them. The insistence on secrecy was also self-defeating. It spurred reporters to redouble their efforts to learn about the wedding and the honeymoon.

Whether Ralph had a hand in the *Sun's* coverage is not known, but the charge that the press harassed Cleveland and other public figures bothered him. It obscured the fact that by the 1880s it was not always the press that did the pursuing. "While there are reporters who 'hound' public men," said Ralph, "there are also public men who badger the newspaper folk" in hopes of favorable attention. The attacks on the press also ignored the reciprocal relationship that had developed between reporters and public figures. Critics of the "modern newspaperman" overlooked two points:

> One is that nine times in ten, when a man's affairs become of interest to the public, he is as anxious to see the newspaperman as the other is to see him. The other is that a shrewd man, who recognizes the place the press has taken and the power it has, will easily manage to make it serve him to some extent while he is serving it.

If the furor over the reporting of President Cleveland's marriage was excessive, a wave of indignation in the same period over invasions of the privacy of lesser-known citizens was more justified. The *Sun's* penchant for exploiting private embarrassments in rich detail, a practice shared in varying degrees by numerous other newspapers, usually served no conceivable purpose other than to titillate readers at the expense of the hapless souls involved.

Probably no *Sun* reporter could escape doing such stories on occasion. Through most ran the theme of seemingly respectable people caught in circumstances that made them ridiculous or pathetic. Marital discord within a sedate brownstone, a rift over money between a wealthy father and his son, public tipsiness by a member of an upstanding family—all this was front-page news in the *Sun*. When a rich man's daughter eloped with the coachman, it was a surefire story. So, indeed, was almost any case of a daughter from a prominent family rebelling against her father and marrying a suitor he disapproved of, a situation that seems to have arisen with great regularity in Victorian households.

In February 1883, for example, under the headline "MISS KITTY GETS MARRIED," there appeared the tale of the marriage of Kitty Kernochan of 384 Fifth Avenue to Herbert C. Pell. Pell was anything but a coachman—he was a blueblood at home on Wall Street and in the best clubs—but Kitty's father, James P. Kernochan, nevertheless "forebade him the house and ordered the young lady to have nothing to do with him." After Kitty had slipped away and married Pell, a helpful "friend of the family" told a *Sun* man that "many of her intimate friends have been aware that the acquaintance was kept up and was ripening into that love which laughs at parental orders. . . . The consternation of the family at the news was quite dreadful. Mr. Kernochan was said to have become quite prostrated."

It is barely possible that James Kernochan was such a dictatorial ogre of a father that he deserved to be pilloried, but there were other *Sun* stories that can be described only as undiluted cruelty. In June 1887 this headline appeared on the front page:

HE COMETH NOT, SHE SAID

An Expectant Bride's Vain Wait
For Her Truant Lover

The story beneath described how all had been in readiness in a Brooklyn household for the wedding of one of the family's three daughters. There were flowers in abundance and a display of handsome presents, and on the evening of the wedding, guests filled the house. But 8 P.M., the hour for the ceremony, came, and the groom was not in evidence. Shortly after nine o'clock the guests began to drift away, and "the priest soon followed and left the young woman weeping bitter tears of disappointment. At 10 o'clock the family was alone and the house was hushed. No tidings came from the missing bridegroom. Miss McCoy was inconsolable." She was undoubtedly more so when her humiliation was broadcast in the *Sun*.

Such stories provoked strong criticism. "The press is overstepping in every direction the obvious bounds of propriety and decency," declared an 1890 article in the *Harvard Law Review* coauthored by a future Supreme Court justice, Louis Brandeis. "Gossip is no longer the resource of the idle and the vicious, but has become a trade, which is pursued with industry as well as effrontery."

Other critics told horror stories of families already devastated by private sorrows having their anguish compounded by press intrusions, and they denounced reporters who did this kind of work. Such a reporter, said one contributor to an exchange on the subject in the *Writer* magazine in 1888–89, "comes to one's fireside like an angel of light; yet it is his intention prepense to betray one to the gibbering world in leaded type and terrible head-lines." Another contributor, claiming to know of an episode in which forty reporters had tried to force their way into a household that had suffered some unspecified misfortune, concluded: "I cannot believe that any gentleman or lady would do such work."

A reporter named John Arthur attempted a defense of his calling against the attacks in the *Writer*. "Reporters on all reputable papers . . . are almost always gentlemen, and are possessed of more honor and brains than they are generally given credit for. They are neither liars nor scandalmongers. They do not invade the sanctity of homes." Reporters could also argue that it wasn't always a case of their pressuring or duping people into revealing their innermost secrets; it was amazing how eager some people were to share confidences in the most unlikely circumstances.

But even many of these must have been mortified when they saw the results in print, and in general the apologies ring hollow. Granted that Victorians were stuffy and afflicted with an exaggerated sense of decorum, they did not deserve what their newspapers did to them when reporters exposed their private follies and woes to public view.

The controversy over privacy paralleled another over reporters' use of the interview—or, as the critics sometimes wrote it, the "interview." The quotation marks dripped scorn and distanced the critics from what they regarded as a vulgar new application of an old word.

From the days of the earliest newspapers, journalists must have ventured forth from time to time to talk to people in pursuit of information and opinion. But through the middle of the nineteenth century American newspapers gave little direct evidence of this practice. Their news columns were filled with reports of speeches and public meetings, wordy letters from wandering correspondents, and reams of political and other matter presented on the writer's own authority and often reading more like informed gossip than a news report. If reporters asked people questions and recorded their responses, the stories seldom reflected it.

This began to change after Horace Greeley's celebrated question-and-answer session with Brigham Young for the New York *Tribune* in 1859. Other newspapers took up the practice, and by the end of the 1860s the interview was a full-fledged journalistic fad. Reporters interviewed statesmen, artists, scientists, and preachers, along with those who had emerged into momentary prominence because of catastrophes, crimes, and scandals. Reporters also were assigned to patrol hotels and to meet arriving ships in hopes of encountering visiting notables who might say something interesting.

Even in the days when reporting was a relatively new and rather suspect profession, pioneering interviewers sometimes met with surprising success in extracting responses from prickly characters and people in trying circumstances. A likely explanation is the absence of telephones. In a face-to-face encounter it was harder to rebuff a reporter. Also, without telephones reporters seldom gave their targets advance notice. Instead, they simply showed up at the door and began firing questions, with the result that a person who might not have given a reporter the time of day if allowed to gather his wits found himself deep into an interview before he knew what was happening.

Charles Russell told of a New York *Herald* reporter who used a variation of this tactic when sent to interview General William Tecumseh Sherman, a man given to brushing reporters away like flies. Sherman was staying at the Fifth Avenue Hotel, and the *Herald* man's assignment was to get the general's comments on an already published newspaper article on the Army. Proceeding directly to the door of Sherman's suite, the reporter circled the article in a copy of the newspaper, wrote "What have you to say about this?" in big letters in the margin and, "as if throwing a lighted bomb," tossed the newspaper through the open transom. He then retreated a short distance.

A moment later Sherman stuck his head out of the door, held up the paper, and bellowed: "Did you throw this into my room?" The reporter admitted that he had. "Well, come here then," said the general. "I want to see you." The resulting interview ran a column and a half.

Such enterprise pleased newspaper editors—the *Herald* man was paid double the usual space rate—and the public, but the *Nation* magazine deplored the very idea of interviews. "The 'interview,' as at present managed," it asserted in 1869, "is generally the joint production of some humbug of a hack politician and another humbug of a newspaper reporter." A few years later Richard Grant White, a noted magazine writer, called "this new thing"—the interview—"the most perfect contrivance yet devised to make journalism an offence, a thing of ill savor in all decent nostrils." And in 1886 a Washington reporter of forty years' experience, Ben: Perley Poore of the Boston *Journal* (he always wrote his name that way), was still insisting that "the pernicious habit of 'interviewing' is a dangerous method of communication between our public men and the people."

Why the fuss? Partly it was the novelty of printing words spoken in conversation; the practice took some getting used to. George Alfred Townsend, a leading Washington correspondent who had begun his career in 1860, eventually adopted "the interview system," but in 1891 he remembered that the first interviews he read made him "shudder at their audacity: they looked like breaches of confidence." The uproar over interviews was also related to the privacy issue. Richard Grant White complained that interviewing "elevates prying into an art" and "attempts to dignify intrusion with the mantle of the teacher who ministers to the noble desire of knowledge." White further complained, along with others, that interviewers were too insistent and pushy. Certainly few would have denied that a reporter covering the funeral of Henry Ward Beecher in 1887 went too far when he sprang into the street to interview the presiding clergyman as he led the procession taking Beecher's coffin from his house to Plymouth Church to the beat of muffled drums.

Nor could it be denied that many interviews were a waste of space. "The merest charlatans are raised to a temporary eminence," charged an article in the *Forum* in 1886, "and the veriest twaddle is thrown abroad as if it was wisdom. If deeper waters are ventured into, nothing is preserved but what is entertaining." Some reporters agreed that interviewers' questions were often inane. Elizabeth Banks, like Nellie Bly a pioneering woman reporter on the *World,* noted that important visitors from abroad scarcely set foot ashore before they were asked: "What do you think of America?" When Theodore Dreiser, as a reporter in St. Louis, called at hotels to interview visiting evangelists, musicians, scientists, and prizefighters, he inquired of each "what did they think of life, its meaning." John L. Sullivan replied: "Write any damned thing yuh please, young fella, and say that John L. Sullivan said so."

Although some of the criticisms of interviews were valid, none justified the sweeping condemnations of what was, in large part, sheer common sense—talk to people with interesting or important things to say and print the results. The real basis for the antipathy lay deeper. Interviews were part of the new kind of journalism that stressed news over opinion, and they made some of those accustomed to the old-style journalism uneasy. The editors of the *Nation* enjoyed their own oracular role, looked upon newspaper reporters with condescension, and fretted as the journalistic spotlight swung toward reporters' interviews and away from what editors had to say. Interviewing, said the magazine, helped to establish the reporter "as a person . . . not at all under editorial control," and this was the chief reason it was to be condemned.

Similarly, an old reporter like Ben: Perley Poore was uncomfortable with interviews. Poore had begun covering Washington during the Polk administration, and he had a golden vision of reporting before the Civil War.

"Washington correspondents in those days were neither eavesdroppers nor interviewers, but gentlemen, who had a recognized position in society, which they never abused," he wrote sadly in his memoirs. His sort of reporting consisted of moving among great men in gracious social intercourse, then setting down his reflections on what they had said—not straining to take down a senator's words with a pencil stub like some hovering secretary.

Objections like Poore's or the *Nation's* are hard to fathom now. Particularly in the realm of public affairs, interviews introduced a new element of accountability, allowing public figures to be measured against their words and spurring some reporters to take greater pains to be accurate. Younger reporters in the late nineteenth century were enthusiastic interviewers. Even if the reporter had to take notes on a shirt cuff, said Henry Grady in 1879, the year before he became managing editor of the Atlanta *Constitution*, interviews were "the neatest and handiest things in journalism." Besides eliciting material that otherwise might be overlooked, interviewing "enabled the correspondent to preserve the flavor of the great man's individuality, and carry his subtle characteristics into print."

Julian Ralph acknowledged that interviews were not foolproof. He recalled interviewing a vestryman of a wealthy church on some sensitive matter—most likely a dispute within the congregation—only to have the vestryman deny that the interview had ever taken place after his words appeared in print. When Ralph pressed him, he conceded that the story had been accurate "but declared that he had been too impulsive, and his words had placed him in a very disagreeable position." In this instance at least, Ralph shrugged and composed a "correction" that eased the situation.

Still, for Ralph the usefulness of the interview was beyond dispute. Certainly in the case of a public figure, it was infinitely superior to a reporter's speculation and conjecture about "what a great man thinks and feels." That was "only slightly more valuable than a promising novel broken off by a great novelist's death and finished by a friend or some hack hired by a publisher."

Ralph and other *Sun* reporters had their share of interviews with great men, and, like reporters at other newspapers, they also pursued a variety of others who came into the news. Lily Langtry arrives on the steamer *Arizona* and reveals that what she likes most about acting is the money. A director of a failed fire insurance company explains that the central problem was nepotism: the president had given his nephew a job, and the nephew had stolen $39,000. Grant's doctor acknowledges that the general has given up cigars because of a swelling at the base of his tongue but will not yet say if the diagnosis is, as rumored, cancer.

One of the more distinctive uses of interviews by the *Sun* was in the stories that were "news" only under Dana's sweeping definition—explorations of fads, social customs, eating habits, strange professions, or almost any other out-of-the-way subject that stirred the curiosity of a staff member. A reporter looks into why most sailors can't swim, and an old salt encountered on a wharf explains that a sailor's "business ain't in the water." Someone at the *Sun* has a sudden urge to find out if fat men, who usually look jolly and good-natured, commit many crimes, and a warder at Sing Sing comments to an interviewer: "I should not say that the percentage of fat criminals would go higher than one in 1,000—not really fat ones." A chat with an official of an institution for the treatment of alcoholics yields the insight that the most effective approach is to regard drunkenness not as a disease but as a sin. Looking into another facet of the treatment of drunks, a *Sun* reporter interviews bouncers at New York bars and restaurants. At Delmonico's, on West Twenty-sixth Street, he comes across a bouncer so smoothly efficient at his work that he can eject even boisterous young drunks "without ruffling his cuffs or his temper."

Some *Sun* interviewers were skilled writers, employing great selectivity and producing artfully shaped stories that were a far cry from the verbatim style of questions and answers used by Horace Greeley in interviewing Brigham Young. Indeed, so skillful was a *Sun* reporter who interviewed Cornelius Vanderbilt back in 1875 that he wrote a revealing story even though the old commodore said little that was relevant to anything.

INTERVIEWING VANDERBILT
Another Reporter Comes Away Freighted With Valuable Information

Commodore Vanderbilt was eighty-one years old yesterday. He spent the day in his Fourth Avenue offices, taking his usual drive in the afternoon. A *Sun* reporter visited him in the evening to inquire about a favorable time for selling a few thousands of New York Central.

"This," said the commodore, slowly and solemnly, as he entered the drawing-room, "is my birthday."

"Indeed!" said the reporter. "Do you think the preferred stock—"

"To-day," the commodore interrupted, "I am eighty-one years old. I am stronger—"

"Is there any prospect of an immediate rise?"

"I have never gone into the late-supper business," the commodore answered, apparently not catching the drift of the question; "and I have always been a very temperate man. But how did you find out that this was my birthday?"

"You hinted at the fact yourself," the reporter replied. "Will the Erie troubles—"

"The Erie troubles will not prevent me from beginning my eighty-second year with a young heart and a clear conscience."

"And with the prospect of seeing a good many more birthday anniversaries?" the reporter asked.

"That, my dear boy," said the commodore, "is one of those things that no fellow can tell about."

"Do you think that this is a good time to sell?"

"No, it's never a good time to sell after banking-hours."

"Good evening!"

"Good evening! Drop in again."

9. The Age of Corruption

When Ralph was in Albany covering the New York state legislature in 1885 and 1886, he stayed at the Delavan House. The Delavan was a sprawling old hotel, opened in the 1840s and expanded haphazardly over the years until it filled an entire city block at the foot of the steep slope rising from the Hudson River. It was handy for travelers—across the street from the railroad station and a short omnibus ride from the steamboat landing—and out of convenience, as well as custom, a large share of the legislators, lobbyists, and others who came to Albany on political business put up there. When the legislature was meeting, the hotel was a center of political activity, a place reeking of cigar smoke and backroom deals.

Although the Delavan was rather down at the heels by the 1880s, it must have seemed inviting as the legislative sessions got under way each January. Winter could be brutal in Albany; during Ralph's first stint there thick ice plated the streets so long that some of those descending the hill toward the river became bobsled runs, with huge sleds rumbling down at all hours. But inside the Delavan coal fires glowed in parlors and bedrooms, and in the front room a bartender known as "the Doctor" dispensed warming potions across a bar backed by a great mirror. There were always people about, clustering in knots on the checkered marble floor of the lobby, scanning the latest New York papers at the newsstand, organizing all-night poker games. And there was always talk—endless political talk that was grist for a reporter's mill. One January day in 1885, said Ralph, "the big hotel buzzed like a fly trap in a butcher's shop in midsummer."

Every half hour horsecars climbed the hill to the new Capitol. It was unfinished; though work had begun in 1867, the last of the construction sheds would not be dismantled till 1898. But the Capitol had been in use since 1879 and the essential structure stood complete in the mid-1880s. Architectural critics called it a hodgepodge of styles, reflecting the contributions of a succession of architects with tastes varying from Victorian Gothic to French Renaissance. Laymen found the Capitol a pretty impressive pile of granite. It resembled an immense French chateau, heavily ornamented and replete with peaked roofs, dormers, and tall chimneys. Inside, the embellishments were almost oriental in their lushness—gilt, red damask, carved oak and mahogany, onyx, Siena marble.

The Assembly and Senate chambers were on the third floor. The acoustics were terrible in the Assembly chamber; it had a soaring vaulted stone ceiling that swallowed much of what was said on the floor, sometimes causing great confusion about what was happening. Otherwise, reporters worked under good conditions. They had their own cloakroom, and their seats were right on the Assembly and Senate floors, handy for buttonholing members. The arrangements were so casual, in fact, that anyone could wander onto the legislative floors, and Ralph once related how business was disrupted for two days when a stunning young woman with black hair and black eyes visited both chambers to sell a book. In the Senate she occupied a red-leather seat while the senators lined up and "took turns, one after another, in questioning her about the gorgeous volume in her dimpled hand."

The two Albany assignments lasted from January through May. Most weekends Ralph took the New York Central south to see Belle and the children—by now there were five—but the rest of the time during those five-month stretches in 1885 and 1886 his world essentially comprised the Delavan and the Capitol. The work was not the sort of journalism Ralph preferred—ranging from assignment to assignment and place to place. Day after day he was at the Capitol keeping track of a flood of bills dealing with everything from the disposal of manure and the regulation of roller-skating rinks, which some upright citizens viewed as dens of iniquity in the 1880s, to the major political and social issues of the day, such as civil service reform and child labor. (In 1885 a proposal to bar the employment in the state of children under fourteen in factories for more than ten hours a day failed to pass.) In the evenings, back at the Delavan, there were tidbits of political gossip to be picked up in the lobby and the barroom and then a story to be written. Some nights Ralph was still telegraphing copy at 1 A.M.

There were compensations. In the opening weeks of the 1885 legislative session Ralph chatted almost daily with twenty-six-year-old Theodore Roosevelt, cementing a journalistic relationship that continued as Roosevelt's political stature grew. Starting in 1882, Roosevelt had served three terms as a reforming assemblyman from Manhattan, acting as the driving force behind the state's first civil service law in 1883. After a dreadful personal blow—the death of his wife and his mother on the same day in 1884—

Roosevelt had given up his seat and sought solace in Dakota Territory, but in January 1885 he was back in Albany ready to reenter the political wars. "He says that since he has snuffed the battle he is sorry he has got to go back to raising grizzlies on his ranch, and wishes he was in the Legislature," Ralph reported.

There was also the challenge of exposing the corruption that pervaded Albany. In the New York legislature the breakdown in public morality in the United States in the decades after the Civil War plumbed new depths. The best that could be said was that by the mid-1880s the graft was not quite as brazen as when Boss Tweed dominated both New York City and New York state politics in 1870, and that was not saying much. Legislators belonging to the "Black Horse Cavalry," a band of rogues dating from Tweed days, still routinely sold their votes. Sometimes they engaged in blackmail, threatening a business or an industry with an investigation or damaging legislation, then exacting money for backing off. New schemes surfaced regularly in the legislature to pad government payrolls, hand over public property for private exploitation, and send legislators on lavish junkets.

For a reporter, however, the corruption could mean something other than the chance for professional glory. Journalists themselves could get caught up in it. That had happened to one of Ralph's predecessors in Albany, and in 1885 one of the agents of corruption sought to lure Ralph himself into his net. At stake for a reporter in such an encounter was his freedom to tell the truth as he saw it. Such freedom, as it happened, was not of great moment for a considerable number of nineteenth-century journalists. Nor, indeed, was truth itself.

Even after newspapers' main focus shifted from political advocacy to the dissemination of news in the mid-1800s, the notion that their primary mission was to seek out and print the truth—simply because it was the truth—was far from universally accepted. Probably most editors and reporters made a reasonable try for accuracy, often in the face of the formidable travel and communication difficulties impeding early news-gathering. But a significant minority lacked any serious concern for the truth. The results ranged from minor dressing up of the "facts" and sophomoric irresponsibility to gross distortions of important news and utter venality.

A glance at almost any newspaper from the 1880s, even those relatively temperate in tone, shows the political biases of publishers and editors continuing to warp political news. "FRAUD AND FORGERY REPUDI-

ATED BY THE AMERICAN PEOPLE," crowed a headline over the story in the Republican New York *Times* proclaiming the victory of James A. Garfield in the 1880 Presidential election. At the *Sun,* even though Charles Dana and his editors did not insist that the staff agree with their editorial views, in 1884 they relied on some reporters to bolster their assault on Grover Cleveland. Sent out to interview factory workers just days before the New York governor won the Presidential election, one *Sun* man found all but unanimous disapproval of Cleveland. "The ground of opposition among the workingmen I have talked with," the reporter quoted John Brady of the Reedy Elevator Works in Jersey City as saying, "is that he is a narrow-minded, selfish tool of the monopolies, and has shown himself such by every one of his official acts as Governor where the interests of men who work were arrayed against the interests of men who reap enormous profits from that work." Talk of "objectivity" was not heard in newspaper circles even as late as the 1920s, according to Michael Schudson, a journalism historian.

In the post–Civil War period, the fierce competition among newspapers for readers, and among reporters for survival, also played havoc with the truth. "Faking," as the invention or twisting of "news" eventually became known, grew widespread. Out of the West in 1866–67 came dramatic descriptions of Indian raids and massacres that were largely the products of correspondents' imaginations. One of the reporters who covered the Chicago fire of 1871 confirmed long afterward that the tale of Mrs. O'Leary's cow kicking over the lantern and starting the conflagration was fiction. Not even sermon reports, that staple of Monday morning editions, were immune from faking. Ordered to attend the Sunday service at an unfashionable, out-of-the-way church, an assignment not befitting his senior status, John Finerty of the Chicago *Tribune* spent Saturday night composing a sermon abstract in a saloon. A fellow newspaperman, perhaps indulging in a bit of faking himself, later claimed that the clergyman credited with the sermon was so pleased with its eloquence that he called at the *Tribune* to thank its author.

Following the example of the early *Sun,* which back in the 1830s had pulled off a widely believed hoax about the discovery of strange creatures on the moon thanks to a marvelous new telescope, one November morning in 1874 the New York *Herald* devoted all of its first news page to a bloodcurdling account of carnage in Manhattan following the escape of all the lions, tigers, elephants, and other beasts from the Central Park zoo. Forty-nine persons were dead, many others mutilated. Not till readers reached the very end did it become clear that the story was a bad joke.

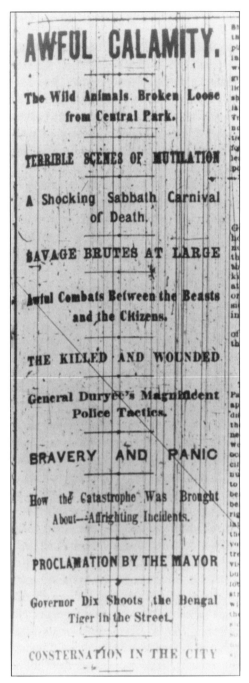

The headline of the lead news story in the New York *Herald* for November 9, 1874. The story was a hoax. *Newspaper Collection, The New York Public Library, Astor, Lenox and Tilden Foundations*

Interviews were routinely faked. If reporters sent to hotels in search of newsworthy visitors found the pickings slim, they sometimes simply conjured up quotable characters. Theodore Dreiser admitted that he did this as a young reporter in St. Louis. At other times reporters put words in the mouths of real persons who were uncooperative or uninspired. "I always made it a rule, when imagining or exaggerating an interview, to make it fit," said William Salisbury, who started his reporting career at the Kansas City *Times* in 1895 and later worked for William Randolph Hearst's Chicago *American*. It is highly probable that most of the *Sun's* interview with Commodore Vanderbilt on his eighty-first birthday was fabricated—and also that it fit nicely. A common practice when public figures held themselves aloof was to string together second- and thirdhand quotations and pass the results off as exclusive interviews. The *Nation* observed that this had the side benefit of allowing newspapers to save on rail and hotel bills.

The pressure to invent was particularly strong in the crime, scandal, sex, and human-interest stories that many late-nineteenth-century newspapers relied on to lure readers. Under Dana the *Sun* went after stories of this sort, but all-out sensationalism—extracting every last drop of drama, sentiment, shock, and titillation from such material—was the contribution of Joseph Pulitzer. Headlines like "LOVED THE COOK," "A FORTUNE SQUANDERED IN DRINK," and "SCREAMING FOR MERCY" in his St. Louis *Post-Dispatch* and New York *World* delighted him.

Reporters who worked for Pulitzer, and reporters who emulated them, found it hard to resist reaching for the little details so useful in rounding out such tales. The gist of contemporary professional advice was that everybody was doing it and there was no need to agonize.

Faking, said an article in the *Writer* in 1887, was "an almost universal practice"; "hardly a news despatch is written which is not 'faked' in greater or less degree." With the "constant demand for picturesque stories," the situation could not be otherwise. "Descriptive details are expected from the correspondent, and he must do his best to supply the demand." With the merest hint of irony, the magazine explained that faking differed from "ordinary lying." Ideally, it did not entail making up "the important facts of a story" but rather "the supplying, by the exercise of common sense and a healthy imagination, of unimportant details, which may serve an excellent purpose in the embellishment of a despatch."

A handbook for young journalists published in 1894 offered much the same advice about faking:

In spite of the fact that editors come to grief once in a while by its use, this trick of drawing upon the imagination for the non-essential parts of an article is certainly one of the most valuable secrets of the profession at its present stage of development. Truth in essentials, imagination in non-essentials, is considered a legitimate rule of action in every office. The paramount object is to make an interesting story.

Space writers with short strings were quick to get the message. But as faking sometimes worked out in practice, once a reporter got in the habit of embellishing his stories a bit—a touch of dishabille here, a pinch more poignancy in a deathbed statement there—it was hard to know where to stop. At the New York *World,* despite wall placards in the newsroom enjoining "Accuracy, Accuracy, Accuracy!," Theodore Dreiser decided a struggling young space writer had to go pretty far just to get a story in the paper. Early in his brief career at the *World* in 1894–95 Dreiser had one assignment after another fizzle. He found a rumor of a graveyard apparition too flimsy to build a story on. A visit to the morgue to view the body of a beautiful girl who had mysteriously drowned produced no copy when the girl turned out not to be beautiful.

Dreiser's lack of creativity exasperated his editors until one night when he was sent to look into a report of a fight in a tenement. It proved to have been a totally unexceptional brawl between two neighbors who had drunk too much beer. But, in desperation, Dreiser let his imagination run. One neighbor, he scribbled back at the *World's* new gold-domed tower on Park Row, was a musician who was composing a waltz on the piano at midnight when a next-door tenant's loud snoring disturbed his concentration. A piano-banging, glass-smashing uproar ensued, culminating in a neighborhood riot that required a contingent of police to quell. The story ran on page 1. "Rather well done," said the city editor, who was Charles Russell, his flood-reporting days over.

Dreiser saw that faking was one road to success at Joseph Pulitzer's *World.* But he was disinclined to take it, even though he had sometimes faked in the past. He soon quit the *World* and—following a failed attempt to land a job at the *Sun*—fled journalism altogether after only three years as a reporter to take up the writing of fiction labeled as such.

Dana's stress on the importance of accuracy—"of knowing, for instance, that it is two and one quarter and not two and three eighths, and saying so"—may have had more effect than the *World's* "Accuracy!" signs, but faking undoubtedly crept into some of the polished tales the *Sun* printed in the eighties and nineties. No *Sun* reporter appears to have owned up to it publicly, but a celebrated reporter for its sister *Evening Sun,* Richard

Harding Davis, did. Davis, who joined the two-year-old *Evening Sun* in 1889 at the age of twenty-five, alternated between fiction and journalism throughout his career, and sometimes he blended the two in what has been called "documentary fiction." One of his first widely noticed stories for the *Evening Sun* contained a richly detailed description of the scene of the suicide of a young woman that he later acknowledged was imaginary. "As a matter of fact, they would not let me in the room, and I don't know whether it abounded in signed etchings or Bougereau's nymphs," he said in a note to his brother accompanying a clipping of the story.

At least one human-interest story that ran in the *Sun* in the 1890s was a fake from beginning to end. It was reprinted from the Kansas City *Times* rather than written by a member of the *Sun's* staff, but the *Sun* editor who spotted it and suspended disbelief long enough to send it up to the composing room must bear some responsibility. The author was William Salisbury, the reporter who prided himself on the verisimilitude of his phony interviews. As Salisbury recalled in an inside account of journalistic faking published in 1908, one dull Sunday afternoon in Kansas City he dreamed up a neat little fiction about a chance meeting and reconciliation at the Union depot of an Australian millionaire and his long-alienated son. The father, wrote Salisbury, had banished the youth for marrying the daughter of a rival in politics and gold-mining. Salisbury prudently ended the story by putting the pair on a train for San Francisco. The Kansas City *Times* ran the story under the headline "TALE OF TWO COUNTRIES." It appeared in the *Sun* as "A ROMANCE OF TWO LANDS." At the time, Salisbury noted, the top of the *Sun's* front page carried the slogan "If You See It in *The Sun,* It's So."

This sort of faking might seem harmless, though it was maddening to anyone who liked to draw a line between fact and fiction, and bias in political news was usually detectable. Financial corruption in the press was another matter. Although the press exposed some of the major scandals of the age of corruption—the Tweed Ring, Crédit Mobilier, the Whiskey Ring—it also participated in the corruption. Distortions and omissions of news caused by newspapers' venality concealed wrongdoing and kept important information from the public.

The problem began in the offices of the publishers and their business managers. At most major American newspapers, "the publisher is everything; the writer is nothing," complained James Parton in 1888. Newspaper business offices frequently shaped news with little attempt at subtlety.

As newspapers came to depend increasingly on advertising income in the 1880s and 1890s, solicitude for the sensibilities of advertisers grew, and some editors kept handy in a desk drawer a list of businessmen and firms to be treated respectfully. The system could work in reverse, too; it was not unknown for a department store that refused to advertise to be the target of a damaging concocted article.

Literary and theatrical reviews were particularly susceptible to the influence of advertisers. In the late 1880s the professional publication the *Journalist* charged:

> In nine cases out of ten, the critical notices are carefully measured to accord with the size of the advertisement handed in at the business office. If a publisher advertises, his books receive notice; twenty lines secure a good review, forty a better one. If a play is ever so bad, the astute critic can find much good in it if he looks through the greenback lorgnette furnished by the business office of the mighty organ of public opinion by which he is employed. The book reviewer's judgment is warped in the same way; his favor is bought at the cashier's desk.

More than a few newspaper writers profited directly from corruption. "I hear of critics . . . whose houses are full of costly presents from those they have 'puffed' and those they have spared," said Julian Ralph. It was assumed that financial journalists would use their positions to facilitate their own speculations and advance their personal fortunes, even though common sense suggested that a writer who did so risked letting his private interests outweigh the interests of his readers and color what he reported. "To be a money-writer is considered to be on the direct road to wealth; and the road is seldom missed," summed up Junius Henri Browne, a reporter for the New York *Tribune,* in 1869. Even so revered a figure as Henry Grady of the Atlanta *Constitution* saw nothing amiss in using inside information gained as a result of his work for personal gain. Grady interviewed the president of the Louisville and Nashville Railroad in 1880 and established a continuing relationship that enabled him to profit handsomely in L&N stock.

Some powerful interests simply put journalists on the payroll. The Pennsylvania Railroad kept a number of reporters on retainer, and under the Tweed Ring the Board of Councilmen of New York City paid seventeen reporters two hundred dollars a year *not* to report their activities. In the 1872 Presidential campaign the Republicans paid off three hundred reporters.

Newspapers as reputable as the New York *Times* seemingly were not immune from contamination by corruption. John McDonald, the architect of the Whiskey Ring fraud during the Grant administration, told in his confessional memoir of an evening in 1875 when he dined at the Washington home of Orville Babcock, Grant's scheming confidential secretary. A man came to the door. Babcock went to see his caller and presently returned with "a receipt for $500, signed by Krounce, the Washington correspondent of the New York *Times.*" The *Times* then had a reporter named Lorenzo L. Crounse. Babcock told McDonald the money was payment for an article useful to the administration.

As for the *Sun,* no one ever accused it of kowtowing to advertisers; indeed, Dana said he would prefer to be rid of them altogether. Also, the most serious charges ever made against the integrity of the *Sun* apparently were groundless. These were contained in an anonymous pamphlet, published in 1870, alleging that high-level figures at the *Sun* had accepted bribes from Boss Tweed and from Jay Gould and Jim Fisk, the buccaneering financiers. Amos Cummings, the printer-turned-managing-editor, was said to have received $6,500 from Tweed on a single occasion. Dana dismissed the pamphlet, entitled *The Biter Bit,* as the work of a blackmailer, and most outsiders seem to have regarded it as a fabrication inspired by some of Dana's many enemies.

But the *Sun* did not escape untainted. Thomas Hitchcock managed to amass great wealth while serving as the *Sun's* financial editor over several decades. Hitchcock, one of Dana's numerous backers when he took over the *Sun* in 1868, did not conceal that he speculated actively in the stock market. Nor can there be any doubt that, like so many other financial writers, he profited much more from the Wall Street intelligence he gathered in the course of his work than did most of his readers. Hitchcock owned a town house on East Twenty-ninth Street in Manhattan and a Newport "cottage," and his fortune eventually amounted to more than ten million dollars. His two sons devoted their lives to polo.

Activities like Hitchcock's raised few eyebrows, but even by the undemanding moral standards of the time the conduct of the corrupt *Sun* legislative reporter in Albany before Ralph's era was outrageous. His name was A. M. Soteldo, and he was assigned to Albany in 1870, when Tweed was ramrodding through the legislature a new charter tightening his grip on New York City. Tweed was spending freely to buy votes, and at one point he met with five cooperative Republican senators in his rooms at the Delavan House to parcel out $50,000 to each for use in swaying other legislators. Just as the stacks of bills were being distributed, Soteldo walked in. Instantly he sized up the situation and demanded a share. Otherwise, he threatened, he would expose the transaction, including the names of the senators.

In the words of William Hudson, an Albany correspondent for the Brooklyn *Eagle:* "Tweed, indignant as he was over being held up in this dishonorable manner, yielded, and the reporter went off with $40,000 as his share." Within twenty-four hours, Hudson added, Soteldo had been inveigled into a poker game with a senator who was a cardsharp and relieved of his new fortune. The story of Soteldo's extortion became generally known, and he soon left the *Sun.* A dozen years later he died after being shot in a dispute in a newspaper office in Washington.

Ralph was not cut out to be a legislative reporter. Compared with his earlier assignments, the work was often tedious. He lacked the patience to do a consistently thorough job of explaining legislation, and, given his occasional laxness and the *Sun's* limited space, some of his stories amounted to little more than perfunctory lists of bills. At times he was bored and exasperated, and, in the free-wheeling style of nineteenth-century political reporting, he let his feelings show. He fumed at the obtuseness of the "hayseed" upstate legislators and at the arch, heavy-handed humor that marked debate in the senate. "The Senate was stupider than ever," began his account of one day's proceedings in February 1885. The snail's pace of legislative business also vexed him. "Day follows day," he wrote in March 1885, "and still the Senate and Assembly fritter time away in code amendments and discussions on the advisability of substituting the guillotine for the scaffold."

The problem with this attitude was that the code amendments that glazed Ralph's eyes were probably important to some *Sun* readers. If they really wanted to find out what was going on in Albany each day, they were better off reading the New York *Times.* The *Times* had an experienced, workmanlike correspondent named George Spinney and was willing to allot more space than the *Sun* to dull but important details.

All the same, there were days when Ralph made Albany spring to life. In the two years he covered the legislature the Republicans controlled both houses. Their intraparty fights to choose the speaker of the Assembly and, in 1885, a United States senator—until 1913 state legislatures elected U.S. senators—inspired some of Ralph's liveliest stories. He covered the party battles much as a sportswriter of a later era might cover baseball. He sprinkled his stories with politicians' nicknames—Wood Pulp Miller, the Bald Eagle of Westchester, the Jobber from Kings—and reached for bold metaphors of band contests, rival theatrical troupes, and raffles.

Sometimes the metaphors got out of hand. "The raffle is especially interesting to the Republicans, because the prizes are about the only plums in the Republican orchard this year," Ralph reported as the speakership contest began in 1886. Other times they illuminated. In 1885 backers of the Senate candidacy of William Evarts, the defender of Henry Ward Beecher, carried the day when the forces of Evarts's chief opponent, Levi P. Morton, a future vice president, overreached themselves by grabbing all the key committee posts in the Assembly. The action rankled many uncommitted Republicans, and these were ushered into a parlor at the Delavan by Evarts's supporters, who included Theodore Roosevelt. "They went among the soreheads and combed their aching heads with prongs of red-hot steel," reported Ralph. "A man who felt a little sorry when he came to the hotel was pretty sure to be as spiteful as a hornet after one of these sympathizers had interviewed him."

Some stories strip away the veneer and leave the sense that this is the way politics and politicians really were in Albany in the 1880s. A Senator Plunkett, the tool of assorted private interests, introduces a complicated bill redrawing horsecar routes in New York City and acknowledges that he does not have the slightest idea what the point of it is. (Ralph spelled the senator's name wrong; he was George Washington Plunkitt, the Tammany man who would be immortalized for coining the phrase "honest graft.") An assemblyman calls for prohibiting alcoholic beverages in the Capitol restaurant; members of the committee on banks, accustomed to beer with lunch, retaliate by opposing his bill regulating savings banks. High-minded assemblymen clamor to serve on a committee to investigate corruption in New York City—until it is proposed that the hearings be held in Albany rather than amid the fleshpots of Manhattan.

Posturing, self-important politicians were regularly deflated. Twice a week Mr. Raines of Ontario, no matter what the topic of debate, took the Assembly floor to speak "upon the late war of the rebellion, the abolition of slavery, and hallowed name of Lincoln." William Evarts, another of Dana's partners when he took over the *Sun,* was a man of notable achievements, but he was also a windbag, even by the standards of audiences accustomed to speeches lasting hours. At a banquet at an Albany club celebrating Evarts's election to the U.S. Senate, Chauncey Depew, the chief public representative of the Vanderbilt interests and briefly a rival for the Senate seat himself, introduced Evarts with clumsy humor to the effect that maybe the only way to defeat him was to shoot him.

Mr. Evarts replied in a sentence. It was not an ordinary sentence, such as he would unwind in a Supreme Court trial, or a mere passing remark like the one that made half a yard of agate type in the papers last week while he was in New York. He was touched by Mr. Depew's queer conceit, and gave the club a full, well-recounted, healthy, complete, and perfect regulation sentence that seemed for a long time likely to prove as extraordinary as the ceaseless noise of Niagara Falls, softened by distance. The reporters went down town, filed their despatches, and took the thread of it up when they returned. Men passed from sobriety to positive hilarity as they drank. The table which was well laden when the great man began his remark bore a mere heap of fragments when he had done. But still the sentence ran on, filling the great club house, and piling up its sound under the roof and its meaning in the minds of the audience until it seemed, a long while before he came to its end, that the great man must stop or fall exhausted upon the floor.

Ralph professed immense satisfaction with his reporting on the overriding issue in Albany, the endemic corruption. "Of all my work I am proudest of my service as a legislative reporter during two corrupt sessions of the Legislature of New York," he wrote toward the end of his life. It had been calculated, he said, that he and a handful of other correspondents "had saved the people of the State many millions of dollars" by "simply disregarding our own opportunities for gain and protecting the public treasury against the scoundrels who tried to rob it."

Ralph's stories sometimes make palpable the atmosphere of corruption and the pervasive role of money in Albany. At the opening of the 1885 legislative session, sniggers ripple through the Assembly as members, taking the oath of office in small groups, swear that they bought no votes in their election campaigns and then kiss a Bible. As action nears on some bills lobbyists flit from desk to desk in the legislative chambers, all but openly handing out packets of cash. At the Delavan House an assemblyman from New York City flashes diamonds and hands the Doctor a thousand-dollar bill to buy a round of drinks.

Needling asides must at least have made some of the participants in corruption squirm. Watching assemblymen line up for their customary free railroad passes, Ralph wonders if the railroads get a fair return, since the members of the Black Horse Cavalry "make no reductions on account of passes whenever the companies want favors or protection." In Ralph's stories a bill carefully tailored to expand the field of operations of a crooked public works official becomes simply the "bill to give Roland M. Squire the earth." A legislative committee proposes to spend a summer junketing about investigating taxes at taxpayer expense and Ralph observes: "Last year it investigated Mount McGregor, a new watering place near Saratoga, and reported it to be a most delightful spot."

Along with some of his fellow Albany reporters, on at least two occasions in 1886 Ralph could legitimately claim credit for contributing to a climate of pressure that led to major defeats for the forces of corruption. One involved an attempt by a new cable-traction company to slip through the legislature a franchise that would have allowed it to operate on seventy miles of New York City streets without paying a cent for the privilege. The other involved an effort by a Manhattan horsecar company that had obtained its franchise by bribery to defeat a bill annulling the franchise.

Ralph explained both schemes at length in the *Sun* and hinted at more bribery in the offing. As the horsecar franchise bill neared a vote, he began one story with a somewhat ponderous warning: "The Legislature need not be surprised if, in a few days, the New York newspapers are obliged to deal sharply with those who may be influenced in favor of Jacob Sharpe, the Philadelphia syndicate, and the Broadway Surface Railroad." The story would have been more impressive if it had contained specifics about the bribery plans and less editorializing, but it apparently helped deter legislators from colluding with the horsecar line.

Sadly, Ralph's role in the victories over corruption in 1886 is overshadowed by his puzzling failure to expose wholesale bribery affecting one of the most important bills to come before the legislature in 1885. Knowledge of the bribery appears to have been widespread, and Ralph, in particular, had to have known that something fishy was going on.

The legislation at issue was aimed at several gas utilities that divided the gaslighting business in New York City. Each enjoyed a monopoly in its area of the city, and all were charging exorbitant prices. Using watered stock, they vastly exaggerated the size of their investments and concealed stratospheric returns. The proposed bill would have ended the deceptive practices and slashed gas prices.

Public support was strong and passage seemed assured. Early in April, as the ice was breaking up on the Hudson, the gas bill breezed through the Senate. Late in the month it began a three-step voting process in the Assembly. In the first vote, on April 28, the gas bill prevailed by a vote of 105 to 1. Then, on the second vote, the very next day, a remarkable shift in sentiment began. Although supporters of the bill still had the edge, their ranks dwindled from 105 to 68. In the final vote, on April 30, the gas bill lost, 64 to 52. Over three days, with no change in the legislation and no significant debate, the gas bill had lost more than half its supporters.

Ralph's story reporting the outcome offered no explanation for the astounding reversal. A week later, as an attempt to revive the gas bill was failing, he remarked in a story that a representative of a gas consumers' group had contributed to the defeat of his cause by offending legislators in some fashion. A week after that he made a passing reference to press reports of bribery involving the gas bill. But he pursued the matter no further, even showing more interest in a baseball game between Democrats and Republicans in the legislature. (The Democrats won 56–20, two players caught "sky scrapers," and there was some confusion over the differences between the rules for baseball and rounders.)

The New York *Times* presented a sharp contrast to the *Sun*. The morning after the defeat of the gas bill in the Assembly George Spinney reported in the *Times* that the gas companies had paid assemblymen to vote against it. Members from New York City and Brooklyn who went along with the utilities each received $2,000. "Country" members came cheaper—they got $1,000 apiece for their votes. The bribe-takers' performance, said a *Times* editorial, "deepens the disgrace which has been brought upon the Legislature of this State by the conscienceless greed of men chosen to represent the people."

The reason Ralph had to have been aware of skulduggery was that the gas bill had led to his personal brush with corruption. As the issue came to the fore, he was taken aside by an assemblyman in league with the gas companies and offered money to tailor his reporting to suit them—in other words, to compromise the truth. Eight years later in *Scribner's Magazine* he reconstructed the encounter with the assemblyman:

He began by offering me a cigar, and then putting this question:
"Which would you rather do, take cigars from men or have cigars to give to others?"
"I do both," said I; "I take a cigar when I want one, and I give cigars to others when they want them."
"Well, which would you prefer, to take a carriage ride or own your own carriage? Very well, then, why don't you own your own carriage, buy cigars by the box, and live as well as any man in Albany, with money to spare?"
"I wish I could," said I.
"Very well, then; I like you and I can do you a service. Now, there's so-and-so's gas bill affecting the price of gas. You are favoring it and making a fuss about the efforts of the lobby to kill it, and all that sort of thing. Stop that. Either change your tone or drop the whole matter and say nothing, and I will get you fifteen hundred dollars to-morrow morning—the price that is paid to all who help to defeat the bill. That is only a drop in the bucket to the money I can get for you as the session wears

along. I will put you in the way to own a carriage and live as a man of your ability ought to live. What do you say?"

I thanked him and said, in a few words, that I preferred to buy cigars one at a time for many years to come rather than drown myself at once, as I would certainly have to do after taking the money; "because," I said, "I couldn't live to let an infernal rascal like you point me out as one of your kind."

"Oh, well," said he, as little ruffled as if I had paid him an empty compliment; "every man to his own liking. Go ahead and be poor, as you please."

Ralph was striking a more heroic pose than his record warranted. The *Sun* duly reported the charges that the gas companies had engaged in deception and the arrival at the Capitol of petitions demonstrating public backing for the gas bill, but Ralph never really focused on the subject. Nothing he wrote as the bill worked its way through the legislative preliminaries should have seriously alarmed the utilities. Probably the offer of a bribe to Ralph was part of a general effort by the gas companies to arrange blanket insurance against probing articles in newspapers. A year later it was disclosed that many small newspapers around the state had taken money in return for opposing the gas bill editorially.

But if Ralph edited history in the *Scribner's* article, he must be believed when he says he turned down the bribe. It is hardly conceivable that someone who took a bribe would dredge the matter up years later in a magazine. Moreover, accepting a bribe would have been completely out of keeping with everything that can be gleaned about Ralph's character. While acknowledging that newspaper offices contained men who valued money more than truth and that reporters must sometimes practice deception in the service of a higher cause, he generally clung to a lofty, idealized—and unrealistic—view of his profession. A reporter, he said, was "a knight of the pen" who "works only for the right, the truth, and justice, and will not pen a single word that does not rhyme with his convictions." A man who could unblushingly write those words was not the sort of man to take a bribe.

Then why on earth did the *Sun* not print an account of the attempt to bribe Ralph and of the entire bribery scheme? Ralph must have realized that the assemblyman's overture to him was part of a broad plan involving legislators as well as journalists. The money involved as Ralph recalled it—$1,500 "to all who help to defeat the bill"—was roughly in line with the bribes reported by George Spinney in the *Times*.

Assuming Ralph's copy was not drastically reshaped in the *Sun* office without his assent—an unlikely occurrence in view of his standing by then as a reporter and his recollections of the affair—the most plausible explanation for his dereliction is that he fell in line with the *Sun's* editorial policy. The editorial page opposed the gas bill, arguing that such regulation was "paternal government with a vengeance." The real explanation for its opposition, according to advocates of the bill, was that financial editor Thomas Hitchcock, an influential figure on the paper, owned a lot of stock in gas companies.

Most of Ralph's stories from Albany probably were not affected by the editorial page. Despite the *Sun's* vicious campaign against Grover Cleveland, for example, Ralph had nothing unkind to say about the President-elect when he handed over the governor's office to the lieutenant governor in January 1885 preparatory to leaving for Washington. But in the case of the gas bill Hitchcock may have exerted special pressure. Perhaps in letters or when Ralph came down from Albany for the weekend, he pressed the wisdom of the editorial position on Ralph. Perhaps Ralph, unable to shake entirely the old notion that a political writer took his cue from the editorial page, consciously or unconsciously went along with Hitchcock's arguments and let them blur his reportorial vision when the gas companies resorted to bribery. If that was indeed what happened, it could be said that the venality of the age, operating through Hitchcock, kept Ralph from reporting the whole truth.

There may be a supplementary explanation. Given his idealized conception of the reporter, the bribe offer must have left Ralph feeling dirtied and demeaned. Illogical as it might seem for a reporter, his initial, unthinking reaction may have been to want to put the offer behind him as quickly as possible, to sweep it out of sight like something disgusting. The assemblyman who offered him boxes of cigars and a carriage of his own had regarded him as a likely partner in the squalid business of corruption. He had looked upon Ralph as a member of a group always in need of a dollar and not overly fastidious about how it was obtained—a member of the bribable class. When a corrupt politician put you on his level, it only underscored the low esteem in which most people held your calling.

10. 'Drunkards, Deadbeats, and Bummers'

I t was true, Julian Ralph acknowledged after he had reached the pinnacle of his profession, that there had been a time when respectable citizens could have been excused for looking down their noses at journalists. They were all too often somewhat disreputable—irresponsible in the management of their daily affairs, never entirely clean, never entirely sober. A certain measure of unconventionality and raffishness had even come to be considered a hallmark of journalistic ability, something to be borne with as the price of talent.

But, writing in 1893, Ralph said all that had changed. The reporter could no longer ignore the ordinary rules of conduct. "The day has gone by when either his employers or associates will put up with any form of unreliability or blameworthiness in his habits or his principles," he declared. "The need of a barber and a bath, and the tenancy of an attic with a bottle in lieu of other furniture, are no longer recognized as the outward proof of even poetic ability." In contrast to earlier reporters, he added, "The correspondents of to-day must be and are welcome at the houses, clubs, and business places of the men who lead in public affairs. They must be men of good parts and of good appearance and behavior."

Julian Ralph himself may have been welcome at the best places. As he entered middle age—he would turn forty in 1893—he was a substantial, imposing figure, his forehead increasingly high-domed as his hair receded, his great mustache flourishing in its full luxuriance. His own reputation was such that he could move easily among the famous and powerful. But he protests too much when he claims that journalism in general had entirely shed its scruffy image. In truth, reporters commanded little public respect throughout the late 1800s. With a few exceptions—most notably, the small contingent of correspondents who had established themselves in Washington—they had second-class status. Ralph's repeated insistence that any

such stigma belonged to the distant past only confirms his nagging aware-
ness that it did in fact linger.

A degree of wariness toward reporters on the part of the public was
understandable. Their sometimes cavalier way with the truth and their
frequent invasions of domestic privacy solely for the sake of titillation
soured thoughtful citizens on both reporters and their newspapers. There
was also the sheer novelty of the reporter's role. When a *Sun* man was
dispatched to a Long Island convent on a story, the nuns all filed by to look
at him because, it was explained, they had never seen a reporter before. In
the wider world as well, the idea of making a living by poking into others'
business—going where you were not wanted, asking annoying questions,
writing it all up in a newspaper—took some getting used to. "Impertinent"—the word recurs again and again when Victorians, habitually deferential to their betters, speak of reporters.

Nor did certain other aspects of reporting comport with prevailing notions of respectability. At times the work seemed unserious, more like a
game than an adult occupation. Reporters often spent their days pursuing a
snippet of gossip as if the fate of the world depended on it. Reporting could
be undignified. Reporters were always having doors slammed in their
faces, or waiting outside closed doors while important men within made
weighty decisions that they might or might not deign to reveal. Reporters
stood watch in the rain outside mansions, derbies dripping, ulsters soggy,
and they scurried down the street at the heels of great men—anything for a
scrap of news. Victorians, who stood much on their dignity, could not
imagine self-respecting persons stooping to such activities.

Reporters also had to contend with the popular impression of their field
as a refuge for social outcasts. "Geniuses, ne'er-do-wells, Bohemians—
often men of disorderly lives or irresponsible natures" who resembled
actors in their flouting of convention—was the way Ralph described them,
even while insisting that reporters of this kind belonged to an earlier era.
That many reporters were former printers, a trade known for both bibulous-
ness and rootlessness, did nothing to enhance reporters' social standing.

It sometimes seemed that the outcasts set the tone in the newspaper
world. Around 1870 the city editor of the Chicago *Times,* which specialized in seamy scandals, boasted: "I have a great force in the city
department. Two of my men are ex-convicts, ten of them are divorced
husbands, and not a single one of them is living with his own wife." Junius
Henri Browne of the New York *Tribune* wrote in 1869:

Bohemian, particularly in New-York, has indeed come to be a sort of synonym for a newspaper writer, and not without reason, as he is usually no favorite of fortune, and his gifts, whatever they may be, rarely include that of practicality. His profession, enabling him to see the shams of the World and the hollowness of reputation, renders him indifferent to fame, distrustful of appearances, and skeptical of humanity.

Ralph to the contrary, the bohemians hung around newsrooms for a long time. Charles Rosebault joined Ralph on the *Sun* reporting staff in the mid-1880s. "Most newspapermen of that time," he said decades later, "were strays in the social sense, for whom the irregular habits imposed by their calling were not its least attraction. Not a few of them had drifted into journalism from other vocations for the very reason that they could not tolerate the conventional life."

Journalism, said James Parton in 1888, was for "educated tramps," and most reporting staffs did in fact include men who had tried their hand at other work—former lawyers, doctors, clergymen, teachers, soldiers. At the Chicago *News Record* in 1892, one of the youthful Ray Stannard Baker's reporting colleagues was an ex-minister, a man who apparently had left the pulpit after losing his faith. The newspaper office, he told Baker portentously one day, "is the haven of shipwrecked ambitions." Just as they had failed in other fields, such men often failed at newspaper work. But Baker felt that for a time they imparted to newsrooms a variety and spice whose eventual disappearance was something to be regretted.

The common thread running through the lives of many of the drifters was alcohol, and at least in this regard they found newspapers congenial. Steady, heavy drinking was commonplace. In the 1860s the New York reporting fraternity all but lived at Pfaff's, a cellar saloon on Broadway in Greenwich Village, drinking, smoking pipes, and talking. At the Chicago *Times,* from the 1860s through the 1880s, even though petty rules were enforced on such matters as using pencils down to the merest stubs, it was perfectly acceptable to run across the street every now and then for a drink. Franc Wilkie, a Chicago *Times* reporter and editor, said he often slipped out with every intention of having one quick glass of beer only to be trapped by a friendly crowd at the bar. Six to ten beers later Wilkie would make his way back to the office.

Like Ralph, Wilkie maintained that over the years newspapermen turned more temperate. "There is still too much indulgence in stimulants among newspaper attachés," he said in 1891, "but it can be truthfully said that the vice is not nearly as prevalent and deep-seated as it was ten years ago."

One wonders how much change had really occurred. Reflecting on his experience as a *Sun* reporter in the 1880s and 1890s, Charles Rosebault concluded that drinking went with the job.

Owing to their irregular hours of work, as well as their peculiar vocation, most workers on morning newspapers lived a life apart from other men. Working when others played, sleeping when others worked, they, like the people of the stage, were apt to drift into peculiar habits. It took strong will and firm purpose to keep to the narrow path of sobriety, for one thing. It was all very well for the editorial writers and those others who had day jobs, and could live like other folks, to keep their balance, but for the great majority, emerging after long arduous labors into dark, deserted streets, perhaps into the rigors of bitter winter weather, there was almost irresistible lure in the friendly lights of the ever-open saloon and the cup that cheers.

As a matter of course, Thomas Campbell-Copeland's 1889 manual for journalists warned editors about hard-drinking reporters.

A reporter who drinks to excess is never to be trusted. He may be a smart man, or good news-gatherer, and seldom or never incapacitated for duty by his unfortunate habit, but such a man cannot be relied on, and as soon as the discovery is made, he is sternly cautioned that his discharge will follow any omission, however trifling, which might have been avoided had he been a temperate man.

Despite such advice, drinking was widely tolerated. Alcohol was thought to lubricate the creative machinery and make the words flow. Even Ralph fortified himself during a long night of writing with a jolt of brandy. In retirement Chester Lord recalled that in his years as managing editor of the *Sun* in the late 1800s and early 1900s many reporters routinely started work with a drink. "The notion that alcohol stimulates to more brilliant thought is very common among newspaper writers," he said.

As a very young reporter for the Kansas City *Times* in the 1890s, William Salisbury took up drinking simply because it seemed the thing for a reporter to do, even though he had no taste for liquor. He preserved the beginning of a story he wrote after attending the annual Priests of Pallas ball and then, as was the custom, stopping at a bar on the way back to the office.

It was a cosmopolitan assemblage when last night the votaries of fair Pallas Athene danced the hours away. The wit, the beauty, the wealth, the fashion of the Missouri Valley shone resplendent, intermingled with some of the representative citizens of the Old World, in whose veins the noble blood of ancients coursed. There were fair women and brave men treading the measures of stately waltzes, the music of which, borne upon perfumed air, from a concealed orchestra, intoxicated the senses of all. There were charming debutantes in the first flush of the primal persuasive pulchritude of young womanhood. There were haughty dames of proud lineage, indisputable descent from revolutionary sires, and some descended from the Mayflower Pilgrims. There were leaders in the business world—financiers whose banks contain the wealth of fair provinces—heads of live-stock importing firms whose bellowing herds dot the prairies for numberless miles—packing-house presidents in whose establishments are slaughtered legions of bovine and porcine creatures daily. . . .

An exchange reader at the *Sun* spotted Salisbury's story, and the *Sun* reprinted part of it, commenting: "The progress of empire in the great West, it seems, bids fair to be equaled by the progress of letters, if this bit of journalistic descriptive work be a fair sample."

Whether alcohol transmuted prose into poetry or into drunken prose was a subjective matter, of course. There were more serious concerns. Drinking, said James Parton back in 1874, was contributing to inaccuracy in newspaper stories.

Alcohol, among other pernicious effects, renders the mind inexact, disposed to exaggerate, and reckless of the consequences of what it utters. Watch a man who is going down this steep decline to ruin, and you will observe, as one of the symptoms of a moral lapse along the whole line of character, a growing insensibility to the claims of truth, and a growing inability to discern truth.

Parton recounted a minor journalistic scandal of the previous year. Fifteen New York reporters had traveled to the sedate suburb of Morristown, New Jersey, the evening before they were to witness a hanging at the local jail. A number got roaring drunk and engaged in running disputes with the sheriff and warden in charge of the proceedings—raging, for example, when the sheriff refused to advance the hour of execution so they could catch an earlier train back to the city. After the hanging, several reporters who had caroused through the night wrote accounts that bore no resemblance to what had really happened, describing the hanging as a totally bungled job when in reality, according to Parton, it was carried out with unusual smoothness and speed. "Such are the possibilities of falsehood and riotous indecency to brains weakened and crazed by the fumes of alcohol!" commented Parton.

There were also tales of missed assignments and monumental binges. At the *Sun* a reporter named Robert McAlpin was dispatched to Harlem one afternoon to cover a suicide. He did not reappear in the office for a year and a half, apparently having spent the interim drinking. The day of his return he showed up at the usual hour around midday and remarked to John Bogart, the city editor, "Very good paper this morning, John." McAlpin received an assignment.

Another *Sun* tale involved a reporter keeping the death watch on General Grant at the upstate New York resort of Mount McGregor in the summer of 1885. When Grant died no story arrived from the *Sun* man, and the office could not reach him by telegraph. Apparently no full explanation was ever forthcoming, but the next day, as *Sun* veterans remembered the episode, Bogart received a telegram from the reporter: "Doesn't the *Sun* permit its reporters to get drunk once in a while?"

Bogart replied: "Yes—once in a while."

This was not one of those times.

If some of the criticism of reporters was warranted, surely it was getting out of hand when Charles W. Eliot, the president of Harvard, was widely quoted in 1890 as dismissing the whole breed as "drunkards, deadbeats, and bummers." All the same, the comment was probably a fair reflection of the attitudes toward the profession then prevalent among large segments of the public, including the upper reaches of society as epitomized by Harvard.

Although growing numbers of college men were entering journalism in the 1880s and 1890s, few graduates of an elite institution like Harvard would have seriously contemplated a career as a reporter. An 1888 article in the *Harvard Monthly* asked in its title "What Inducements Has Journalism to Offer to Young Men Leaving College?" and seemed to conclude that it had few, even though the author was a Harvard man who had at least dabbled in newspaper work. He deplored Harvard's haughtiness where newspapers were concerned—as exemplified by a sign reading "No Loafers or Reporters Admitted!" that was displayed for a time at the crew's headquarters—and he acknowledged that *owning* a newspaper might be a worthwhile goal for a Harvard graduate. "Once he builds up or inherits a thriving newspaper, he can, if he choose, reside thousands of miles away, and by sending telegraphic messages now and then, manage the property." But for the present educated men should look upon the lower levels of journalism, such as reporting, mainly as a broadening experience, a stepping-stone, "to fit them for useful life, in law, in trade, in letters, in politics, or in finance."

Reporters were aware of the low esteem in which they were held. The phrase "gentlemen of the press," they knew, was laced with irony. Indeed, the public was convinced, said *Sun* reporter Franklin Matthews in 1893, that "the metropolitan newspaper reporter of to-day" was "not a gentleman." On the stage, said Matthews, the reporter was always "loudly dressed, ill-mannered, nauseously obtrusive." From this and other portrayals the public was persuaded that the reporter was "coarse and almost loathsome and a member of a guild which as a life-calling must of necessity be most undesirable."

Saloonkeepers and traveling salesmen could have made similar complaints, but reporters more often, in the course of their work, had to move in circles where the condescension was palpable. Although, as Ralph noted, such public figures as Chauncey Depew of the Vanderbilt empire had early recognized the value of cultivating reporters, lesser personages were more inclined to scorn them except on the rare occasions when the cooperation of the press might be useful. A reporter named Henry Blake complained in the *Writer* in 1887:

> The rich man who has crawled up the night-entrance stairs to ask that his sudden failure or the glaring wickedness of his son may be handled tenderly, and who is willing that the reporter should have a place at his daughter's wedding provided he eats his escalloped oysters and boned turkey unobtrusively and does not assume familiarity with the real guests, this man, as soon as he has no immediate use for the craft, is ready to speak contemptuously of "those cattle of the press."

Slights and small insults were part of the reporter's daily round. In New York reporters assigned to elegant banquets sometimes had to listen to the speeches from behind a screen, hidden from the others present. Early women reporters, sent to cover society balls, found themselves hustled back out into the night as soon as they had finished their notes on the guest list, the decorations, and the dresses. Now and then reporters were offered tips—the amounts were too small to be dignified as bribes—for publicizing a lecture or a social affair. A. E. Watrous, a Philadelphia newspaperman, visiting an estate to write about a hunt around 1880, was handed a five-dollar bill for his trouble by the lord of the manor. Watrous politely declined the money, saying, "There was a time when it was done, but we've done away with it."

Ralph recounted an experience of a reporter friend named Roland Folger Coffin. Coffin was one of those who had come to reporting from another field, but he had more success at it than the general run of drifters. Of Nantucket stock, he had served as master of vessels in the Liverpool trade until berths were scarce after the Civil War, when he cast about for another way to earn a living. Having passed idle hours at sea learning shorthand, Captain Coffin decided to try reporting, and in 1868, when he was about forty years old, he started working for the New York *World*. Ralph must have encountered him during his own brief stay at the *World,* and the two were also thrown together in the small press contingent that joined President Arthur on his St. Lawrence River fishing trip in 1882. On the occasion about which Ralph told his story Captain Coffin had been sent to a mansion to report on the meeting of a fashionable club. As Ralph recalled it:

The lady of the house saw him seated in the drawing-room, which opened upon a dining-room that had been arranged for a large dinner-party and was lustrous with plate and crystal. She called up to her husband to know who was "the person" in the drawing-room, and the captain heard his host reply that he was a reporter. Upon hearing this, the lady crept into the dining-room and, gathering up all the silver spoons and forks, made off with them out of his reach.

Ralph did not bother to reconcile the incident with his claim that reporters had lived down their unsavory reputations, but whatever explanation he might offer, Coffin's experience was in fact yet another illustration of nineteenth-century Americans' disdain for the people who gathered the news they so voraciously consumed. The irony of the situation was largely overlooked, but it was noted by one William Hobart Beebe. Beebe, a Long Islander who liked to have his reflections on diverse subjects printed up in little books, sounds like an odd character, but reporters would have appreciated some of the sentiments he expressed in an 1880 essay entitled "The Ill-Used Reporter."

"The reporters of the present day are abused and misused by the very same persons who are always glad to read those very same reporters' notes and newspaper articles," wrote Beebe. The reporter's life was rigorous, demanding late hours and exposure to foul weather, and getting the facts of a story straight was harder than a layman might think. While some might regard reporters as "regular bummers, lovers of lager beer and champagne suppers," that was certainly not true of all reporters. Moreover, if the public did look down on reporters, why did it not evince more concern for uplifting them? Referring to a recent week of prayer in New York City, Beebe said that churches had devoted one day to the press but had failed to pray for "that neglected class of men called newspaper reporters."

Are we not an ungrateful people? With how much interest we read the daily and weekly reports, that are made up by these very same reporters, and then not take enough interest in their welfare to lift up our voices in prayer for them, that they may be guided aright. Is this not a spirit of ingratitude shown towards them? If the reporters knew that we took enough interest in them to lift up our voices in prayer in their behalf . . . would they not in return be much encouraged and also endeavor to give us better reports than before.

Sometimes it seemed that reporters didn't get much appreciation back at the office either. At some newspapers the old view of reporting as a relatively mindless, mechanical chore was slow in dying. It was "item gathering," work that a printer—almost anyone, for that matter—could pick up in no time. That attitude, along with the old notion that the whole paper was a reflection of its editor, contributed to the continuing absence of bylines in most newspapers. In contrast to successful unionization by printers, early attempts by reporters to improve their status through organization sputtered out.

The editors of the *Nation* even found it pretentious to call reporting a "profession," and in their darker moments reporters agreed. After thirteen years in the field, a New York reporter named J. W. Keller wrote in 1893: "Journalism in its essential qualifications is a learned profession; in its exactions, its limitations to income and its insecurity of employment, it is more nearly a trade." The reporter "is simply a wage-earner, a hired man."

Campbell-Copeland's 1889 guide to journalistic practice reinforces the view of reporters as hired help. The ideal newsroom, as Campbell-Copeland describes it, sounds more like a stove factory than a place where creative spirits exercise their talents. Punctuality and neatness are of central importance. The city editor must "break up the habit of lounging and idle conversation." As the member of management who supervises reporters' day-to-day work, he must keep his distance from them lest they forget their place.

The less a City Editor has to do with his reporters outside of the office the better he finds it to be for himself and the better for the paper. It may be necessary for him to attach himself to the journalist clubs which exist in all large cities, but he should make it clear at all times that he is the City Editor, and that if he unbends socially it is for the occasion only, and that no familiarities will be tolerated as the result of it.

According to Franc Wilkie, Wilbur F. Storey, the editor of the Chicago *Times,* insisted that his subordinate editors not even acknowledge the existence of staff members encountered outside the office. It remained to James Gordon Bennett, Jr., of the New York *Herald,* however, to perfect the imperial style of newspaper management.

Whereas the elder Bennett, the *Herald's* founder, has been described as "a man of explosive temper but kindly heart" toward those who worked for him, his son treated *Herald* employees with all the consideration of the Czarist nobility for their serfs. He never shook hands with any of them. In utterly peremptory and arbitrary fashion, he hired, fired, and reassigned, often just to demonstrate his power or to underscore that James Gordon Bennett, Jr., was the only indispensable man at the *Herald*. Each day *Herald* reporters received cards from the city editor giving their assignments over Bennett's printed name. Bennett was so firmly convinced that he alone deserved credit for every word in his newspaper that he seethed at the acclaim lavished on his man Stanley after he returned from risking his life to find Livingstone in central Africa. "Who was Stanley before I found him?" Bennett raged. "Who thought of looking for Livingstone? *Who paid the bills?*" When Stanley reached New York after his triumph, Bennett scarcely acknowledged his return.

At many other newspapers besides the *Herald*, reporters could seldom feel entirely confident that they would have a job the next day. Though *Sun* reporters had few grounds for complaint, Ralph railed against publishers and editors elsewhere who "establish business rules and talk of 'discipline,' who suspend and fire and lecture the writers who are under them. . . . These martinets can decimate their forces, they can weed out the talent and hold fast to the sticks, and they can crush down *esprit de corps* and greatly weaken a newspaper; that is all. Newspaper making is not a business, except in the publication office."

Mass firings of reporters—sometimes with an editor thrown in for good measure—were standard management procedure in the 1890s. The practice was said to keep people on their toes. Stories of wholesale dismissals circulated regularly on Park Row and elsewhere in the newspaper world— twenty at a crack at a New York morning daily, seven in one afternoon at a Boston paper, seven in the course of a morning in a Chicago city room. Because so many were flocking into reporting in the late 1800s, editors lost no sleep over filling their suddenly depleted ranks. An article in the *Arena* said: "An editor in any of the metropolitan centres of to-day would have no more hesitation, if he chanced to feel in the mood, in ordering out seven or eight men than in hurriedly clearing waste 'copy' from his desk. For he knows that, early next morning, perhaps twenty men, not freshlings, but capable writers and copy-handlers, would be in his office beseeching him for the positions vacated."

Disciplinary suspensions, even of reporters of established ability, were similarly routine. Jacob Riis, the most dedicated of reporters, was suspended from the New York *Tribune* for missing a single development in a celebrated grave robbery case that was front-page news for months in 1878 and 1879. Using proscribed words and phrases could also bring suspension at the *Tribune;* a reporter from the 1880s remembered, for example, that "a sea of upturned faces" meant instant punishment. At the New York *Herald*, after a rash of adverse libel judgments, James Gordon Bennett, Jr., for a time decreed that any reporter involved in such a suit be suspended until his forfeited salary or average weekly space bills equaled the libel award. One reporter who had made an admittedly serious mistake—after two decades of outstanding work—calculated that his suspension would last seven years and five months. He quit.

Jacob Riis had the delicious experience of having a big story fall into his lap while he was on suspension, forcing the *Tribune* to relent and welcome him back with open arms. As he was "sulking" at home in Brooklyn one evening during his enforced idleness, a fire broke out at a large warehouse within sight of his house. It soon raged out of control. Putting aside his injured pride, Riis hurried to the scene, gathered the particulars, and reached the *Tribune* with them after midnight. The night editor, overcoming his initial surprise at seeing a suspended reporter walk into the newsroom, cleared his own desk for Riis to use to write the story. Riis's suspension was lifted the next day.

Things did not work out so well for a *Herald* reporter in similar circumstances. His name was Indian Brown, and during a two-week suspension he was bound from Albany to New York when his train came to a sudden halt, because, it turned out, another train had hurtled off the tracks up ahead. Brown telegraphed an exclusive story to the *Herald*. Afterwards, still smarting from the suspension, he wired James Gordon Bennett, Jr.: "That is the sort of man you suspend." Bennett ordered Brown paid handsomely for his story and then fired him. "I can hire all the brains I want for twenty-five dollars a week," Bennett liked to say.

Reporters often complained bitterly about their pay. With too many applicants chasing too few jobs, reporting unquestionably looked like a buyers' market. A reporter who had been tossed out on the street along with several of his colleagues in a mass firing obviously was in no position to bargain and had to settle for whatever he could get. The struggling space writers who in some weeks earned only five or ten dollars lived on the edge of destitution. In New York they could scarcely get by even if they shared a room at the shabbiest of rooming houses and took their meals at greasy Park Row eateries that dished out "beef 'n' beans" for a dime.

As a young space writer at the New York *Commercial Advertiser*, Charles Russell discovered it was even possible to work hard and end up in the hole, thanks to the management's penny-pinching on expenses. One bitter January day he was dispatched to Jamaica Bay on Long Island, where a hunting party was said to be lost in a blizzard. Russell failed to get a story—the hunters turned up quickly—but in the course of the day he nevertheless walked many miles, suffered frostbitten ears, and at one point had to spend his last dollar to hire a carriage. When he presented a chit for the carriage at the *Commercial Advertiser* the next morning, it was rejected with the explanation that reporters were not authorized to hire carriages. Since he had not earned a space payment, and since the *Commercial Advertiser,* unlike many papers, paid no time allowance, Russell was out a dollar for his day's work.

Even reporters with relatively good incomes sometimes grumbled that the peculiar requirements of the job made it hard to get by. The only way to obtain a story might be to loosen tongues with a round or two of drinks, an expense the newspapers of the time, perhaps wisely, were not inclined to pick up. Reporters also had to dress well enough to be able to move easily in lofty social and economic circles when the need arose. Ralph noted that male reporters assigned to cover society balls seldom had the requisite evening clothes. He told of one who bought a white tie, an opera hat, and white gloves and circulated at such affairs with his coat buttoned and his hat under his arm. When the reporter changed newspapers he said of his new employer: "It is a perfect establishment. They always keep a man with a dress suit on the staff."

Reporters' complaints about their financial pinch, some far more serious than the lack of a dress suit, were clearly justified in many cases. And yet, the truth is that they complained too much. In seeming contradiction to the supply-and-demand situation and to the callous attitudes of some editors and publishers, newspapers placed a rising value on reporters' services. In some quarters the realization was obviously dawning that good ones were not to be found on every street corner, and as a result between 1872 and 1892, a period when prices were actually declining, reporters' pay virtually doubled. Increasingly, those reporters who survived the initiation of the lean early days could look forward to earning a decent living.

Pay rose to the highest levels in New York, though living costs were also highest there. James Gordon Bennett, Jr., at one time might have been able to hire all the proven reporters he wanted for the *Herald* at twenty-five dollars a week, but by 1895, according to a study of journalistic pay by the *Forum* magazine, the earnings of New York reporters averaged forty dollars a week and often ranged up to sixty dollars. A couple of years earlier Franklin Matthews of the *Sun* had estimated the earnings of New York reporters at forty to eighty dollars a week. A few prolific space writers topped a hundred dollars in good weeks.

These incomes, amounting to $2,000 or more a year, were high for the 1890s, and they represented a big jump in the economic status of reporters. The *Forum* said that the handful of reporters functioning around 1840 had ranked economically on a par with stage drivers. By the 1850s reporters had climbed to the level of "the better grades of mechanics," such as printers. Although later generations of reporters would sometimes complain that they had once more fallen behind the printers who set their stories in type, the *Forum* maintained that in the economic pecking order of the 1890s journalism stacked up well against a number of other fields.

It was true, said the magazine, that doctors and lawyers had a better chance of earning very large incomes—$10,000 or more a year. But journalists, editors as well as reporters, were more assured of at least reaching the fairly comfortable $2,000–3,000 range. In law, medicine, and other professions, larger proportions were well below that level. Many doctors managed on $1,000 a year in the 1890s. Teachers averaged $800 a year, and many clergymen scraped by on $500.

Convincing as the *Forum's* case was, many reporters would have argued that it ignored the long-term shortcomings of a reporting career. Reporters were very apt to achieve their peak earnings quickly and then to face the prospect of years of grinding labor with no further increase in tangible reward. A talented reporter, said J. W. Keller, might earn $500–700 the first year, double that the next, and before long $3,000 a year. "But three thousand dollars is his income the next year and the next and the next, until he realizes one day that he has grown old." Only a few reporters could expect to move into one of the relatively small number of editors' positions—one reason being, according to a reporter's complaint in the *Writer* in 1887, that a disproportionate share of these appointments went to "inside men," such as copy readers.

Many reporters, including some of the best, eventually departed for business, government, and the developing specialty of press agentry. A man who started at the Boston *Globe* in 1872 as a reporter kept track of his colleagues and found that of the forty-nine reporters in the *Globe* newsroom in 1872, only seven were reporting fifteen years later. J. W. Keller said in 1893 that in the newsroom of his New York daily only one man was over fifty and the staff averaged under thirty-five. Reporting, almost everybody agreed, was "a young man's game."

Those who did continue as reporters into middle age, either because they loved the job or because they couldn't fit in elsewhere, were not allowed to grow old gracefully. Newspapers offered few sinecures. For a reporter working on space, what was produced each day was all that counted, and sometimes youthful energy could outdo wisdom gained from experience. Said Ralph: "There is no resting on one's oars in this profession—no period of ease, no matter how well earned—no drowsy evening in the day of any correspondent's life."

Sometimes older reporters saw their incomes dwindle. Allan Forman, editor of the *Journalist,* said in 1891 that no one should count on making a decent living as a newspaper writer past the age of fifty, for "after that you will surely be crowded to the wall." Pensions were almost unheard of, and some reporters, said Keller, were reduced to "gray ghosts that haunt Newspaper Row asking for work that is seldom given, begging a little from this friend or that."

In the end some died penniless. The New Yorkers among them were buried in Cypress Hills Cemetery in Brooklyn, the expenses paid out of a fund maintained by the New York Press Club, which was headquartered over a saloon on Nassau Street, just behind Park Row. Buoyant as his natural disposition seems to have been, Ralph must now and then have harbored some fears of such a fate. In 1885 he journeyed back to Red Bank and paid seventy-five dollars for a plot in Fair View Cemetery, located across the Navesink River from the town. It appears to have been the only piece of real estate he ever owned.

Ralph should not have been particularly worried about money in 1885. That was the first of the two years in which he covered the annual sessions of the New York legislature, and he remembered that while in Albany he earned seventy-five dollars a week, far more than most New York reporters would earn even a decade later. The assignment must have been one of those calling for a fixed salary rather than space rates.

Seventy-five dollars a week—about $4,000 a year assuming his space payments when not in Albany averaged roughly the same—entrenched Ralph solidly in the middle class. Like many New York family men, he had crossed the East River and was living in Brooklyn in the 1880s. He and Belle and the children had made the move about the time the Brooklyn Bridge was opened in 1883. The bridge provided an alternative to the ferries, which were subject to disruption by ice in the winter, and it spurred the growth of Brooklyn. Its population rose from just under 400,000 in

1869, the year construction of the bridge began, to 900,000 a decade after its completion.

Brooklyn was still a separate city in the eighties; it would not become a borough of New York till 1898. It was an important city in its own right, with shops, offices, factories, and shipyards. But to Ralph, as to the tens of thousand of others who commuted daily to jobs in Manhattan, it was a suburb. It was a place, Ralph wrote in *Harper's Monthly* in 1893, that "works for New York, and is paid off like a shop-girl on Saturday nights," a place where people found "elbow-room and a hush at night, and where they see trees and can have growing flowers."

Brooklyn had endless miles of streets lined with brick and frame row houses, most with high stoops and small dooryards. They rented for twenty-five to fifty dollars a month. The Ralphs lived in at least two such houses in Brooklyn in the eighties, both in a neighborhood some two and a half miles east of the Brooklyn end of the new bridge. One house was on Kosciusko Street, the other on Hart. Opposite the Kosciusko Street house a man named Isaac Smith ran what he advertised as "The first Infirmary that was ever established in Brooklyn with practical remedies for LAME HORSES," but otherwise the neighborhood consisted of the residences of shopkeepers, lawyers, salesmen, brokers, engineers, and clerks, plus an occasional skilled tradesman such as a glassblower or wheelwright. The more affluent households, among which the Ralphs' must have been counted, included maids and nurses.

Horsecars provided a link to the bridge and the East River ferries, and starting in 1885 there were steam-powered elevated trains as well. With the swift el and with cable cars crossing the bridge in five minutes, Ralph could descend his stoop late in the morning and reach the *Sun* building—a short block from the Manhattan end of the bridge—in little more than half an hour. If he worked late, however, the return trip could take longer. The Brooklyn el stopped running at midnight, and if Ralph missed the last train he had to make his way home through the dark streets of Brooklyn at the clopping pace of a tired horsecar team.

Aside from Julian's unorthodox working hours and sudden departures for out-of-town assignments, the Ralphs led a life much like those of their neighbors. Belle very likely took part in one of the women's literary clubs that thrived in Brooklyn. The Ralphs attended an Episcopal church with some regularity, and in May the Ralph children probably marched in the annual Sunday school parade, a major Brooklyn event in which armies of youngsters flooded through the streets led by bands and carrying silken banners embroidered in gold, after which they gorged themselves on ice cream and cake.

Even so Ralph had to concede that reporters were not regarded in quite the same light as the lawyers and salesmen and clerks who were their neighbors. He told of an occasion when, on an assignment and in need of help to find his way, he stopped at the shop of a bearded German cobbler to ask directions.

> I cleared my throat and said:
> "I beg your pardon, but I am a reporter of the *Sun*—"
> "Well, well," he said soothingly, before I could finish the sentence, "you cannot help dot."

11. The Joy of the Chase

anhattan did not lack for licensed saloons in the late 1800s, but for some reason—perhaps the appeal of the mildly illicit—one of the favorite drinking spots of New York reporters of the period was a Park Row drugstore run by a man named Charley Perry. Located first in the *Herald* building at Broadway and Ann Street, then, starting in 1887, on the ground floor of the *Sun* building, "Doc" Perry's place stayed open all hours. It was particularly popular with young reporters on the morning newspapers. After handing in their last copy around midnight, they would gather in the back room, hidden from the front of the drugstore and the soda fountain by a screen marked "Prescriptions." There, remembered Willis Abbot from his days as a beginning reporter on the New York *Tribune,* they sipped whiskey from green glasses and talked shop.

The talk often went on till dawn. Much of it was about "the work of those who were journalistic giants in our eyes," said Abbot. "When the first editions were brought in to Doctor Perry's, we would look eagerly for the articles which showed the style of Ralph or Brisbane, of Townsend, Davis, Carvalho or Creelman.* If one of us were lucky enough to have been given an assignment which had been covered for his paper by one of the journalistic aristocracy, there would be eager comparison, and careful estimates of the difference in quality." Sometimes the great men themselves would drop by and join the discussion, though for Ralph such visits must have come mainly at times when he was not living in Brooklyn and rushing for the last Brooklyn elevated train at midnight.

When the group finally broke up, said Abbot, the future editor of the *Christian Science Monitor,* the young reporters would walk uptown to their boardinghouses, through the Bowery, then up Broadway, "deserted, silent and romantic in the early dawn."

*Besides Julian Ralph, the references are to Arthur Brisbane, Edward W. Townsend, Richard Harding Davis, S. S. Carvalho, and James Creelman. All were leading lights on Park Row in the late 1800s.

There is something impressive about the spectacle of city streets that one knows as crowded and noisy lying empty and silent just before the higher windows begin to reflect the rosy sunrise. It was at such moments that we youngsters, after usually fourteen hours of work, walked gayly home discussing the news of the day still unknown to the sleeping thousands around us.

That reporters, their grumbling to the contrary, had a fair prospect of earning a decent living did not explain why for many, at least for a period in their lives, the job held an appeal that other lines of work could not match. If making money was the prime goal, there were more direct ways to go about it, and bigger fortunes to be made, in business. Moreover, even those reporters who complained of miserable pay and tyrannical editors usually ended their recital of woes by affirming that reporting was nevertheless the best job on earth. Beyond the wages picked up at the cashier's window each Saturday, beyond the superficial glamor that lured some young men into newsrooms—"free tickets to the theatres . . . the gay little suppers with pretty actresses," in the words of one 1890s observer of the field—the life of a reporter obviously offered special satisfactions.

Willis Abbot touched on one. Everybody enjoys being an insider, and the young reporters who discussed the news as they walked home at dawn were savoring that pleasure. "We were the first to know what had happened in the world," said Alexander Noyes, another young *Tribune* reporter of the 1880s who went on to journalistic success. For reporters, news, including the behind-the-scenes variety that would never see print, was the stuff of office gossip. More important, a reporter's own daily assignments allowed him to observe a variety of men and events close up in a way that most people could never do.

This could be disillusioning, as Noyes learned at the very start of his career. Assigned to report the fiftieth anniversary meeting of the New York Abolition Society, Noyes, the product of a fervently antislavery, pro-Union upbringing, was shocked to realize that the old slavery fighters now occupied themselves mainly with petty internal disputes. Similarly, attending a meeting of a local post of the Grand Army of the Republic, he encountered "uncouth and beery veterans" chiefly concerned with exacting bigger pensions from Washington.

But if such experiences gave rise to the cynicism said to mark the profession, they also heightened the reporter's sense, admittedly not always warranted, that he was in touch with reality. This was a heady feeling for a youth out in the world on his own for the first time. As a new reporter in Chicago in the nineties, Ray Stannard Baker wrote about fires, murders, robberies, sermons, banquets, champion watermelons, golden weddings, and an escaped elephant.

I had a wonderful feeling of not being dependent for my knowledge of what happened upon hearsay, or upon speculation. . . . The sense of being taken into an event is surely one of the greatest lures of journalism: the satisfaction of the appetite for knowing life at first hand.

There was also the satisfaction of telling others the news. The urge to pass along news is inborn—most people who come across a juicy item fairly burst to share it—and gratification of that urge was the reporter's daily lot. At its most mundane, reporting differed little from what anyone did who rushed to spread the word about an accident observed or a domestic spat overheard. On a more exalted level, where momentous events were involved, a veteran reporter once wrote, "One experiences the joy . . . which must have been Paul Revere's when, as a sort of morning newspaper extra, he made the midnight ride to Lexington. So long as the tribe of reporters persists, this must be its chief reward."

Sounding the alarm, whether about menacing foreign armies or home-grown problems, has always been one of the crucial roles of a free press. From the Civil War through the turn of the century the domestic front pro-vided ample material for this sort of journalism—rampant corruption, squa-lor at the bottom of society, outrageous excess at the top. The uncovering of the scandals of the postwar years rank as particularly notable achievements. In more than twelve columns on September 4, 1872, for example, the *Sun* laid bare for the first time the Crédit Mobilier fraud. Unscrupulous business-men had bought the cooperation of politicians in Washington in draining the treasury of the Union Pacific, a railroad lavishly subsidized by the federal government. The Vice President, the Speaker of the House, the chairmen of leading House committees—"all of them," declared the *Sun*, "are proven, by irrefutable evidence, to have been bribed."

From time to time almost every reporter experienced the satisfaction of spotlighting wrongs and contributing to the betterment of the human condi-tion—or at least alleviating the misery of one human being. Sometimes, as Ralph believed had happened when the authorities in Newcastle, Dela-ware, refrained from flogging a woman in the presence of reporters, the mere threat of publicity could have a salutary effect. Other times an assignment that for the moment did no more than prick a few consciences, such as Ralph's report of the high death rate for New York foundlings, might in the long run advance social reform.

Occasionally a story could produce a quick, dramatic result. In his autobiography Ralph told of a time when managing editor Chester Lord ordered him to look into a murder. Lord appears to have become convinced that the police, unable to track down the real murderer, were trying to cover up their failure by blaming the crime on an innocent youth.

The murder had occurred early on the morning of March 7, 1889, in a drugstore on Third Avenue in mid-Manhattan. The victim was a man who had clerked in the drugstore and slept each night in its back room. The druggist also employed an errand boy, an orphaned youngster of seventeen, who customarily arrived at the store at 7 A.M., was let in by the clerk, and shortly thereafter went out to buy rolls for his employer's breakfast. On the day of the murder a neighbor entered the store at the time the errand boy was usually out fetching the rolls and discovered the clerk lying on the floor of the back room near death, "his skull chopped into flinders," said the *Sun's* account, and his blood spattered everywhere. A hatchet lay at the clerk's side, and the store's cashbox had been emptied. The errand boy presently returned, at which time it was noted that his clothes—the only ones he owned, according to Ralph—were spotless. Moreover, before expiring the clerk had said that "after the boy went out I stooped to tie my shoe and a *man* struck me."

Exoneration of the youth, whose name was Willie Krulisch, would seem to have been in order, but the police were determined to pin the murder on him. In a day when the fist and the club were among the principal tools of criminal investigation, the police pressured Willie relentlessly to confess. Failing to shake his assertions of innocence, they nevertheless charged him with the murder, and on April 1 he went on trial. Ralph claimed that only his intervention, at Chester Lord's behest, saved the boy from becoming the first to die in New York State's new electric chair.

Ralph's story filled two columns of the *Sun* on Sunday, April 7, after the trial had been under way for a week. It devastated the police case. "By concealment of some facts, and the distortion of others, the case against the boy had been made to appear convincing," Ralph later wrote, "but when the whole truth was massed candidly against the unbroken good record of the prisoner's life, the police fabric fell to pieces like a house built of cards." Ralph's story reported that the murder victim's dying declaration that he had been attacked by a "man"—"not Willie, whom he had worked with every day for two months, but a man"—had been suppressed by the police; they lamely explained that an officer's notes on the statement had been "lost." As for the question of how Willie could be wearing clothes showing not a trace of blood only minutes after committing a murder that caused blood to jet over the walls up to a height of eight feet, the police simply ignored it.

Further, a police claim that a hardware dealer had identified Willie as the purchaser of a hatchet like the one found at the murder scene could not be taken seriously; instead of bringing the storekeeper to police headquarters and asking him to make an identification out of a lineup of persons of similar size and age, as was customary in such situations, detectives had taken Willie to the hardware store and announced, "This is the boy," upon which the owner had agreed that yes, it was. Efforts to extract a confession that would obviate quibbles over such matters had come to naught, said Ralph's story, even though Willie "was put through what the police call 'the third degree,'" in the course of which during one twenty-four-hour period more than half a dozen detectives hammered away at him nonstop.

Whether or not Ralph really deserves all the credit for freeing Willie Krulisch, the prosecution seemed to lose its zeal after his story appeared, and two days later, on April 9, the jury acquitted Willie. Ralph commented: "The incident . . . demonstrates the power of a journalist—that power which lends to his calling so much of its fascination."

Despite occasions such as this when Ralph's reporting served a higher cause, righting the world's wrongs was not his overriding passion. There were some reporters for whom it was. Jacob Riis, whose reporting career in New York spanned roughly the same period as Ralph's, was one. Ray Stannard Baker, just getting started in Chicago in 1892, would turn out to be another, and so would a scholarly young man from a comfortable California background who joined the New York *Evening Post* as a reporter the same year, Lincoln Steffens.

In the end none of these men would be known primarily as newspaper reporters. All would achieve their reputations with other writings and as social reformers. Riis's specialty was the plight of the big-city poor, depicted most tellingly in his 1890 book *How the Other Half Lives*. Baker and Steffens would become part of the "muckraking" school of magazine journalism in the early 1900s. Baker wrote about railroads, labor, and the status of blacks; Steffens was best known for his exposés of municipal corruption.

All the same, the newspaper careers of these writer-reformers—even the brief ones of Baker and Steffens—laid the foundations of the work for which they would be remembered. When Baker started out as a reporter in Chicago, he was struck by the contrast between the drab life of the city's poor and the glamor and excitement of the "White City" created on the shore of Lake Michigan for the 1893 world's fair. So, while others focused on the fair, he was "lifting a flap of the gorgeous tent, where the music was, and the warmth and the feasting, and looking into the cold, wet and littered alleys outside." More prosaically, Steffens, as a novice New York *Post* reporter, sought "facts of scientific value" about slums and labor and other aspects of urban life.

Jacob Riis kept at newspaper reporting far longer than Baker or Steffens—more than two decades—and his major achievements as a social reformer flowed much more directly from daily journalism. His work as a police reporter, he said, shaped "the point of view" from which he wrote *How the Other Half Lives* and his other books about New York's poor.

Riis was a good reporter; otherwise an organization as demanding as the *Sun* would not have employed him as the chief police reporter for its evening paper from 1890 to 1899. He was tireless, aggressive, and clever, not above plotting to waylay an official in a dark hall and pop a question before his quarry had time to gather his wits. His assignment embraced not only police matters but also health and sanitation. One of Riis's triumphs as an *Evening Sun* reporter was an investigation showing that New York faced the threat of cholera because of sewage in its water supply, a revelation that forced fundamental improvements in the system. What captured most of Riis's interest, however, was the slums of New York's Lower East Side, which were just steps away from police headquarters on Mulberry Street and the building across the way where police reporters had offices. Riis used his broad mandate as a police reporter to prowl the swarming streets, the tenements where four families shared a single room, and the dives where a few pennies' worth of beer entitled a patron to curl up on the floor for the night.

Riis came by his concern for the poor naturally. He himself had been poor. He had arrived in the United States in 1870 as a twenty-one-year-old immigrant from Denmark, his assets limited largely to a good command of English and a carpenter's skills. For several years he wandered the country restlessly, never quite sure what he wanted to do with his life, working sometimes at his own trade of carpentry, other times at odd jobs, lumbering, brick-making, and peddling. Usually he lived from hand to mouth, and often he was penniless. During a period of destitution in New York he spent a degrading night in one of the city's police lodging houses, noisome dormitories in police station cellars where the homeless—tramps, jobless young men, sometimes girls—slept on bare planks.

That night, climaxed when a policeman bashed out the brains of a dog that had attached itself to Riis, determined him to become a reporter. "Some one had to tell the facts," said Riis, for the way to change things for the better was "to make the facts of the wrong plain." The "reporter's calling," he became convinced, "was the highest and noblest of all call- ings; no one could sift right from wrong as he, and punish the wrong." Lincoln Steffens, who modeled his work after Riis's, said Riis "not only got the news, he cared about the news."

He was anything but a cool, detached reporter. A small man with "a voice like a squeaky cellar-door" and birdlike energy, he was hot-tempered, impatient, emotional, and enthusiastic. Covering a public meeting on tene- ments in 1888, he had to remind himself that he was a reporter and stifle the impulse to shout "Amen!" when a reformer made a rousing speech. More and more, as his role in the reform movement grew, he did cross the line from observer to participant, serving on committees and giving lectures that took his audiences into dark slums via magic lantern slides he had made with the aid of a new photographic flash powder. (Once he set himself afire using it.) Riis's activism, combined with his relentless exposure of slum conditions in his reporting and writing, bore fruit by the 1890s. Some of the most notorious slums were leveled, parks and playgrounds were opened, and the police lodging houses were closed.

The lodging house victory was especially sweet. One night in 1895 Riis took Theodore Roosevelt, now the new president of the New York Police Board, on a tour of the lodging houses. At 2 A.M. they arrived at the police station where Riis had spent the night a quarter of a century earlier. It was cold and raining—much like the earlier night—and among those sleeping on the filthy planks was a youth who reminded Riis of his younger self. Roosevelt was appalled. To Riis—"Jake," Roosevelt called him—he said: "I will smash them tomorrow."

Riis left a touching picture of his chief at the *Evening Sun,* Charles Dana. A reporter passionately committed to a cause could sometimes be a trial to editors, but Dana, cynical, disillusioned, and skeptical about reform him- self, looked upon Riis with kindly tolerance. Although Riis had few direct dealings with Dana, he happened to encounter him on the day in 1897 when Dana, succumbing to illness after a lifetime of robust health, was leaving the *Sun* office for what turned out to be the last time. Dana was descending the stairs as Riis was ascending.

I took off my hat and we shook hands.

"Well," he said, "have you reformed everything to suit you, straightened out every kink in town?"

"Pretty nearly," I said, falling into his tone of banter; "all except the *Sun* office. That is left yet, and as bad as ever."

"Ha!" he laughed, "you come on! We are ready for you. Come right along!" And with another hearty handshake he was gone.

Sometimes Julian Ralph must have bumped into Riis on those stairs, but Ralph's recollections do not mention him. Nor does he loom large in most newspaper histories and memoirs. Pivotal a figure as he was in social reform, Riis was out of the mainstream of journalism, and the things that attracted him to the field were not the primary concern of most reporters. True, other reporters liked to taste power on occasion and to have their printed words reverberate in the larger world, but for them reporting was not an endless crusade. Riis crossed the line and became more reformer than reporter. For many others the appeal of the job lay not so much in a story's impact as in reporting itself.

Joseph Ignatius Constantine Clarke took up reporting as a young Irish immigrant and became one of the New York *Herald's* stalwarts in the 1870s. When he looked back on those years decades later, he grew positively lyrical. "Given youth, strength and enthusiasm for the things of life, for the footsteps of beauty, for the broad reaches of freedom," he wrote, "it would be hard to hit upon a career more seductive, more satisfying than that of a footloose reporter on a great paper, whose compensation was mainly in what new fine things he saw, what people of achievement he met, and what rich emotions stirred him."

Clarke had put out of his mind the tedious assignments, the waiting outside closed doors, and the frustrations of chasing stories as elusive as a drop of mercury. Nor were all reporters quite as footloose as Clarke, who moved easily from a female murderer's cell to a cardinal's palace to a baseball field, where he covered the sport with aplomb despite the "considerable drawback . . . that I had never seen the game played." Specialization continued to grow. "Sporting writers" were common by the nineties, one of the *Sun's* first experts in this area being a former copy boy who had been patiently taught to write "the players were" instead of "the players was." Moving from the New York *Tribune* to the *Commercial Advertiser,* young Alexander Noyes stumbled into financial journalism because he happened to be the only reporter available when word reached the office of the failure of the investment firm in which General Grant had been duped into sinking his money. Noyes, who on that day had to ask a policeman where the stock exchange was, thus took his first step toward his future job as financial editor of the New York *Times*.

But even within some of the specialties, such as police reporting, the raw material was immensely varied. And as for general reporters, who constituted the bulk of the news-gathering staffs, it was rare for a reporter to deal with the same topic two days in a row. Here is a list of assignments of David Graham Phillips, a leading *Sun* reporter in the early nineties, during one stretch in 1893 (unless Phillips was for some reason exempt from the general rule of two stories a day, the list must include only those regarded as his principal efforts):

March   1—Joseph Jefferson's Lecture on the Drama
   "   2—Bear Hunt at Glen Cove
   "   3—Special stories for the Sunday *Sun*
   "   6—Obituary of W. P. Demarest
   "   7—Meeting of Russian-Americans
   "   8—Mystery at New Brunswick, New Jersey
   "   9—Special Stories for Sunday
   "   10—Accident in Seventy-First St. Tunnel
   "   11—More Triplets in Cold Spring
   "   12—Services in Old Scotch Church
   "   13—Furniture Sale
   "   14—Opening of Hotel Waldorf
   "   15—Married Four Days, Then False
   "   17—Dinner, Friendly Sons of St. Patrick
   "   18—Parade and Show, Barnum & Bailey
   "   19—Church Quarrel, Rutherford, N.J.

Nothing on the order of Paul Revere's ride here—in fact, nothing that would linger in the minds of most readers for more than a day or two. Nevertheless, for a keenly aware reporter like Phillips, who in time became a popular novelist as well as a celebrated muckraker, almost every story, even the most trivial, etched some new impression on the mind—a pungent personality, a curious fact, a new understanding of the way a small part of the world worked. To a far greater degree than most jobs, and to a degree that compensated for some of its shortcomings, reporting was an intrinsically interesting way to make a living. You never knew what the day might bring. Approaching the city editor's desk for an assignment, said

Will Irwin, who joined the *Sun* as a reporter shortly after the turn of the century, was "a prelude to adventure."

It was an obvious case of arson—a farmhouse and separate outbuildings had burned. Ralph got the assignment. The police had arrested a suspect, a black vagrant, and Ralph managed a private talk with him. Something— Ralph's looming physical presence or perhaps his knack for getting all sorts of people to bare their souls to him—led the man to confess to Ralph that he had indeed set the fires. What to do? If Ralph relayed the confession to the police, they would quickly inform the rest of the press that they had solved the crime. If Ralph said nothing to the police, the suspect might neverthe- less decide that the game was up and tell them of his guilt himself, in which case the story would also get out. Ralph struck a bargain with the police: he would induce the culprit to repeat his admission for their benefit in return for their keeping the news quiet until Ralph's account had appeared.

The story sounds fairly minor, but it pleased Ralph inordinately because no one else had it. Like his all-night interview with a murderer on a Fall River Line steamboat, it was a "beat."

Ralph liked to dwell on the romantic aspects of reporting, and "beats"— also known as "scoops" or, in proper Boston, "exclusives"—were part of the romance and legend of the newspaper world. Newspapers, so the legend held, lived or died according to their success in printing news their rivals did not have, or at least in printing news first. The tale was told of how the *Sun* once went so far as to print an obituary before its subject had expired. This happened in 1874 when the *Sun* alone learned that an eminent New York state abolitionist, Gerrit Smith, who had given John Brown financial backing before the raid at Harper's Ferry, lay gravely ill. An eloquent four-column tribute to Smith was prepared, and then, unable to forgo the opportunity to show up the rest of Park Row, the *Sun* went ahead and ran it under the headline "GERRIT SMITH'S DEATH-BED" without waiting for Smith to breathe his last. ("As we pen this line he may already have passed within the veil.") Smith cooperated by dying a few hours after his obituary appeared. "One of the grandest newspaper beats that ever happened in New York!" declared a *Sun* editor.

Reporting, it followed from the stress on beats, was an all-out, no-holds- barred competition. According to this view of the job, there could be no cooperation with rivals, no sharing of news. " 'Self-reliance' is the maxim of a good reporter," said Thomas Campbell-Copeland in his little instruc- tional book. "When on duty he asks no favors from 'the enemy.' " Giving news to "the representative of a rival paper" is "an inexcusable breach of trust."

Such unremitting competition may actually have prevailed in some situations. Theodore Dreiser claimed, for example, that reporters for competing newspapers in St. Louis in the early 1890s would scarcely speak to each other when out on assignment, lest they give away a scrap of news. Also, there were some reporters—Jacob Riis, for one—who shunned cooperation and operated as loners. By and large, however, beats were not nearly as important in the life of a reporter as Ralph and other purveyors of legend suggest.

The public was largely oblivious of them. With the rise of national news-gathering services and of city news bureaus that sold local news to any buyer—often as a sort of tip sheet to stories newspapers might want to cover more fully themselves—the great bulk of important stories became widely available. The basic menu of news consequently differed little from one paper to another: whether New Yorkers bought the *Herald* or the *Sun* or the *Times* in the morning, they learned about the latest tariff debate in Washington and the latest murder in Manhattan. If one paper did come up with a truly significant exclusive story, its competitors could usually cobble together reasonable facsimiles and rush new editions onto the streets before the public was any the wiser.

Nor for most reporters did the notion of uncompromising competition bear much relation to reality. They quickly learned that on the general run of assignments—fires, accidents, strikes—there was little to be gained by constantly trying to outdo others in digging up news and considerable to be risked. In cities where reporters from half a dozen or more papers found themselves covering the same story, it was highly unlikely that a reporter working alone would be able to come up with everything the rest of the group learned. If, on the other hand, he hit upon a significant piece of news and withheld it from his colleagues, thereby damaging their standing with their city editors, he could be sure that they would take advantage of the first opportunity to make him look bad. Survival generally dictated cooperation.

Ground rules evolved. Reporters who covered "departments" such as the police or city hall always worked in "combinations," the *Writer* magazine explained. "That is, they agree to exchange news in order to lighten their labors and, at the same time, avoid being beaten by one another." A reporter assigned to the municipal courts, for example, could not follow every trial, so he and his fellows would divide the load and share their findings. Edward W. Townsend of the *Sun* said that New York reporters covering the same story routinely divided it into segments called "ends." Each reporter covered his end and then all met to exchange material. City editors professed to disapprove of the practice, said Townsend, but in reality winked at it.

Turning Campbell-Copeland's ethical code inside out, reporters who joined combinations viewed as inexcusable any member's *failure* to share news. "Woe to the man who tries to be independent of a 'combination,' or, being in it, withholds and exclusively publishes an iota of news," warned the *Writer*. "Every hand is instantly raised against him, and if he is not so unmercifully 'scooped' before the next sun rises as to warrant his city editor recalling, if not discharging, him, he can be counted lucky." Townsend told of a reporter who held back part of his end on one story and subsequently was treated with such scorn by other reporters that he quit the profession.

Cooperation in reporting did not rule out competition in writing, Townsend stressed; there were usually many ways to tell the same story and some were better than others. But as for beats, Townsend, rated one of the *Sun's* most talented reporters and writers in the nineties, dismissed them as hardly worthy of serious concern. "Reporters who work year after year, side by side, seeking news under cheerless, disagreeable, and not infrequently dangerous conditions, develop a character of comradeship which destroys desire to beat or scoop each other," he said. "Indeed, most scoops result from accident or chance, and not from design, and are heard of more in the shop talk of novices than among experienced reporters."

Ralph was no novice when he wrote glowingly of beats, but Townsend gave a more accurate picture of the life of the typical reporter for a daily newspaper. Ralph must have covered his share of ends as a reporter in New York, and he must not have crossed up his colleagues, since if he had he would not have been as universally respected in the profession as he seems to have been. But by the time he began to reflect on his career and on journalism in general that sort of routine reporting was largely behind him. And even Ralph, writing in *Scribner's* magazine in 1893, acknowledged that some of the excitement had gone out of the quest for beats. In an earlier day an enterprising reporter could often score a beat by racing to the scene of a story aboard a hired locomotive or by using any means short of outright violence to monopolize the telegraph wire. But such tactics rarely paid off anymore, Ralph suggested, for "the great press associations now scatter the news of important happenings indiscriminately." What beats remained, said Ralph, were "more and more a product of intimate acquaintance with public men, and less and less a result of agility of mind and body."

Nevertheless, he continued to insist that a beat was still "the highest aim and the proudest achievement of a correspondent." And if Ralph lays too much stress on beats, Townsend dismisses them too quickly. Most of those who worked at reporting for any length of time could remember at least one occasion when they experienced an exhilarating sense of triumph at being first with an important story. Rivals may have scrambled so fast to catch up that the public never noticed, but within the newspaper world the achievement would be acknowledged and remembered.

Charles Rosebault remembered such an occasion. It occurred in January 1885, when he was a rank beginner at the *Sun,* only twenty years old. Like so many stories that represented professional success for the reporter, the news was sad: the country's foremost hero, General Grant, had cancer.

Managing editor Chester Lord assigned the story to Rosebault late on a Saturday night. It was rumored in Washington that Grant, now living in Manhattan, was suffering from cancer of the throat as a result of his heavy cigar smoking, and Lord wanted Rosebault to pursue the matter immediately. Grant and his family were believed to be out of the city, and all Rosebault had as a starting point was Lord's suggestion that a friend of Grant's on lower Fifth Avenue might know something.

Rosebault rang the friend's doorbell at 11:30 and was relieved when the man proved civil despite the hour. He had heard the general was ill but knew nothing further. Why didn't Rosebault try Grant's doctor—wasn't it a Dr. Fordyce Barker? A check of a city directory in a drugstore showed that Dr. Barker lived uptown, in the forties. Rosebault leaped aboard a horsecar. It seemed to crawl.

The doctor was still up. More luck yet, he was a courteous, gracious fellow, an Englishman, who seemed willing to talk about Grant. Ushering Rosebault into his library, he stopped short of an unequivocal diagnosis of cancer but left little doubt that this was indeed his diagnosis. Rosebault was ready to bolt for the door and race to the *Sun.* But hold on. Dr. Barker, it turned out, was a stickler for accuracy, and if the *Sun* was to report on the matter, it must be precise. So, as the minutes ticked away, he sat at the library table and wrote out all the facts about Grant's illness. Half a century later Rosebault recalled his churning emotions:

Already it was after midnight and the *Sun* office miles away. Will the old codger never finish!

Yes, he is done with his writing, he has read it over, but even with the surrender of the precious bit of paper the ordeal is not finished.

"Read it aloud, so that we may be sure you can master my writing," says the physician, smiling amiably. "I write such a wretched hand."

In calmer moments the reporter wondered how he had held back from throttling him. Here was a big news story, a sure beat on all the other papers, and he was being done out of it by a doddering old fossil!

At last! At last! He is out and free again. Little does he reck the biting night as he runs like a hound through slush and ice to the nearest station of the Third Avenue elevated road. His one chance is to catch a train within the next few minutes. He can give no heed to the probabilities that he will come a cropper on the slippery pavements. Panting, thoroughly winded, he forces his tired legs to forget their weariness, his sopping feet to skip like a fairy's as he leaps up the steps to the platform. Thank God! Virtue is rewarded. He lands on the train just as the guard is closing the gate!

No sooner in his seat than he has his roll of copy paper on his knee and his numbed fingers are racing the pencil across sheet after sheet. When the train rolls into City Hall station, his article is finished. Again he forces his stiffened body to the courser's pace, bounding up the two flights of stairs to the city room. Is he in time, after all?

The omniscient Clarke [the night city editor] is standing at the little dumb waiter which carries copy to the composing room, his omnipresent pipe tipped at an impertinent angle. He has just sent up the final item.

But there are still a few minutes' grace, and emergency only stimulates to action. Without moving from his place, he dashes off a heading . . . and skims the pages with a glance. It is all over in a jiffy and the manuscript is on its way.

"Looks like a beat," he remarks, with just a suggestion of satisfaction.

Sensational murders also brought the competitive instinct into play. Reporters may have gladly worked with combinations to cover run-of-the-mill robberies and mayhem, but when a headline-catching murder occurred some disregarded the usual rules and bent every effort toward staying a step ahead not only of other reporters but also of the police in solving the crime.

Staying a step ahead of the police was sometimes not difficult. Detectives, in the view of most reporters, were incompetents, "distinctly a lower order of men," as Ralph put it. In New York, according to Jacob Riis, the police said nothing to reporters about many crimes for fear of calling attention to the embarrassingly small number they solved. Will Irwin found that the police also solved few crimes in San Francisco, where he worked for the *Chronicle* before joining the *Sun*. But they took the opposite tack with the press, revealing all they knew in the hope that reporters would carry on from there with the investigation. "They appeared to proceed on the theory that if they gave reporters free access to all sources of information—like witnesses, the room where the crime occurred, the suspect, even the corpse—there was so much the less work for them," said Irwin.

In either situation, the field was wide open for reporters who wanted to play detective, and some reporters became specialists known as "detective-reporters." In Chicago there was the reporter—slender and rather frail and, of all things, a Harvard graduate—who, so the tale went, got so caught up in a trunk murder mystery that he traced the trunk in which the body had been found to a tenement flat and burst in upon the three men there with, "I say, are you the fellows that killed that man and put him in a trunk?" They were and he barely escaped with his life, but they were eventually hanged. In New York in the 1870s, according to an account left by Julius Chambers, he and half a dozen other *Herald* reporters set to work one evening at 11 P.M. investigating the bludgeon slaying of a Wall Street banker and by 2:30 A.M. had gathered enough evidence to beat the police to the punch with a story correctly pointing to a nephew as the killer. In 1891 when a would-be extortionist confronted financier Russell Sage in his Broadway office with a bomb—blowing up himself and Sage's clerk but not the elderly financier—the assailant's identity remained a mystery until a New York *World* reporter traced one of his suspender buttons and a scrap of his trousers to a tailor in Boston. He turned out to have been a young note broker who lived quietly with his parents, the last person on earth one would have suspected of such violence.

It was on this sort of case, not involving ordinary criminals, that reporters did best, Ralph suggested. Detectives knew criminals well, he said, and "Newspaper men cannot do as clever work as they where the case requires a knowledge of the faces, haunts, and habits of the evil-doers whom they pursue. It is when a crime is committed by some one not known to the police that the journalist and the detective are evenly matched." Ralph's theory was also borne out by a celebrated bit of sleuthing by one of his *Sun* colleagues, Charles W. Tyler, in an 1886 murder case.

The murder, vaguely reminiscent of the one Ralph had covered in a rural New Jersey village three years earlier, had occurred in Hackettstown, New Jersey, forty-five miles west of Manhattan. The victim, Tillie Smith, nineteen years old, had lived and worked as a kitchen maid at the local seminary, a coeducational Methodist boarding school. She was beaten, raped, and strangled on an April night, and her body was discovered in the morning by a passerby just beyond the rear grounds of the seminary. No signs of a struggle were found there, suggesting strongly that she was murdered elsewhere and her body carried to the spot.

The story initially drew a swarm of reporters from New York, Tyler among them. It had the ingredients both to titillate readers and to send shivers of horror through them. Tillie had violated the school matron's rules and sneaked out for a night on the town. She had dallied with two traveling salesmen, who, when questioned by the police, claimed they had last seen her heading up a dimly lit walk leading to the seminary, a forbidding red-brick building with a mansard roof surmounted by a clock tower. Tyler noted that within the seminary grounds Tillie would have had to pass through "a dark cluster of evergreens which whistle and moan dismally with every breath of wind."

But very quickly the story began to peter out. The most obvious suspects, the two salesmen, had convincing alibis. Similarly, in the first days after the murder, other suspects—another pair of transients, some young men of the town—were considered and dropped. The possibility that tramps, since vanished, had abducted Tillie and then killed her in a nearby unused barn was raised but left dangling inconclusively.

After only a week of investigation, the police, whose lackadaisical attitude lent substance to reporters' scorn for the calling, professed bafflement and, with a shrug, turned to other matters. A Pinkerton man who had been called in also gave up. And, in this instance showing no more enterprise than the police, so did most reporters. An exception was Charles Tyler of the *Sun*.

Tyler, a graduate of Kenyon College in Ohio who had worked in Cleveland before joining the *Sun* in 1885, had become obsessed with the murder of Tillie Smith. Over the next two weeks, with the *Sun's* readers looking over his shoulder each day, he worried the case like a dog with a bone. He reexamined old clues and hunted new ones. Again and again he turned over in his mind possible scenarios.

The beginning of the solution came as Tyler ruminated on the theory that Tillie had been killed by tramps in the barn. The theory was implausible, he decided. If the tramps had murdered Tillie in the barn, it would have made no sense for them to carry her body to the spot on the edge of the seminary grounds where it was found; almost certainly it would have been discovered later if left in the barn. Also, there was straw on the floor of the barn, which Tyler apparently visited several times, but no straw had been found on Tillie's clothes. On the other hand, there *was* dust on her clothes—this had given rise in the first place to the suggestion that a barn or shed might have been the scene of the murder, since the spring thaw had left the countryside muddy. And the dust confirmed that Tillie had indeed been killed in *some covered place,* though not the barn.

What place? It is obvious from Tyler's stories that the seminary presented itself almost immediately as the most likely possibility. Among the many shortcomings of the police investigation had been its failure to pursue inquiries there vigorously. But after all, Tyler reasons, if the traveling salesmen are to be believed—and they seem believable—when they last saw Tillie she was headed toward the seminary. Moreover, on his own he has come up with what he thinks may be an important clue. The night of her murder Tillie had been wearing buff-colored kid gloves with three pearl buttons. She was not wearing them when found. Does this not suggest that she had reached home that night and removed them—that she was killed not on her way home but *after* she had reached home?

Tyler's suspicions are soon focusing on the seminary's janitor and night watchman, James Titus. Titus is a family man with a decent reputation, and until now no one has implicated him. But Tyler had chatted with Titus not long after first arriving in Hackettstown and learned, though he made nothing of it at the time, that Titus had known Tillie planned to be out late the night she was killed. He knows further that Titus's janitorial quarters are just off a rear basement entrance by which Tillie would have returned to the seminary.

He assembles pieces of evidence. Reexamining the coat Tillie had been wearing, he finds that the dust on it appears to be from ashes—like the dust he notices around the furnace in surreptitious inspections of Titus's quarters. There is a red smudge on the coat; he runs his hand across a spill of red lead on the floor near the janitor's workbench and comes up with a matching smear. He takes another look at a hank of Tillie's long hair cut off in the autopsy. It contains tiny bits of wood shavings and, it turns out, there are similar shavings on the floor of Titus's room.

As Tyler reveals his detective work in print step by step, the *Herald* resumes interest in the case long enough to scoff, reporting that the insinuations against Titus are widely believed to be baseless. Tyler hints that prominent Methodists connected with the seminary are discouraging any moves to implicate the institution further in the affair. But he makes clear that he now has no doubts as to the murderer. Titus must be under great strain, Tyler writes. "It would be difficult to appreciate the sufferings of a man who, if he were guilty and shaken in nerve by the knowledge that many people suspected him of being guilty, should be obliged to go in the lonely hours of the night to the dismal spot where he did his awful deed."

The police are showing signs of life again, and a detective says that, come to think of it, the dust on Tillie's dress *had* struck him as like the dust found in furnace rooms. And so two and a half weeks after the murder Titus is arrested, the *Sun* story duly noting that the prosecutor had credited it with solving the case. Titus eventually confessed and was sentenced to life in prison.

Ralph had no particular appetite for writing about crime. "Neither criminals nor police have ever attracted or interested me, and detective-reporting has taken little of my time," he said, although he had been "obliged to give these people and subjects some attention." Nor, for that matter, did some of the other lures of reporting—the sense of being a privileged insider, the occasional taste of the power of the press, the thrill of a beat like young Charles Rosebault's—entirely capture the appeal the job held for Ralph.

Certainly, however, he must be counted among those who found the everyday business of reporting itself challenging and satisfying. The ideal reporter, as far as Ralph was concerned, was the one who stood ready to cover anything, anytime, anywhere. Such a paragon, said Ralph in one of his swaggering moods, "can make no appointment with wife or friend, even a day in advance. . . . He is not surprised, on coming back from a wearisome journey at midnight, to find that he is ordered to start on another expedition in five hours." Around the *Sun* office this selfless attitude was epitomized by a traveling correspondent named John R. Spears. Spears was sent off on an assignment to South America that lasted almost a year. He had scarcely crossed his threshold after returning when he received a telegram from the *Sun* saying "Please come to the office as soon as you conveniently can." He responded instantly, bag packed, and was dispatched on another journey.

For a thoroughbred reporter, subject matter was irrelevant. The chase was what mattered. "Until he has a thing to do," said Ralph of such a reporter, "it may not interest him at all; he may even congratulate himself that he is not called upon for the work in question. But when the order is given he is elated, nerved up, and pushed forward in a degree which swells with the difficulty of the task."

Given a modicum of talent, a reporter of this sort could be highly useful to a newspaper. He would undertake any assignment, unencumbered by ideological baggage or worries about whether the topic at hand comported with notions of professional dignity. It is less obvious, on the other hand, what satisfaction a reporter would draw from such a role, aside from earning a living. It demanded an almost childlike willingness to submit to the control of others. It also required, as Ralph made clear, frequent efforts to work up forced-draft enthusiasm—despite Will Irwin's cheerful view of the profession, not *every* assignment rose to the level of adventure—and for most reporters this became harder over time.

Ralph's reason for accepting the job's drawbacks seems to be that he drew immense satisfaction from being one of the best at his trade and at being recognized as such by his fellows. He was the supremely competent professional, the reporter a great newspaper counted on to bring back the story—to get what he was sent for. Achieving that standing in the hard business of reporting was Ralph's reward.

12. 'The Bright Young Men'

From the *Sun* for August 9, 1885:

> There have not often been gathered in one place so many men whose names have been household words, and whose lives have been inwoven with the history of a grave crisis in a great nation's life, as met yesterday in this city. The scene was before General Grant's tomb in Riverside Park; the space was less than goes to half an ordinary city block, and the names of the actors were William T. Sherman, Joe Johnston, Phil Sheridan, Simon B. Buckner, John A. Logan, W. S. Hancock, Fitz John Porter, Chester A. Arthur, Thomas A. Hendricks, John Sherman, Fitz Hugh Lee, John B. Gordon, David D. Porter, Thomas F. Bayard, John L. Worden, and a dozen others naturally linked in the mind with these greater men. Among them, like children amid gray heads, or shadows beside monuments, were other men more newly famous, and famous only for deeds of peace in times of quiet and plenty—a President, an ex-President, Governors, Mayors, and millionaires. And all were paying homage to the greatest figure of their time, whose mortal remains they pressed around with bared, bowed heads.

So began Ralph's account of the funeral of Ulysses S. Grant, who had died of cancer six months after Charles Rosebault's midnight interview with Dr. Fordyce Barker. The story filled the front page of the *Sun*. In rich detail it painted the events of "a beautiful golden day" on which a "madcap breeze" billowed the crepe and the world *would* "look gay in spite of the sombre drapings." It implied without saying that it was Grant the war hero, not the failed President, who would be remembered, and *Sun* readers, sharing in that unspoken consensus and also in the Victorian fascination with the ceremonies of death, could be counted on to devour every word.

Little escaped Ralph's notice. From early morning crowds of people, some wearing badges bearing Grant's portrait that they had purchased from vendors, were "jostling and pushing" for vantage points along Broadway, the initial line of march for the funeral procession. As the military units that would accompany the massive black hearse containing Grant's coffin assembled near City Hall Park, the air filled with "the blare and clash of great bands, the shrill, thin music of fifes, the rat-a-plan of drums, and the sound of thousands treading in unison."

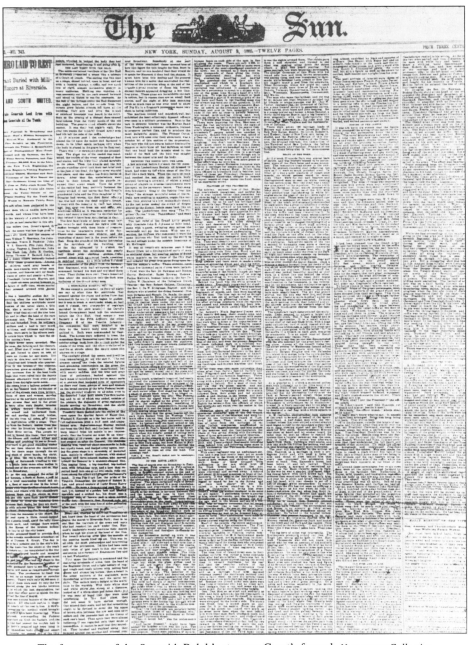

The front page of the *Sun* with Ralph's story on Grant's funeral. *Newspaper Collection, The New York Public Library, Astor, Lenox and Tilden Foundations*

Just before ten o'clock the nine-and-a-half-mile march up Manhattan to the tomb began, led by a general on horseback and his "clattering cavalcade of aides." Spit-and-polish contingents of soldiers and militia followed one after another, but the spectators' favorites were a bunch of sailors who looked as if they had never set foot on a drill field. Periodically a squad of the sailors "would career toward the people on one sidewalk, and then catch itself and lurch the other way, like the dying motions of a spinning plate." Less appreciated by the crowd were the New York policemen lining the route, who, Ralph observed, once again showed themselves constitutionally incapable of asking citizens to move "without a poke of the club here and there."

The cortege moved up Manhattan at a solemn pace, and not till late in the afternoon did all the elements reach the tomb site overlooking the Hudson at 122nd Street. Ralph, having gone on ahead, was waiting, and he watched as the procession traversed a final stretch of raw earth in the unfinished park along the river and "the approaching dust and bustle resolved itself in a mass of glittering steel and gay clothing." Moments later chaos threatened. A stream of carriages was disgorging a multitude of dignitaries, but no one seemed to be in charge of shepherding them to their places on the platform before the tomb, a temporary structure of brick and asphalt. The result was a stampede in which some of the most important personages were left behind. President Cleveland sat in his carriage, forgotten, until an army officer led him to the forefront of the assemblage.

Decorum returned. Two old foes—William Tecumseh Sherman and the Confederate general Joseph Johnston, whose armies had fought in Georgia—were seen to link arms. A bishop spoke, but his words did not carry from the platform even as far as the stand erected nearby for reporters. Taps sounded, lines of riflemen snapped off volleys, and cannon thundered. Soon the crowd was melting away, and in the early evening an ironworker named Patrick Cregan began bolting shut the steel case in which the coffin had been placed inside the tomb.

Even though the story would be remembered as one of Ralph's prodigious one-man feats, another *Sun* man must have picked up that last detail. Surely by then Ralph would have rushed for the Ninth Avenue elevated and hurried back to Park Row. Behind him lay a wearying job of reporting—being everywhere, seeing everything through the course of a long day. Ahead lay the even more wearying task of getting it all down on paper—seven columns of copy, in longhand, with a pencil, in an evening, six hours at most. It was a task requiring, to borrow the phrase of another

Sun reporter, "blazing concentration." His faculties galvanized by the knowledge that a story of great importance rested on his shoulders, Ralph must have found the sentences and paragraphs taking shape in his mind as fast as his hand could fly across the paper.

The result was far from perfect, but few other reporters would have had the eye, the stamina, and the fluency to match it. The measured rhythms of the opening paragraph—dashed off in minutes and probably never given a second glance—echo the slow beat of muffled drums. The rest of the thousands of words capture the majesty and pomp of the day, the homely touches, the jarring notes. It was the sort of performance that made the young newspapermen who gathered behind the prescription screen at Doc Perry's think of Ralph, in Willis Abbot's words, as the "most titanic of reporters, to whom a page of the paper written out in longhand was an 'ordinary stunt.' "

That Ralph was assigned to cover Grant's funeral confirms his high standing at the *Sun* in 1885. As newspaper offices went, the *Sun* was a fairly democratic place. Novice reporters occasionally got a crack at some of the better stories, and proven men could not expect to have every assignment just suited to their tastes. Earlier in 1885 Ralph had done the first of his two stints of writing about the legislature in Albany, important work perhaps but not the sort he normally preferred. When an event of such great moment as Grant's funeral came along, however, democracy went out the window, and the assignment fell to a reporter who had demonstrated beyond all doubt that he could handle the most demanding and important stories. At the age of thirty-two, moving into his second decade on the *Sun,* Ralph had established a solid claim to those credentials. Many years later he observed wearily that "the higher you go the harder you must work," but for the moment what could be finer than to be acknowledged as one of the best of a small circle of talented journalists who turned out a newspaper they were convinced was the best?

By the late 1880s the *Sun* had taken a step or two in the direction of the look and feel of a modern newspaper. Some days the major story of the day ran in the far-right column instead of on the left, where it invariably appeared in the 1870s. The four-page *Sun* was a thing of the past. Weekdays the paper was six or eight pages, Sundays twenty. Charles Dana having long since abandoned his notion of a paper supported entirely by circulation revenues, advertisements for nerve tonics, French underwear, and hundred-dollar building lots on Long Island filled the back pages. On the whole, however, the *Sun* of the late eighties did not look remarkably different from the *Sun* of the seventies. The front page remained as conservative as ever, with seven single columns running from top to bottom and the most modest of headlines. Although illustrations—cuts of bare-knuckle boxers, a diagram of a ship collision, drawings made from Jacob Riis's slum photographs—were more common than formerly, they remained rare; as late as 1894 Dana was still insisting that extensive use of pictures in newspapers was "a passing fashion."

Change also came only slowly to the *Sun* office. In the mid-eighties electric lights dangling from a jungle of overhead wires replaced the gas jets in the newsroom. (A *Sun* reporter who witnessed an early demonstration of Thomas Edison's bulb burst into the office at midnight and exclaimed: "He's got it—we are going to have the electric light in every part of every house and over every desk in this room.") Also, starting in 1880 you could ask central for Nassau 61 and get the *Sun* newsroom on the telephone. As at most newspapers, however, for many years use of the office telephone was extremely sparing, because of both the limited reach of the network and the initial uneasiness about conducting interviews except in face-to-face encounters.*

Another product of nineteenth-century technology, the typewriter, would make no headway whatever in the *Sun* office till after the turn of the century. Following the introduction of the first satisfactory machines around 1880, most newspapers had initially shared the *Sun's* reluctance to switch to them, despite the obvious advantage in legibility. One prominent editor declared typewriters fit only as "servants of commerce." But by the early 1890s they were in use in many newsrooms. At the *Sun,* however, managing editor Chester Lord was convinced that the machines resulted in a "diffuse" style, and his reporters continued to write their copy in pencil long after reporters elsewhere were tapping out their stories on typewriters.

In other ways as well, the working conditions of *Sun* reporters changed little over the years. The newsroom was still a shambles in the late 1880s, reflecting to some extent the indifference of editors and reporters to their physical surroundings on the job but also a powerful emotional attachment

---

*Besides the usual argument that it was necessary to see a news source to assess the truth and meaning of spoken words, William Salisbury offered another ground for caution. He told of interviewing James J. Hill, the railroad tycoon, by telephone only to have Hill, after his remarks had unfavorable repercussions, disown them by denying that he had "seen" a reporter on the day in question.

to them—a feeling that a place so conducive to artistic journalism should not be tampered with. The desks had only become more battered, the wastebaskets still overflowed onto the floor, and the walls were as begrimed as ever with smoke and soot. Once every decade or so a crew of painters came in after the last edition had gone to press and slapped a coat of yellow calcimine over the dirt on the walls, but the yellow quickly decayed to the normal dingy brownish hue.

In 1889 Joseph Pulitzer of the *World* began building his new skyscraper headquarters across Frankfurt Street from the *Sun*. When finished in 1890 it towered twenty stories above Park Row and was capped by a magnificent gilded dome. It made the *Sun's* squat red-brick home—a "shabby little building," said the *World* in the course of the editorial sniping that had been going on between the two papers ever since Pulitzer came to town in 1883—look more insignificant than ever. It also symbolized Pulitzer's victory over the *Sun,* as well as the rest of Park Row, in the battle for circulation supremacy in New York.

With an occasional setback, and some renewed competition from the *Herald,* the *Sun* under Dana had led the morning field in circulation through the 1870s and into the 1880s. The *Sun* attained its peak sales, something over 150,000 copies a day, early in the eighties. The *Herald* was close on its heels, but the *World,* the *Tribune,* and the *Times* trailed far behind. Then Pulitzer bought the *World.*

Pulitzer represented a new wave in journalism; indeed, his innovations came to be called the "new journalism." Some of his ideas had clearly been inspired by the *Sun,* which back in 1871 Pulitzer had called "the best newspaper in the world." But Dana never stopped professing scorn. In 1894, with obvious reference to Pulitzer—whose rival in sensationalism, William Randolph Hearst, had not yet arrived on the New York scene— Dana said in a lecture at Cornell that an editor had to decide whether he wished to produce a newspaper for sensible men or for fools.

> Now I would not be understood as intimating that there is anything unworthy or below anybody's dignity in making a newspaper for fools. In the first place, there is impressive evidence to show that the fools form a large part of any community. . . . So that it is perfectly right to provide for the fools in special newspapers; and that duty, as you may have noticed, is extensively and conscientiously performed by gifted and conspicuous individuals; and I have heard that some of them make money by it.

The *World* did print some cheap sensations, and, as Theodore Dreiser found in his brief tour as a *World* reporter, it sometimes stretched the truth for the sake of entertaining the public. Nevertheless, Dana did not give Pulitzer due credit. Besides the crime and scandal, which the *Sun* itself exploited, besides the lavish use of illustrations and the attention-getting crusades, such as an enormously successful one to raise money for a pedestal for the Statue of Liberty in 1885, the *World* offered solid coverage of important news and a consistent, liberal editorial policy that championed the cause of the poor and attacked corrupt wealth.

What was really troubling Dana was that in the decade following Pulitzer's acquisition of the *World* in 1883, the circulation of the *Sun* had plummeted. From the peak of around 150,000, it slid to 80,000 in the late eighties, then dropped to 70,000 by 1893. During the same period the circulation of the *World* was growing tenfold, from 20,000 to 200,000. The *Sun* also fell behind the *Herald* again and even lagged behind two newcomers in the morning field, the *Press* and the *Journal,* though it held its own against a modestly resurgent *Tribune* and still had a wide lead over the *Times.* Contributing to the *Sun's* troubles were moves by its competitors to match its two-cent price and its assaults on Grover Cleveland in the 1884 Presidential campaign, which put the paper out of step with the thousands of its readers who were loyal to the New York governor. But whatever the reason or reasons, the *Sun's* period of greatest prosperity was clearly over by the mid-1880s.

Considering that a large part of the reading public obviously disagreed, one might wonder why those who wrote for the *Sun* in the eighties and nineties were so cocksure of the superiority of their newspaper. But cocksure they were, and a core of loyal readers backed them up. Moreover, many who worked for other newspapers continued to acknowledge the *Sun* as a model for their craft, reinforcing its reputation as "the newspaperman's newspaper." Paradoxically, in fact, the mid-eighties marked the beginning of a period that would come to be remembered as a sort of golden age for the *Sun.* "By this time," said Frank O'Brien, the paper's historian and an unabashed partisan, "Dana had framed a newspaper organization more nearly perfect than any other in America."

Grouping about him men suited to the *Sun,* to himself, and to one another, he had created a literary world of his own—a seeing, thinking, writing world of keen objective vision. Men of a hundred various minds, each with his own style, his own ambition, his own manner of life, the *Sun* staff focused their abilities into the one flood of light that came out every morning.

Charles Dana turned seventy in 1889. Still straight-backed and sturdy, he had by then taken on a patriarchal appearance—bald dome fringed with white, flowing white beard, and small wire-rimmed spectacles, through which he peered at copy with his head tilted back. Despite the *Sun's* circulation losses, he had become a wealthy man. Though seemingly oblivious to his surroundings at work, he had an exquisitely furnished town house at Sixtieth Street and Madison Avenue in Manhattan and a country home set amid lavish gardens on a forty-acre private island linked to the north shore of Long Island by a bridge. He delighted in fine wines, raised rare orchids, and on trips to Europe collected Chinese porcelains and paintings by Corot, Millet, Rousseau, and Courbet.

Perhaps he departed from the *Sun* office a bit earlier in the afternoon than he had as a younger man, particularly when catching a steamboat to commute to Long Island in the summer. But he was still in full command. He chatted with callers and with his editorial writers, summoned the city editor with a bell when he picked up an idea for a story, and strode with "masterful tread" into the newsroom at 2 P.M. to inquire of his managing editor, "Well, Mr. Lord, what is the news?" He dictated his own editorial contributions to his secretary, Tom Williams, and edited the proofs of editorials with bold, quick strokes of his pencil, his body swaying back and forth as he made corrections.

To the public, which knew Dana only as he was reflected by his editorial page, he remained an often mean-spirited, vindictive man. Though feuds between editors were common throughout the nineteenth century, Dana's attacks on Joseph Pulitzer embarrassed even some on the *Sun* staff. The *Sun* called the *World's* proprietor "Judas Pulitzer" and "a renegade Jew," cried "Move on, Pulitzer, move on!," and once printed a Pulitzer speech in dialect (Pulitzer had emigrated from Hungary as a young man and retained a slight accent).

Pulitzer was capable of fighting back and giving as good as he got—for a time the *World* gleefully changed Dana's middle name from Anderson to Ananias, the name of the Biblical liar—but another of the *Sun's* prime editorial targets in the eighties, Rose Elizabeth Cleveland, was not so resilient. Miss Cleveland, the President's sister and his hostess in the White House before his marriage, was a woman of some literary pretensions. She made the mistake of using her new prominence to advance her literary fortunes, eventually going so far as to assume the editorship of a Chicago literary magazine.

In 1885 and 1886 she published her reflections on such varied topics as the nature of poetry, Joan of Arc, and the perils of alcohol, the style running heavily to French phrases, exclamation points, and interminable sentences. The *Sun's* editorial page pounced on her mercilessly, printing columns of the awful stuff and commenting on it with mock seriousness. "It is gratifying to observe that Miss Cleveland's daring excursions into some of the most difficult regions of thought and speculation are regarded with almost universal respect," said one of the tongue-in-cheek editorials. "Nearly all admire the courage with which she attacks great problems of life and faith that have been for centuries the despair of some of the wisest men the world has seen."

Admittedly, to a large extent Rose Elizabeth brought her troubles on herself. All the same, the cruelty of the *Sun's* ridicule, which soon led Miss Cleveland to withdraw from the literary scene—"entirely broken down" in health, according to her physician—is undeniable. So is the broader charge that Dana sometimes took perverse delight in cutting public idols down to size simply for the sake of a good rumpus. But it must also be acknowledged that in a generally pompous age the *Sun's* editorial page had the redeeming virtues of wit and playfulness. It did not even take the *Sun* seriously all the time. Once when a "flimsy" of an important Presidential message fluttered out a window near the telegraph editor's desk on a warm evening and never made it into print, Dana delightedly accepted the suggestion that the *Sun* explain the omission to readers by announcing that the message had been eaten by the office cat. For years thereafter, whenever the *Sun* missed an important story, that was the explanation offered. The cat, said one editorial, had a particularly voracious appetite for speeches on tariffs and "twelve-column articles on the restoration of the American merchant marine."

Within the *Sun* office, Dana inspired only greater devotion as the years went by. "He hated all that was dull," said his eventual successor as editor, Edward Mitchell, and thus made the *Sun* an interesting place to work day after day. Moreover, said Mitchell, Dana "would blithely risk a libel suit any day" to expose a humbug, and when a *Sun* staff member provoked the fury of powerful interests he remained unperturbed. Ralph said that Dana once turned away a delegation demanding Ralph's discharge because of something he had written while assigned to Albany. "I suppose he does make mistakes," Ralph quoted Dana as saying, "but we will keep him because he is honest."

On another occasion a leading merchant called on Dana to complain that

Charles A. Dana in 1894 at the age of seventy-five. *From* Memoirs of an Editor *by Edward Page Mitchell (Charles Scribner's Sons, an imprint of Macmillan Publishing Company, New York, 1924), p. 230.*

a *Sun* reporter had rejected the merchant's denial that he was involved in a certain financial deal. "This morning he printed the story and made me out a liar," protested the merchant, according to one account of the incident.

"Wasn't the story true?" mildly insinuated Mr. Dana.

"Well, er, yes, I suppose so; but I did not want anything said about it."

"Ah, um," said Mr. Dana, meditatively, "that is bad, very bad; I will see what can be done. It won't do to have a man on the newspaper who insists on telling the truth, will it?"

The merchant got the point and withdrew, muttering about "impertinent" reporters as he went out.

Dana had little day-to-day contact with most of the *Sun's* reporters and lower-level editors, though he never became a remote figure like Pulitzer, cruising the world on a yacht. But while words like "love" would usually be out of place in the cynical atmosphere of a newsroom, Dana's unyielding support for his staff in the face of pressure, coupled with his quickness to give credit for good work, can only be said to have made him loved in the *Sun's* ramshackle third-floor newsroom. In 1915, many years after his death, when the *Sun* was at last moving to more respectable quarters, veterans of the old days gathered there one last time for a farewell dinner. They reminisced about Dana, and when one called him "the kindliest man that ever was supreme in a great newspaper" he seems to have summed up the feelings of all those who ever worked for Charles Dana.

Of the editors who sat in the newsroom by the windows overlooking Park Row and City Hall Park, two loomed particularly large starting in the 1880s. One was Chester Lord, the managing editor from 1880 to 1913. The other was Selah Clarke, the night city editor over almost the same span.

Lord had the overall responsibility for filling the *Sun's* news columns. From his rolltop desk he surveyed the globe for potential news each day and ensured that the *Sun* stood ready to cover it. As a magazine of the period put it, "He sets the vast engines of his department at work as easily as the chief engineer of an ocean steamship sets his ponderous and complicated machines in operation." That was a bit grand, considering the relatively modest size of his staff. In the early nineties the *Sun* had some two dozen reporters in New York, plus correspondents in Washington, Chicago, and London; beyond these, it relied heavily on part-time correspondents scattered around the United States and abroad.

But Lord, in his mature years a stolid, imposing man with a graying walrus mustache, managed his limited resources superbly. Having mastered the temper that in his first days on the *Sun* in the early 1870s had almost caused him to come to blows with Amos Cummings, the managing editor at the time, Lord was an island of calm amid the crises that are a daily part of the newspaper business. Among reporters, he was appreciated for his trust in the judgment of men sent off on distant assignments and for his steadying encouragement. David Graham Phillips, catapulted with no notice one summer day in 1892 into a violent coal miners' strike in Tennessee, his wardrobe limited to the dandyish white summer suit he happened to be wearing when he showed up for work, got this telegram from Lord after wiring his first story:

Take the entire matter into your hands. Do exactly what you think should be done. Go anywhere you like only continue to send us the magnificent news that you have been sending if such a thing is possible. We are tickled almost to death. You have laid out every other newspaper in the country.

Powerful as Lord's impact could be in such a situation, day in and day out Selah Clarke played a larger role in the lives of the reporters in the *Sun* newsroom. As night city editor, "Boss Clarke" took over from the city editor each afternoon around five o'clock. He sent men out on late assignments, assessed stories as they were turned in, and took a vigorous hand in editing them through the course of the evening. "The city editor of a New York newspaper sows seeds; the night city editor re-seeds barren spots, waters wilting items, and cuts and bags the harvest," explained Frank O'Brien.

Tall, thin, and nervous, Clarke puffed rapidly on a clay pipe as he worked and made trips to the water cooler every ten minutes. An introverted man who sought relaxation in solving problems in higher mathematics and writing Greek limericks, he was so shy that when his *Sun* colleagues staged a testimonial affair after his retirement he refused to attend. He didn't "see how a common, decent man" could show up at a dinner in his own honor, he said in a note of regret. Clarke, a bachelor, was particularly shy where women were concerned. When Lord hired the first woman for the regular newsroom reporting staff after the turn of the century—before that women employed by the *Sun* were limited to submitting articles written outside the office, mainly on fashions and society—her presence completely unnerved Clarke. Lord had to move the woman, first to a desk behind the bookshelves in the *Sun's* library, then to an uptown office the *Sun* had opened by then.

Not all memories of Clarke were fond. His own service as a reporter at the pre-Pulitzer *World,* where he had briefly been Ralph's reporting colleague, lay far behind him, and he sometimes placed unthinking demands on reporters. Charles Rosebault recalled an occasion in 1884 when a body was found buried in an ash heap in the basement of a Chinese laundry a block from the *Sun* office. Clarke summoned a young reporter.

"Feel all the bones, they may have been broken," he directed. "And look carefully at the teeth for gold fillings."

The body had been buried a long time and looked like a mummy, with the ashes clinging like a cere-cloth. The mouth was firmly closed, the lips tight against the teeth. Even the police pitied the poor reporter. But the man was not yet born who dared return and face Clarke with his duty unperformed.

Judging from the revoltingly graphic story that appeared on the front page of the *Sun* the next morning, the reporter did indeed do exactly as he had been told. "The teeth were good, and none of them was missing or filled," he dutifully reported.

Boss Clarke's nervousness could drive to distraction a reporter racing to finish a story late at night. Will Irwin recalled covering a horrendous train wreck in New Jersey after the turn of the century and returning to the *Sun* around seven o'clock in the evening with a wealth of vivid material. Clarke told him to "let it run." Irwin began writing, turning in his copy a sheet at a time, and almost immediately Clarke started pestering him with questions. How did Irwin know the exact moment of the crash? He had checked the clock in the engine and obtained the statement of the train crew. How did he know the speed of the train? From the indicator in the engine. When would the casualty list be ready?

"He was like a sticky, persistent fly when one is trying to sleep," said Irwin. As the evening wore on toward midnight and the deadline for the first edition neared, Clarke grew still edgier, and the interruptions came at shorter intervals. Finally Irwin could bear it no longer. He leaped up and screamed, "For God's sake, will you leave me alone!"

Clarke retreated and said no more. Irwin's story was well received—even by Clarke, though that had to be deduced from his manner the next day, since it was not his style to praise. And Irwin conceded that Clarke, for all his chivvying, was an exceptional editor. He had a memory that seemed to embrace everything the *Sun* had ever printed and could often dredge up a fact that snapped a story into sharp focus or prevented an embarrassing error. Sometimes he could put his finger on the point of a story when the reporter had lost his way in a thicket of facts. Sometimes, in Frank O'Brien's words, "by the eliding stroke of his pencil and the insertion of perhaps a single word he could change the commonplace to literature."

In the end, most *Sun* reporters came to revere Clarke. "No reporter ever worked on the *Sun* but wished, at one time or another, to thank Clarke for saving him from himself," said O'Brien. "Clarke had the faculty of seeing instantly the opportunity for improvement that the reporter might have seen an hour or a day later."

In the 1880s and 1890s, as in the 1870s, youth was the rule among *Sun* reporters. Arthur Brisbane joined the staff at the age of eighteen and became the *Sun's* London correspondent at twenty-two. David Graham Phillips was an established star at twenty-three. Reporters in their thirties— in the late eighties Ralph was in his mid-thirties—were old-timers. With the passing of time, a rising proportion of the reporters had attended college. Dana had always valued higher education, and Chester Lord was convinced that college fitted a reporter to cope better with the personalities and issues newspapers dealt with—though he probably wouldn't have pressed the point with an old printer like Ralph. Lord, who had spent some time at Hamilton College without graduating, relieved Dana of most of the burden of hiring reporters after 1880.

Dana habitually referred to his reporters as "the *Sun's* bright young men." He once described them as "accomplished men, men familiar with every branch of study that intellectual young men ordinarily devote themselves to, men who have prepared themselves either by college studies or by practical life . . . for the peculiar duty they have undertaken . . . men of extraordinary talent, knowing the world well, able to see through a deception, and sometimes able to set one up."

If "bright young men" sounds a trifle patronizing, and if Dana in general appears to lay it on a bit thick, no matter. The reporters treasured his every word of praise, and it served only to build a loyalty that embraced the entire *Sun* organization as well as Dana himself. In a field in which tender egos are the norm and complaining and backbiting endemic, *Sun* staff members worked together in astounding harmony. Surely on occasion professional rivalries produced flare-ups of jealousy and pique in the newsroom, but few hints show up in the recollections of those who knew Dana's *Sun* best. Each day, so the rosy legend ran, reporters gathered around the desk of the colleague who had produced the day's best story to offer their congratulations.

In respites from labor *Sun* men gloried in each other's company. Charles Rosebault remembered delightful supper breaks at a French restaurant on Fulton Street where editors and reporters gathered around a big table— "merry, jostling fellows, rattling off quip and story," dining well for fifty cents or lavishly, complete with wine and a ten-cent cigar, for a dollar. The *Sun* was like a club, said Ralph. "No taint of caste poisons its atmosphere or forces its workers into cliques, and when its men have no work to do they play together, at cards, or chess, or gymnastics, or whatever."

Sometimes *Sun* men must have struck outsiders as arrogant. It was widely acknowledged by most journalists, wrote *Sun* man Julian Ralph in 1893, that his newspaper was "the most brilliant and most wide-awake product of their profession." *Sun* men lorded it over reporters on other papers, confident that they would always come up with offbeat tales missed by their rivals and that on any widely covered story the *Sun's* version would be superior. "There were some excellent writers on all the big papers," Rosebault conceded. "But it was beyond dispute that usually the *Sun* yarn did seem to be the best. Otherwise the paper would not have won the reputation it had in newspaper offices throughout the country for being the best-written paper extant."

However much such self-congratulation may grate, it was in truth easy to make a case that the *Sun* was in a class by itself. One indication was that other newspapers constantly sought to hire away men trained by the *Sun* and that many who left became leading figures elsewhere. One of the best known was Arthur Brisbane, recruited first by Joseph Pulitzer, then lured away from Pulitzer by William Randolph Hearst to become one of his top editors and writers. Another was Carr Van Anda, a *Sun* reporter and editor for sixteen years until Adolph Ochs made him managing editor of the rejuvenated New York *Times* in 1904.

Moreover, a remarkable number of men who worked at the *Sun* at some point in their careers won at least passing fame as writers, one reason being that the atmosphere at the paper was unusually hospitable for those who wanted to try their hand at something beyond the daily assignments. The Sunday edition, which regularly carried fiction by such writers as Henry James, Bret Harte, Robert Louis Stevenson, and Rudyard Kipling, welcomed sketches and short stories by staff members, who thereby obtained not only an outlet for their creative energies but also extra income.

Ralph, for one, took advantage of the opportunity, giving birth in the early 1880s to a character known as "the German barber," who for some time spouted his opinions on all manner of topics every Sunday. The pieces were written in an all but impenetrable dialect for an age that had a taste for such things, but they are interesting as revelations of some of Ralph's peeves and prejudices. He was annoyed by the rich man who went to Delmonico's and bought "a tinner vich gosts so much vot he bays his glerk a whole veek to lif." And he was convinced that the Wall Street of his day was rigged against the ordinary citizen: "der negst ding ve vill all vake up some tay und find dey got a gorner in larker peer." Also, New York cops were bullies, prizefighting was a stupid sport, and there was something unsavory about politicians who lived in mansions and made a big display of giving free coal to the poor.

The German barber sketches and later character-based series by others won followings and made the *Sun* talked about. Like news stories, however, they carried no bylines, and the *Sun* men who attracted notice as writers from the public pursued other avenues. In the 1890s, Ralph, while still a reporter, would become well known as an author of magazine articles and books. Franklin Fyles, who covered the Beecher trial for the *Sun* as a reporter and later served as the paper's drama critic, wrote successful Broadway plays while still showing up in the newsroom each day. Edward Townsend and Jesse Lynch Williams, reporting colleagues on the *Sun* in the nineties, became the authors of both popular plays and novels. Among the other graduates of the *Sun* newsroom in the same era who made names for themselves as novelists were David Graham Phillips and Samuel Hopkins Adams. For a time, said Edward Mitchell, the newsrooms of both the *Sun* and the *Evening Sun* "were somewhat of a preparatory school for writers of fiction." Even if they made their mark after leaving the *Sun,* such writers remained identified with the paper, contributing to its reputation as a hotbed of creativity.

What counted most with Dana and Lord and Clarke, of course, was the literary talent that showed up in the news columns of the *Sun.* And with newswriting conventions not yet rigidly established in the late 1800s and early 1900s, there was considerable opportunity for a reporter to display originality and a personal style in covering a murder, a flood, or a society wedding.

One convention that definitely had not taken hold at the *Sun* in those days was that you should jam all the essential facts into the beginning of a story. If there was any characteristic approach at all at the *Sun* for stories beyond the most routine, it was the narrative. The *Sun,* said Frank O'Brien, avoided "leading paragraphs which told over again what was in the headlines and were merely a prelude to a third and detailed telling. The *Sun* reporter began at the beginning."

Sometimes the result could be maddening, with the reader forced to wade through several paragraphs before getting even a glimmer of the point of the story. But it could be highly effective with the right story, such as David Graham Phillips's account of the hunt for a child lost in the Catskill Mountains in 1890. Under the headline "Lost Baby Found"—so readers knew they could look forward to a happy ending—the story began with an account of the forming of a friendship between a small boy and his dog, told how they wandered off into the woods one day and of the agonizing two-day search that followed, and climaxed after a column and a half with the child's return to his mother's arms.

In a refinement of the style, some *Sun* reporters, including Ralph, were learning to start their stories at the climactic point and then backtrack to the events leading up to it, a technique that sharpened the focus and enhanced clarity but retained drama, suspense, and narrative interest. That was, for example, the approach Ralph used in covering Grant's funeral in 1885 and would also use to great advantage in his account of the day the jury returned its verdict in the trial of Lizzie Borden in 1893.

Whatever the precise technique, "To invent some new way of presenting an old topic was the thing," said Chester Lord. He described the *Sun's* reporters as "a delicious aggregation of mental acrobats" who went about their assignments with a daredevil spirit, always reaching for the original, vivid way to tell a story. Sometimes their reach exceeded their grasp and the results were embarrassing, but they succeeded often enough to give the *Sun* in its golden age a reputation for literary flair that no other newspaper matched.

"Some one said of Ralph," recalled Frank O'Brien, "that he 'could write five thousand words about a cobblestone.' If he had done that, it would have been an interesting cobblestone. He had a passion for detail, but it was not the lifeless and wearisome detail of the realistic novelist. When he wrote half a column about a horse eating a woman's hat, the reader became well acquainted with the horse, the woman, and the crowd that had looked on."

O'Brien doesn't say when Ralph wrote the story about the horse that ate the hat, so there is no practical way to find it. But the reference does underscore the range of material a *Sun* reporter was allowed to exercise his talents on, and O'Brien is more specific about two stories written by Ralph in the late 1880s that also illustrate the diversity of assignments a reporter like Ralph undertook.

One was the *Sun's* principal front-page story on the late-winter blizzard that paralyzed New York in March 1888. Snow began falling in the early hours of a Monday. By morning a wind that reached at least seventy-five miles an hour—at that point the Weather Bureau's gauge atop a building on Lower Broadway broke—was piling the snow into drifts that eventually mounted to the second-story windows of brownstones and touched elevated tracks. The temperature was near zero. Both elevated trains and horsecars had stopped running and most people did not try to get to work, but Ralph struggled the two and a half miles from his house in the heart of Brooklyn to the Brooklyn Bridge on foot. The bridge trains, it turned out, had also come to a halt, and the pedestrian walkway was closed. Ralph crossed the East River on a Fulton Street ferry that felt its way through the blinding snow.

Around noon Ralph arrived at the *Sun,* which must have been as shorthanded as other businesses. He spent the day reporting as best he could. Most telephone and telegraph lines were down. He drew on his own experiences in the morning, braved the storm again to explore the immediate environs of the office, and surveyed the scene from the newsroom windows. His story began:

> It was as if New York had been a burning candle upon which nature had clapped a snuffer, leaving nothing of the city's activity but a struggling ember.

And from a bit further on:

> The wind howled, whistled, banged, roared, and moaned as it rushed along. It fell upon the house sides in fearful gusts, it strained great plate glass windows, rocked the frame houses, pressed against doors so that it was almost dangerous to open them. It was a visible, substantial wind, so freighted was it with snow. It came in whirls, it descended in layers, it shot along in great blocks, it rose and fell and corkscrewed and zigzagged and played merry havoc with everything it could swing or batter or bang or carry away.

The rest of the two columns assembled the images he had accumulated through the day—shuttered businesses; the moonscape presented by Printing House Square, where snow was burying abandoned horsecars; a fire engine floundering through snowdrifts toward a blaze; men stumbling along in outlandish getups of fur and oilskin and anything else that could keep out the weather; sparrows huddled on the windowsills of the *Sun* building. "What a storm! What a day!" Ralph exclaimed at one point.

Getting out a paper as usual in such circumstances must have been satisfying, though it probably reached only a handful of readers. When the *Sun* staff finished its work late at night, snow was still falling—the city would remain tied up for days—and going home was out of the question. The nearby hotels were long since overflowing with people stranded by the storm. Doc Perry's was almost certainly open, however, since Charley Perry lived at the Astor House, located on Broadway at the foot of Park Row, and would have had little trouble making it to his drugstore. By then he was doing business on the ground floor of the *Sun* building, and one suspects that Ralph and his colleagues gathered in the back room behind the prescription screen, sipped whiskey from green glasses, and swapped tales about covering the Blizzard of Eighty-eight.

Chester Lord was said to have valued reporters with specialized knowledge of politics, finance, or some other field, but at the same time there was a swaggering attitude around the *Sun* office that a good reporter could handle anything. Thus, the job of covering one of the big football games of the year, a festive Thanksgiving Day contest between Yale and Princeton, was passed from one top reporter to another as a sort of reward, knowledge of the sport not being a prerequisite. The tale was told that when Ralph's turn came he wrote a description of the affair that so captivated the copy desk that his failure to mention the score was overlooked.

The lead story about the 1889 Yale-Princeton game sounds like Ralph. It runs two columns and, sure enough, never does spell out the final score (neither does the headline). It is followed by two and a half columns of more detailed analysis of the game obviously written by someone other than the author of the principal article. The supplementary material must have been judged necessary because the author of the principal article, presumably Ralph, like many *Sun* readers, still had only the haziest understanding of the relatively new game of football.

All the same, the account that appears to be Ralph's work, which fills the right-hand column of page 1 and continues on page 2, has an innocent charm. It begins:

A huge mud-covered oval with a rectangle faintly indicated upon it in white, two swaying groups of canvas-jacketed young men facing each other, a big melon-shaped ball, now out of sight as the two groups plunged savagely at each other above it, now soaring aloft far over their heads; on every side, bank on bank of human beings, more than 25,000 in number, jumping up and down in their places, throwing up their hats, waving canes and umbrellas, and a flutter of bunting, while the air trembled and the welkin rang with such yells and screams and bellowing of horns as are indescribable—that was the entertainment at Berkeley Oval, on the hillside back of Morris Dock station on the Hudson River Railroad.

Most of the rest of the material on page 1 focused on the crowd—the array of coaches drawn up on one sideline, the small boys selling seats on benches they constructed from barrels and boards, William K. Vanderbilt and party passing around a large goblet of champagne. Just before the reader turned to the continuation on page 2, the author remembered that a football game was the cause of all the excitement. The Yale team, "in white shirts and dark blue stockings, appeared, and began pitching practice balls about the field and dropping on them somewhat gingerly, being willing to wait until business required it before wallowing in that mud."

The Princetons were right on their heels and for full six minutes there was a steady roar of voices with no special cry to be distinguished. It might have lasted longer, but the two handsome gentlemen who were to judge the game got out among the players, and straightway the two teams stripped for the fight and got in line, with Princeton and the ball at the east facing Yale and the wind, and there they stood for a minute, swaying about, lifting first one foot and then the other, swinging their arms and clutching the air with their fingers, while some of them worked their jaws as if anxious to bite something or somebody.

From there on the story grows increasingly vague about what is happening on the field. There are rushes and dropkicks and loud cheers, and, summing up, "everyone who understood the game looked on in wonder at the science and skill displayed on both sides, and those who didn't understand the game grew excited over the dash, the pluck, and the endurance displayed."

Those who cared to know the final score could find it in the last line of the supplementary analysis: Princeton 10, Yale 0.

An all-rounder at the *Sun* could also expect to write about politics from time to time. Ralph had covered a President, Chester Arthur, as far back as 1882 and had mingled with politicians in Albany in the mid-eighties. In the late eighties and early nineties he would plunge more deeply into political reporting.

13. At Washington City

Election nights were exciting, demanding times at the *Sun* in the eighties and nineties. Memories of the protracted dispute over the results of the contest between Hayes and Tilden for the White House in 1876 remained fresh, and vote-counting was still a drawn-out and often subjective process. Many political bosses did not hesitate to doctor returns. Some partisan newspapers added to the confusion by indulging in wishful thinking and giving their side the benefit of every doubt.

As far as the *Sun* was concerned, Chester Lord had resolved when he became managing editor to have no part in such practices. In the close presidential election of 1884 he startled some in the newsroom by sending the paper to press with an early indication of a victory by Grover Cleveland, whom Dana had bitterly opposed. Soon, however, the whole staff was taking pride in the *Sun's* reputation for sorting through the conflicting, sometimes manipulated figures that flooded into the newsroom on election nights and coming up with quick, honest counts. The swift calculations of results, said Ralph in an account of such an evening he wrote for *Scribner's Magazine* in 1894, were made "as sparks might be counted while they fly from the shapeless iron on a blacksmith's anvil."

Throughout the evening leather cups stuffed with telegrams bringing fragmentary vote figures shot from a pneumatic tube "like bullets from a rapid-fire gun" until desks and floor were awash in paper. Editors and reporters assigned to individual races—federal, state, local, varying with the year—recorded the numbers and searched anxiously for trends. Cheers and shouts drifting up from Park Row, where crowds filled the street to watch the election bulletins flashed by stereopticons on huge canvas screens outside the *Sun* and other newspaper buildings, were constant reminders of the keen public interest in the newsroom's work.

After midnight, when managing editor Lord began ticking off the minutes until the first-edition deadline, concentration became total and cold sweat broke out on some brows. Men following elections where the picture was still blurred took a deep breath and made instant resolutions of conflicting figures, educated guesses based on past voting where there were no figures at all. With time running out, everyone added up totals, dispatched the vote tables to the composing room, and finished up stories roughed out earlier. A sip of beer, a bite of a sandwich, a moment to stretch the legs, and a copy boy was slapping a *Sun* with the ink still damp on the managing editor's desk. Members of the staff clustered round to look at their efforts in cold, unforgiving type, praying they had not gone too far wrong. Then, sifting through a new deluge of telegrams, they began polishing and refining their work for the second edition.

One feature of the evening, as Ralph described it, was the presence in the newsroom of a variety of visitors. Public men—a senator, a visiting editor, a judge or two, a general—showed up to learn the news before lesser mortals. The New York correspondents of large newspapers in other American cities and representatives of the English press were there to get an early line on the election outcome as the *Sun* saw it. And always on hand was the Washington correspondent of the *Sun*. He was, said Ralph, "a nabob in the estimation of the staff, which grades the editor first, the managing editor second, the city editor third, the Washington correspondent fourth, and the London correspondent nebulously, with awe, as the pagans consider one of their gods that operate and yet are never seen."

This Washington correspondent brings an unfamiliar, enviable atmosphere with him. Well-salaried, in command of a "bureau" and a staff of his own, he supports not only an elegance of attire, but an ease and a pride of bearing that are eloquent of a calmer atmosphere than the boiler-room energy of the home office. He has been heard of as smoking on the back porch of the White House with a President, and it is noticed that the editorial writers not only come out of the inner sanctum to gossip with him, but that they listen keenly and keep saying "Oho!" "Ah, indeed!" and "If that leaks out there'll be a stir."

If there is more than a suggestion of mockery here, it probably does not mean that Ralph bore any particular ill will toward the *Sun's* Washington correspondent in the nineties, David S. Barry—who, as it happened, counted himself among Ralph's admirers. Reading between the lines, however, does suggest something about the attitudes of Ralph and most other non-Washington reporters toward Washington correspondents in general.

Washington correspondents often struck other reporters as self-important, like many of the political figures they covered. From this flowed a certain condescension toward reporters in the home office—bright young men, the Washington men might have generously acknowledged, but not equipped to deal with the weighty matters of state and infinite subtleties of politics that were their daily diet. As for the editorial writers' delighted clucking over the Washington correspondent's inside tales from the capital, it only underscored that his private gossip was vastly more interesting than the stories he wrote for public consumption. And that, in turn, reflected a fundamental problem with Washington reporters. They were so much a part of the world they covered—participants as well as observers, intimates of the powerful and the pretenders to power—that they were often hamstrung when it came to presenting a rounded picture of what went on in national government and politics. Sometimes they gloried so in their role as insiders that they boasted more about the news they withheld than the news they printed. Sometimes they seemed almost to forget they were reporters.

Nineteenth-century Americans joined political clubs, marched in campaign parades, and listened to two-hour political speeches. They turned out at the polls at a far higher rate than would the electorate in the twentieth century—or rather the men did, since women could not vote. Considering this zest for politics, it is at first surprising to scan random issues of the *Sun* from Ralph's era and find that often there is little significant news from Washington. Days sometimes pass without a substantial Washington story on the front page.

The basic explanation is that the federal government was not the factor in American life that it would later become. Washington played almost no role in coping with the nation's major social and economic problems. It was minimally involved abroad. Some years in the late 1800s one of the government's major challenges was figuring out what to do about a massive surplus of revenues. There were, in short, many days when there was not much for a Washington correspondent to write about. What news there was came mainly from partisan clashes in Congress; the Capitol was so much the focus of Washington coverage throughout the nineteenth century, in fact, that some early Washington correspondents had regarded the job as seasonal and left town when Congress was not in session. As for the White House, Presidents in Ralph's day had almost nothing to do with the press and generated little news. There were no Presidential press conferences or press secretaries, and on the rare occasions when a President spoke to a reporter it was usually understood that his words could not be printed. "A President is never interviewed" was the generally accepted rule, according to one of Ralph's contemporaries on the *Sun*.

Washington reporters did have to supply enough political analysis and speculation to satisfy the many readers for whom politics was a serious avocation, and periodically they also had to grapple with a few perennial issues of the late 1800s—tariffs, civil service reform, and "free silver." But reading the Washington correspondence of the *Sun* of the eighties and nineties often leaves the impression of reporters dealing not with the government of a vast nation but with the affairs of a small town. Tedious accounts of utterly inconsequential congressional routine have the ring of minutes of a meeting of a local library board: "The Chair placed before the Senate to-day the resolution submitted yesterday by Mr. Riddlebergh and the substitute for it by Mr. Pugh, relating to the relations between the President and the Senate in regard to . . ."

News from the executive departments features annual report summaries every bit as dry as the report of a drainage district. Who will be the doorkeeper of the House or the consul in Asuncion is a matter of some moment, and considerable space is devoted to the appointments of postmasters and lighthouse keepers. The President, we learn, took a walk with a friend the other day, and the First Lady rode down Pennsylvania Avenue in her carriage. Also, a large mirror used to represent a lake as part of a centerpiece for the table in the White House state dining room has been broken by a careless servant, who "received a deserved scolding from the President."

Supplying the nation's newspapers with such items did not require an army of correspondents. In 1893 the *Congressional Directory's* press roster listed only 132 Washington correspondents, including press association correspondents who served many newspapers. In 1874 Ben: Perley Poore of the Boston *Journal* had described in *Harper's Monthly* how an industrious correspondent could keep abreast of the entire federal establishment in the course of a day, making the rounds of the White House, the Cabinet departments, and Congress and finding time along the way to chat with promenaders on Pennsylvania Avenue, eavesdrop on fellow horsecar passengers, and dine with foreign diplomats. Despite Ralph's reference to the Washington man's "bureau," the *Congressional Directory* indicates that in the nineties the *Sun* was still getting by with only one full-time Washington correspondent.

But Washington correspondents had grounds other than their small numbers for considering themselves something of a journalistic elite—"a not inconsiderable fraction of the flower of journalism," as one of them immodestly put it. Most were older and more experienced than other reporters and, as Ralph suggested, better paid. In the early nineties many were earning substantially more than the $5,000 annual salary of a member of Congress, a level that put them near the top of the journalistic heap at the time. Further, for all the dreary or trivial things they wrote, Washington correspondents could nevertheless claim with some justification that on the whole their work mattered more than that of most other reporters; keeping the citizens of a democracy informed about their government was more important than covering titillating divorces and dark deeds in back alleys.

Washington correspondents could also claim a heritage of staunch defense of freedom of the press against assaults by Congress, the principal source of news in the capital in the 1800s. As late as 1839 the Senate was still debating whether reporters should be granted special seats in the chamber; one opponent called them "miserable slanderers, hirelings hanging on to the skirts of literature, earning a miserable subsistence from their vile and dirty misrepresentations of the proceedings here." But Washington reporters had prevailed against all attempts to limit their access to the ordinary proceedings of Congress, and in other clashes over the years they frustrated repeated congressional efforts to punish or curb them because of things they had written. The matters at issue ranged from a New York *Tribune* description of a backwoods congressman eating a lunch of sausage on the House floor, wiping his greasy hands on his hair and picking his teeth with a jackknife, to accounts of secret Senate proceedings.

Wherever the merits lay in the individual disputes, the message of the retreats by Congress in the face of press defiance was clear: senators, congressmen, and others in positions of authority could expect hard going if they tried to use their powers of office to prevent journalists from reporting and writing freely. Further, the assumption must be that the Washington press would find ways to penetrate official secrecy; it is significant that "leak" seems to have first gained currency as a journalistic term in Washington. Finally, and most specifically, Washington reporters were going to insist on their right to keep some sources secret as an essential tool of their trade.

If all this suggests that Washington reporters and the political establishment were destined to live in a perpetual state of confrontation, the impression would be misleading. By the late nineteenth century, Washington correspondents were, to a considerable extent, smoothly functioning parts of the system. Other reporters spent most of their time with their noses pressed to the glass; Washington reporters were often invited into the parlor.

Many politicians in Washington, in common with politicians elsewhere, learned relatively early that getting along with reporters could be worthwhile. "Public men," observed a Washington correspondent named E. J. Gibson in 1894, "realize the advantage of having published in their home papers facts that would be useful to their constituents as well as of advantage to themselves, and they no longer look upon the newspaper man as their natural enemy or as one to be shunned." One leading public man of the late nineteenth century, James G. Blaine—congressman, senator, Secretary of State, Presidential candidate—commented that "it's a better thing to have the boys who write about you dip their pens in the ink of friendship than in that of gall."

Favorable publicity was obviously to be preferred, but some politicians took the view that any publicity was better than none. Francis B. Spinola, a Tammany Hall congressman known as "Shirt-collar" Spinola because a towering starched collar was his only distinction, once reproached a *Sun* reporter for ignoring him. "What's the matter with you, my young friend? What have I done to you? My name hasn't appeared in the *Sun* in a year." Told that he had done nothing worth reporting, Spinola responded: "Mebbe so, mebbe so, but abuse me, pitch into me, don't let me die in oblivion like this."

For some three decades, the 1870s through the 1890s, the mutuality of interests between reporters and politicians—one group got stories, the other public attention—was institutionalized on Washington's "Newspaper Row." This was a formerly residential block of Fourteenth Street between F Street and Pennsylvania Avenue where most important out-of-town newspapers, including, for many years, the *Sun,* rented rooms for offices. Political figures took to stopping by Newspaper Row in the evening. Senators and congressmen, many of whom lived at two hotels on the block, Willard's and the Ebbitt House, were most numerous, but there were also Cabinet members, visiting governors, and an occasional ambassador. They would call at the offices of their journalistic acquaintances, and sometimes reporters and politicians would adjourn to the bar of Willard's, one of the most popular in town.

On warm evenings everyone would sit outside under the elms lining Fourteenth Street, sipping tall drinks served by black waiters from the hotels. Later the correspondents would write their stories and dispatch them from the Western Union office, conveniently located at one end of the block. It was a sad day for the Washington press when politicians could no longer find the time to come visiting and the reporters had to chase after

Newspaper Row in Washington as depicted in *Harper's Monthly* for January 1874. The *Sun* had an office on the ground floor of the Ebbitt House, the large building with the flag. Willard's Hotel was on the opposite side of the street, at the corner of Fourteenth Street NW and Pennsylvania Avenue. *Newspaper Collection, The New York Public Library, Astor, Lenox and Tilden Foundations*

their sources. Stores eventually replaced the correspondents' offices on Newspaper Row.

Close relations with sources were an accepted part of a Washington man's job. Unlike a reporter who dashed from one unrelated assignment to another, dealing with a constantly changing cast of characters, a Washington correspondent, like a city hall reporter, sought news from the same people day after day. If he failed to maintain friendly, or at least civil, relations with them, his sources would soon dry up. Ralph did enough of this sort of reporting to know how the system worked. "The best Washington correspondents work upon a friendly basis with cabinet officers and senators . . . and are recognized as men pursuing an honorable calling," he said.

Partisan ties often cemented such relationships. Major newspapers no longer served as subservient party organs, but they remained highly partisan and this partisanship spilled over from the editorial page into the news columns. By the late eighties and early nineties the *Sun* was making feeble attempts to break itself of this habit. In the days before Presidential elections, balanced assessments of the campaigns were sometimes interspersed among the customary cheerleading articles in support of the *Sun's* candidate. But the Washington reporting of the *Sun,* and of other newspapers as well, was in general still expected to reflect editorial biases, which meant that Washington reporters often had to work closely with their employers' political allies. At Dana's nominally independent and sometimes unpredictable *Sun,* more often than not this meant support for the Democrats as the party of "honest toilers" and opposition to the Republicans as the party of privilege.

Understandable as these constraints on a reporter's independence may be, they often made it impossible to produce decent journalism. Flattered by confidences and bewitched by a heady sense of sharing in power, reporters became excessively sensitive to the feelings of their politician friends and reluctant to print anything that might annoy them. Moreover, their partisan involvement was not limited to mere journalistic support. While continuing to work for newspapers, Washington correspondents wrote speeches for congressmen, served as paid congressional clerks, and sat in on party strategy sessions. Chester Lord, despite his insistence on objective reporting of election returns, saw nothing wrong with Washington correspondents' earning money on the side by writing campaign literature.

By its very nature much Washington news was vague and unsatisfying. "News coming out of Washington," wrote Elmer Davis in his history of the

New York *Times,* "is apt to represent not what is so but what might be so under certain contingencies, what may turn out to be so, what some eminent personage says is so, or even what he wants the public to believe is so when it is not." The web of confidences and political obligations entangling Washington reporters only compounded the problem. It meant that the public learned only part of some interesting stories and missed others altogether. It also meant that readers never learned the source of many stories, information that was often essential for assessing them. From the start Washington stories were larded with phrases like "it is believed," "it is understood" or, in a quaint *Sun* formulation, "it is the opinion of persons with opportunities for knowing." "This more than anything else is responsible for the sort of fog, the haze of miasmatic exhalations, which hangs over news with a Washington date line," said Davis.

Swept up in their own little world of politics, smug in the knowledge that *they* knew the real story even if their readers didn't, Washington reporters tended to lose touch with the rest of the country. One of the best of the Washington correspondents of the eighties and nineties, Frank Carpenter of the Cleveland *Leader,* acknowledged as much. "Washington City is the poorest place in the United States from which to judge the temper of the nation," he wrote. "Its citizens have a different outlook on life from those of the individual states, and its atmosphere is artificial and enervating."

For editors the problem was that such an atmosphere put Washington correspondents out of tune with the interests of readers. Shaking up his Washington bureau, Joseph Pulitzer of the New York *World* once instructed an associate not to consider a particular reporter for the chief correspondent's post because he "is a politician only. . . . I believe a little less politics and a few more thrilling stories from real life, even if they contain some ghosts and blood and thunder, might be advisable."

Dana, who did not like the *Sun* to print columns of copy that nobody read, must have had similar misgivings about Washington stories. Most of the stories eaten by the office cat came from Washington. The *Sun's* antipathy toward the tedious and vapid may explain why it continued to employ only one correspondent in Washington at a time when some of its competitors had two or three. One man could usually supply all the Washington copy the editors wanted. There were times, however, when that was not so, and special correspondents from the New York office took over some of the work. Ralph did this on a number of occasions.

Sixty-eight Washington correspondents arrived at Minneapolis on June 3, 1892, to cover the Presidential nominating convention of the Republican Party. They traveled on a special train made up of six luxurious Pullman cars. The train, according to Ralph, who had reached Minneapolis earlier from New York, had been "placed at their absolute disposal" for that year's national conventions by the Pennsylvania Railroad.

Washington correspondents took the lead in covering the conventions even though they met away from the capital, but for such a major political story so many other reporters were assigned that the Washington men were outnumbered. A total of 300 reporters assembled in Minneapolis for the Republican convention, and the Democratic convention later in the month in Chicago attracted 350. These were enormous aggregations of journalists for the time.

The conventions generated more suspense and drama—and thus more genuine news—than they would after Presidential primaries began playing a large role in determining nominees. Covering them for a daily newspaper meant twenty-hour days. "The reporting of the great national political conventions requires unceasing effort for a week or more, the utmost vigil through night and day," said Ralph's boss, Chester Lord. "There is no sleep for the unfortunate correspondent." Ralph commented: "There is nothing in all the business that compares with a national convention for trying the body and mind of a man who essays to master and report it."

Still, things could have been worse. As in Washington, reporters were accepted as part of the political landscape, men with a useful job to do, and some effort was made to ease their burden and perhaps win their favor. In the early-summer heat waves that always seemed to strike at convention time and turn the cavernous halls into seas of perspiring faces, shirtsleeves, and swaying palm-leaf fans, the reporters sweltered along with everybody else, but they at least had the best seats in the house, right on the platform. There they could hear the proceedings, which the delegates beyond the first few rows could do only when an orator of exceptional power held forth. Scores of telegraphers waited in the bowels of the auditoriums to speed the reporters' copy to their newspapers, and at Minneapolis in 1892 Ralph found that the Republicans had thoughtfully provided female stenographers to take down the stories of weary reporters.

Away from the convention hall, in barrooms and hotel suites, campaign managers courted reporters and sometimes even did their work for them. After a visit to the Cleveland headquarters at the Grand Pacific Hotel during the Democratic convention in Chicago in 1892, one correspondent wrote incredulously: "It is a picnic for the newspaper men to visit this bureau. The Cleveland . . . men interview themselves. They dictate to the type-writers, and then anxiously await the appearance of reporters, when the interviews are solemnly handed out."

Ralph attended the 1888 conventions—the Democrats met in St. Louis that year and the Republicans in Chicago—as one of several writers working under the direction of Ambrose W. Lyman, the *Sun's* Washington correspondent at the time. Most days Ralph did not write the principal story, and it is sometimes difficult to sort out his work from that of his colleagues. What Ralph did, however, must have impressed Dana and Lord. In 1892 they placed him rather than David Barry, the *Sun's* Washington man by then, in charge of the convention staff, and much of the paper's coverage that year bears his stamp. Ralph was in his element—once more at the center of a large event, taking in everything from debates over tariff planks to parades by delegates costumed in dusters and top hats, getting it all down on paper, three or four columns on an easy day, six on a busy one.

The stories were sometimes rambling and untidy, but, taken together, they did a pretty good job of putting the reader right in the middle of the swirl and confusion of the national conventions. There was evanescent political gossip and speculation; at the Republican convention in Minneapolis, Blaine was on top one day, McKinley the next—until President Harrison was renominated on the first ballot. There were capsule descriptions of politicians; visiting party leaders' hotel suites in Minneapolis late at night, Ralph came across Senator Matthew Quay, the unscrupulous Republican boss of Pennsylvania, "in his shirt sleeves, with one eye very slightly closed and the other very wide open, saying nothing and absorbing everything."

As was permissible at the time, there were freewheeling assaults—splendidly nonpartisan on this occasion, since in 1892 the *Sun* had no particular love for the powers in charge of either the Republicans or the Democrats—on various politicians who grated on Ralph's sensibilities. Senator Spooner of Wisconsin "perpetrated an oration" at the Republican convention; one speaker at the Democratic convention in Chicago was "a single-tax crank from Ohio"; and the chairman of the Democratic convention, an utterly ineffectual fellow in Ralph's view, "showed about as much nerve and backbone as an oyster."

There was also the irrelevant but interesting. One Minneapolis hotel opened a vast bar, manned by sixty bartenders, that could accommodate all the delegates "if they have patience and follow the old rule of war, 'to fire and fall back.' " Also in Minneapolis, a "comely" woman reporter caught Ralph's eye as she edged through the swarms of delegates "with her fashionable skirt upheld in one hand."

For Ralph, however, the great challenge in reporting a convention lay in spinning a running account of a night nominating session, jamming as much matter as possible into each successive edition of the *Sun*. The 1892 Democratic convention in Chicago, held in a vast, hastily built wooden shed on the lakefront called the Wigwam, provided such a test. That Grover Cleveland, evicted from the White House four years earlier by Harrison, would be given another opportunity to run for President was never in much doubt. But the nominating process dragged out through most of one night, beginning at 9 P.M. and ending at 4 A.M., the worst possible timing for a morning newspaper. The hall was stifling. Periodic rainstorms gave no relief, but the rain did leak through the roof of the Wigwam, dripping on reporters' desks and causing some delegates to raise umbrellas. Thanks partly to the ineffectual chairman—at one particularly chaotic point, said Ralph, he idly munched a sandwich "as calm and complacent as a frog in a rainstorm"—the convention often verged on a mob scene, with last-ditch foes of Cleveland trying to outyell his supporters.

All this was still fresh in Ralph's mind when he described the rigors of such an assignment in *Scribner's*.

Then the reporter of the main story selects the ablest man on his staff and asks him to stand beside him and whisper everything that he sees. The reporter is seeing for himself, but must write as well, and so may miss a word or a tableau. He is writing as for his life. He has a man to keep sharpening his pencils and to hand his copy to the telegraph boys, who are throwing themselves at him and away from him like balls out of cannon. Sometimes he is allowed to finish twenty words on a sheet, but more often the pages are torn from under his pencil with only eight or ten words on each one. His desk is a board; men are clambering over him, the place is in a tumult. But all that and the strain conduce to good work. The strain! He knows that the hungry maw of the printing-press in New York is wide-open, that the wires are loaded, that his matter is being seized and flung into extra editions, and that all around him are men as able as himself, doing the same work, and determined to excel him at it if they can. The fevered pencil flies, every nerve is strained, every brain-cell is clear. Comment, description, reminiscence, dialogue, and explanation, flow upon the impatient sheets in short paragraphs, like slivers of crystal. There is no turning back, no chance for correction or rearrangement, no possibility of changing a word that has been written. Yet there must be no mistakes, no confusion or complexity. For two or three hours, perhaps even longer, this race is kept up. That is the hardest task that falls to the lot of a "special," and it is the most intoxicating. Whoever does it is glad that he has lived to drink so deep a draught of that matchless elixir, which keeps us all young till we die—excitement.

In that same 1893 *Scribner's* article, which dealt with many aspects of the life of a special correspondent, Ralph mentioned, with studied casualness, that there had been "several Presidents who have honored me with their friendship or acquaintance." The Presidents Ralph is known to have encountered up to 1893 were Chester Arthur, Grover Cleveland, and Benjamin Harrison. From all indications he did not get much news from them, but then neither did anybody else. The White House was an exception to the generally easy relationships that prevailed between politicians and reporters in Washington.

Presidents before Lincoln more or less systematically kept the public abreast of their views through semiofficial administration organs, Washington newspapers that were subsidized by government printing contracts and whose authoritative articles were widely copied by other newspapers around the country. During the Civil War Lincoln sometimes took the time to chat with reporters (one Cabinet member complained he allowed the "little newsmongers" entirely too much familiarity), and his successor, Andrew Johnson, granted a number of interviews that were devoted mainly to defending himself against impeachment charges but also to denying tales that he drank to excess. Grant usually said little to anyone, including the press, but from time to time he would see reporters sent to elicit specific information. Also, on one occasion he talked to a reporter inadvertently. Taking a stroll about Washington on a Sunday, Grant was joined by a "stranger" who engaged him in conversation about a pending foreign affairs matter. Grant was astonished when his remarks appeared in print; the "stranger" had been a reporter.

After Grant news from the White House dried up almost completely until the administration of Theodore Roosevelt, who took the modern view that the press could be a useful tool for advancing his interests. Arthur, Cleveland, and Harrison were particularly tight-lipped. Considering that within relatively recent memory two Presidents had been assassinated, access to them was remarkably casual—once a week anyone not obviously a lunatic could call at the White House and shake the President's hand—but all three were disinclined to say anything of substance to a reporter. They gave the public almost nothing beyond their formal pronouncements.

Arthur would not respond to questions touching on politics when Ralph joined him on the fishing trip to the Thousand Islands in 1882, and despite his apparently otherwise congenial manner toward Ralph on that vacation, he resented the press most of the time. "You cannot realize what it is to feel that you cannot turn around or do anything without being watched by newspaper men, ready to blazon to the world every act or move that can be construed to your disadvantage," a Washington reporter quoted him as saying.

Cleveland's reticence with the press was not limited to personal matters, such as his marriage or, in his second term, an operation for cancer of the jaw that he managed to keep secret till long afterward. He "seldom if ever talked to a newspaper correspondent," according to David Barry, and a friend recalled that Cleveland was even nervous about distributing advance copies of his speeches lest they help his foes in the press attack him when the words were scarcely out of his mouth.

As for Benjamin Harrison, he was unassuming enough to refresh himself at a soda fountain on a stroll around Washington, just as he might have done back home in Indianapolis, but, said David Barry, he could never even be brought to the point of accepting reporters as "at least a necessary evil that he and others must tolerate." On one occasion Julian Ralph would receive a reception from Harrison so chilly that Ralph had to be stretching a point if he classed his relationship with Harrison as one of his Presidential "friendships."

Ralph took time off from his legislative assignment in Albany in 1885 to cover the first inauguration of Cleveland, and he returned to Washington to report the inaugurations of Harrison in 1889 and Cleveland again in 1893. Most large newspapers sent teams of special correspondents to help their Washington bureaus with the inaugurations, which then took place on March 4, but Ralph apparently supplied the *Sun's* report largely by himself. Covering an inauguration, he said, was hard work but nothing compared with a national political convention. At a convention a reporter had to be constantly alert to developments behind the scenes; at an inauguration the story lay in plain sight before him and he simply served as the reader's eyes. Ralph described covering the inauguration of 1893, when Cleveland succeeded Harrison:

I had myself called at five o'clock in the morning, and having a cab at hand, mounted the box with the negro driver and travelled about the city from end to end and side to side. I did this to see the people get up and the trains roll in and the soldiers turn out—to catch the Capital robing like a bride for her wedding. After a breakfast, eaten calmly, I made another tour of the town and then began to approach the subject more closely, calling at the White House, mingling with the crowds in the principal hotels, moving between the Senate and the House of Representatives to report the hurly-burly of the closing moments of a dying administration. I saw the old and the new President, and then witnessed the inauguration ceremonies and the parade. Then, having seen the new family in place in the White House, I took a hearty luncheon and sat down at half-past one o'clock to write steadily for twelve hours, with plenty of pencils and pads and messenger boys at hand, and with my note-book supplemented by clippings from all the afternoon papers (covering details to which I might or might not wish to refer). Cigars, a sandwich or two at supper-time, and a stout horn of brandy late at night were my other equipments.

The *Sun's* Washington correspondent might have felt compelled to read deep political portents into the events surrounding a presidential inauguration; Ralph saw the affairs simply as grand spectacles. There is a certain sameness about his accounts. The weather varies—"a glorious golden Southern spring" day in '85, "spiteful, slanting rain" in '89, and snow, slush, and polar winds in '93. But there are always crowds, bands, drunks, troops, political clubs, and bunting. Ralph loved to write about such scenes, and the descriptions come tumbling out as they do in his story about Grant's funeral. Reflecting the stereotypes of the time, there are also condescending references to the capital's many blacks, such as those along the parade route in '93 who delightedly "rolled their heads at every band of music and every corps of marching men."

Ralph displays a measure of disdain toward politicians, particularly the ill-mannered congressmen who always bolted for the best seats at the proceedings. But he never became so jaded as to be unmoved by the ceremony of a President taking office. He was especially struck by the sight of Grover Cleveland, a huge, stolid man whom the *Sun* had often treated contemptuously, standing bareheaded in the bitter cold on the platform outside the Capitol in 1893.

There was no friend of Grover Cleveland who ever dreamed for a moment that he would put his hat on. They knew that he felt that he was in the presence of the majesty of our country, the people, and that he considered it incumbent on himself to remain bareheaded when introducing himself as their servant. . . .

It was a marvellous sight to see that one man, bareheaded, standing in a bitter gale, with the little hair that's on his head blown in every direction, as he turned, now this way, now that. . . .

It was so cold that the people could see Mr. Cleveland's breath leave his mouth in a white vapor at the end of every sentence.

Despite their general antipathy toward the press, Ralph seems to have had some degree of personal relationship with Chester Arthur and Grover Cleveland. In 1885 he went to see Cleveland in Albany after he had re-

Ralph rides about Washington as he covers the Presidential inauguration of 1893. The illustration accompanied his article on the life of a reporter in *Scribner's Magazine* for August 1893. *Newspaper Collection, The New York Public Library, Astor, Lenox and Tilden Foundations*

signed as governor of New York and was preparing to leave for Washington for his first inauguration. Ralph apparently had called at the White House sometime previously during Arthur's residency there, and Cleveland asked him to describe the executive mansion. When Ralph got to Arthur's bedroom, Cleveland stopped him. "There," said Cleveland, slamming his fist down on a table, "that settles it. That thing's got to stop when I get to Washington. I am not going to have my house turned into a public museum." The public, said Cleveland, could see the Blue Room, the East Room, and the Red Room, but not his bedroom.

In connection with his inaugural coverage, Ralph made a practice of calling on the outgoing President on his last full day in office. The calls, which yielded no quotations from the Presidents and no real news of any sort, seem to have been almost ceremonial, perhaps serving more to flatter Ralph's ego than anything else. They did, however, provide some glancing impressions of the Presidents as human beings. Arthur, passed over for renomination by the Republicans, was clearly dejected about leaving the White House in 1885, in large part because he thoroughly enjoyed the social life there. Four years later, Cleveland, departing in defeat after his first term, was stoic, shaking Ralph's hand and expressing no regrets.

And in 1893 Benjamin Harrison remained true to form, relenting not the slightest in his scorn for the press. Ralph's story in the *Sun* on the morning of inauguration day gave away nothing about what really happened in his encounter with Harrison. "The reporter of the *Sun* . . . was one of those who went in to bid the President Godspeed," wrote Ralph. Harrison was sober, even "a trifle sad. What he said of his experience as President was like all else that he says upon a subject that interests him. It was eloquent, thoughtful, and framed in such well-chosen words that no writer, choosing every phrase for public scrutiny, could better a word of it."

David Barry had accompanied Ralph when he called on Harrison, and many years later he set down a rather different account.

While waiting in an anteroom to be admitted into Harrison's private office, Mr. Ralph regaled me with tales of how he had been received by former Presidents when making his farewell call, and we both were somewhat eager to see Harrison unbend. When "Lige" Halford, Harrison's private secretary, suddenly opened the door and said, "Walk in, Gentlemen," we were still laughing over some anecdote of a former President, but the laughter froze on our lips when we came face to face with Harrison. He was seated at a little desk writing notes of farewell on black-bordered paper [Harrison's wife had died two weeks before the 1892 election] to personal friends. Having finished one, he said, "Sit down, Gentlemen," and then in characteristic icy tones, "What can I do for you?" Ralph, who was a cheery, friendly soul not easily abashed, started in to tell the President of his innocent penchant for writing presidential valedictories, but was cut short by Mr. Harrison's abrupt condemnation of the newspaper press generally for what he described as their cruel, unfair, and discourteous references to himself and Mrs. Harrison for having accepted from John Wanamaker, of Philadelphia, Postmaster-General in Harrison's cabinet, a gift of a summer cottage at Cape May Point. It was true that newspaper comment had been severe, especially on the part of the *Sun,* and undoubtedly it had rankled in the bosom of the President more bitterly than the public had imagined. When Ralph had partly recovered his wits from the unexpected attack he attempted to apologize for the press. He said he thought it a mistake to say that they had ever criticized Mrs. Harrison and that perhaps their criticism of the President had been more caustic than the facts had warranted, or perhaps that the facts were not entirely understood. He failed, however, to puncture the President's cuticle, and after a few pointless remarks back and forth, we were shown out. It was quite dark by this time, and as we went down the old historic stairway, the one that in those days served on all occasions, public and private, official and social, and were ushered into the cold, Ralph said, "Well, I am cured of my desire to visit Presidents on their last day in the White House."

Ralph's failure even to hint at the true nature of Harrison's reception suggests that at this stage in his career he couldn't bring himself to acknowledge in print that he had been all but thrown out of the President's office. He was fond of saying that reporters of the first rank, of which he most certainly was one, could now meet on terms of equality with important men. His treatment by Harrison, however, rudely reminded him that now and then every reporter could expect a humiliating rebuff—even Julian Ralph, special correspondent of the New York *Sun.*

Later in 1893 Ralph went down to Washington to cover a major congressional battle. His stories on this occasion display enough familiarity with Capitol Hill to suggest that he must have undertaken such assignments a number of times, but this is the only one of which there is a record.

The issue was "free silver," which toward the end of the nineteenth century removed government monetary policy from the realm of the abstract to the arena of fierce public controversy. Backed by Western silver miners, financially strapped farmers in the Midwest and South had pressed for unlimited coinage of silver—"free silver"—as a way of putting more money into circulation and raising the prices of the commodities they produced. Eastern business interests feared that flooding the economy with silver and silver-backed currency would undermine the gold standard and cause financial instability. Shaken business confidence stemming from fears about the gold standard did, in fact, contribute to a surge in business failures shortly after Cleveland took office—the Panic of 1893—and the President's response was to call a special session of Congress to consider repeal of an 1890 law that authorized liberal, though not unlimited, coinage of silver.

The special session ran from August through October. Majorities in the House and Senate, both controlled by the Democrats, clearly went along with the President in opposing free silver, and the House quickly voted to repeal the bill in question. The Senate was another story. It as yet had no procedure for cutting off debate, and the minority of senators opposing repeal, a combination of members from agricultural and Western mining states, blocked repeal by filibustering. Day after day the struggle was front-page news in the *Sun,* which backed repeal, but as the debate ground on and got nowhere it was increasingly hard to make the stories interesting, which may explain why Ralph was dispatched to Washington. He appears to have spent much of September and October there.

As at other times, his stories occasionally went off on tangents, his attention caught by things that passed unnoticed by reporters who spent most of their time at the Capitol. Glancing into a Senate office one day, he saw stenographers shouting floor speeches into the horns of Edison phonographs, after which they would be transcribed by typists; the stenographers, he noticed, unconsciously mimicked the gestures and speaking styles of the senators who had made the speeches. Another day, having been barred from a room in the Capitol by a "Negro flunkey" who told him no one may "intrude where a Senator is," Ralph let fly at the privilege and luxury that seemed to him to envelop senators. They had a private restaurant, "for the Senators will not eat where the people will." They were shaved at the taxpayers' expense in the lavish Senate barber shop, and in the Senate's private baths they soaked in marble tubs filled with perfumed water. They had personal clerks, a frivolous waste of money in Ralph's view, and they did little work themselves, preferring instead to entertain "friends in their golden committee rooms, or to read novels and smoke and drink in their private apartments." "It is a great thing to be a Senator," said Ralph.

Most of the time, however, he focused on the business at hand. At first the proceedings on the Senate floor were mildly entertaining. Watching from the press gallery behind the rostrum, he noted the gentlemanly way in which senators called each other liars. One day in early September he described the ritual of quorum calls, used by the filibusterers to waste time. Senators materialized to respond to their names, then quickly melted away, so that by the time it was announced that a quorum was present, it was no longer present and another quorum call was requested. "This is the way the day was consumed in the United States Senate, and the comedy is to be played each day for some time to come," he wrote.

The show soon grew tiresome, at least from the point of view of the forces opposing free silver, which Ralph's stories reflected. At mid-September a move to set a date to end debate failed and he reported: "Thereupon the Senate relapsed into the state of coma that has characterized it since Mr. Stewart began to speak a week ago and did not emerge from this condition during the day." Weeks later, with nothing changed, a free-silver senator made a speech that Ralph called a "rambling, incoherent and illogical harangue." On October 16, the seventieth day of the special session, a silver senator from Kansas droned on, "but no one was listening to him except the stenographer, whose pen trailed lazily over his pad in slow keeping with the drawling utterances of the speaker. . . . The galleries were half filled by a crowd of men and women whose faces wore a surprised and puzzled expression, such as might be looked for on their faces had they entered a church and found a vaudeville troupe making professional use of its chancel."

Something had to be done, and if no one else was ready to jolt the Senate out of its rut, Ralph was willing to try. He had heard a suggestion that even though the Senate had no formal cloture procedure, it was conceivable that its presiding officer, Vice President Adlai Stevenson, who naturally supported President Cleveland's call for repeal of the silver-coinage bill, might have it within his power to end the filibuster by simply cutting off debate and ordering a vote. Ralph, in effect, began to promote this idea around the Capitol. He asked a number of people, including Senator Henry Cabot Lodge of Massachusetts and Representative Thomas B. Reed of Maine— known as "Czar" Reed for his iron control of the House when Speaker— what they thought of it. The responses were generally skeptical, but Reed asserted that the Vice President could do whatever he pleased if he had a majority behind him. What it came down to, Ralph decided, was that although no Senate rule said the presiding officer *could* cut off debate, none said he could *not*.

Ralph put the matter to Senator Isham G. Harris of Tennessee, a Democrat who was a leading free-silver advocate and who was president pro tem of the Senate. Ralph began by asking Harris, who was "seated like an emperor" in an ornate committee room, if there was any possibility of cloture in the silver debate. "If you ask," said Harris, "whether closure can be established in this chamber during this debate on the silver question, I can say it would be easier to pluck the sun from the firmament."

Ralph persisted. Why, he asked, could not the presiding officer call for a vote whenever he wanted it? The rules did not authorize such action, responded Harris. Then the following:

"But," said the reporter for the *Sun,* "do not think me obtuse for pressing the question. What is to prevent the Vice President from simply doing it without rule or authority? Why can't he simply call for or order a vote?"

"Why, sir," said the President pro tempore, speaking with impressive gravity, "I don't believe he would live to accomplish it."

It was the kind of foolish, indiscreet remark that a regular Washington correspondent, sure to be encountering Senator Harris for a long time to come, would have tucked away for use over the bar at Willard's. Ralph included it in his account of the interview in the *Sun*.

David Barry, who had sat in on the interview, recorded what followed:

A few minutes after the Senate met on the morning of its publication, Senator Harris arose and with solemn mien and his voice quavering with honest emotion repudiated Mr. Ralph's story *in toto*. No such interview had taken place, he said, or had been sought; he had a recollection, he admitted, of running across a newspaperman in the corridor whose face he seemed to know and of having made some offhand reply to a half-understood question, but beyond that there was no basis for the fanciful story.

Following up in the *Sun,* Ralph noted that "this is not the first time that Senators have denied the reports of reputable and responsible correspondents," thereby tarnishing "that which must always be the chief stock in trade of a correspondent," his reputation for accuracy. But Harris would not prevail.

Unfortunately for his denial he gave the interview to the special correspondent of the *Sun* in the presence of its regular Washington correspondent. . . . It is too bad for the pretended dignity of the Senate that there has grown up in that body an impression that Senators, unlike other men, may deny their own words without losing the respect of the people. They think it fair and honorable to discredit reports which convey what they say in warm blood, but which they do not afterward like when they see these utterances materialized in cold type.

As events turned out, Senator Harris's assault on Ralph's veracity was one of the last signs of fight on the part of the free-silver senators. They soon gave up and repeal passed. Ralph, having given the Senate the benefit of his thinking on its procedures and trod on just about every toe in that august body, went home and left the windup of the coverage of the special session to Barry. In his memoirs Barry called Ralph "the greatest newspaper reporter who ever lived," but one wonders if on this occasion he didn't heave a small sigh of relief when Ralph boarded the train back to New York.

14. Last Days at the *Sun*

Even as Ralph was solidifying his reputation as one of the outstanding reporters of his day, there were times when he was not entirely content with his life on Park Row. Knowing that a great newspaper counted on him to take on some of the most demanding assignments and that he had won the respect of his fellows was gratifying, of course, and often as he tossed aside his pencil after writing the final paragraph of a big story that had gone well it must truly have seemed that nothing could be better. But the satisfactions of being a reporter for the *Sun* were not always enough.

Perhaps there was validity in the complaint that reporting had its shortcomings as a long-term career—that reporters, even the best, reached a plateau fairly early and then could look forward only to more of the same. In the case of a prolific space writer like Ralph, whose weekly earnings must have regularly topped a hundred dollars by 1890, as much as the pay of all but the top editors, misgivings of this sort would probably have focused mainly on professional responsibilities. Reporters, no matter how well regarded, do not have the final say in shaping a publication. That may explain why Ralph and another *Sun* reporter launched a literary magazine called *Chatter* as a part-time undertaking in 1890. Despite free, if involuntary, contributions from such noted English writers as Thomas Hardy and A. Conan Doyle, who in the absence of international copyright protection in 1890 could not collect when their work was reprinted abroad, financial troubles led to *Chatter's* demise after only six months.

The yearning to sit at the editor's desk reflected by Ralph's magazine venture must surely have extended to the *Sun* on occasion. It may well be that Ralph would not have been a very good editor; he might have lacked the sense of balance and proportion that an editor, faced with a dozen competing claims for space, must have. Or it may be that Ralph never became an editor at the *Sun* simply because Charles Dana and Chester Lord regarded him as too brilliant a reporter to waste in any other role. Henry Grady of the Atlanta *Constitution,* who himself was always torn between reporting and editing, at his death left behind in his desk a note observing:

"A good reporter who subsides into an able editor marks a loss to journalism." Still, whatever the reason that Ralph's career took the direction it did, his failure to join Lord or Selah Clarke as one of Dana's subordinate editors meant that his influence within the office was more limited than it might have been.

At the same time, the absence of bylines blocked Ralph from achieving wide recognition beyond the office. In Dana's era the Sunday edition of the *Sun* printed a few signed features, often by outside writers, but the *Sun's* news stories never carried bylines. Scanning many hundreds of issues of the paper from Ralph's long service there turns up his byline only once—on a Sunday piece about New York music halls, one of his extracurricular interests. He may have written a handful of other signed articles, but for all practical purposes Ralph was as anonymous in the *Sun* as the greenest reporter in the newsroom.

Possibly because a few newspapers, including the New York *World* and the Boston *Globe,* had expanded the use of bylines, the *Sun's* editors felt compelled to defend their policy of anonymous authorship in 1893. It allowed articles to be judged strictly on their merits, an editorial explained. "Under the anonymous system of journalism, an article is admitted into a newspaper on its deserts, and, therefore, a high standard of excellence can be more easily maintained than where the reputation or notoriety of an author enters into an editor's calculations." For the *Sun* this rationale may have sufficed, and it is undeniable that bad writing bearing the name of a well-known figure often finds its way into print more easily than good writing by an unknown. But for the newspaper world generally, the underlying reason for the absence of bylines was tradition—the lowly origins of reporting, the preeminence of editors.

In any case, the no-byline policy clashed with human nature. Reporters shared the universal craving to stand out from the crowd and gain public credit for work well done. A contributor to the *Writer* complained in 1888 that the only way a journalist could truly make his mark was "by impressing the superiority of himself upon the appreciation of the world," but this was impossible under "the present order of things" because "Only the journalist's immediate friends ever heard of him as a journalist." The real reason newspapers favored anonymity, the author suggested, was that it weakened writers' bargaining power and saved publishers money. "Anonymous journalism is profitable to the owners of newspapers. That is the reason it exists." Richard Harding Davis, who lost little time in fleeing the reporting staff of the *Evening Sun* for more visible lines of work, grumbled in 1892 that newspaper owners "who cannot tell a display head from a third alarm of fire" got all the attention while "the real newspaper men" were unknown except to their colleagues.

Ralph did not quarrel publicly with anonymity for reporters, but he chafed under it. At the end of the eighties he began taking occasional breaks from the *Sun* to travel and write magazine articles. With the flexibility allowed by the space system, which meant that the *Sun* didn't have to pay him if he didn't turn in a story, Ralph stepped up this activity until in the nineties there were periods when he relegated newspaper work to a sideline and focused almost exclusively on magazines. As with any editorial ambitions Ralph may have harbored, money would probably not have been a significant motive, at least in the beginning. Although eventually he must have commanded much more substantial fees, in 1890 magazines seldom paid more than a cent a word—twenty-five to fifty dollars for most articles. What magazines did offer Ralph from the outset, however, was the opportunity to sign his work. For the first time he enjoyed a measure of recognition not just within his profession but from the public at large.

In his autobiography Ralph said that he submitted articles to magazines for thirteen years before his first acceptance. When this occurred is not known, but by 1889 he was making regular sales and felt confident enough about magazine writing to begin taking time off from the *Sun* to pursue it. Before long he was among the most productive magazine writers in the country. From 1890 through 1895, the last year he was affiliated with the *Sun*, Ralph published almost 150 pieces in important American magazines.

In the course of his magazine work he delved into almost every conceivable field—history, politics, international affairs, economics, education, journalism, travel, sports, Indians, immigration, architecture, religion, technology. He wasted nothing. When he visited a meat-packing plant in Chicago for an 1892 article, he came away impressed by the way the industry found a use for every last scrap of a slaughtered animal—"without particularizing too closely," bone for knife handles, gut for sausage casing, hoofs for glue. But as a magazine writer Ralph operated in very similar fashion.

When his train derails just as he settles down in the diner to roast chicken, hashed potatoes and a double portion of stewed tomatoes, the result is an article on train wrecks. A chat with a retired sheriff in Montana becomes the germ for an article about the lawless days in the old West.

When Ralph is bored to tears on an ocean voyage, he sells a piece about boredom at sea. Sometimes leftover odds and ends from his notebooks even turn up as short stories and sketches in magazines—no more enduring than most magazine fiction but occasionally interesting a century later for the light they shed on some of the little-known corners of existence that Ralph explored in his journalistic research. After Ralph had accumulated a number of related magazine articles or stories, he would recycle them between hard covers. All told, he would eventually publish more than a dozen books.

At one time or another Ralph contributed to *Scribner's,* the *Century,* the *Review of Reviews,* and even *Scientific American,* but mostly he wrote for *Harper's Weekly* and *Harper's Monthly.* Ralph's association with Harper and Brothers, the publisher of both the popular weekly and the more literary monthly, began to flourish after he sailed to England in the summer of 1889 with a commission to write a series of "letters" for *Harper's Weekly.* He gathered so much material in his ten weeks in England that the weekly was still printing articles from the trip in 1891. They touched on matters as varied as the accessibility of public toilets, his puzzlement over the leasehold system, and English speech ("an English sentence is uttered like the blade of a Holland skate, in a long straight bar with a curl at the end").

Over the next several years the Harper magazines sent Ralph on journeys to various parts of the United States and to Canada. Seemingly delighted to print anything he offered them, they occasionally even ran two Ralph pieces in a single issue. Harper and Brothers also published the books that collected Ralph's magazine work, and, in an altogether cozy arrangement, *Harper's Monthly* usually greeted each with a laudatory review.

Harper kept an army of artists busy producing drawings to illustrate the articles in its magazines, and one of those with whom Ralph sometimes worked was Frederic Remington. Remington was eight years younger than Ralph but had been contributing Western sketches to *Harper's Weekly* regularly since the mid-eighties. Their professional association began in 1889. Both were members of the Players, a new club made up of men from the theatrical, artistic, and literary worlds, and as they drank before a fire in the clubhouse on Gramercy Park one Saturday night shortly before Christmas they were struck with the improbable notion that they should go moose-hunting in Canada. Hastily arranging to defray at least part of the expense by producing something for Harper, they took a train north the next day. Ralph, who had been hunting only once before in his life, as a boy, was never able to get warm in the week they spent camping in the frozen Hudson Bay country, and he quickly tired of the fried salt pork that was a dietary staple. But he got a moose and articles for both *Harper's Weekly* and *Harper's Monthly,* the latter illustrated by Remington.

Ralph and Remington subsequently cooperated on numerous other projects for Harper, including a lengthy expedition through western Canada that produced a series of articles for the monthly and a book entitled *On Canada's Frontier.* Their professional relationship was accompanied by a personal friendship. Ralph and Remington had similarities. Both were vigorous and outgoing. Both were big men: Remington, though only five feet nine inches tall, weighed two hundred and thirty pounds, and Ralph, perhaps three inches taller, weighed two hundred pounds. Despite Ralph's protests that journalists' taste for alcohol was exaggerated, he seems to have shared with Remington a considerable capacity for liquor.

But Remington must have been a trying friend at times. He was self-indulgent and undisciplined about everything but his work, and his drinking often went beyond all bounds. When William Randolph Hearst's New York *Journal* sent Richard Harding Davis to Cuba with Remington in 1897 to report on the insurrection against Spain, Davis was relieved when Remington left for home after only a week; Remington, he said, "always wanted to talk it over and that had to be done in the nearest . . . cafe, and it always took him fifteen minutes before he got his cocktails to suit him."

Even the loyal Ralph must have found that Remington's behavior sometimes crossed the line from the adventurous and playful to the irresponsible. On their trip to western Canada Ralph was horrified when a chief of the Blackfoot Indians offered to order his braves to perform a "sun dance" involving self-torture at a charge of five dollars a warrior, but Remington, according to his biographers, slipped the chief some money when Ralph wasn't looking and then sketched the ritual. At times, moreover, Remington, who had studied art at Yale, appears to have treated Ralph—a former printer, after all—rather demeaningly. With his wife, a woman of some social pretensions, the artist lived on an estate in New Rochelle, and Ralph's reception there was not always warm. Once when Ralph proposed a visit to discuss a business matter Remington headed him off, telegraphing that he would prefer to meet him at the Harper office in the city.

In general, however, as he became known through his magazine writing, Ralph seems to have moved easily in exalted circles. At the Players his fellow members included the actors Edwin Booth and John Drew, the

Ralph, left, poses with Frederic Remington against a painted backdrop in a photographer's studio. Remington worked from the photograph in drawing an illustration for an article by Ralph on their moose-hunting expedition to Canada.
Kansas State Historical Society

architect Stanford White and the painter Eastman Johnson, plus a host of prominent writers and editors. He was welcome at the literary salon of Ella Wheeler Wilcox, the poet who wrote "Laugh, and the world laughs with you;/ Weep, and you weep alone." When he organized an excursion to the Thousand Islands for a group of his newspaper friends, the New York Central laid on a special train, most likely because Ralph was on close terms with Chauncey Depew, who ran the railroad for the Vanderbilts. And a magazine article that Ralph wrote about Theodore Roosevelt in 1895 gives evidence of time passed rocking on the veranda of Sagamore Hill, Roosevelt's house overlooking Long Island Sound at Oyster Bay.

Around 1890 the Ralph family moved from Brooklyn back to Manhattan, more fashionable and considerably more expensive. During the next few years the Ralphs rented a succession of Manhattan row houses, including places on East Forty-seventh Street, West Sixtieth, and West Thirty-eighth. Julian drew on his domestic life for a *Harper's Weekly* article entitled "City House of Today." The first-class Manhattan rental dwelling, said Ralph, boasted electric lights, fireplaces with gas logs, and a bathroom that could fairly be described as "a beautiful chamber." The householder who was so inclined—and Ralph apparently was so inclined—scarcely need lift a finger. There was a man to sweep the walk and another to tend the furnace and roll the barrels of ashes out to the curb. The butcher, the grocer, the baker, the milkman, and the laundryman paraded to the basement door. If the woman of the house did not feel up to supervising the cooking, to say nothing of doing it herself, she could order meals sent in from a nearby hotel.

Between his work for the *Sun* and for magazines and his evenings out at the Players, Ralph spent much time away from home. He was even gone for a couple of Christmases, once when he went moose-hunting with Frederic Remington and another time when he was out west on his own for Harper. In his writings Ralph took little care to set Belle's mind at ease about his absences. His travel articles usually cast an appraising eye on the local women, and he generally found something to admire. They, in turn, seem to have spent some time appraising him. A brief news item in the New York *Times* in 1895 recounted an incident in which an impostor posing as Julian Ralph checked into a Pittsburgh hotel. When word of the noted journalist's supposed presence somehow spread around town, said the *Times,* "Several ladies from the east end telephoned . . . that they would like to see Mr. Ralph."

On the other hand, Ralph's frank appreciation of attractive women has a guileless quality about it, and now and then he even sounds rather strait-laced. When he visited England for *Harper's Weekly* in 1889, he made a side trip to France. Although he judged the women of Paris "magnificent," he was offended by the "perverted morals" and "degenerate tastes" he found there. Sometimes he also comes across as a man with strong ties to home and family. On his trips to Indian country he always returned home laden with tomahawks, war clubs, and beaded costumes that delighted his children. And around 1894 he wrote an intimate and touching poem on the subject of married love. In their youth, it suggested, Julian and Belle had scarcely known the meaning of love, but in later years their marriage had ripened into a powerful, fulfilling union. The poem ended:

> What if we did not love at first?
> Thank God, sweet wife, we thought we did.

True to form, he sold the poem to a magazine, the *Critic*.

In a letter to a friend Remington described Ralph in the wilds of western Canada: "Ralph is a large fat man & he had a little runt of a pinto—it was his first experience in the saddle and with a funny hat with a piece of cheese cloth on it, pants worked up to his knees, he did an act which made one think of Mark Twains Doctor in the Holy Land." Remington was in no position to ridicule anyone for being fat and it could hardly be true that Ralph had never mounted a horse before, but it is true that he was often out of his element as he traveled in remote places on behalf of magazines.

His element was New York City. Watching "a rushing, howling torrent of excited braves on the plains," Ralph, according to a self-description, wore his "derby hat and awkward New York clothes." Like Englishmen dispatched to the outposts of empire, he strove to maintain his accustomed way of life; a review of *On Canada's Frontier* in the *Nation* observed that when Ralph "goes into the backwoods" he "takes a good cook with him." And although, as a review of one of his other books put it, Ralph's "good nature and his happy faculty of taking a kindly interest in everybody with whom he comes in contact" contributed greatly to his success as a reporter, an underlying condescension marked his view of the world beyond Man-hattan. He always seemed mildly surprised when he found streetcars and running water and tall buildings in backwaters like Minneapolis, Chicago, or Denver, and he was forever judging restaurants and hotels and fashions by his New York standards. Chicago newspapers once complained that

Ralph was incapable of writing about the Midwest without making slighting comparisons to the East.

His provincial outlook must occasionally have grated on readers of national magazines. But more often than not Ralph's clear-cut New York point of view—his comparison, say, of a strange city's traffic to the bustle of Fulton and Broadway—sharpened the focus of his magazine articles. It accomplished the same end in his work for the *Sun,* and it was only one of the characteristics of his magazine writing that helped explain why he was such a valuable newspaper reporter. There was also the bottomless, wide-ranging curiosity, the fascination with how the world works—from the building of a ship or the supplying of water to a city to the functioning of railroad monopolies and federal Indian policies. And there was the willingness to tackle any subject, the ability to get a story out of anything; he could indeed, as his admirers said, have gotten copy out of a cobblestone.

Most important, there was his eye for incident, character, and telling detail. He visits Buffalo Bill's Wild West Show and notes that Buffalo Bill has a telephone in his tent. He learns of an Englishman living deep in the Canadian wilds, where he represents the Hudson's Bay Company, a man whose mail is delivered only once a year; having arranged to receive a complete set of the *Times* of London for the previous year in his annual mail, each morning at breakfast he peruses the year-old issue of the *Times* for that date. Ralph enlivens what could have been a very ordinary account of an excursion by American tourists to Clovelly on the Devon coast by weaving in a lovers' spat between two young members of the group, who end up going their separate ways.

The truth is, however, that bright bits such as these stand out in part because so little of Ralph's magazine work is memorable. Character sketches of public figures such as Theodore Roosevelt and Chauncey Depew are bland and deferential, demonstrating that a journalist can know those he writes about *too* well. Much of the travel writing is flat and pedestrian, reading like copy produced to order—a few statistics on lumber production and bank deposits dressed up with touches of local color, then on to the next assignment.

In short, Ralph's magazine work lacks the spontaneity and life of the newspaper stories he wrote under the spur of events. That apparently was the view on Park Row of most of his efforts outside daily journalism, though perhaps attitudes there reflected a touch of sour grapes. "There is better quality in the things he wrote hastily and anonymously for the *Sun* than in some of the eight or nine published volumes"—the actual total was considerably higher—"that bear his name," said Frank O'Brien, "and the reason for this is that he was primarily a newspaperman." Certainly it was Ralph's newspaper work, not his magazine articles and books, that made him a legend among his journalistic contemporaries. The magazine articles, for the most part, could have been written by any number of writers. On the other hand, few could have matched some of Ralph's newspaper-reporting feats.

He continued to work as a reporter in the nineties, but because of his magazine work he did not show up at the *Sun* at noon every day to take an assignment from the city editor. He seems to have worked out his own special arrangements. While traveling for Harper he sent the *Sun* occasional pieces, such as an account of an 1892 range war in Wyoming, and he scheduled his life so that he could represent the *Sun* on some big stories of which there was advance notice. At other times he made himself available when he could. An article in *Munsey's Magazine* in 1893 entitled "The Men Who Make the New York *Sun*" described Ralph, who had won "repute as the best of American reporters," strolling into the office in the early evening "with ponderous and yet graceful, swinging gait." He is "received with something of awe by the young reporters" and "greeted with cordiality" by managing editor Chester Lord, with whom Ralph pauses to chat.

Perhaps, while he is talking to Mr. Lord, there comes over the wires the report of some world stirring calamity, some news of momentous import. He eyes his managing editor for a moment. . . . Mr. Ralph says: "Shall I go?" and if Mr. Lord replies "Yes, at once," it may be that within the next twenty four hours Ralph is five hundred miles away, prepared for an all night session with the telegraph operators, whose wires he is sure to make hot.

Although Ralph retained his ties to the *Sun* till 1895, 1893 is the last year that anything is known about his work there. That was the year he reported the second inauguration of Grover Cleveland as President in March and the free-silver fight in the Senate in late summer and early fall. In between he took on at least two important assignments for the *Sun:* the opening of the 1893 world's fair in Chicago and the trial of Lizzie Borden in New Bedford, Massachusetts.

Long before the World's Columbian Exposition opened on Chicago's lakefront on May 1, Ralph had written extensively about the fair for Harper. The fair boasted a large publicity apparatus—the first extensive undertaking of this sort Ralph had encountered—that flooded journalists with material, and much of the copy Ralph produced for Harper was glowing stuff that could just as well have been turned out by the fair's promoters. Indeed, when Harper collected a number of Ralph's magazine articles about Chicago and the fair in a book, it noted that the chapters on the fair had been "approved by the Department of Publicity and Promotion of the World's Columbian Exposition."

The department would not have approved the articles he wrote for the *Sun* in the fair's first week. In time, they acknowledged, the fair would undoubtedly live up to its advance billing—an assemblage of white plaster palaces dazzlingly outlined in electric lights by night, mechanical marvels ranging from the dynamo to the Ferris wheel, art that included works by Manet and Rodin. But for the present almost nothing was ready and the place was a mess.

President Cleveland spoke on the opening day amid rain, cold, and mud. "The speech," Ralph reported, "was delivered from the front of the exposition grounds, and a great concourse gradually sunk into the mud while listening to it." The mud sucked rubber overshoes off the feet of many of the President's listeners, and afterwards a black man dug them up for resale. Everywhere stood unfinished buildings, unopened packing cases containing the exhibits, and heaps of debris. "If our entire American navy had been wrecked in the lake and all the wreckage had floated on the Exposition beach, there would not have been more litter and rubbish than is piled there now," said Ralph. On the midway he spotted a sign reading "Forty Beauties from Forty Nations Welcome You—Not Open," and outside the harems on the Avenue de Turk two hundred men peered through lattice screens trying vainly for a glimpse of the "beautiful black-eyed odalisques" rumored to be inside.

Aside from the exhibits and entertainments, Ralph reported that Chicago hotels were doubling and tripling rates and that food prices were extortionate. He was also irked by an order forbidding the smoking of cigars on the fairgrounds, and he kept calling attention to it in the *Sun* until the authorities rescinded it. Ralph's comments on the locals reflected unabashed New York snobbery. The Chicago waiters were too familiar for his tastes, and the women's dresses appeared to have been "fashioned in the heart of the woods." As for the men: "One remarks that they are peculiar. They wear soft hats, they carry no canes, and they do not use gloves."

By Ralph's standards, the people of "the interior" were also innocents when it came to art. Nude statues of males shocked them. "Wives drag their husbands away, and mothers and sisters, after one startled glance, tug at their children to lead them out of danger before they have seen the statues and it is too late." In the Palace of Art a man escorting two women inquired of a stranger: "Sir, can you tell me whether this next gallery is for gentlemen or both sexes?"

In a gesture reminiscent of Henry Ward Beecher's performance at his adultery trial eighteen years earlier, Lizzie Borden showed up in court one day carrying a bunch of pansies, which she left lying in her lap. "Ophelia's words, 'there is pansies, that's for thoughts,' leaped to the mind," wrote Ralph in the *Sun*. "What thoughts were these delicate flowers dedicated to upon this occasion? If to the prisoner's, who would dare to say what was their nature? Were they guiltless as those of the poor mad girl in the play, or deep and damned like Lady Macbeth's?"

In the 1890s a reporter covering a sensational murder trial—and few were more sensational than Lizzie's for the ax murders of Andrew and Abby Borden, her father and stepmother—was still expected to provide more than unadorned facts. A medical expert from Harvard testified and Ralph commented: "He had held converse with blood, had interviewed bones, had cross-examined half-digested food in human stomachs, and was on speaking terms with infinitesimal specks of gore that had been spattered during the murders." Andrew Borden's hacked skull was displayed. "It was done up in a white handkerchief, and looked like a bouquet such as a man carries to his sweetheart," said Ralph. His stories were also laced with speculation and opinion, and although some began with summaries of the previous day's proceedings or with their climactic point, there was much narrative and drama.

The trial ran for two weeks in June in the courthouse in New Bedford, twelve miles from Fall River, the scene of the murders in August 1892. Ralph—described by a history of the affair as "possibly the most distinguished newspaper correspondent at this time"—was one of some thirty reporters and artists present. Special telegraph facilities and operators had been installed for the press in a carriage shed behind the courthouse. Throughout the trial Ralph sat in a seat in the first row of journalists, not far from Lizzie. His daily stories filled three or four columns in the *Sun*. They were stories to savor, perhaps to read at leisure in the evening.

The circumstantial case against Lizzie was strong. She had a motive: unmarried and living at home, she feared her father's considerable wealth might slip into the hands of her stepmother, with whom her relations were decidedly chilly. She had the opportunity: she was present at the Borden residence when the murders were committed there. Her account of her movements about the property during this time was utterly implausible. Moreover, both before and after the murders she had engaged in suspicious behavior, making an abortive attempt to buy poison the day before, burning the dress she apparently had worn the day of the murders in the kitchen stove three days after.

And yet, in another similarity to the Beecher trial, some of the same attitudes that had protected the celebrated clergyman were working in Lizzie's favor in the New Bedford courtroom. Many people simply found it impossible to accept that a respectable member of society like Lizzie—a plain, plumpish figure in black who was active in Christian Endeavor and retreated behind a fan when the testimony turned grisly—could have committed the atrocious acts she was charged with. There was also the matter of the frailty of the female sex; many, apparently including Ralph, doubted that Lizzie would have been strong enough to deliver the savage ax blows that killed the Bordens—eighteen for Abby, ten for Andrew, according to the Harvard expert. And so, at the midpoint of the trial, the *Sun's* man was in a quandary: "He only knows that after studying the testimony and talking to the lawyers on both sides, he is convinced that the Bordens were brutally slain, but could not have been murdered by the prisoner nor yet by anyone else than the prisoner."

Inconsistent, contradictory testimony by the Fall River police undermined the prosecution's case. Their stories "were not as uniform as the clothes they wore," observed Ralph. Lizzie had hired a masterful lawyer, a former governor of Massachusetts named George D. Robinson, and again and again he tripped up police witnesses. After a particularly devastating cross-examination of one officer, Robinson dismissed him "with a wave of his hand, as one might fling away an orange after tasting it and finding it insipid." At another point, wrote Ralph, "The operation could almost be likened to a pigeon-shooting match, in which District Attorney Moody kept flinging up the birds and defying his antagonist to hit them, while the ex-governor as constantly fired, and often, but by no means always, wounded or brought them down." Robinson had hit the mark often enough, however, to convince the lawyers questioned by Ralph as the trial neared its end that "the jurors will not find the rich maiden of Fall River guilty of the butcheries."

"We don't burn witches in Massachusetts now," said Governor Robinson during closing arguments on Monday, June 19. The prosecutor insisted:

"We must face these cases as men, not as gallants." The next day the jury returned with its verdict.

"Lizzie Andrew Borden," said the Clerk of the court, "stand up." She rose unsteadily, with a face as white as marble.

"Gentlemen, have you agreed upon a verdict?" said the clerk to the jury.

It was so still in court that the flutter of two fans made a great noise.

"We have," said Foreman Richards boldly.

The prisoner was gripping the rail in front of the dock as if her standing up depended upon its keeping its place.

"Lizzie Andrew Borden," said the clerk, "hold up your right hand."

"Jurors, look upon the prisoner. Prisoner, look upon the foreman."

Every juryman stood at right about-face, staring at the woman. There was such a gentle, kindly light beaming in every eye that no one questioned the verdict that was to be uttered. But God save every woman from the feelings that Lizzie Borden showed in the return look she cast upon that jury. It was what is pictured as the rolling gaze of a dying woman. She seemed not to have the power to move her eyes directly where she was told to, and they swung all around in her head. They looked at the ceiling; they looked at everything but they saw nothing. It was a horrible, a pitiful sight to see her then.

"What say you, Mr. Foreman?" said the gentle old clerk.

"Not guilty," shouted Mr. Richards.

At the words the wretched woman fell quicker than ever an ox fell in the stock yards of Chicago. Her forehead crashed against the heavy walnut rail of the dock so as to shake the reporter of the *Sun* who sat next to her, twelve feet away, leaning on the rail. It seemed that she must be stunned, but she was not. Quickly, with an unconscious movement, she flung up both arms and threw them over the rail and pressed them under her face so that it rested on them.

The verdict, commented Ralph, "left the people where they began— asking one another who killed Mr. and Mrs. Borden."

Toward the end of the summer of 1894 Ralph undertook an assignment for Harper that was to mark the beginning of the end of his association with the *Sun*. He went to Asia to write about a war that had broken out between China and Japan in Korea, where both countries sought to exert control.

Ralph traveled first to Japan. He crossed Canada on the Canadian Pacific Railroad to Vancouver, where he embarked on a new Canadian Pacific steamer, the *Empress of Japan*. Characteristically, he squeezed pieces for *Harper's Weekly* out of both the rail journey and the ocean passage. Aboard the train were 350 Chinese workers starting their return trip to China with the small fortunes they had earned abroad and a small contingent of

Japanese military officers; Ralph found the Japanese quick and sharp and the Chinese "very dull and commonplace." The big news aboard the *Empress of Japan,* a new white-hulled vessel whose deck was furnished with wicker settees and little tables to hold drinks, was that Ralph's fellow passengers included Lord and Lady Randolph Churchill, bound on a leisurely trip around the world. Lord Randolph did not look well—he would be dead within a few months—but his vivacious wife, the former Jennie Jerome of New York, entertained on the piano in the grand salon.

Ralph reached Yokohama on September 10. He quickly learned that correspondents were to be allowed nowhere near the fighting, in which Japanese troops would push into Chinese territory and by the next spring completely rout the Chinese. But his inability to see the war he had been sent to cover did not noticeably cramp his style. On the basis of two weeks in Japan and two months in China—all in and around Shanghai, well out of the war zone—Ralph produced some two dozen magazine pieces. The stay in China, which included a brief venture into the interior aboard a houseboat on the Grand Canal, also yielded a book. The *Nation* described it as "a delightful book of travels in the form of stories and sketches" but hinted that it was a bit superficial. "Despite the facile pen of the writer and his chameleon-like power of quickly catching and reflecting the colors of a region visited by him for but a few months," said the reviewer, "there is to one long familiar with 'chit-book,' 'tiffin,' 'boy,' and 'cumshaw,' a curious sense of limitation in both the text and its writer."

Ralph's writings from Asia touched on many matters—military and political analysis, missionaries, the cultural clash between East and West, and a dinner given by a magistrate in Shanghai at which Ralph, as an honored literary man, had been seated on a throne, from which his legs "stuck straight out, as if I was a baby in an arm-chair." In the end, however, one brief dispatch from Shanghai that was printed in the December 1, 1894, issue of *Harper's Weekly* overshadowed everything else.

The article dealt with an incident arising out of the United States' assumption of a loosely defined responsibility for Japanese nationals caught in China after the war began. Believing he was acting in accord with the obligation, the U.S. consul at Shanghai gave asylum to two young Japanese students accused by the Chinese of spying. But subsequently Secretary of State Walter Gresham informed the consul that he had overstepped the bounds of his country's role and ordered him to turn the Japanese youths over to the Chinese immediately.

Their fate remained unknown until Ralph reported in *Harper's Weekly* that the students had been horribly tortured and then beheaded by the Chinese. Ralph waxed indignant. "A higher influence than law—that of common humanity—seemed to demand that a country which we officially characterize as semi-civilized should not be allowed to wreak its anger upon our wards until we were satisfied that they had offended that nation's laws," he wrote. "But we missed that fine point of humanity and surrendered the men." Sounding very much like a budding imperialist, Ralph said that to avoid such humiliation in the future the United States should make its armed presence felt in Chinese ports. "If this publication result in the sending of some war-ships here to enable us to command the respect that is now denied us, I shall feel that nothing I have ever written in my life has been of such value to my country as this."

Ralph's article was front-page news in the New York *Times.* A condescending story from a *Times* Washington correspondent, reflecting the views of Secretary of State Gresham, suggested that Ralph simply didn't understand the situation. "In so far as the Secretary was able to judge from the language used by Mr. Ralph," said the story, "he was compelled to believe that Mr. Ralph was not fully in possession of the facts of the case, and that while it may have seemed to him to be very easy to prevent the Chinese from taking possession of the men, and afterward killing them, there were unfortunate complications which had been overlooked."

But the *Times* reprinted most of Ralph's *Harper's Weekly* article, and his old paper, the *Sun,* declared in an editorial: "We can assure the Government and people of Japan that in this shameful business it is Mr. Julian Ralph, and not Secretary Gresham, who represents the heart and conscience of the United States." Early in 1895, in response to a resolution offered by Senator Henry Cabot Lodge of Massachusetts, the administration presented all the records of the affair to the Senate. *Harper's Weekly* commented: "The correspondence shows conclusively that Mr. Ralph was entirely right in every accusation that he made, and in all his statements of fact."

By December 1894 Ralph was back in New York. In the ensuing months he spent some of his time cleaning out his Chinese notebooks for pieces in *Harper's Monthly* and *Harper's Weekly.* He worked on readying the China book for publication, as well as two other books, one a collection of articles about the South and the other a series of fictional sketches set on the Lower East Side in which he showed that somewhere along the way he had picked up considerable knowledge about the life of New York's poor. He dashed off other articles for Harper, including an embarrassingly flattering piece for the weekly about Frederic Remington ("Of powerful build, with half his life yet unspent, with such a temperament and such health as to keep the bloom of boyhood on his face and heart, what bounds should narrow his field?"). He also undertook new travels around the United States for Harper, crisscrossing the country from East to West and North to South. These journeys yielded articles on subjects ranging from the Southern Pacific monopoly in California and coeducation at the University of Michigan to Ralph's experiences in the Sierra Nevadas on "Norwegian snowshoes," nine-foot boards that sound like primitive cross-country skis. "There is much to be learned before a snow-shoer becomes adept," observed Ralph.

Presumably, when he was not off learning to ski or editing proofs of a book, he undertook an occasional assignment for the *Sun*—as always, anonymously. But if his days were full, they must have seemed tame after Asia and the stir caused by his reporting there. He had tasted the life of a foreign correspondent at the center of world events and he liked it, but clearly the place for a foreign correspondent who wanted to make his impact felt on a regular basis was on the staff of a major daily newspaper. Possibilities at the *Sun* were limited. It was no longer thriving as it once had, its foreign staff was tiny, and just possibly there was some resentment against Ralph on the *Sun*—a feeling that he had deserted the cause.

But a whole new prospect was opening up for journalists in New York. William Randolph Hearst, who had turned the San Francisco *Examiner* into a roaring success, was coming to town to take on Joseph Pulitzer and his *World*. In September 1895 Hearst bought the struggling New York *Journal*. He immediately set about building a strong staff for his new enterprise, and soon leading New York journalists were receiving cards reading "Mr. Hearst would be pleased if you would call." "They are trying to get all the well-known men at big prices," said Richard Harding Davis, whom Hearst hired away from an editorship at *Harper's Weekly*. Another of those successfully wooed by Hearst was Ralph. His specific duties remained to be decided, but an assignment abroad was clearly in the works.

15. Foreign Correspondent

Ralph's initial assignment for Hearst took him only as far as St. Thomas's Episcopal Church on the Upper East Side of Manhattan. The occasion was the wedding of Consuelo Vanderbilt, the old commodore's great-granddaughter, to the ninth duke of Marlborough. Ralph's account of the splendiferous affair, which climaxed a spate of transatlantic exchanges of American fortunes for European titles, filled most of pages 1 and 2 of the New York *Journal* for November 7, 1895, the first issue turned out under Hearst's command.

The story resembled those Ralph had often done for the *Sun* on great ceremonial occasions, but as it appeared in print in the *Journal* there were differences. A huge drawing of the wedding party—lavish illustration was a Hearst trademark—slashed diagonally through the copy on the front page. And at the start of the story, in type as large as a headline in the *Sun,* was a line reading "Described by Julian Ralph." After two decades of anonymity in the *Sun,* such public credit in the columns of his newspaper had to be gratifying.

But while bylines may have increased the *Journal's* appeal for Ralph, they would not have been a decisive consideration for him, nor for some of the other prominent writers who signed on with Hearst. By now, at the age of forty-two, Ralph was already fairly well known from his books and magazine articles. Two other men lured by Hearst soon after he took over the New York *Journal*—Stephen Crane, whose novel *The Red Badge of Courage* appeared in 1895, and the dashing Richard Harding Davis—were even better known and would have been still less likely to be tempted merely by more fame and celebrity. What had to have captured the interest of all three was the "big prices" Davis spoke of—money in amounts unheard of in the newspaper world. Hearst had millions of dollars from his family's mining fortune to pour into journalism, and he was prepared to spend unstintingly to make his newspapers the biggest and most powerful.

Raiding other newspapers—particularly Pultizer's *World*, his archrival for mass readership—Hearst was credited with driving up the already respectable newspaper pay level in New York by 25 percent. Stars could command princely sums. Richard Harding Davis would earn $500 for covering a football game, $3,000 for a month's work in Cuba. Arthur Brisbane, who had started at the *Sun* and then switched to the *World,* became a Hearst editor in 1897 and soon was making $1,000 a week. Davis and Brisbane were exceptional cases, but it is likely that a reporter of Ralph's standing would have been offered, in salary or some sort of gilt-edged space-payment guarantee, upwards of $10,000 a year, enough to qualify him for membership in the economic elite in the mid-nineties.

Although in time it became obligatory for many of those who took Hearst's money to let it be known that they nevertheless loathed his journalism, when Ralph was hired in 1895 the depths to which Hearst would sink in sensationalism and faking as he battled Pulitzer for circulation were not yet apparent. Moreover, on a personal level, the megalomania that would come to dominate Hearst's character was not yet full-blown. On the contrary, the William Randolph Hearst of 1895—he turned thirty-two that year—had appealing qualities. Born to wealth, he had somehow acquired a concern for the poor and the underdog that seemed genuine. He was a shy, polite man who listened intently to what his subordinates had to say, phrased his orders in the form of "suggestions," and exuded a contagious enthusiasm for the newspaper business. It is easy to imagine him charming a veteran like Ralph, recalling his stellar feats for the *Sun,* speaking admiringly of the stir caused by his reports from China for *Harper's Weekly,* and conjuring up visions of the exciting prospects at the *Journal.*

Having recruited a galaxy of stars, however, Hearst sometimes seems to have had difficulty keeping them busy. In the weeks following the Marlborough-Vanderbilt wedding, Ralph wrote a number of other articles, including lengthy interviews with Police Board President Theodore Roosevelt, who over dinner denied reports that crime was on the rise in New York, and with a noted visitor to the city, Henry M. Stanley—although now a bored member of Parliament in London, once, in Ralph's eyes, "the greatest of newspaper correspondents."

But for the "crime and underwear" copy ("TORTURED BY HER MANIAC HUSBAND," "CHOPPED HER SISTER ALMOST TO PIECES," "ROBBED OF WIFE BY THE DENTIST") that Hearst relied on to entice readers day in and day out, the *Journal* called on swarms of anonymous reporters whose contributions were blended into stories by editors and rewritemen in the *Journal's* rented quarters in the *Tribune* building. An old

Sun man like Ralph, proud of his ability to handle the most challenging assignments on his own, did not fit easily into this scheme of things, and in mid-December Hearst told Ralph to take a week off. One evening a few days before Christmas he was strolling from his house on West Thirty-eighth Street to the theater when the "sixth sense" he prided himself on went into operation.

> I had gone about four blocks from my home, out of a quiet residence street into the boisterous stir of Sixth Avenue, in New York, when I saw a district messenger lad propelling himself head foremost, as boys and bullets have a way of doing. Something prompted me to put out an arm and stop him. "Where are you going with that message?" I asked.
> "Ralph," said he; "19 West Thirty-eighth Street."
> "Give it to me," I said, and he did so. It was a request from my office to know whether I could start the next morning at seven o'clock to fill the post of correspondent in London for my paper.

A diplomatic crisis had erupted between the United States and Britain. The border between British Guiana and Venezuela was in dispute and London was hinting it might resort to force to settle the matter; Washington, for its part, was threatening to invoke the Monroe Doctrine's prohibition against European intervention in the Americas. Ralph presumably abandoned his theater plans, returned home to pack, and in the morning sailed for England, leaving Belle and the rest of the family to celebrate yet another Christmas without him and then to follow.

Ralph never said much about his experiences as Hearst's man in London, at least in his surviving writings. In the digression on journalistic status in his 1894 magazine article on election night in a newspaper office, however, he had ranked the job near the top of the pecking order, observing that the staff regarded the London correspondent "nebulously, with awe, as the pagans consider one of their gods that operate and yet are never seen." Even though his tongue was partially in his cheek, it is clear that he had an exalted notion of his new assignment and that he crossed the Atlantic with high expectations. But it is also clear that these expectations were disappointed. Within a year and a half he had quit.

The files of the *Journal* for the year after Ralph began work in London early in 1896 show that the problem was not a lack of things to write about. In the 1890s news from the Continent and the British empire as well as from England flowed through London, and Ralph's byline turns up on a broad assortment of stories dealing with matters large and small. Besides the South American border dispute, which was eventually settled by arbitration, Ralph reported on a political crisis in France and a papal encyclical, on the Jameson Raid in South Africa and plague in India. There were dull stories about British trade prospects and interesting stories about a miraculous new device from Germany called the X ray, and Ralph regularly chronicled the social triumphs of "our duchess," as the *Journal* styled the former Consuelo Vanderbilt. The London correspondent of the *Journal* did not, of course, overlook tales of crime and scandal, particularly those involving Americans. When a prominent American man arrived in London with his paramour, Ralph made page 1 with the news, and he made it several days running when a proper American couple from San Francisco were arrested for shoplifting in London.

It was true that there was little time for firsthand reporting, which meant that Ralph's keen powers of observation went largely unused. The scope of the assignment was so broad that, like his fellow foreign correspondents in London, Ralph had to get most of his copy by rewriting stories in the British press. Still, he did manage an occasional interview with a newsworthy figure in London, traveled some in England, and on a handful of stories visited such Continental capitals as Paris, Budapest, and Vienna. Moreover, Ralph was almost certainly responsible for a reporting coup that resulted in an important *Journal* exclusive in 1896—the secret text of the treaty on arbitration of the border controversy between Venezuela and British Guiana. (Probably to protect a source, he received no public credit.) In any case, his work pleased Hearst sufficiently so that when the *Journal* ran a page of portraits of its leading contributors in November of 1896, Ralph was there, along with Stephen Crane and William Dean Howells.

Ralph's disenchantment with his role as Hearst's London correspondent, despite such recognition and despite high pay, may in part reflect his limited involvement as a reporter with the events that were dominating the news in this period—at least news as defined by the New York *Journal*. At the *Sun* he had become accustomed to being called on regularly to take on the day's big story, but now he was sometimes crowded off the front page of the *Journal* for long stretches. Except for the border dispute, the big stories, including the 1896 Presidential contest and the Cuban revolution, a cause that was increasingly an obsession with Hearst, were not in London.

Another situation almost certainly rankled even more. On some occasions when the prospect of a major story did come Ralph's way, he was upstaged by one of the stars of still greater magnitude attracted by Hearst's money. That very likely was the case in May of 1896.

Nicholas II was to be crowned czar of Russia with great pomp. It was a story made to order for Ralph; moreover, by way of buttressing his claim, somewhere along the way he had acquired the title of European editor as well as London correspondent. But the *Journal* sent Richard Harding Davis to Moscow instead. Davis wrote two front-page stories from Moscow, both topped by two-column sketches not of the czar but of the handsome, firm-jawed author. Back in England, as Davis was preparing to cover the coronation, Ralph was reporting the opening of the Oxfordshire Agricultural Show by the Duchess of Marlborough. The story, one of the few that Ralph covered in person, was amusing. Consuelo was so intent on blurting out her two-sentence speech before she forgot it that she all but ignored the waiting reception committee as she charged onto the platform, and later, when she was handing out prizes, an official stood behind her and frantically signaled the winning farmers to doff their caps as they approached the duchess. But the Oxfordshire Agricultural Show was no substitute for the coronation of a czar.

Ralph was not to be denied a visit to Russia, however. Early in 1897, he did the same thing he had done when he became restless at the *Sun*—he took time off to write magazine articles. Arranging for a leave from his London post, for a month he traveled through Russia from St. Petersburg in the north to the Caucasus in the south for *Harper's Monthly*. He gathered enough material to fill the lead spot in the magazine for three successive issues. He had made his point. If Hearst didn't think he was good enough to send to Russia, Harper did.

In the spring of 1897 the long-standing enmity between Greece and Turkey flared into open hostilities. From the perspective of history, the resulting war was utterly without significance. It lasted little more than a month, from mid-April to May 20. In the principal action of the war, Turkish troops moved south from Macedonia—then part of Turkey, later divided among Greece, Yugoslavia, and Bulgaria—into the Greek district of Thessaly and won a series of battles. After an armistice ended the fighting, the Turks withdrew, leaving the situation to return essentially to the status quo.

History aside, from the perspective of Julian Ralph, now back in the *Journal's* office in London, the Greco-Turkish war of 1897 had considerable significance. What at first looked like an opportunity to turn his

descriptive talents to the drama of battle ended up as a professional humiliation. This time he was not left behind, but once again he was destined to be
upstaged by a more celebrated star—Stephen Crane.

As the conflict loomed, Hearst had diverted his attention from Cuba long
enough to assign seven correspondents to the story. Six, including Crane,
were to report from the Greek side, which had wide support in the United
States. One, Ralph, was to report from the Turkish side. Besides appearing
in the *Journal* and Hearst's San Francisco *Examiner,* their war dispatches
had been purchased by a number of other large newspapers around the
country.

The correspondents assigned to the Greeks were warmly received and
allowed wide freedom of movement. Ralph, who had equipped himself
with a camp bed and an alcohol stove and armed himself with a revolver, as
was the custom among war correspondents of the day, was stymied from
the start. Smarting from accounts in the foreign press of Turkish atrocities
against the Armenians—Ralph himself had written of "the filthy Turk"—
Turkish officials had no intention of letting correspondents get a close look
at their troops in action. The Turkish consul in London was unhelpful in
clearing the way for Ralph to join up with the Turkish army, and for several
days he was delayed in leaving for the Continent and a train to Salonica, the
seat of Turkish rule in Macedonia. Once in Salonica, he had to call repeatedly at the military governor's office before he was finally granted credentials declaring him "a good friend of the Sultan" who was "anxious to witness the glories of Turkish arms." One of his few consolations as he prowled
the narrow, crowded streets of Salonica during five days of waiting was the
companionship of his eldest son, Lester, who, at the age of twenty, was
taking up the trade of sketch artist and hoped to try his hand at war drawings.

It was not until the end of April, when the war was almost half over, that
Julian and Lester headed south for Thessaly and the war zone. Traveling in
a landau with a mounted Turkish escort, they jounced over rocky roads at a
leisurely pace and paused frequently to rest and feast on roast lamb and
wine. It soon became evident that the Turks were taking Ralph on an
excursion carefully planned to ensure that he saw none of the fighting. "I
was being played with," Ralph said later. The Turks, while unfailingly
polite, kept him "waiting unconscionably everywhere." Time and again
Ralph arrived at battlefields long after the last shot had been fired and there
was nothing to see but deserted breastworks, abandoned Greek equipment,
and spent shells. One day toward the end of his guided tour he heard the
distant rumble of cannons and spotted some Greek corpses stripped of their

trousers—a sight the Turks would have preferred that he not see—but that was as close to the war as he got.

In any case, Ralph could not send the *Journal* a line of copy that displeased the Turks. They required that all his stories be telegraphed via Constantinople, where they were censored by Turkish officials. Moreover, since the censors were more fluent in French than in English, all dispatches had to be written in French. The French that he had picked up as a boy, perhaps reinforced on excursions across the channel from his London post, allowed him to get by; at least he makes little of the requirement in his autobiography when he describes lying on the dirt floor of a tent in Thessaly, along with a handful of other correspondents, composing a story with the aid of a French-English dictionary. But the Turks' insistence on French—which, of course, had to be translated into English at the other end—surely would have prevented Ralph from passing along more than a few bare bones of information. Combined with the other constraints imposed by the Turks, it made his assignment all but impossible.

As a result, Ralph's contribution to the *Journal's* coverage of the Greco-Turkish war of 1897—at least the part that made it into print—was embarrassingly small. Only a handful of his stories ran in the *Journal,* and all were brief, insubstantial, and late, reporting little more than that he was making his way to the front and that no information about the progress of the war was available. Any hopes he may have harbored of writing panoramic descriptions of battles and armies—of covering a war the way he covered parades and inaugurations—were dashed.

Back in his London office, as he flipped through back issues of the *Journal,* Ralph could not have avoided comparing the fragments of his work that survived with the stories of Stephen Crane, then twenty-five years old, from the Greek side. Some reporters did not regard Crane as a professional; they complained that he obtained lucrative journalistic assignments only because of his reputation as a novelist. But on this occasion he outshone Ralph. Although his reporting was thin and his output limited, the few stories he did write were far more dramatic and vivid than anything of Ralph's. Hearst made the most of them. "CRANE AT VELESTINO" read the headline over an account of one battle, and the description of a Greek retreat widely blamed on the weak-kneed leadership of the Greek commander was heralded by "THE BLUE BADGE OF COWARDICE." As was the case with Richard Harding Davis in Moscow, large drawings of the author accompanied Crane's stories.

On his way back to London, just as the armistice was about to take effect,

Ralph had cabled an uncensored story from Serbia forecasting that Turkey henceforth would be a power to reckon with because of the confidence it had gained in the brief war. Ralph's piece and a Crane story about wounded Greek soldiers ran side by side in a fat Sunday *Journal* under "STEPHEN CRANE AND JULIAN RALPH TELL OF WAR'S HEROES AND TURKEY'S BOLD PLAN." Ralph's dry analysis paled next to Crane's moving description of a hospital ship. Moreover, beneath the stories by Crane and Ralph was one by another Hearst reporter bearing the headline "HOW NOVELIST CRANE ACTS ON THE BATTLEFIELD—Journal's War Correspondent's Sangfroid under Fire Described by a Fellow Worker." It told how Crane sat on an ammunition box on a hill and coolly smoked a cigarette as he watched a battle raging before him. Ralph would have given anything to trade places.

Only a month after his return to London from Greece, Ralph found himself working in the shadow of another famous novelist. The occasion was Queen Victoria's Diamond Jubilee. The celebration of the sixtieth anniversary of Victoria's ascent to the throne was another of those vast ceremonial affairs so suited to Ralph's talents. But Mark Twain happened to be in London at the time and in need of money to pay off debts, and Hearst signed him up to write Jubilee articles.

Since a celebrated author like Mark Twain could not be expected to rush about London with a notebook, the detailed reporting of Jubilee events fell to Ralph, aided by three other *Journal* reporters dispatched to England for the affair. On June 21, Jubilee eve, Ralph strolled among the immense throng gathering in London, took sour note of the drunken, rowdy behavior of many in its ranks, and witnessed the arrival of Victoria from Windsor castle at Paddington Station, where she made "one of those womanly simple speeches about her son and other dear children which so delight the cockles of the hearts of the British people." On Jubilee day, having gone to bed at 3 A.M., he was on his way to St. Paul's Cathedral by 7 A.M. to take up his vantage point for observing Victoria's royal progress around London with an escort of troops from every corner of the empire. The queen passed so close, Ralph later recalled, "that I could have touched the door of Her Majesty's carriage with my walking-stick."

The contributions of Ralph and his colleagues were substantial. Indeed, Ralph's marvelously detailed account of Jubilee day—from a petulant display of temper by the Archbishop of Canterbury over some trivial matter to the fast-stepping procession that "left an impression of a great blur of

red, white, gold, silver, plumes, velvet, medals, orders, swords and splendid men"—had to be one of the best stories he wrote for the *Journal*. Still,
Twain's three articles were the centerpieces of the *Journal's* coverage.
Although they contained some wry and thoughtful reflections on the real-
ities that lay behind the imperial pomp, for the most part they were about
what might be expected of a Mark Twain presented with the opportunity to
earn a quick dollar with a minimal investment of time and energy—
contrived humor, superficial philosophizing. It had to bother Ralph to have
his diligent reporting eclipsed by Twain's facile efforts.

Besides bruising anew an ego still recovering from the blows inflicted in
Greece, the experience seems to have made Ralph step back and take a
harder look at Hearst's brand of journalism. The sensationalism was becoming ever more blatant; in time someone would liken a Hearst newspaper to "a screaming woman running down the street with her throat cut."
By 1897 Hearst's utter unconcern with the truth had also become evident;
as he fanned the flames of war for Cuban independence from Spain, manufactured "eyewitness" accounts of Spanish atrocities—Cubans beaten to
death, fed to sharks, roasted alive—appeared regularly in the *Journal*.
Pulitzer's New York *World* for a time was guilty of the same sort of yellow
journalism. But after the Spanish-American War Pulitzer would pull back
from the fraud and the worst of the sensationalism. Not so Hearst; such was
the essence of his journalism.

Richard Harding Davis had broken with Hearst earlier in 1897 after one
of his dispatches from Cuba was distorted by *Journal* editors in New York.
By the middle of 1897 Ralph, who would later write that yellow journalism's "methods belong more naturally to the circus business than to our
profession," had also had enough. Soon after the Jubilee celebration in
June he quit as the *Journal's* London correspondent.

———————————————

In 1898, when he had been in London for more than two years, Ralph
went to a photographer's studio and had a formal portrait made. In the
three-quarter-length photograph he is approaching baldness, and the hair at
his temples is graying, as is his luxuriant mustache. He wears a frock coat,
an elegant waistcoat with lapels, and a high wing-collar with a wide cravat.
A stickpin—a diamond perhaps?—adorns the cravat, and his gloved left
hand holds the other glove and a tall silk hat. He is the picture of a London
gentleman.

Life in England had taken some getting used to. Yards were gardens, rare

The front page of the *New York Journal* for June 23, 1897. *Newspaper Collection, The New York Public Library, Astor, Lenox and Tilden Foundations*

Ralph in London in 1898. *Dr. Joseph E. Ralph*

beef was underdone, and drapers sold cloth. London winters brought "black fog," the choking, impenetrable mixture of fog and soft-coal smoke that made nearby pedestrians look like ghosts at midday. Winter also meant enduring the bone-chilling cold of English houses. "The English heat themselves instead of their houses," said Ralph, explaining the English penchant for vigorous walks. In the social realm Ralph was bemused by the English practice of never bothering to make introductions when guests assembled for dinners or country weekends, and he never stopped feeling a trifle foolish addressing a mere mortal as "lord."

As the photograph suggests, however, on the whole Ralph fitted comfortably into English life. Only days after his arrival in London, while the diplomatic crisis between England and the United States over the British Guiana–Venezuela border was still at a boil, he had attended a large dinner and had been called upon to speak. He responded with aplomb, provoking "great applause," according to an account of the affair, by holding up a glass of red wine and praying that "no liquid of that color will ever be shed between the countries except in such toasts." There was much about England that he liked—bobbies, English maids, the regard of the English for individual liberty, "the precision with which they choose their words in speaking." He liked to stroll in Hyde Park. He even liked English cooking.

Such attitudes probably explain why Ralph decided to remain in London after his departure from the New York *Journal*. For the first time since he had taken the steamer from Red Bank to New York as a nineteen-year-old seeking to make his way in metropolitan journalism, he had no exclusive affiliation with a newspaper. This must have been by choice. His reputation would have assured him a job on the staff of another newspaper if he so chose, but perhaps the right paper did not have a job open in London at the time. In any case, for two years he earned his living from a variety of sources—magazines, books, and assignments from different newspapers.

Judging from the way he lived, he prospered as a freelancer. After residing in two West End flats earlier in his London days, by 1898 Ralph and his family were renting a six-floor, twenty-room house in the same area. After a stay there, the Ralphs moved to their final London residence, a rented red-brick house at 70 Holland Road in Kensington. This house was not quite as grand as the preceding one, but it was spacious enough to serve as a hotel many years later. With the houses went full complements of servants. At the twenty-room establishment, Ralph listed as full-time employees a cook, a waitress, a parlormaid, and a housemaid, as part-timers a butler, a charwoman, a laundress, a gardener, and a man to do heavy lifting.

Work for Harper paid some of the bills. Both the weekly and the monthly regularly printed articles by Ralph. He wrote on a wide range of subjects— his unhappy tour of Thessaly, English life and manners, London newspapers, his reflections on China. One of his most extensive undertakings for Harper was a trip to India that lasted from January of 1899 till spring and produced a dozen articles for the magazines.

As in the past, Ralph also tried his hand at fiction. Harper ran some of it in the monthly and published two books, a collection of short stories and a novel. Ralph's earlier stories and sketches had generally been journalism thinly disguised as fiction, passable attempts to get more out of material gathered in his reporting by dressing it up with fictional touches. In his newer productions he relied more heavily on his imagination, even to the point of constructing the novel around the efforts of supernatural beings called "Etherians" to prevent a beautiful young heiress named Laura Balm from being done out of her fortune. In general the results were dreadful. The plots creaked and the dialogue was sometimes otherworldly. ("I was all downcast, Harry, but your splendid courage picks me up again," says Helen, the heroine of a romantic short story set in London.) Even *Harper's Monthly's* own book reviewer suggested that fiction was not Ralph's calling. "Mr. Ralph is not by nature a fictionist," he commented when the short story collection was published. "He is a brilliant reporter, and we hope he will not be offended at our saying so."

Although to keep up his large domestic establishments Ralph apparently supplemented his income from Harper with considerable reporting for both British and American newspapers, only the sketchiest of details about this work can be turned up. It is known, for example, that in 1898 Ralph covered the funerals of two of the era's towering figures, Germany's Otto von Bismarck and Britain's William Gladstone, for newspapers, but which ones remains a mystery. It is also known that for a time he wrote for the New York *Herald,* but *what* he wrote is a mystery because the *Herald* still scorned bylines. Indeed, the only newspaper journalism of Ralph's during these years that can be pinned down is a Sunday column titled "Julian Ralph's London Letter" that ran for a while in 1899 in the Brooklyn *Eagle,* a paper of modest circulation but high quality. The freewheeling column touched on whatever was on Ralph's mind—English entertainment, sports, fashions, politics, art, books, and social issues. Among the social issues discussed was the death penalty; Ralph, who had witnessed hangings as a young reporter, said "the general trend of enlightenment" opposed it as ineffectual in deterring crime.

One major story Ralph covered in 1899 for an unknown newspaper, as well as for *Harper's Weekly,* was the second trial of Captain Alfred Dreyfus in Rennes, France, in August and September. Dreyfus was the Jewish officer in the French army who in 1894, amid an atmosphere of anti-Semitism, had been falsely convicted of treason by a military court and sentenced to Devil's Island for life. A new trial was forced on the army by proof that the conviction had been based on forged evidence.

Ralph's comments in *Harper's Weekly* on the proceedings, which re-sulted in a second conviction that was subsequently overturned by a pardon from the president of France, were unremarkable; like most observers, he judged Dreyfus innocent and French military justice a farce. But the trial did provide another of those instances when Ralph claimed clairvoyance helped him in his newspaper reporting. He was walking to court early one morning with another reporter, he later wrote, when he turned to his companion and said on impulse: "Will you wait a minute? I think I will telegraph my paper that I expect exciting news today." Minutes later Ralph heard cries of alarm. Hurrying in their direction, he found that Dreyfus's lawyer had been shot and wounded on his way to court.

The reporter with Ralph that morning was George W. Steevens, a brilliant young correspondent for the London *Daily Mail.* Possibly through his friendship with Steevens, or possibly because the *Daily Mail's* propri-etor, Alfred Harmsworth, was aware of his reputation, after the Dreyfus trial Ralph was invited to return full-time to daily journalism as a member of the *Mail's* staff. Britain and the Boer republics of the Transvaal and the Orange Free State in South Africa were moving inexorably toward war, and Ralph was to play a central role in the *Mail's* coverage of the conflict.

It was not unusual for American reporters to serve stints on British newspapers; a number of well-known ones did so, including Richard Harding Davis. Moreover, Ralph's work would not be lost to American readers. Harmsworth had sold the rights to the *Mail's* cabled dispatches from South Africa to the New York *Herald,* and longer mailed articles by Ralph—limited cable service forced all Boer War correspondents to resort to the mail even though it took more than two weeks to reach England—would eventually be published in books in the United States.

Nevertheless, Ralph's decision to join the staff of a London newspaper represented a considerable change of heart. Despite his fondness for most things English, he had always taken a condescending view of British journalism. Most British newspapers continued to stress editorials over the aggressive pursuit of news, and Ralph complained that what little news they did contain was stodgily presented. Britain had produced some outstanding foreign correspondents—George Steevens of the *Mail* was one who had recently come to the fore—but by and large Ralph judged English reporters timid and unenterprising. He told of meeting one who acknowledged that during almost twenty years of covering Gladstone he had never spoken a word to the great Liberal statesman except once when he had inadvertently encountered him in a railroad car and could not avoid an introduction. "But I never presumed upon that, you know," the English reporter said to an incredulous Ralph.

Alfred Harmsworth, a budding press lord who later became Lord Northcliffe, had founded the *Daily Mail* only three years earlier. At first glance, it did not seem to break sharply with tradition. A morning paper, in appearance it resembled the most staid of its rivals, the *Times*. The front page was filled with classified advertisements for Continental tours, false teeth, and lost dogs, and the headlines did not exceed one column. In other ways, however, the *Mail,* which was thriving, embodied a movement away from English journalistic practice toward that of popular American newspapers. Indeed, Harmsworth was often called an English version of William Randolph Hearst. He had the same craving for mass readership, spent freely to send reporters wherever there was a story, and did not shy from tales of steamy scandals, bizarre tortures, and the like. Unlike Hearst, however, Harmsworth rarely let crime and sex dominate his news columns. His idea, said Ralph, whose memories of Hearst were unhappy and who was perhaps being too kind to Harmsworth, was to create a morning daily with "the brightness and enterprise of an American journal, combined with sobriety and trustworthiness."

The Boer War, which began on October 11, 1899, was a bonanza for the *Mail.* Although historians have viewed the conflict as one provoked by England in a grab for Boer gold and territory, at the time it was heralded in Britain as a noble effort to bring the blessings of empire to the benighted Afrikaner republics. Before the realization dawned that this would entail a long, costly struggle, the war stirred rousing popular support, and Alfred Harmsworth, a flag-waving imperialist, was delighted to cater to the demand for news from South Africa.

Fourteen *Mail* correspondents were soon on the scene. Ralph's friend George Steevens was among those assigned to the British forces opposing a Boer invasion of Natal, the crown colony on the Indian Ocean. Ralph, who along with Steevens was accorded the rare distinction of a byline in the *Mail,* was part of the contingent deployed in the Cape Colony, which the Boers had also invaded. Reaching Cape Town in late October, he was soon five hundred miles to the northeast filing reports on the early confrontations between the British and the Boers who had crossed the border of the Orange Free State into the Cape. Thanks to the war news, the *Mail's* circulation began passing one million on some days, making it by far the largest newspaper of its day in Britain.

The initial goal of the British troops in the Cape Colony was to relieve the diamond-mining center of Kimberley, located in the Cape just across the Free State border and under siege by the Boer invaders since the outset of the war. Advancing north toward Kimberley, the British won a quick succession of battles in late November of 1899. Ralph's cabled account of the last of these, the battle of Modder River on November 28, appeared in the New York *Herald* under a banner headline.

Belmont, Tuesday—Lord Methuen's force fought a big engagement at Modder River to-day with the Boers.

The enemy numbered at least 8,000, having been reinforced from the force investing Kimberley.

Our men found them very strongly intrenched on both banks of the river, and also in the broad bed of the stream. They were especially strong on the northern bank, which being heavily lined with thick mimosa bushes, formed an ideal position for the Boers, who had been in possession of it for several weeks, and had been busily preparing for to-day's battle.

The fighting was simply terrific and raged for hours, being especially hard in the afternoon.

Our men, however, although inferior in numbers, showed magnificent gallantry, and drove the enemy out of his position on the south side of the river, and forced him across the stream.

Then they cleared him from the other side, until he was driven off in full retreat.

This is an enormous gain and opens the road to Kimberley.

General Methuen now has a large force firmly established across the river.

JULIAN RALPH

The story of the battle of Modder River was unusual not only in that it was signed, contrary to the *Herald's* usual policy, but also in that it was fairly complete. Coupled with the inadequate transmission facilities, military censorship generally prevented correspondents from cabling full reports of the fighting, particularly in the early days of the war. "Alas! The days of newspaper enterprise in war are over," complained a twenty-five-

year-old correspondent for the London *Morning Post* named Winston Churchill. "What can one do with a censor, a forty-eight hours' delay and a fifty-
word limit on a wire?" Ralph did not find the situation as frustrating as in
the Greco-Turkish war, but it was pretty bad. Once a censor cut everything
from one of his cables except the description of a sandstorm.

The mailed dispatches, by contrast, were largely uncensored and could
run on at length, allowing a correspondent to display his talents freely.
Ralph's "letters" are sprinkled with striking passages. Far across the veldt
five hundred Boer horsemen loom into view; they halt, then ride on again,
"like theatrical cavalry moving across a stage." In the half-light of dawn
Boers ensconced on a ridge of hills open up with their rifles on a British
force below them, and the muzzle blasts are "quick, vivid jets of fire, like
jewels flashing on a coronet on the hills' brow." Defeated Boers retreat
down the far side of a hill "like flowing water." British troops confront
Boers who have taken up a defensive position along the near bank of a
river, "down on their knees, Mausers in hand, like a three-mile jaw of
sunken teeth." Opposing riflemen peg away at each other and the sound is
"like the frying of fat." Parched after a hard fight in the broiling sun,
British soldiers line up to fill their canteens at a white canvas tank in which
water shimmers "like melted diamonds, touched with emerald shadows by
some sprays of foliage above." Ralph peers through the telescope of an
artillery piece and sees Boers "all over the hills in numbers, like plant-lice
on a leaf."

One letter painted a dramatic and disturbing picture of a British defeat
during the fighting in the Cape Colony toward the end of 1899. The
occasion was the battle of Magersfontein, fought on December 11, two
months after the start of the war. At Magersfontein the British forces
seeking to lift the siege of Kimberley experienced their first setback when
they ran head on into a reality of modern war, which was that the traditional
tactic of making a frontal attack with troops in close formation did not work
when the foe was protected by trenches and equipped with rapid-firing
magazine rifles capable of laying down sheets of bullets. The British
suffered some nine hundred casualties, most of them in the first few
minutes of fighting, according to Ralph, and their advance toward Kimberley, just twelve miles farther on, was halted.

Ralph dashed off a cable that spoke of the Boers' "murderous fire" and
the "fearful loss" suffered by the British but did not spell out the extent of
the rout or its cause. (The New York *Times* blithely lifted the story from the
Daily Mail and ran it on page 1, crediting Ralph, despite the exclusive

rights Harmsworth had granted the New York *Herald* in the United States.) In his subsequent mailed dispatch Ralph set forth a fuller account of the day. This said that the Highlanders, who had been assigned the principal role in the assault on the Boers at Magersfontein, set out believing the main Boer force to be on a rocky hill well beyond the place where they were actually entrenched on the veldt.

> Therefore it happened that they were at perfect ease, swinging along without a thought of immediate attack, chatting—even to such an extent that their officers bade them make less noise. Neither officers nor men knew of the existence of the formidable trenches that ran along the veldt in front of them. . . .
>
> Suddenly . . . a Boer rifle was fired on the left, and the whole long-hidden trench belched flame, and riddled our ranks with bullets.
>
> Nothing could have been more of a surprise, more unexpected.
>
> A panic seized the troops, and would have possessed any other regiments in any other army—so fearful was the fire, so completely were the men taken off their guard, and so like a general slaughter must it have seemed to those who saw their comrades dropping on both sides, and before them.
>
> They turned and ran, literally colliding and climbing over one another in their confusion.
>
> A chaplain forward in their ranks was knocked down and trampled; as brave a man as any, and yet one who declared that there lived no men who could have behaved differently.
>
> It had been as if the earth had opened, and from a cleft that ran as far as our men reached fire had belched, and shot had swept the veldt.

When the dispatch was reprinted in one of Ralph's Boer War books, it included a passage suggesting that the general in command of British forces at Magersfontein, Lord Methuen, had known about the trenches but for some unfathomable reason had failed to pass the intelligence along to the Highlanders. This was missing from the version of the story that appeared in the *Mail*. Perhaps, unlike most letters, this one came to the attention of a censor, or perhaps an editor wielded his blue pencil. Still, Ralph's description of the disastrous attack could only have contributed to doubts about the caliber of British leadership. Before long Lord Methuen was demoted.

Despite such high points as the Magersfontein story, much of Ralph's reporting from South Africa was flawed. Blind zeal for the imperial cause marked the coverage of the Boer War from the British side, and most of the time Ralph, a thoroughgoing Anglophile by now, was as guilty of such bias as any of his British colleagues. Bias was still commonplace in journalism, of course, and would remain so in war reporting, but even at the turn of the century it could be carried too far for some tastes. Ralph had "no word of praise for any man who fought for the two republics, and never a word of dispraise for those on the other side," complained an American reviewer of one collection of his articles.

That was something of an overstatement, but it was not far off the mark. In his *Daily Mail* dispatches Ralph seldom strayed from his initial impression of British officers, whose khaki uniform and peaked helmet he and his fellow correspondents wore, as "splendid, dashing fellows" always champing at the bit to get into battle. "Tommy Atkins," the British rank-and-filer, was equally admirable—stolid, resourceful, brave, the salt of the earth. The Boers, on the other hand, were cruel, ignorant, and unsportsmanlike; they fired at ambulances and waved white truce flags to draw Tommies into the open, where they made easy targets.

Sometimes Ralph's South African stories also betray a lack of industry. Too often the rich detail that marked the *Sun* stories that made his name on Park Row—Grant's funeral, the political conventions, the trial of Lizzie Borden—is missing. Perhaps to some extent he was coasting on his reputation, despite his contention that there was "no resting on one's oars" in his profession. Another explanation may be that, at least until he began to be weighed down by physical afflictions, he was simply having too good a time.

For the most part, correspondents in the field roughed it in style. Carts filled with their gear—tents, bedding, private stocks of food and drink—accompanied them. Soldier-servants reached through their tent flaps in the morning with mugs of cocoa. The officers' messes, which somehow managed to maintain their traditional punctilio even when rough boards served as the table and soap boxes as seats, welcomed them.

On occasion conditions did turn more rugged, but then there was satisfaction in coping and making do, particularly for someone like Ralph who had come to the war from a soft city life. He recounted a day when he rigged a makeshift shelter out of a waterproof covering from an ammunition cart and sprawled in its shade writing and offering a sociable drink of water from his canvas waterbag to passersby. When it was too dark to write he did his laundry. It is obvious that he thoroughly enjoyed himself, even while he was washing his socks. From time to time, to be sure, there were complaints—of the dust that seemed always to fill the air, of the heat by day and the chill by night, of the monotony of the South African landscape. ("All places on the veldt are the same, but they have different names," Ralph commented.) The complaints, however, come across mainly as echoes of the ritual grousing of the soldier rather than as anything to be taken very seriously.

In Ralph's first days in South Africa, as he went about Cape Town applying to various officers for assistance in traveling to the front, he had some bad moments. He was treated, he said, like a stranger who had wandered into an exclusive club and suddenly started making demands for all sorts of services. In the end, however, he obtained the logistical help he needed, and by the time he reached the war zone the officers' upper-class hauteur had faded along with the gleam of their brass. Although eventually he concluded that many were "amateurs" when it came to soldiering, for the present they were fine companions—courageous, hospitable, convivial. Soon he was sharing his pipe tobacco with them, and they were calling him "old chap" and inviting him to join them in their tents for a tot of whiskey.

In particular, Ralph enjoyed the camaraderie of the mess, and he waxed positively maudlin when he described Christmas dinner at a camp to which the British had withdrawn to lick their wounds after the defeat at Magersfontein. "The pudding is perfect, the coffee and Benedictine taste like nectar, and all are now so cheery and near to Christmas spirit that it is an hour later than usual when the little band of brother braves scatters in the darkness and the desert dirt," his *Mail* article about the day concluded.

There were occupational hazards, of course. At least thirteen correspondents died in the Boer War. George Steevens, Ralph's fellow *Daily Mail* correspondent, succumbed to typhoid in January 1900 while trapped in Ladysmith in Natal with the British troops under Boer siege there. In the first battle Ralph covered, a correspondent for the London *Morning Post* lost an arm from a gunshot.

Ralph, who did not carry a revolver in South Africa as he had in Greece, professed a commonsense attitude toward the dangers of battle. It was foolish, he said, to rush "into the forefront of each fight, there to risk death, and limit one's knowledge of the battle to the narrowest possible point." Moreover, a correspondent was paid to keep safe so he could write stories. At the same time, it is clear that he got a certain thrill from brushes with danger, and also that he was not above swaggering and letting readers know of his daring.

The most detailed accounts of Ralph's experiences with the perils of war involve the battle of Modder River in late November of 1899. The first incident occurred on the day of the battle. Ralph and another correspondent, though well to the rear of the British front line, found themselves, along with a Tommy, pinned down on the open veldt by Boer sharpshooters. Every time Ralph or one of his companions lifted his head bullets whistled by. At the Tommy's suggestion, they extricated themselves from their plight by simultaneously jumping up and sprinting in three different directions—"so the blooming Boers won't know which one to peg at," as the Tommy explained. The sharpshooters concentrated their fire on the other correspondent, but they missed and both reporters and the Tommy reached cover safely.

The second incident occurred the day after the battle. Ralph, on horseback, tagged along with a troop of British Lancers entering a village supposedly abandoned by the retreating Boers. Suddenly, from the windows and garden walls of the houses, rifle fire was directed at the Lancers, who swung off their horses, dropped to one knee, and returned the fire. The Lancers quickly prevailed. As for Ralph, as he related it in a magazine article, "Bullets flew all around me, and I sat upright among the kneeling soldiers, a superb target, motionless—in a funk." The "funk" only added a nice touch of modesty to the picture of Ralph in the thick of things.

In episodes such as these it becomes evident that in South Africa Ralph was enjoying a sense of kinship with the great adventurers of his field—men like Stanley—and that he reveled in the experience. Even while turning out work that fell short of his best, he was coming as close as he ever did to realizing his romantic notion of the reporter—the knight-errant, risking danger and enduring hardship in pursuit of the story. He was living his own great adventure.

After the British defeat at Magersfontein in December, there was a lull in fighting in the Cape until February. Then the British, under new leadership, resumed the offensive. When a cavalry force finally succeeded in lifting the siege of Kimberley on February 15, Ralph was a member of the accompanying press contingent. Cecil Rhodes, diamond magnate, empire builder, and siege victim, served champagne to the correspondents.

The festivities at Kimberley were cut short for Ralph, however, by the first of the physical misfortunes that were to prove his undoing in South Africa. As he alighted onto sloping ground from a Cape cart, the heavy two-wheeled vehicle toppled over on him, injuring one leg so severely that he was laid up in Kimberley for almost a month. Meanwhile, British troops who had invaded the Orange Free State were fighting their way towards its capital, Bloemfontein.

By March 11 Ralph had recovered sufficiently to travel. With another correspondent, he hurried a hundred and ten miles across the veldt in a Cape cart to join the British force advancing on Bloemfontein. Passing dead horses, tattered uniforms torn from wounded men, bully beef tins, and discarded letters from home along the way, Ralph caught up with the British just outside Bloemfontein. On March 13 he entered the city, which the Boer army had fled, with British cavalrymen. Watching the infantrymen who followed, "I turned aside and whispered under my breath, 'God bless Tommy Atkins,' " wrote Ralph, as moved as any Englishman.

For six weeks the British paused in Bloemfontein to prepare for the drive north to Pretoria, capital of the Transvaal. Ralph would retain some fond memories of his stay in Bloemfontein. Once more he had the wartime companionship of his son Lester, who was in town working as a sketch artist for *Harper's Weekly.* At the behest of the British commanding general, Lord Roberts, Julian teamed with three other correspondents to produce a daily newspaper, the *Friend,* to inform and entertain the British troops and the local citizenry, and he enjoyed the joint effort. (A book he later wrote about the undertaking was entitled *The Brighter Side of War.*) The correspondents devoted two or three hours every morning to the paper, and Ralph said that although the employers of his colleagues complained about the time they were spending on the extracurricular project, Alfred Harmsworth, the owner of the *Daily Mail,* did not object.

Interesting people passed through Bloemfontein, among them Winston Churchill of the London *Morning Post.* Churchill had achieved much publicity early in the war by abandoning his noncombatant status, plunging into action in Natal, getting himself captured by the Boers, and then making a dramatic escape. Rudyard Kipling and A. Conan Doyle, both enthusiastic imperialists, also spent time in Bloemfontein. The two writers contributed to the *Friend,* and Ralph came to know Kipling, who lived across the hall in the Free State Hotel, quite well. They collaborated on an editorial, printed in both English and Afrikaans, assuring Free Staters of the beneficence of British rule, and when the correspondents who edited the *Friend* gave a banquet at the Bloemfontein railroad station for Lord Roberts and his staff, Ralph introduced Kipling as one of the after-dinner speakers.

Unfortunately, Ralph's enjoyment of the congenial life in Bloemfontein was considerably dampened by his physical problems. The leg injured in the Cape cart accident still pained him. In Bloemfontein he was also plagued by a finicky digestive system—the product, Ralph said, of months of hard living in the field—that sometimes rebelled at any nourishment other than milk diluted with soda water. In a photograph taken at this time

Ralph, seated behind desk, in Bloemfontein, South Africa, in 1900, with fellow contributors to the *Friend*. Rudyard Kipling is perched on a corner of the desk reading proofs. *General Research Division, The New York Public Library, Astor, Lenox and Tilden Foundations*

showing Ralph seated at a desk in the *Friend* office with one of his fellow editors standing alongside and Kipling perched on the front of the desk reading proofs, Ralph looks shrunken.

The culminating blow came toward the end of March. As a preliminary to the general advance on Pretoria, British troops on March 29 attacked a Boer position just north of Bloemfontein on the railroad line to the Transvaal capital. Ralph and Kipling went along to observe. On the way, Ralph's horse, a spirited mount named Rattlesnake that was totally unsuited to a horseman of Ralph's abilities, bolted. Ralph was catapulted into a wire fence. Both arms and both legs were badly lacerated, and he suffered an unspecified internal injury.

He somehow continued with the attacking force, which drove the Boers off at the cost of many British casualties, and afterwards he hung on in Bloemfontein through most of April. But when, toward the end of the month, the doctors recommended that he go back to England, he took their advice and boarded a train to Cape Town. The romance of it all had largely faded. From a train window he saw Tommies without tents shivering in a cold, driving rain—it was now fall in South Africa—and their plight saddened him. He had become "unutterably sick" of the war.

And yet, for all his dark thoughts, it is certain that he would not have exchanged his seven months in South Africa for anything. He predicted, correctly, that the war would drag on for some time—as it turned out, two years would pass before the last shots were fired in the guerrilla skirmishing that ended the fighting—and he told Frederic Remington in a letter written from Cape Town on May 9 that he planned to return to South Africa when his body had mended. Sometime around mid-May he sailed for England, and by early June he was home. But he never went back to South Africa. He had, in fact, carried out his last important reporting assignment.

Epilogue

R alph, who turned forty-seven in May of 1900, had a little more than two and a half years to live.

In London he rejoined his family in the big red-brick house on Holland Road in Kensington. For a time he was a semi-invalid, mainly because of the leg injured at Kimberley. Every afternoon, he wrote Frederic Remington, he took a carriage ride "to get a little of what the b——y British call 'fresh ayah.'" The rest of the day he was "tied to a chayah." He had heard that New York newspapers had printed drawings purporting to show the interior of his bad leg. "I wish somebody would send me one. I consider it rude for others to peer into my works unless at least I can see 'em for myself."

So far as is known Ralph did no further significant work for the *Daily Mail*. It is likely, however, that even if he did not Alfred Harmsworth continued to pay him till he was well enough to get around again. Harmsworth was a generous employer, and after George Steevens died in South Africa during the siege of Ladysmith Harmsworth had arranged for a lifetime pension for Steevens's wife. Still, Ralph wasted little time in getting back to his writing, not only for the money it brought in, which, considering his elaborate way of life, he could always use, but also because writing was what Ralph did.

There were two more Boer War books, both published in 1901, to be added to the one already drawn from his South African material. In 1902 a second novel, a continuation of the saga of the beautiful young heiress (now called Laura Lamont) showed that his fiction was not improving with age. There was also his autobiography, which he had begun in 1899 but which would not be published until after his death in 1903. When not occupied with the books, Ralph found time to turn out a steady stream of magazine articles and to resume his weekly column in the Brooklyn *Eagle*.

Two snippets of Ralph's writing in this period seem to confirm that his pride had indeed been injured during his time with the New York *Journal*.

At least he appears to go out of his way to take pokes at two of the writers who upstaged him there.

Stephen Crane was the target of a comment appended to the second collection of Ralph's Boer War dispatches, *An American with Lord Roberts*. His experience in South Africa, said Ralph, showed that the "imaginative descriptions of battle which make up such books as *The Red Badge of Courage*" have little to do with the real thing. (Crane was past hurting; he had died in June 1900 at the age of twenty-eight.)

Richard Harding Davis had served briefly as a *Daily Mail* correspondent in South Africa, replacing George Steevens in Natal and covering the relief of Ladysmith. But he had quit his *Mail* assignment and gone over to observe the war from the Boer side, in the process becoming a fervent supporter of the Boers. Wrote Ralph in an *Eagle* column: "How lonely an American pro-Boer must have been in South Africa, where all the Americans who knew the Boers and who were worth a pinch of salt were solidly against them."

An *Eagle* column in the fall of 1900 provides another of those instances when Ralph's life seems to be interwoven with the fabric of history. His fellow Boer War correspondent Winston Churchill had just been elected to Parliament. Ralph spent a day with Churchill as he made the rounds of his constituency, accompanied by his mother, Lady Randolph Churchill. Churchill made eleven speeches and Ralph concluded that he had the makings of an excellent speaker, but Churchill seemed to take the most pleasure that day from a superb kick he made to open a football match:

He got it and himself just right and he let fly and it flew—high skywards. Then he grinned with delight and every now and then for two or three hours, between speeches, he chuckled either to me or his mother, and said: "I kicked that ball well, didn't I? It would never have done to make a fluke of that."

In 1901 South Africa was still much on Ralph's mind. After Lord Roberts returned from there early in the year—he had mistakenly believed the war was almost over—Ralph and the three other correspondents who had edited the *Friend* in Bloemfontein invited him to join with them in establishing the Order of the Friendlies. Lord Stanley, who as Roberts's chief censor had won the correspondents' respect for his reasonableness and fairness, also became a member of the group, as did Rudyard Kipling. Kipling designed a gold and enamel badge for the order, and a jeweler made up copies for the seven members. Even if the Order of the Friendlies served no other purpose, it allowed Ralph to recapture something of the camaraderie he had known in South Africa.

Ralph received a less welcome reminder of South Africa when reviews of *An American with Lord Roberts* came out. Two important periodicals, the *Dial* and the *Atheneum,* raised the issue of Ralph's pervasive bias, and the latter went further and questioned his overall accuracy. "There is a good deal in Mr. Ralph which fills us with astonishment as coming from a man of his experience," said the reviewer. No one had ever said anything like that about Ralph before. Adding insult to injury, the *Atheneum* also suggested that Ralph's style was dated. "Mr. Ralph," said its reviewer, "has a somewhat old-fashioned and full-flavoured style."

In the summer of 1901 there was a still less pleasant reminder of South Africa. The digestive system troubles that Ralph had attributed to the rough life in the field apparently had never disappeared, and now they became acute enough for him to seek new treatment. The waters at the health spa of Carlsbad in Bohemia were reputed to help those "who suffer liver and stomachic derangements," and so Ralph decided to spend the month of August there. Early every morning he joined the parade of ailing visitors who streamed from their hotels and lodging houses, mugs on straps hung over their shoulders, to an enormous pavilion housing the springs. There, while a band played, he and the others lounged about sipping the warm water, lining up to have young girls refill their mugs until they had drunk their quota.

Ralph got a magazine article out of Carlsbad, but that was all. Neither the waters nor the prescribed bland "white diet"—no beef, wine, or beer—could cure Ralph's illness. He had abdominal cancer.

It had been obvious for some time that Ralph would not be able to adhere to his plan to revisit South Africa, and in March of 1902 he returned to the United States. For several months he made the rounds of resorts, starting in Summerville, South Carolina, and moving north as the weather turned warmer. He stopped for a while in Lakewood, New Jersey, and then he took up residence at an inn in Brandon, Vermont. In August he made an excursion from Brandon to Saratoga Springs, New York, and he subsequently wrote a rather stuffy magazine piece unfavorably contrasting the fast life of the racing and gambling crowd there with the simple pleasures of Vermont—hiking, fishing, reading, games. At least some of his five children, all now in their twenties, appear to have been with him in Vermont, and it must have been a bittersweet pleasure for Ralph to watch them enjoy themselves, for by now he knew that he did not have long to live.

While Ralph was in Brandon the New York *Times* and the Springfield *Union* engaged in a genteel literary dispute in which Ralph became involved. Pondering the link between journalism and literature, the *Times* book section had concluded there was none. "The work of a newspaper reporter has no more relation to literature than that of a house and sign painter has to the art of Michael Angelo [*sic*]," declared the *Times*. When the Massachusetts paper begged to differ, the *Times* held its ground and in passing observed, "Julian Ralph is not a literary man." Ralph read the passage while sitting on the porch of his inn and sent off a bemused reply that the *Times* ran under the headline "JULIAN RALPH ANSWERS THE ACCUSATION OF NOT BEING LITERARY." He was not sure, said Ralph, whether he should be pleased or distraught that he was not "a literary man." But there was no concealing that the *Times* comment had touched a nerve.

The *Times* was right, of course. Ralph was not a literary man. He was a reporter, a very good one most of the time, sometimes a great one. "He could see and remember and write," said *Harper's Weekly* in an obituary. At the New York *Sun,* where he had made his reputation, years after his death people could still point out where his desk had been, and those who had served on the staff with Ralph remained in awe of him. It was Charles Rosebault, as a young *Sun* reporter the midnight pursuer of General Grant's doctor, who as an old man would remember Ralph as "the prince of reporters."

Fall found Ralph back in Manhattan at last. His writing energy running low and very likely his money as well—he said his sixth sense never worked to his advantage in his personal affairs—Ralph dragged himself aboard a train in November and went to St. Louis, where he had himself appointed "Eastern representative" of the Louisiana Purchase Exposition, the world's fair scheduled for St. Louis in 1904.

"Eastern representative" was probably a euphemism for press agent, but in any case Ralph could have attended to his duties very little if at all. He experienced stomach hemorrhaging in St. Louis, and after returning to New York he was confined to his bed. On the evening of Tuesday, January 20, 1903, four months shy of his fiftieth birthday, he died at 118 West Seventy-sixth Street—a boardinghouse, according to newspaper obituaries. Belle and Ralph's son Lester were at his bedside, and the other children were in an adjoining room.

Ralph's funeral was held the following Friday at Christ Church, an

Episcopal church at Broadway and Seventy-first Street. Many from the *Sun* attended, including Chester Lord, the managing editor, and John Bogart, the city editor, now retired, who many years earlier had planted the notion in Ralph's mind that a mysterious force guided a few fortunate reporters to news. There were also people from other newspapers and from magazines, and Frederic Remington was present.

Ralph was buried in New Jersey in the plot he had purchased in 1885 in Fair View Cemetery, across the Navesink River from Red Bank, where he had entered journalism as a printer's apprentice. No one ever got around to marking his grave with a headstone.

Notes
Bibliography
Index

Notes

Newspaper circulation figures for the nineteenth century are spotty. The *American Newspaper Directory,* published starting in 1869, is specific for the 1870s but for the 1880s and 1890s provides only vague categories, such as "not exceeding 100,000" or "exceeding 100,000." Other figures are scattered through journalism histories. The numbers used here are taken from a combination of sources. Although they are not as satisfactory as if a definitive central source existed, the general trends are clear.

Obvious typographical errors have been corrected in the newspaper stories quoted, but they were rare.

Complete authors' names, titles, and publishing information for items cited in the Notes are given in the Bibliography, pp. 293–300.

Newspapers cited are New York newspapers unless otherwise indicated.

The notes are keyed to the text by page number and catch phrase.

1. A Summons from Mr. Dana

Much of the material on the atmosphere and setting of the trial of Henry Ward Beecher comes from the pages of the New York *Daily Graphic,* including its richly detailed illustrations as well as Julian Ralph's stories. Robert Shaplen, *Free Love and Heavenly Sinners,* details the events leading up to the trial. A retrospective analysis of the trial that appeared in the New York *Times* on July 3, 1876, was also helpful. Two books by Milton Rugoff, *The Beechers* and *Prudery and Passion,* supplied useful background on Beecher, including the trial, and the Victorian era.

1 "We aim to give": *Daily Graphic,* Jan. 16, 1875.
2 "wholly alienated": quoted in Rugoff, *Beechers,* 475.
3 "more reporters": quoted in *Graphic,* Jan. 29, 1875.
3 "When counsel paused": *Graphic,* Jan. 11, 1875.
4 "would abound in indelicacies": *ibid.,* Jan. 12, 1875.
4 "The ferry-boats": *ibid.,* Jan. 22, 1875.
4 "The gallery is all attention": *ibid.,* Jan. 19, 1875.
5 "keeps intruders": *ibid.,* Jan. 26, 1875.
5 "smiling pleasantly": *ibid.,* Jan. 14, 1875.
5 "look of unconcern": *ibid.,* Jan. 13, 1875.
5 "crossed his legs": *ibid.,* Jan. 12, 1875.
5 "walked in slowly": *ibid.,* Feb. 3, 1875.
5 "hard, cold face": *ibid.,* Jan. 12, 1875.
7 "girlish": *ibid.*
7 "The jury looked": *ibid.,* Jan. 21, 1875.

7 "deferring to each other": *ibid.*, Jan. 14, 1875.
7 "never surrenders": *ibid.*, Mar. 12, 1875.
7 " Mr. Sherman came in": *ibid.*, Jan. 22, 1875.
7 "The two larger tables": *ibid.*, Jan. 29, 1875.
7–8 "Oh, gentlemen": *ibid.*, Jan. 13, 1875.
8 "There is a forced calmness": *ibid.*, Feb. 2, 1875.
8 "He puts his questions": *ibid.*, Feb. 9, 1875.
8 "measured out each sentence": *ibid.*, Jan. 18, 1875.
8 "When Mrs. Moulton left": *ibid.*, Feb. 19, 1875.
8–9 "Charity has always considered it": *ibid.*, Feb. 5, 1875.
9 "rich young man": *ibid.*, Jan. 21, 1875.
9 "Bessie Turner": *ibid.*, Feb. 15, 1875.
9 "veiled lady": *ibid.*, Feb. 6, 1875.
9 "the duty requires": *ibid.*, May 24, 1875.
10 "to look more and more at home": *ibid.*, Feb. 3, 1875.
10 "She is very clear": *ibid.*, Mar. 11, 1875.
10 "The Rev. Henry Ward Beecher": *ibid.*, Apr. 1, 1875.
10–11 "The turning point": *ibid.*, Apr. 2, 1875.
11 "tendrils of her affection": *Times*, Apr. 3, 1875.
11 "there was a mesmerism": *Graphic*, Apr. 2, 1875.
11 *Graphic* tally: *ibid.*, July 2, 1875.
11 "stood between two tables": *ibid.*, Apr. 19, 1875.
11 "He is said": *ibid.*, Apr. 23, 1875.
11 "any gentlemen": *ibid.*, May 24, 1875.
12 "gives the impression": *ibid.*, June 1, 1875.
12 "speaks as a clock ticks": *ibid.*
12 "the general impression": *ibid.*, June 24, 1875.
12 "He hit me": *ibid.*, June 25, 1875.
12 "Imagine eight hundred": *ibid.*, June 26, 1875.
12 "looking like the pale ghosts": *ibid.*
12 "there is a depth": *ibid.*
13 "This is, we believe": *ibid.*, July 2, 1875.
13 Reporter—Mr. Hull: *ibid.*
13 "dull as a cloister": *ibid.*
14 "the prince of reporters": Rosebault, 174.

2. The Item Gatherers

Frank Luther Mott, *American Journalism*, still provides an invaluable overview of the history of newspapers in the United States, sweeping in scope yet encyclopedic in detail. Edwin and Michael Emery, *The Press and America: An Interpretive History of the Mass Media*, has also been drawn on repeatedly. Other histories consulted include William Grosvenor Bleyer, *Main Currents in the History of American Journalism;* James Melvin Lee, *History of American Journalism;* Michael Schudson, *Discovering the News: A Social History of American Newspapers*; and Thomas C. Leonard, *The Power of the Press: The Birth of American Political Reporting.*

15 "If I have done": Ralph, *Making of a Journalist*, 189.

15 Between 1870 and 1900: Emery and Emery, 231.

15 In 1875: figures on number of newspapers in various cities from the *American Newspaper Directory* for 1875. Also see Mott, *American Journalism*, 411, 506–9.

16 "The prestige": Parton, "The New York Herald," 375–76.

16 "For the majority": Lesperance, 180.

17 "exhortations to the malefactors": quoted in F. Hudson, 57.

17 "He was the first": Lee, 154.

17 "first professional reporters": Mott, *American Journalism*, 155.

17 "four seats": Elizabeth Gregory McPherson, "Reporting the Debates of Congress," *Quarterly Journal of Speech* (April 1942): 141–48, quoted in Emery and Emery, 119.

18 Braddock's defeat: Pennsylvania *Gazette*, July 24, 1775.

18 "the Post-Chaise": *ibid.*, July 10, 1755.

18 "the papers of the Revolutionary period": Mott, *American Journalism*, 99.

19 "I never admit": Jerry W. Knudson, "The Jefferson Years: Response by the Press, 1801–1809" (Ph.D. dissertation, University of Virginia, 1962), 54, quoted in Leonard, 143.

19 "gazettes and journals": Thomas, *The History of Printing in America* (Worcester, Mass., 1810; rev. ed. Albany, N.Y., 1874), II, 189, quoted in Mott, *American Journalism*, 200.

19 "even on the largest papers": *ibid.*, 205.

19 "sustained vituperation": Emery and Emery, 94.

20 "the unhappy Transactions": Boston *Evening-Post*, Apr. 24, 1775, quoted in Mott, *American Journalism*, 80.

21 By 1850: *American Newspaper Directory* for 1875, 31.

21 "more interested in *news*": Emery and Emery, 142.

21–22 Day founds *Sun:* drawn largely from O'Brien, 21–138.

22–23 Bennett founds *Herald:* from Carlson, *The Man Who Made News*, 3–223, 300, supplemented by Crouthamel, 1–55.

22 "the Stock Exchange": Carlson, 124.

24 Greeley interview with Young: Parton, *Life of Horace Greeley*, 422.

23–25 Raymond founds *Times:* from F. Brown, 3–102.

24 "I fear": *ibid.*, 32.

25 "Raymond's contribution": Emery and Emery, 153.

26 "hired reporters": *The Diary of John Quincy Adams*, ed. Allan Nevins, (New York: Frederick Ungar Publishing, 1969), 543, quoted in Schudson, 24.

26 "was compelled": Halstead, 712.

26 "there was mingled": *ibid.*, 713.

26 "These were conservative times": *ibid.*, 714.

27 "Bread and the Newspaper": Holmes, 346.

3. Country Journalist

A multiplicity of sources—city directories, census records, occasional personal references in his articles and books, obituaries—provide clues to Julian Ralph's otherwise undocumented personal life. A sense of the atmosphere in which he grew up emerges from material on New York and Red Bank in the mid-1800s. Dr. Joseph E. Ralph of Red Bank, a great-nephew of Julian, was able to shed light on Julian's family circumstances, and further hints were gleaned from studies of the economic status of doctors in the nineteenth century. Similarly, printers' manuals and other material on printing contribute to a picture of young Julian entering journalism as a printer's apprentice.

28 "where I belong": letter to Frederic Remington, May 9, 1900, New York Public Library.

28 "is very worldly": Remington, "Julian Ralph."

28–29 "Traffic jams": Rosebault, 150–51.

29 "I still hate": letter, May 9, 1900.

29 "He drops into a Canadian forest": Remington, "Julian Ralph."

30–31 Status of doctors: Starr, *The Social Transformation of American Medicine,* deals with the economic and social status of physicians in the United States in the nineteenth century.

31–32 1869–70 high school enrollment: Cubberley, 627.

32 During the Greco-Turkish war: Ralph, *Making of a Journalist,* 79.

32 Favorite books: *ibid.,* 10.

33 Hunter material: drawn largely from Hunter, *The Autobiography of Dr. Thomas Hunter.*

33 "warned the boys": *ibid.,* 124.

33 "There was a general deficiency": *Times,* July 11, 1870.

34 "No man born": Ralph, *Making of a Journalist,* 8.

34 "Newspapermen are born": *ibid.,* 175.

34 "he could not help": *Times,* Dec. 5, 1903.

34–35 "The principal source": quoted with no source in H. Wilson, I, 356.

35 "Mrs. Ralph desires": New Jersey *Standard,* Dec. 23, 1870.

36 Information on New Jersey *Standard: American Newspaper Directory* for 1870.

36 "Men who appreciate": *Wisconsin Press Association Proceedings* for 1862, 110.

37 "School masters": *ibid.,* 108.

37 "For my own part": *ibid.,* 109.

37 "I'd a damned sight": Chambers, 3.

37–38 "The idea prevailed": Lord, "Reminiscences," 9.

38 "of the old-fashioned": Baker, 312.

38 "I cringe": *ibid.,* 262.

38 "Has he had": MacKellar, 103.

38 "should understand": *ibid.,* 180.

39 "essays to empty": *ibid.,* 104.

39 "Pick and click": *ibid.,* xii.

39 "such as swinging": *ibid.,* 104.

39 Congdon on printing: Congdon, 324–25.

39 "his mind": *Wisconsin Press Association Proceedings* for 1862, 109.

40 "The handling": *Times,* Dec. 5, 1903.

40 "I became": Ralph, *Making of a Journalist,* 12.

40 "When found": New Jersey *Standard,* Feb. 11, 1870.
40 Toms River incident: Ralph, *Making of a Journalist,* 134–35.
40 *Leader* fails: F. Ellis, 604.
41 One tale remains: Ralph, *Making of a Journalist,* 136–37.

4. 'I Have Pictured It as I Saw It'

Four books were especially useful for their accounts of the experiences of young reporters starting out in New York: Julius Chambers, *News Hunting on Three Continents;* Theodore Dreiser, *A Book About Myself;* Alexander Dana Noyes, *The Market Place: Reminiscences of a Financial Editor;* and Charles E. Russell, *These Shifting Scenes.* A pamphlet by Selah Merrill Clarke, *Frivolous Recollections of the Humble Side of Old Days in New York Newspaperdom,* contributed several anecdotes.

44 "steep and dark" stairs to "kid reporters": Chambers, 3–4.
44 "We had pictured": Russell, 35.
44 "We climbed": *ibid.,* 31.
45 "How on earth": *ibid.,* 35.
45 On a second visit: Chambers, 5–6.
45 "frightful barrack": Russell, 37.
45 "Whoja wanta see?": Dreiser, 463.
45–46 Dreiser-Brisbane encounter: *ibid.,* 466–67.
47 "The *Tribune*": Noyes, 5–6.
47 "an applicant": *ibid.,* 6.
47 "unconquerable persistence": Ralph, *Making of a Journalist,* 99.
48 *World's* press falls: S. Clarke, 22.
49 "Imagine a young fellow": *ibid.,* 10.
49 "I thought": *ibid.*
49 "It is thought: *World,* May 25, 1873.
49 "lively style": *ibid.*
49–50 Oysters caused insanity: *ibid.,* Nov. 9, 1873.
50 "whatever rots": *ibid.,* May 29, 1873.
50–51 Corporal punishment: Barnes, 57.
51 Ralph was one of six: Ralph, *Making of a Journalist,* 126–27.
51 Brief item on whippings: *World,* May 25, 1873.
51–53 Second whipping story: *ibid.,* May 27, 1873.
53 Vanderbilt encounter: Ralph, *Making of a Journalist,* 7.
54–55 *Graphic* history: Horgan, 360–62.
54 "among families": *American Newspaper Directory* for 1875, 143.
54 "childish": *Nation,* May 7, 1896: 356, quoted in Bleyer, 287.
55 "An unparalleled feat": *Graphic,* May 27, 1875.
55 "the most complete pictorial history": Horgan, 360.
55–57 Bungled hanging: Ralph, *Making of a Journalist,* 32–33; *Graphic,* Jan. 15, 1875; *Times,* Jan. 16, 1875.
56 "If the neck is not broken": Barnes, 238.
56–57 "writhing in agonizing contortions": *Graphic,* Jan. 15, 1875.

57 "down the side of the gully": Ralph, *Making of a Journalist,* 33.
57–58 "I pursued": *ibid.,* 6.

5. Dana and the *Sun*

Three books powerfully evoke the atmosphere of the *Sun* in the late 1800s: Frank M. O'Brien, *The Story of the Sun;* Charles J. Rosebault, *When Dana Was the Sun;* and Edward P. Mitchell, *Memoirs of an Editor.* Candace Stone, *Dana and the Sun,* follows the twists and turns of the *Sun's* editorial policy. Most useful of all in getting the flavor of the *Sun* were the files of the newspaper itself.

59 "In my opinion": *Sun,* Aug. 24, 1871, quoted in Stone, 53.
59 "Dana was the *Sun*": James H. Wilson, 393.
59–60 "No citizen": John A. Cockerill, "Some Phases of Contemporary Journalism," *Cosmopolitan* (Oct. 1892), quoted in Stone, 115.
60 "Your articles have stirred": O'Brien, x.
60 "I never knew": Mitchell, 198.
60 "model newspaper office": reprint of *Harper's* advertisement in Dyer, 2.
61 "Surroundings were nothing": O'Brien, 248.
63 "the usual commonplace": Mitchell, 124–25.
63 "always had a little grudge": Dana, 28.
64 50,000 "mechanics and small merchants": Bleyer, 295.
64 "The realist": Parrington, III, 44.
65 "Turn the rascals out": Lord, "Reminiscences," 58.
65 "a good man": *Sun,* Oct. 18, 1880.
65 "We wish it": Dyer, 1.
65 "impossible for anybody": Riis, *Making of an American,* 239.
65 "That he ever": Remington, "Julian Ralph."
65–66 "clearness of brain": Ralph, *Making of a Journalist,* 51.
66 "a high art": Dana, 54.
66 "the eye": *ibid.,* 56.
66 "The first thing": *ibid.,* 12.
66 "a good part": Noyes, 31.
66 "Life was everything": O'Brien, 244.
66 "a unique comprehension": Abbot, 26.
67 "that certain kinds of news": Dana, 12.
67 "to encourage originality": Bleyer, 298.
67 "The invariable law": Dana, 102–3.
67 "Mr. Lord": O'Brien, 245.
67–68 "It was a model": Abbot, 26.
68 Bearded women: *Sun,* Nov. 3, 1878.
68 "Another Lunatic": *Sun,* Oct. 18, 1875.
69 Dana and clubs: Mitchell, 126; Rosebault, 185.
70 Advertising editorial: *Sun,* Apr. 3, 1878, quoted in Stone, 47.
70 "To have worked": Abbot, 24.
70 "worked with Dana": Field, I, 97–104.

70 "It was mainly education": Mitchell, 157.
71 "This paper is for people": O'Brien, 267.
71 "I started": Lord, "Reminiscences," 8.
71 "freethinkers": *ibid.*
71 "When a dog bites": O'Brien, 241.
72 " 'I notice' ": *ibid., 282–83.*
72 "when suddenly a current of news": Ralph, *Making of a Journalist,* 66–67.
72 "None except newspapermen": *ibid.,* 64.
72 "an exalted hunch": O'Brien, 335.
73 "this strange gift": Ralph, *Making of a Journalist,* 63.
73 "Let every man": Dana, 52.
73 "It was as natural": James H. Wilson, 511.
73 "I think I would have killed": Lord, "Reminiscences," 52.
73 "Mr. Rosebault must be discharged": Rosebault, 244.
74 "One such looked up": *ibid.,* 253–54.
74 "Mr. Bogart, who wrote": *ibid.,* 256.
74 "to project a violent stream": Mitchell, 122–24.
75 "The application of Mrs. Jane Smith": O'Brien, 279.
75 "Rhetoric becomes": Dyer, 5.
75 "stamp on the cobbles": *A Farewell Dinner to the Old Sun Building,* 4.

6. Marching Through History

77 "treasures": Ralph, *Making of a Journalist,* 93.
77 "all young men": Dyer, 2.
78 "untiring in mind": O'Brien, 331.
78 "he should be familiar": Leslie, 100.
80 Material on early use of telephone from Morris, 208–10; Lockwood, 279; and Mott, *American Journalism,* 498–99.
80 "a rank evasion": Rosebault, 246.
80 "I was told": *Farewell Dinner,* 27.
80–81 "Whatever faults": O'Brien, 284.
81 "There is probably no industry": "The Profession of Journalism," 38.
81 *Tribune* pay: Noyes, 23.
81 *Commercial Advertiser* pay: Russell, 47.
82–83 "Sir," said Ralph: Ralph, "The Sixth Sense of a Newspaper Man."
85–86 "I disobeyed orders": *ibid.*
86 "the chief aim": Ralph, "The Newspaper Correspondent," 162.
86 "There was not a teaspoonful": Ralph, "Sixth Sense."
87 Molly Maguires background material primarily from Broehl, *The Molly Maguires,* and Rhodes, *History of the United States,* VIII, 52–87.
87 Mauch Chunk description from Schneur and Canfield.
87 Ralph concocts rumor: Ralph, *Making of a Journalist,* 23.
88 "Under the shadow": *Sun,* June 20, 1877.
88 "greeted his visitors": *Sun,* June 21, 1877.
88–89 Account of hanging: *Sun,* June 22, 1877.

89 Wake incident: *Sun,* June 23, 1877; Ralph, *Making of a Journalist,* 23–25.
89 Reminiscing about Ralph: Remington, "Julian Ralph."
89–91 History of railroad strike from Rhodes, 13–51, and Nevins, *The Emergence of Modern America,* 385–92.
90 "The action of the mob": Rhodes, 46.
91, 93 "The sun dawned": *Sun,* July 23, 1877.

7. 'Get What You're Sent For'

94 "practical newspaper man": Campbell-Copeland, iii.
94 "A gentlemanly address": *ibid.,* 9.
94 Covering fires: *ibid.,* 22–25.
94 Weddings: *ibid.,* 18–19.
94 "does a reporter need": *ibid.,* 19.
95 "flitting about": *ibid.,* 20.
95 "In writing up": *ibid.,* 33.
95 "A very little effort": *ibid.*
95 "Neatness in dress": *ibid.,* 31.
96 "I had rather take": Dana, 32.
96 "Dana was interested": O'Brien, 251.
96 "must be universal": Dana, 14.
96 "I never saw": *ibid.,* 89.
96 "There is no question": *ibid.,* 33.
96 "the critical faculty": *ibid.,* 35–36.
96–97 "state them exactly": *ibid.,* 54.
97 "or the lack of it": Ralph, *Making of a Journalist,* 9.
97 "Whoever cannot": *ibid.*
97 "perceived instantly": quoted with no source in Nixon, 342.
97 "the light or intuition": Ralph, *Making of a Journalist,* 14.
98 "He must have": Ralph, "Newspaper Correspondent," 154–55.
98 "Unconquerable": Ralph, *Making of a Journalist,* 99.
98 "indomitable": *ibid.,* 140.
98 " 'Follow the copy' ": *ibid.,* 34.
99 "Let me tell you": *ibid.,* 32.
99 "The architect listened": *ibid.,* 47–48.
99 "went poking": Riis, *Making of an American,* 153.
99 "will take the other side": *ibid.,* 154.
100 "One was when": *ibid.,* 154–55.
100–2 Fielders's story on the *Fulda* sinking and the account of the reporters' exploit appeared in the *Times* for Mar. 15 and 16, 1886, respectively.
102 By one account: Russell, 300–1.
102 At a shipboard dinner: Ralph, "Newspaper Correspondent," 161.
102–3 Coal-mine disaster: *ibid.,* 159–60.
103–4 Phoebe Paullin case: Ralph's story appeared in the *Sun* for Nov. 28, 1883.
104 "As I could not judge": Ralph, "Newspaper Correspondent," 161.
104–5 Meighan's career: obituary in *Times,* Mar. 30, 1929.

104–5 James Gordon Bennett, Jr., is vividly depicted in O'Connor, *The Scandalous Mr. Bennett.*

105–7 Political assignment described in Meighan, 575–77.

106 "conversational intercourse": *Herald,* Oct. 3, 1871.

107 "about like turning Niagara Falls": McCullough, *Johnstown Flood,* 102.

107–10 Russell's account of his ordeal in reaching Johnstown comes from Russell, 146–61.

8. Rules of the Game

111–13 Ralph's coverage of Arthur's fishing trip appeared in the *Sun* between Sept. 28 and Oct. 8, 1882.

111–12 "The pernicious and costly example": *ibid.,* Sept. 29, 1882.

112 "At half-past 9 o'clock": quoted *ibid.,* Oct. 2, 1882.

112–13 "with which he pursues the President": *ibid.,* Oct. 5, 1882.

113 "from among the dishes": *ibid.,* Oct. 4, 1882.

113 "Why, that's all right": Ralph, "Newspaper Correspondent," 154.

114 Misrepresentation was fine: Churchill, *Park Row,* 88.

114 At the *World:* Swanberg, *Pulitzer,* 113, 115.

114 Nellie Bly: Ross, 48–59.

114–15 Chambers recollections: Chambers, 26–35, 241–44, 76–80.

115 "never print an interview": Dana, 19.

115 Lord praises reporter: O'Brien, 372.

115–16 Mallon incident: *ibid.,* 382.

116 "the wise city editor": Cobb, 79.

116 Dreiser material from Dreiser, 152–53.

116 "Note-books and pencils": Ralph, *Making of a Journalist,* 46.

117 Fast new train: *ibid.,* 34.

117 Fire hazards in theaters: *ibid.,* 141–42.

118 Room for debate: *ibid.,* 34–35.

118–20 Account of press behavior at time of Cleveland's wedding drawn largely from *Times* for April, May, and June 1886.

119 "but two persons": *Times,* April 22, 1886.

119 "got a severe wigging": *ibid.,* May 17, 1886.

120 "When President Cleveland": quoted anonymously in Bishop, 533.

120 "All in all": *Times,* June 10, 1886.

121 "impudent inquisition": Nevins, ed., *Letters of Grover Cleveland,* 106.

121 "charged with the duty": *ibid.,* 112.

121 "Nobody has a right": *Nation,* June 3, 1886, quoted in Pollard, 509.

121 "the lowest occupation": *Nation,* June 10, 1886, quoted in Pollard, 510.

121 "an impertinent intrusion": *Journalist,* June 5, 1886, quoted in Mott, *American Journalism,* 511.

121 "Suppose that these acts": Bishop, 534.

122 "While there are reporters": Ralph, "Newspaper Correspondent," 156.

122–23 "MISS KITTY": *Sun,* Feb. 23, 1883.

123 "HE COMETH NOT": *ibid.,* June 3, 1887.

123 "The press is overstepping": Warren and Brandeis, 196.

123 "comes to one's fireside": Long, 4.

123 "I cannot believe": Shattuck, 58.

124 "Reporters on all reputable papers": Arthur, 36.

125 Sherman incident: Russell, 264–65.

125 "The 'interview,' as at present": "Interviewing," 67.

125 "this new thing": White, 827.

125 "the pernicious habit": Poore, *Perley's Reminiscences*, II, 525.

125–26 "the interview system": G. Townsend, 634.

126 "elevates prying": White, 827.

126 Beecher funeral: "Hunting Celebrities," 1358.

126 "The merest charlatans": Frothingham, 185.

126 "What do you think": Banks, 198.

126 "what did they think": Dreiser, 149–51.

126 "as a person": "Interviewing," 67.

126–27 "Washington correspondents": Poore, *Perley's Reminiscences*, I, 400.

127 "the neatest and handiest things": Atlanta *Constitution*, Aug. 16, 1879.

127 Vestryman incident: Ralph, *Making of a Journalist*, 46–47.

127 "what a great man": *ibid.*, 40.

127 Lily Langtry: *Sun*, Oct. 24, 1882.

127 A director: *ibid.*, Mar. 1, 1883.

127–28 Grant's doctor: *ibid.*, Jan. 11, 1885.

128 Sailors can't swim: *ibid.*, Oct. 16, 1882.

128 Fat criminals: *ibid.*, Nov. 5, 1882.

128 Drunkenness a sin: *ibid.*, Nov. 9, 1882.

128 Delmonico's bouncer: *ibid.*, Feb. 28, 1883.

128–29 "INTERVIEWING VANDERBILT": quoted in O'Brien, 316.

9. The Age of Corruption

130 Delavan description: Ralph's stories and *Albany Illustrated*, 34.

130 "the big hotel buzzed": *Sun*, Jan. 5, 1885.

130–31 Capitol description from Phelps, Roseberry, and Schuyler.

131 "took turns": *Sun*, Feb. 20, 1885.

132 Roosevelt "has snuffed the battle": *Sun*, Jan. 3, 1885.

132 Background on corruption from Nevins, *Emergence of Modern America*, 178–202; D. Ellis et al.; and Callow.

132–33 "FRAUD AND FORGERY": *Times*, Nov. 3, 1880.

133 "The ground of opposition": *Sun*, Nov. 2, 1884.

133 Talk of "objectivity": Schudson, 120.

133 Out of the West: Watson, 301–10.

133 Chicago fire fake: Bent, 98.

133 Faked sermon: Sprogle, 140.

133 Zoo hoax: *Herald*, Nov. 9, 1874.

135 Dreiser admits faking: Dreiser, 134.

135 "I always made it a rule": Salisbury, 438.

135 *Nation* sees side benefit: "Interviewing," 67.

135 "LOVED THE COOK": Swanberg, *Pulitzer,* 59, 74–75.

135 "an almost universal practice": Hills, 154.

135–36 "In spite of the fact": Edwin L. Shuman, *Steps Into Journalism* (Evanston, Ill.: Correspondence School of Journalism, 1894), 66, quoted in Schudson, 79.

136 "Accuracy" signs: Dreiser, 467.

136 Dreiser's faked fight story: *ibid.,* 483–84.

137 "documentary fiction": Schudson, 64.

137 "As a matter of fact": letter to Charles Davis, quoted in Langford, 103.

137 Salisbury fake in *Sun:* Salisbury, 58.

137 "the publisher is everything": Parton, "Journalism as a Profession for Young Men," 103.

138 "In nine cases out of ten": quoted in Parton, *ibid.,* 104.

138 "I hear of critics": Ralph, *Making of a Journalist,* 142.

138 "To be a money-writer": Browne, 297.

138 Grady profits from stock: Nixon, 352.

138 Pennsylvania Railroad: Bowers, 371.

138 Tweed Ring: Parton, "The Government of the City of New York," 418.

138 Republicans pay off reporters: *Zachariah Chandler: An Outline Sketch of His Life and Public Services,* 315.

138–39 Babcock's caller: McDonald, 149.

139 Pamphlet attacks *Sun:* James B. Mix, *The Biter Bit.* Although the pamphlet was published anonymously, Mix was soon identified as the author.

139 Dana dismissed: Stone, 390; Lee, 326–27.

130 Hitchcock's wealth: Rosebault, 169.

139–40 Soteldo incident: W. Hudson, 24–25.

140 "hayseed" legislators: *Sun,* Feb. 4, 1886.

140 "The Senate was stupider": *ibid.,* Feb. 21, 1885.

140 "Day follows day": *ibid.,* March 4, 1885. Ralph, who visited Washington briefly in March of 1885 to cover the Presidential inauguration, appears to have had stories with both Albany and Washington datelines on this date; the Albany story, which contained no timely news, could have been written in advance.

141 "The raffle": *ibid.,* Jan. 3, 1886.

141 "They went among the soreheads": *ibid.,* Jan. 13, 1885.

141 Plunkett's bill: *ibid.,* Feb. 27, 1885.

141 Capitol restaurant spat: *ibid.,* Feb. 27, 1886.

141 Corruption hearings: *ibid.,* Feb. 5, 1885.

141 Raines's speeches: *ibid.,* Mar. 10, 1885.

141–42 "Mr. Evarts replied": *ibid.,* Feb. 27, 1885.

142 "Of all my work": Ralph, *Making of a Journalist,* 143.

142 Sniggers ripple: *Sun,* Jan. 7, 1885.

142 As action nears: *ibid.,* Feb. 26, May 13, and May 15, 1885.

142 Flashes diamonds: *ibid.,* Jan. 3, 1885.

142 "make no reductions": *ibid.,* Jan. 21, 1886.

142 Crooked public works official: *ibid.,* May 12, 1886.

142–43 "Last year": *ibid.,* May 15, 1885.

143 Defeats for the forces of corruption: Numerous relevant stories ran in the *Sun* between Mar. 17 and Apr. 22, 1886.

143 "The Legislature need not be surprised": *ibid.*, Mar. 26, 1886.

143 Gas bill votes: *ibid.*, Apr. 9, Apr. 29, Apr. 30, May 1, 1885.

144 Ralph blames consumers: *ibid.*, May 8, 1885.

144 Passing reference to bribery: *ibid.*, May 16, 1885.

144 Baseball game: *ibid.*, May 8, 1885.

144 *Times* bribe story and editorial: May 1, 1885.

144–45 Account of bribe offer: Ralph, "Newspaper Correspondent," 165–66.

145 The *Sun* duly reported: *Sun*, Mar. 31, 1885.

145 Arrival of petitions: *ibid.*, Apr. 24, 1885.

145 Small newspapers bribed: *ibid.*, Mar. 2, 1886.

145 "a knight of the pen": Ralph, *Making of a Journalist*, 114.

145 "paternal government": *Sun*, Apr. 10, 1885.

145 Hitchcock stock: *Times*, May 14, 1885.

145 Nothing unkind to say: *Sun*, Jan. 7, 1885.

10. 'Drunkards, Deadbeats, and Bummers'

147 "The day has gone by": Ralph, "Newspaper Correspondent," 155–56.

148 *Sun* man and nuns: Russell, 258.

148 "Geniuses, ne'er-do-wells": Ralph, *Making of a Journalist*, 26–27.

148 "I have a great force": Wilkie, 131.

148–49 "Bohemian, particularly in New-York": Browne, 151.

149 "Most newspapermen of that time": Rosebault, 166.

149 "educated tramps": Parton, "Journalism as a Profession," 105.

149 "is the haven of shipwrecked ambitions": Baker, 313.

149 Drinking at Chicago *Times*: Wilkie, 318–19.

149 "There is still too much indulgence": *ibid*, 319.

150 "Owing to their irregular hours": Rosebault, 166.

150 "A reporter who drinks": Campbell-Copeland, 37.

150 Ralph fortified himself: Ralph, "Newspaper Correspondent," 162.

150 "The notion that alcohol": Lord, "Reminiscences," 55.

150–51 "It was a cosmopolitan assemblage": Salisbury, 56–57.

151 "The progress of empire": quoted in Salisbury, 57.

151 "Alcohol, among other pernicious effects": Parton, "Falsehood in the Daily Press," 276.

151 McAlpin's binge: *Farewell Dinner*, 26–27.

152 Reporter on Grant death watch: *ibid.*, 15.

152 "drunkards, deadbeats": Mott, *American Journalism*, 488.

152 *Harvard Monthly* article: Moore, 129–35.

152–53 "the metropolitan newspaper reporter of to-day": Matthews, 165.

153 "The rich man": Blake, 135.

153 Reporters behind a screen: Keller, 697; Rosebault, 258–60.

153 Early women reporters: Banks, 14–15.

153 Watrous offered five dollars: Watrous, 833.

154 "The lady of the house": Ralph, *Making of a Journalist*, 28.

154 "The reporters of the present day": Beebe, 42.

154 "regular bummers": *ibid.,* 45–46.

154 Are we not an ungrateful people: *ibid.,* 46–47.

155 Unionization: Mott, *American Journalism,* 490, 602–3.

155 Reporting as a profession: *Nation,* June 26, 1879, quoted in Mott, *American Journalism,* 489.

155 "Journalism in its essential qualifications": Keller, 691, 694.

155 Punctuality, no lounging: Campbell-Copeland, 38.

155 "The less a City Editor": *ibid.,* 39.

155 Wilkie on Storey: Wilkie, 112.

155 "a man of explosive temper": O'Connor, 77.

155 Never shook hands: Chambers, 308.

156 Assignment cards: Golding, 10.

156 "Who was Stanley": O'Connor, 114.

156 "establish business rules": Ralph, *Making of a Journalist,* 177.

156 "An editor in any of the metropolitan centres": Wright, 614.

156 Riis, the most dedicated: Riis, *Making of an American,* 143–44.

156–57 Using proscribed words: Noyes, 27.

157 Suspended reporter quits: Russell, 267–68.

157 Riis had the delicious experience: Riis, *Making of an American,* 144.

157 Things did not work out so well: J. Clarke, 106–7.

157 "I can hire": O'Connor, 77.

157–58 Russell out dollar: Russell, 71.

158 "It is a perfect establishment": Ralph, *Making of a Journalist,* 27–28.

158 Pay doubles from 1872 to 1892: Mott, *American Journalism,* 489.

158 Study of journalistic pay: H. King, 587–96.

158–59 Matthews on pay: Matthews, 166–67.

159 Comparisons with other fields: H. King, 595–96; Starr, 84–85.

159 "But three thousand dollars": Keller, 692.

159 "inside men": Nind, 156.

159 *Globe* reporters: O'Meara, 14–15.

159 One man over fifty: Keller, 693.

160 "There is no resting on one's oars": Ralph, *Making of a Journalist,* 139.

160 "after that you will surely": Forman, 17.

160 "gray ghosts": Keller, 693.

160 Ralph's cemetery plot: Fair View Cemetery records.

160 Seventy-five dollars a week: Ralph, *Making of a Journalist,* 143.

160–61 Brooklyn description largely from McCullough, *Great Bridge,* and Ralph, "The City of Brooklyn."

161 "works for New York": Ralph, "The City of Brooklyn," 652–53.

162 "I cleared my throat": Ralph, *Making of a Journalist,* 49–50.

11. The Joy of the Chase

163–64 Midnight sessions at Doc Perry's: Abbot, 23–24.

164 "free tickets": Forman, 16.

164 "We were the first": Noyes, 37.

164 This could be disillusioning: Noyes, 24.

164–65 "I had a wonderful feeling": Baker, 301.

165 "One experiences": Bent, 95–96.

166–67 Ralph investigates murder: Ralph, *Making of a Journalist*, 53–55.

167–68 Sources for muckrakers: Riis, *Making of an American;* Riis, *How the Other Half Lives;* Ware; Baker; Steffens; Kaplan, *Lincoln Steffens.*

168 "lifting a flap": Baker, 319.

168 "facts of scientific value": unpublished short story by Steffens, quoted in Kaplan, *Lincoln Steffens,* 58.

168 Shaped "the point of view": Riis, *Making of an American,* 132.

168 Not above plotting: *ibid.,* 138.

168 Water supply investigation: *ibid.,* 148–49.

168–69 Night in a police lodging house: *ibid.,* 45–46.

169 "to make the facts of the wrong plain": *ibid.,* 169.

169 "reporter's calling": *ibid.,* 62.

169 "not only got the news": Steffens, 203.

169 "a voice like a squeaky cellar-door": Riis, *Making of an American,* 205.

169 Shout "Amen!": *ibid.,* 161.

169 Lodging house victory: *ibid.,* 167–168.

169–70 "I took off my hat": *ibid.,* 240–41.

170 "Given youth": J. Clarke, 108.

170 "considerable drawback": *ibid.,* 104.

170 "the players were": *Farewell Dinner,* 26

170–71 Stumbled into financial journalism: Noyes, 38.

171 Phillips's assignments: O'Brien, 360.

171–72 "a prelude to adventure": Irwin, *Making of a Reporter,* 120.

172 It was an obvious case of arson: Ralph, *Making of a Journalist,* 56.

172 Gerrit Smith obituary: *Sun,* Dec. 28, 1874.

172 "One of the grandest": Parton, "Journalism as a Profession for Young Men," 106.

172–73 " 'Self-reliance' "; "no favors": Campbell-Copeland, 28.

173 "an inexcusable breach": *ibid.,* 37.

173 Competition in St. Louis: Dreiser, 153.

173 "combinations": Leslie, 100.

174 Segments called "ends": E. Townsend, 562.

174 "Woe to the man": Leslie, 100.

174 "Reporters who work": E. Townsend, 562.

174–75 "the great press associations": Ralph, "Newspaper Correspondent," 162.

175–76 Rosebault remembered: Rosebault, 247–50.

176 "distinctly a lower order": Ralph, *Making of a Journalist,* 64.

176 Police said nothing: Riis, *Making of an American,* 132.

176–77 "They appeared to proceed": Irwin, *Making of a Reporter,* 52.

177 Trunk murder: Thompson, 284–85.

177 Bludgeon slaying: Chambers, 81–90.

177 Extortionist confronts Sage: Russell, 299–300.

177 "Newspaper men cannot": Ralph, *Making of a Journalist,* 52.

177–80 Tillie Smith murder: *Sun,* Apr. 10–29, 1886.
179 "It would be difficult": *ibid.,* Apr. 27, 1886.
180 "Neither criminals": Ralph, *Making of a Journalist,* 53.
180 "can make no appointment": Ralph, "Newspaper Correspondent," 152.
180 Spears sent on new trip: Rosebault, 257.
180 "Until he has a thing to do": Ralph, *Making of a Journalist,* 6.

12. 'The Bright Young Men'

184–85 "blazing concentration": Irwin, *Making of a Reporter,* 104.
185 "most titanic": Abbot, 21.
185 Fairly democratic place: O'Brien, 359–61.
185 "the higher you go": Ralph, *Making of a Journalist,* 140.
186 "a passing fashion": Dana, 98.
186 "He's got it": Lord, *The Young Man and Journalism,* 13.
186 Hill denies interview: Salisbury, 437–38.
186 Early typewriters: Mott, *American Journalism,* 499.
186 "servants of commerce": Eggleston, 341.
186 "diffuse" style: Irwin, *Making of a Journalist,* 96.
187 New *World* building: Swanberg, *Pulitzer,* 154, 162–63.
187 "shabby little building": *World,* Apr. 11, 1888, quoted in Swanberg, *Pulitzer,* 149.
187 "the best newspaper": Stone, 53.
187 "Now I would not be understood": Dana, 82.
188 "By this time": O'Brien, 325–26.
189 Dana in his later years: Mitchell, Rosebault, and O'Brien describe Dana in this period, as does Lord, "Reminiscences."
189 "masterful tread": Rosebault, 255.
189 "Well, Mr. Lord": Marcosson, 97.
189 Dana attacks Pulitzer: Swanberg, *Pulitzer,* 139–41.
189–90 Rose Cleveland episode: Rosebault, 229. For an example of Rose Cleveland's work, see *Sun,* May 25, 1885.
190 "It is gratifying": *ibid.,* June 3, 1885.
190 "entirely broken down": *Times,* Oct. 27, 1886.
190 Office cat; O'Brien, 287–89.
190 "He hated all that was dull": Mitchell, 129.
190 "I suppose he does": Ralph, *Making of a Journalist,* 142–43.
190, 192 "This morning he printed": *Times,* Oct. 18, 1897.
192 "the kindliest man": *Farewell Dinner,* 27.
192 "He sets the vast engines": Edwards, 25.
193 "Take the entire matter": Marcosson, 110.
193 "The city editor": O'Brien, 383–84.
193–95 Selah Clarke: Rosebault, O'Brien, and Irwin portray Clarke in their books.
193 "see how a common, decent man": *Times,* Mar. 1, 1917.
193 Clarke and women: Irwin, *Making of a Reporter,* 101.
194 " 'Feel all the bones' ": Rosebault, 173.
194 "The teeth were good": *Sun,* Dec. 3, 1884.

194 Irwin covers train wreck: Irwin, *Making of a Reporter,* 102–5.
195 "by the eliding stroke": "No reporter ever worked": O'Brien, 384.
195 "accomplished men": Rosebault, 261.
196 "merry, jostling fellows": *ibid.,* 264.
196 "No taint of caste": Ralph, "Newspaper Correspondent," 152.
196 "the most brilliant": *ibid.*
196 "There were some excellent writers": Rosebault, 263.
197 "a tinner": *Sun,* Jan. 7, 1883.
197 "der negst ding": *ibid.,* Nov. 26, 1882.
197 "were somewhat of a preparatory school": Mitchell, 282.
197 "leading paragraphs": O'Brien, 321.
198 Phillips's lost child story: Marcosson, 103.
198 "To invent some new way": Lord, "Reminiscences," 58.
198 "a delicious aggregation": *ibid.,* 56.
198 "Some one said of Ralph": O'Brien, 331.
199–200 Blizzard: some details drawn from Werstein, *The Blizzard of '88.*
199 "It was as if New York": *Sun,* Mar. 13, 1888.
200 Ralph's story captivates copy desk: O'Brien, 334–35.
200–1 "A huge mud-covered oval": *Sun,* Nov. 29, 1889.

13. At Washington City

F. B. Marbut, *News From the Capital,* supplied essential background on Washington reporters. For the story of White House reporting, see James E. Pollard, *The Presidents and the Press.*

202–3 Description of vote tally: Ralph, "Election Night in a Newspaper Office."
202 Close election of 1884: Riggs, " 'Boss' Lord."
204 Seasonal job: G. Brown, 333.
204 President never interviewed: Riggs, "The American Newspaper," 494.
205 "The Chair placed before the Senate": *Sun,* Feb. 4, 1886.
205 President takes walk: *ibid.,* Mar. 18, 1889.
205 First Lady: *ibid.,* Dec. 1, 1887.
205 "received a deserved scolding": *ibid.,* Nov. 22, 1887.
205 Industrious correspondent: Poore, "Washington News," 234.
205 "a not inconsiderable fraction": Richardson, 26–27.
205–6 Washington correspondents' pay: Gibson, 720.
206 "miserable slanderers": Sen. John M. Niles, *Congressional Globe,* 25th Cong., 3rd sess., 1839, 100–3, quoted in Marbut, 57.
206 Backwoods congressman . . . secret Senate proceedings: Marbut, 71–72, 85–93, 140–46.
207 "Public men": Gibson, 719.
207 "it's a better thing": W. Hudson, 128.
207 "Shirt-collar" Spinoza: Riggs, "American Newspaper," 476.
207, 209 "Newspaper Row" is described in Marbut, 136–37; G. Brown, 330–41; Richardson, 27.

209 "The best Washington correspondents": Ralph, "Newspaper Correspondent," 156.

209 Earning money on the side: Lord, *Young Man and Journalism,* 10. Creative collaboration between journalists and politicians has a long history. See Leonard, 78–80.

209–10 "News coming out of Washington": E. Davis, 380.

210 "This more than anything else": *ibid.*

210 "Washington City:" Carpenter, 8.

210 "is a politician only": Chambers, 333.

211 "placed at their absolute disposal": *Sun,* June 4, 1892.

211 Twenty-hour days: Riggs, "American Newspaper," 490.

211 "The reporting of the great": Lord, *Young Man and Journalism,* 23.

211 "There is nothing in all the business": Ralph, "Newspaper Correspondent," 162.

211 Female stenographers: *Sun,* June 8, 1892.

211–12 "It is a picnic": *ibid.,* June 17, 1892.

212 "in his shirt sleeves": *ibid.,* June 10, 1892.

212 "perpetrated an oration": *ibid.,* June 11, 1892.

212 "a single-tax crank"; "shows about as much nerve": *ibid.,* June 23, 1892.

212–13 "if they have patience": *ibid.,* June 4, 1892.

213 "comely" woman reporter: *ibid.,* June 8, 1892.

213 "as calm and complacent as a frog": *ibid.,* June 24, 1892.

213–14 "Then the reporter": Ralph, "Newspaper Correspondent," 162.

214 "several Presidents": *ibid.,* 153.

214 "little newsmongers": Gideon Welles, *Diary of Gideon Welles* (Boston: Houghton Mifflin Co., 1911), II, 130–31, quoted in Pollard, 358.

214 "stranger" questions Grant: Nevins, *Hamilton Fish,* 584.

215 "You cannot realize": Gibson, 719.

215 "seldom if ever talked": Barry, "News-Getting," 284.

215 "necessary evil": Barry, *Forty Years,* 219.

215–16 "I had myself called": Ralph, "Newspaper Correspondent," 161.

215 Ralph's inauguration stories: *Sun,* Mar. 5, 1885; Mar. 5, 1889; Mar. 5, 1893.

217 "that settles it": *ibid.,* Mar. 5, 1885.

218 Arthur interview: *ibid.,* Mar. 5, 1885.

218 Cleveland interview: *ibid.,* Mar. 4, 1889.

218 Harrison interview: *ibid.,* Mar. 4, 1893.

218–19 "While waiting in an anteroom": Barry, *Forty Years,* 219–21.

220 Shouting floor speeches: *Sun,* Oct. 19, 1893. "Negro flunkey" to "great thing to be a Senator:" *ibid.,* Oct. 21, 1893.

220 Called each other liars: *ibid.,* Sept. 13, 1893.

220 Quorum calls: *ibid.,* Sept. 8, 1893.

220 "Thereupon the Senate": *ibid.,* Sept 14, 1893.

220–21 "rambling, incoherent": *ibid.,* Oct. 12, 1893.

221 "but no one was listening": *ibid.,* Oct. 17, 1893.

221–22 Harris interview: *ibid.,* Oct. 19, 1893.

222 "A few minutes after": Barry, *Forty Years,* 189–90.

222 "this is not the first time": *Sun,* Oct. 22, 1893.

14. Last Days at the *Sun*

223 *Chatter:* Mott, *American Magazines,* IV, 66.

223–24 "A good reporter": Nixon, 356.

224 Bylined Ralph article: *Sun,* Dec. 25, 1892.

224 "under the anonymous system": *ibid.,* Sept. 24, 1893.

224 "by impressing": McLellan, 273.

224–25"who cannot tell a display head": R. Davis, 856.

225 Cent a word: Mott, *American Magazines,* IV, 40.

225 Submitted articles for thirteen years: Ralph, *Making of a Journalist,* 11.

225 Meat-packing article: Ralph, "Killing Cattle for Two Continents."

225 Train derails: Ralph, "How It Feels to Be Wrecked on a Railway."

225 Chat with a retired sheriff: Ralph, "A Man From Another World."

226 Boredom at sea: Ralph, "A Novice at Sea."

226 "an English sentence": Ralph, "London Street Scenes," 559.

226 Saturday night at the Players: Samuels and Samuels, 128–29. The picture of Remington is taken largely from this book.

227 Davis and Remington: Langford, 180.

227 "sun dance": Samuels and Samuels, 142.

229 Salon of Ella Wheeler Wilcox: Mitchell, 278.

229 Special train: *Times,* June 29, 1890.

229 Theodore Roosevelt: Ralph, "Theodore Roosevelt."

229 Domestic life: Ralph, "City House of Today."

229 "Several ladies": *Times,* July 2, 1895.

230 Women of Paris "magnificent": Ralph, "Eight Days in Paris," 506.

230 Laden with tomahawks: Ralph, "My Indian Plunder."

230 Poem: Ralph, "Why Did We Marry?"

230 "Ralph is a large fat man": letter to Powhatan Clarke, 1890, quoted in Samuels and Samuels, 141.

230 "derby hat": Ralph, "My Indian Plunder," 640.

230 "goes into the backwoods": review of *On Canada's Frontier* in *Nation,* Sept. 15, 1892: 207.

230 Ralph's "good nature": review of *Dixie Sketches* in *Times,* Dec. 1, 1895.

231 Buffalo Bill's telephone: Ralph, "Behind the Wild West Scenes," 775.

231 Learns of an Englishman: Ralph, "Talking Musquash," 502.

231 Clovelly excursion: Ralph, "Quaint Corner of England."

231–32 "There is better quality": O'Brien, 330–31.

232 "repute as the best of American reporters": Edwards, 26–27.

233 "approved by the Department of Publicity": *Harper's Chicago and the World's Fair,* title page.

233 "The speech": *Sun,* May 2, 1893.

233 "If our entire American navy": *ibid.*

233 "Forty Beauties": *ibid.,* May 4, 1893.

233 "beautiful black-eyed odalisques": *ibid.,* May 2, 1893.

233 Snobbish comments: *ibid.,* May 4, 1893.

233–34 "Wives drag their husbands away": *ibid.,* May 3, 1893.

234–35 Background material on Lizzie Borden case from Pearson, ed., *Trial of Lizzie Borden*.

234 "Ophelia's words": *Sun*, June 13, 1893.

234 "He had held converse": *ibid.*, June 14, 1893.

234 "possibly the most distinguished": Pearson, 8.

235 "He only knows": *Sun*, June 12, 1893.

235 "were not as uniform": *ibid.*, June 16, 1893.

235 "with a wave of his hand": *ibid.*, June 10, 1893.

235 "The operation could almost": *ibid.*, June 9, 1893.

235 "the jurors will not find": *ibid.*, June 17, 1893.

235 "We don't burn witches": *ibid.*, June 20, 1893.

236 " 'Lizzie Andrew Borden' ": *ibid.*, June 21, 1893.

236–37 Rail journey: Ralph, "Going to the War in Asia."

237 Ocean Passage: Ralph, "A Voyage to Asia's War Scenes."

237 "a delightful book": review of *Alone in China* in *Nation*, Dec. 31, 1896: 501–2.

237 "stuck straight out": Ralph, "China's Greatest Danger."

238 "A higher influence than law": Ralph, "American Helplessness in China."

238 Front-page news: *Times*, Nov. 28, 1894.

238 "We can assure": *Sun*, Nov. 30, 1894.

238 "The correspondence shows": discussion of "American Helplessness," *Harper's Weekly*, Jan. 26, 1895: 78.

239 "Of powerful build": Ralph, "Frederic Remington."

239 "Norwegian snow-shoes": Ralph, "Twenty Feet of Snow."

239 "Mr. Hearst would be pleased": Swanberg, *Citizen Hearst*, 81–82.

239 "They are trying to get": letter to Charles Davis, quoted in Langford, 166.

15. Foreign Correspondent

240–41 The picture of the young Hearst is drawn largely from Swanberg, *Citizen Hearst*.

240–41 Pay level rises 25 percent: Abbot, 151.

241 Hearst pays Davis lavishly: Langford, 166, 179.

241 Brisbane's pay: Mott, *American Journalism*, 527.

241 Roosevelt interview: *Journal*, Nov. 27, 1895.

241 Stanley interview: *ibid.*, Nov. 10, 1895.

241 Sensational headlines: *ibid.*, Dec. 14, 1896: Aug. 6, 1896; Aug. 19, 1896.

242 "I had gone about four blocks": Ralph, *Making of a Journalist*, 63.

243 Exclusive story on treaty: *Journal*, Dec. 6, 1896.

243 Page of portraits: *ibid.*, Nov. 8, 1896.

244 European editor: *National Cyclopedia of American Biography*, 149.

244 Davis coronation stories: *ibid.*, May 23 and 27, 1896.

244 Oxfordshire Agricultural Show: *ibid.*, May 21, 1896.

244 Ralph's Russian pieces ran in *Harper's Monthly* for May, June, and July 1898.

245 Seven correspondents cover war: Swanberg, *Citizen Hearst*, 107.

245 "the filthy Turk": *Journal*, Feb. 24, 1897.

245 "a good friend of the Sultan": Ralph, "In the Wake of a War," 554.

245 "I was being played with": Ralph, "A Yankee Correspondent in South Africa," 70.

246 Stories in French: Ralph, *Making of a Journalist,* 79.

246 "CRANE AT VELESTINO": *Journal,* May 11, 1897.

246 "THE BLUE BADGE OF COWARDICE": *ibid.,* May 12, 1897.

247 "STEPHEN CRANE AND JULIAN RALPH": *ibid.,* May 23, 1897.

247 Twain in need of money: Kaplan, *Mr. Clemens,* 348.

247–48 Ralph's Jubilee stories: *Journal,* June 22, 23, 1897.

247 "that I could have touched the door": Ralph, "English Characteristics," 572.

248 Twain's three Jubilee articles: *Journal,* June 20, 23, 1897.

248 "a screaming woman": Arthur James Pegler, quoted in Hecht, 144.

248 "the circus business": Ralph, *Making of a Journalist,* 124.

251 "The English heat themselves": Ralph, "Keeping House in London," 869.

251 "no liquid of that color": speech in reply to toast at 179th meeting of the Sette of Odd Volumes, London, Jan. 3, 1896.

251 "the precision": Ralph, "English Characteristics," 562.

251 Full-time employees: Ralph, "Keeping House in London," 877.

252 "Etherians": Ralph, *An Angel in a Web.*

252 "I was all downcast": Ralph, "When the Clouds Fell Down," 474.

252 "Mr. Ralph is not by nature a fictionist": Bangs, sup. 4.

252 "the general trend": Brooklyn *Eagle,* Aug. 6, 1899.

253 "Will you wait a minute?" Ralph, *Making of a Journalist,* 65.

254 "But I never presumed": Ralph, "Newspaper Correspondent," 156.

254 Harmsworth and his London *Daily Mail* are covered in Ferris, *The House of Northcliffe.*

254 "the brightness and enterprise": Ralph, "London Journals," 35.

254–61, 263 Historical material on Boer War from Pakenham, *The Boer War,* and Farwell, *The Great Anglo-Boer War.*

255 "Belmont, Tuesday": *Herald,* Dec. 4, 1899.

255–56 "Alas! The days": Churchill, *Ian Hamilton's March* (London, 1900), 279, quoted in Hohenberg, 113–14.

256 Cut everything but sandstorm: Ralph, *War's Brighter Side,* 5.

256 "like theatrical cavalry": Ralph, *Towards Pretoria,* 150. Ralph's mailed dispatches to the London *Daily Mail* are collected in largely identical form in *Towards Pretoria.*

256 "quick, vivid jets": *ibid.,* 131.

256 "like flowing water": *ibid.,* 132.

256 "down on their knees": *ibid.,* 149.

256 "like the frying of fat": *ibid.,* 220.

256 "like melted diamonds": *ibid.,* 171.

256 "all over the hills": *ibid.,* 216.

256–57 The battle of Magersfontein is described in *Towards Pretoria,* 174–91.

256 "murderous fire": *Times,* Dec. 14, 1899.

257 "Therefore it happened": *Towards Pretoria,* 179–80. A shorter version appeared in London *Daily Mail,* Jan. 9, 1900.

258 "no word of praise": Rice, 341.

258–59 Ralph describes his life in the field at numerous places in his Boer War books.

258 "All places on the veldt": Ralph, *An American with Lord Roberts,* 109.

259 Treated like a stranger: Ralph, "Yankee Correspondent," 70.

259 "amateurs": Ralph, "Lessons of the War in South Africa."

259 "The pudding is perfect": *Towards Pretoria,* 211.

259 Thirteen correspondents died: Hohenberg, 139.

259 "into the forefront": Ralph, "Yankee Correspondent," 67.

259–60 Pinned down: Ralph, *Towards Pretoria,* 242–48. Although Ralph describes the incident in the third person, he was definitely involved.

260 The second incident: Ralph, "Yankee Correspondent," 69.

260–63 Ralph's experiences from Kimberley to his departure from South Africa are described in *An American With Lord Roberts* and *War's Brighter Side.*

260 Rhodes serves champagne: Pakenham, 345.

261 "God bless": Ralph, *An American With Lord Roberts,* 125.

263 "unutterably sick": *ibid.,* 249.

263 Letter to Remington: May 9, 1900, New York Public Library.

Epilogue

264 Letter to Remington: June 5, 1900, New York Public Library.

264 Pension for Steevens's wife: Ferris, 105.

265 "imaginative descriptions": Ralph, *An American With Lord Roberts,* 272.

265 "How lonely": Brooklyn *Eagle,* Nov. 4, 1900.

265 Churchill's kick: *ibid.,* Nov. 11, 1900.

265–66 Order of the Friendlies: Ralph, *War's Brighter Side,* 470–71.

266 Reviews of *An American With Lord Roberts:* Wallace Rice in *Dial,* May 16, 1901: 341; anonymous reviewer in *Atheneum* Feb. 2, 1901: 140. The *Atheneum* reviewed the book under its British title, *At Pretoria.*

266 Ralph at Carlsbad: Ralph, "Famous Cures and Humbugs of Europe," 666, 669–72.

266 Abdominal cancer: Cemetery records list liver cancer as the cause of Ralph's death, but tumors that attack the liver typically spread from other abdominal organs, such as the stomach and the pancreas.

266 Stuffy magazine piece: "The Moral Soundness of American Life."

267 "The work of a newspaper reporter": *Times,* June 7, 1902.

267 "Julian Ralph is not a literary man": *ibid.,* June 28, 1902.

267 Ralph replies: *ibid.,* July 12, 1902.

267 "He could see": *Harper's Weekly,* Jan. 31, 1903: 186.

267–68 Ralph's connection with the fair, as well as his death and funeral, were covered in New York newspapers, including the *Sun,* the *Times,* the *Tribune,* the *Herald,* and the *World* for Jan. 21, 1903, and the *Sun* and the *Herald* for Jan. 24, 1903.

Bibliography

Publications by Julian Ralph

Alone in China, and Other Stories. New York: Harper & Brothers, 1897.
"American Helplessness in China." *Harper's Weekly,* Dec. 1, 1894: 1143.
An American with Lord Roberts. New York: F. A. Stokes Co., 1901.
An Angel in a Web. New York: Harper & Brothers, 1899.
"Awakened Russia." *Harper's Monthly,* May 1898: 817–36.
"Behind the Wild West Scenes." *Harper's Weekly,* Aug. 18, 1894: 775–76.
"China's Greatest Danger." *Harper's Weekly,* Dec. 29, 1894: 1243.
"City House of To-day." *Harper's Weekly,* June 27, 1896: 643.
"The City of Brooklyn." *Harper's Monthly,* Apr. 1893: 650–71.
"The Czar's People." *Harper's Monthly,* June 1898: 2–24.
Dixie; or, Southern Scenes and Sketches. New York: Harper & Brothers, 1896.
"Eight Days in Paris." *Harper's Weekly,* July 4, 1891: 505–7.
"Election Night in a Newspaper Office." *Scribner's Magazine,* Nov. 1894: 531–44.
"English Characteristics." *Harper's Monthly,* Mar. 1899: 562–73.
"Famous Cures and Humbugs of Europe." *Cosmopolitan,* Apr. 1903: 665–72.
"Frederic Remington." *Harper's Weekly,* July 20, 1895: 688.
"Going to the War in Asia." *Harper's Weekly,* Sept. 15, 1894: 874.
Harper's Chicago and the World's Fair. New York: Harper & Brothers, 1893.
"How It Feels to Be Wrecked on a Railway." *Harper's Weekly,* Feb. 16, 1895: 150.
"In the Wake of a War." *Harper's Monthly,* Mar. 1898: 548–65.
"Keeping House in London." *Harper's Monthly,* May 1899: 866–81.
"Killing Cattle for Two Continents." *Harper's Weekly,* July 9, 1892: 670.
"Lessons of the War in South Africa." *Harper's Weekly,* Aug. 11, 1900: 756.
"London Journals." *Harper's Weekly,* Dec. 16, 1899: 35–36.
"London Street Scenes." *Harper's Weekly,* July 19, 1890: 559–60.
The Making of a Journalist. New York: Harper & Brothers, 1903.
"A Man From Another World." *Harper's Weekly,* Aug. 26, 1893: 815, 818.
The Millionairess. Boston: Lothrop Publishing Co., 1902.
"The Moral Soundness of American Life." *World's Work,* Nov. 1902: 2747–79.
"My Indian Plunder." *Scribner's Magazine,* Nov. 1896: 637–45.
"The Newspaper Correspondent." *Scribner's Magazine,* Aug. 1893: 150–66.
"A Novice at Sea." *Harper's Weekly,* Dec. 14, 1889: 1002–3.
On Canada's Frontier. New York: Harper & Brothers, 1892.
Our Great West. New York: Harper & Brothers, 1893.
People We Pass. New York: Harper & Brothers, 1896.

"A Prince of Georgia." *Harper's Monthly,* July 1898: 165–81.
A Prince of Georgia, and Other Tales. New York: Harper & Brothers, 1899.
"Quaint Corner of England." *Harper's Weekly,* May 10, 1890: 373–76.
"The Sixth Sense of a Newspaper Man." *Harper's Weekly,* June 10, 1893: 546.
Speech in reply to Toast of "The Guests" at 179th Meeting of the Sette of Odd Volumes, held at Limmer's Hotel, London, Friday, Jan. 3, 1896. Printed for private circulation by the Sette of Odd Volumes.
The Sun's German Barber. New York: New York News Co., 1883.
"Talking Musquash." *Harper's Monthly,* Mar. 1892: 490–510.
"Theodore Roosevelt." *Review of Reviews,* Aug. 1895: 159–71.
Towards Pretoria. New York: F. A. Stokes Co., 1900.
"Twenty Feet of Snow." *Harper's Weekly,* Feb. 9, 1895: 126.
"A Voyage to Asia's War Scenes." *Harper's Weekly,* Oct. 13, 1894: 975.
War's Brighter Side. London: C. A. Pearson, Ltd., 1901.
"When the Clouds Fell Down." *Harper's Monthly,* Aug. 1898: 465–76.
"Why Did We Marry?" *Critic,* June 9, 1894: 398.
"A Yankee Correspondent in South Africa." *Century,* Nov. 1900: 67–73.

Other Publications

Abbot, Willis J. *Watching the World Go By.* Boston: Little, Brown, & Co., 1933.
Albany Illustrated. Albany: The Argus Co., 1892.
American Newspaper Directory. New York: Geo. P. Rowell & Co., 1869–93.
American Newspaper Journalists, 1873–1900. Dictionary of Literary Biography, Vol. 23, ed. Perry J. Ashley. Detroit: Gale Research Co., 1983.
Arthur, John. "Reporting, Practical and Theoretical." *Writer,* Feb. 1889: 36–37.
Baehr, Harry W., Jr. *The New York Tribune Since the Civil War.* New York: Dodd, Mead & Co., 1936.
Baker, Ray Stannard. *Native American.* New York: Charles Scribner's Sons, 1941.
Bangs, John Kendrick. Review of *A Prince of Georgia and Other Tales. Harper's Monthly,* Oct. 1899: sup. 4.
Banks, Elizabeth L. *The Autobiography of a "Newspaper Girl."* New York: Dodd, Mead & Co., 1902.
Barnes, Harry Elmer. *The Story of Punishment.* Montclair, N.J.: Patterson Smith, 1972.
Barry, David S. *Forty Years in Washington.* Boston: Little, Brown, and Company, 1924.
———. "News-Getting at the Capital." *Chautauquan,* Dec. 1897: 282–86.
Beebe, William Hobart. *Miscellaneum Essayicum.* Orient, Long Island, N.Y., 1880.
Bent, Silas. *Ballyhoo: The Voice of the Press.* New York: Horace Liveright, 1927.
Bishop, Joseph B. "Newspaper Espionage." *Forum,* Aug. 1886: 529–37.
Blake, Henry W. "Reporters: Traditional, Actual, Ideal." *Writer,* Oct. 1887: 134–37.
Bleyer, Willard Grosvenor. *Main Currents in the History of American Journalism.* Boston: Houghton Mifflin Co., 1927.
Bowers, Claude G. *The Tragic Era.* Boston: Houghton Mifflin Co., 1929.
Brockway, Beman. *Fifty Years in Journalism.* Watertown, N.Y.: Daily Times Printing and Publishing House, 1891.

Broehl, Wayne G., Jr. *The Molly Maguires*. Cambridge: Harvard University Press, 1964.

Brown, Francis. *Raymond of the Times*. New York: W. W. Norton & Co., 1951.

Brown, George Rothwell. *Washington, a Not Too Serious History*. Baltimore: The Norman Publishing Co., 1930.

Brown, Henry Collins. *In the Golden Nineties*. Hastings on Hudson, N.Y.: Valentine's Manual, Inc., 1928.

Browne, Junius Henri. *The Great Metropolis: A Mirror of New York*. Hartford: American Publishing Co., 1869.

Bullard, F. Lauriston. *Famous War Correspondents*. Boston: Little, Brown & Co., 1914.

Callow, Alexander B., Jr. *The Tweed Ring*. New York: Oxford University Press, 1966.

Campbell-Copeland, Thomas. *The Ladder of Journalism: How to Climb It*. New York: Allan Forman, 1889.

Carlson, Oliver. *Brisbane*. New York: Stackpole Sons, 1937.

———. *The Man Who Made News: James Gordon Bennett*. New York: Duell, Sloan and Pearce, 1942.

Carpenter, Frank G. *Carp's Washington*. New York: McGraw-Hill Book Co., 1960.

Carson, William E. *Northcliffe: Britain's Man of Power*. New York: Dodge Publishing Co., 1918.

Chamberlin, Joseph Edgar. *The Boston Transcript: A History of Its First Hundred Years*. Boston: Houghton Mifflin Co., 1930.

Chambers, Julius. *News Hunting on Three Continents*. New York: Mitchell Kennerly, 1921.

Churchill, Allen. *Park Row*. New York: Rinehart & Co., 1958.

Clarke, Joseph I. C. *My Life and Memories*. New York, Dodd, Mead & Co., 1925.

Clarke, Selah Merrill. *Frivolous Recollections of the Humble Side of Old Days in New York Newspaperdom*. Reprinted from the American Press, New York, 1932.

Cobb, Irvin S. "I Admit I Am a Good Reporter." *American Magazine,* Aug. 1919: 60–61, 75–83.

Congdon, Charles Tabor. *Reminiscences of a Journalist*. Boston: J. R. Osgood & Co., 1880.

Crouthamel, James L. *Bennett's New York Herald and the Rise of the Popular Press*. Syracuse: Syracuse University Press, 1989.

Cubberley, Ellwood P. *Public Education in the United States*. Boston: Houghton Mifflin Co., 1919.

Dana, Charles A. *The Art of Newspaper Making*. New York: D. Appleton & Co., 1900.

Davis, Elmer. *History of the New York Times*. New York: The New York Times, 1921.

Davis, Richard Harding. "A Newspaperman's Man." *Harper's Weekly,* Sept. 3, 1892: 856.

Depew, Chauncey M. *My Memories of Eighty Years*. New York: Charles Scribner's Sons, 1922.

Dictionary of American Biography. New York: Charles Scribner's Sons, 1936.

Dreiser, Theodore. *A Book About Myself*. New York: Boni and Liveright, 1922.

Dyer, Oliver. *History of the "New York Sun."* New York, 1870.

Edwards, E. J. "The Men Who Make the New York 'Sun.' " *Munsey's Magazine*, Oct. 1893: 20–28.

Eggleston, George Cary. *Recollections of a Varied Life*. New York: Henry Holt & Co., 1910.

Ellis, David M., James A. Frost, Harold C. Syrett, Harry F. Carman. *A Short History of New York State*. Ithaca: Cornell University Press, 1957.

Ellis, Franklin. *History of Monmouth County, New Jersey*. Philadelphia: R. T. Peck & Co., 1885.

Emery, Edwin, and Michael Emery. *The Press and America: An Interpretive History of the Mass Media*. Englewood Cliffs, N.J.: Prentice-Hall, Inc., 1984.

A Farewell Dinner to the Old Sun Building. July 11, 1915. Published by the New York Sun.

Farwell, Byron. *The Great Anglo-Boer War*. New York: Harper and Row, 1976.

Federal Writers' Project, Delaware. *New Castle on the Delaware*. Originally published in 1936. Republished in 1950 by the New Castle Historical Society.

Ferris, Paul. *The House of Northcliffe*. New York: World Publishing Co., 1972.

Field, Eugene. *The Writings in Prose and Verse of Eugene Field*. Vol. 1. New York: Charles Scribner's Sons, 1897.

Forman, Allan. "The Chances in Journalism." *Author*, Feb. 1891: 15–17.

Frothingham, O. B. "The Interviewer." *Forum*, Apr. 1886: 183–90.

Gibson, E. J. "The Washington Correspondent." *Lippincott's Magazine*, Nov. 1894: 715–20.

Golding, Louis. *Memories of Old Park Row, 1887–1897*. Printed for private circulation, 1946.

Gramling, Oliver. *AP—The Story of News*. New York: Farrar and Rinehart, Inc., 1940.

Halstead, Murat. "Early Editorial Experiences." *Lippincott's Magazine*, June 1892: 710–15.

Hecht, Ben. *A Child of the Century*. New York: Simon and Schuster, 1954.

Hills, William H. "Advice to Newspaper Correspondents. IV. 'Faking.' " *Writer*, Nov. 1887: 154–56.

Hoe, Robert. *A Short History of the Printing Press*. New York: Robert Hoe, 1902.

Hohenberg, John. *Foreign Correspondence: The Great Reporters and Their Times*. New York: Columbia University Press, 1964.

Holmes, Oliver Wendell. "Bread and the Newspaper." *Atlantic Monthly*, Sept. 1861: 346–52.

Horgan, S. H. "The Origin and End of the 'New York Daily Graphic.' " *Inland Printer*, Dec. 1906: 360–62.

Hoyt, Edwin P. *The Vanderbilts and Their Fortunes*. Garden City, N.Y.: Doubleday & Co., 1962.

Hudson, Frederic. *Journalism in the United States from 1690 to 1872*. New York: Harper & Brothers, 1873.

Hudson, William. *Random Recollections of an Old Political Reporter*. New York: Cupples and Leon Company, 1911.

Hunter, Thomas. *The Autobiography of Dr. Thomas Hunter*. New York: Knickerbocker Press, 1931.

"Hunting Celebrities." *Independent*, June 13, 1901: 1355–60.

"Interviewing." *Nation,* Jan. 28, 1869: 66–67.

Irwin, Will. *The Making of a Reporter.* New York: G. P. Putnam's Sons, 1942.

———. "The New York Sun." *American Magazine,* Jan. 1909: 301–10.

Kaplan, Justin. *Lincoln Steffens.* New York: Simon and Schuster, 1974.

———. *Mr. Clemens and Mark Twain.* New York: Simon and Schuster, 1966.

Keller, J. W. "Journalism as a Career." *Forum,* Aug. 1893: 691–704.

King, Henry. "The Pay and Rank of Journalists." *Forum,* Jan. 1895: 587–96.

King, Moses, editor. *King's Handbook of New York.* Boston: M. King, 1893.

Knightley, Phillip. *The First Casualty.* New York: Harcourt Brace Jovanovich, 1975.

Kouwenhoven, John A. *The Columbia Historical Portrait of New York.* New York: Doubleday & Co., 1953.

Lambert's New York City Guide. New York: H. G. Lambert & Co., 1873.

Langford, Gerald. *The Richard Harding Davis Years.* New York: Holt, Rinehart and Winston, 1961.

Lee, James Melvin. *History of American Journalism.* Garden City, N.Y.: Garden City Publishing Co., 1923.

Leonard, Thomas C. *The Power of the Press: The Birth of American Political Reporting.* New York: Oxford University Press, 1986.

Leslie, Arthur. "The Making of a Newspaper." *Writer,* July 1899: 99–101.

Lesperance, John. "American Journalism." *Lippincott's Magazine,* Aug. 1871: 174–81.

Lockwood, Charles. *Manhattan Moves Uptown.* Boston: Houghton Mifflin Co., 1976.

Long, J. L. "Statute Regulations for the Press." *Writer,* Jan. 1889: 4–5.

Lord, Chester S. "Reminiscences of Charles A. Dana and the Old New York Sun." *Saturday Evening Post,* July 30, 1921: 8–9, 52, 55–56, 58.

———. *The Young Man and Journalism.* New York: Macmillan Co., 1922.

Lyman, Susan Elizabeth. *The Story of New York.* New York: Crown Publishers, Inc., 1964.

Lynch, Thomas. *The Printer's Manual.* Cincinnati: Cincinnati Type-Foundry, 1859.

MacKellar, Thomas. *The American Printer: A Manual of Typography.* Philadelphia: MacKellar, Smiths and Jordan, 1872 ed. Originally published in 1866.

Marbut, F. B. *News From the Capital.* Carbondale: Southern Illinois University Press, 1971.

Marcosson, Isaac. *David Graham Phillips and His Times.* New York: Dodd, Mead & Co., 1932.

Matthews, Albert Franklin. "The Metropolitan Newspaper Reporter." *Chautauquan,* Nov. 1893: 164–68.

McCullough, David. *The Great Bridge.* New York: Simon and Schuster, 1972.

———. *The Johnstown Flood.* New York: Simon and Schuster, 1968.

McDonald, John: *Secrets of the Great Whiskey Ring.* Chicago: Belford, Clarke & Co., 1880.

McFeely, William S. *Grant.* New York: W. W. Norton & Co., 1981.

McLellan, C. M. S. "The Commonplaceness of Anonymous Journalism." *Writer,* Nov. 1888: 271–74.

Meighan, W. J. C. "The Travelling Correspondent." *Lippincott's Magazine,* May 1892: 573–80.

Mitchell, Edward P. *Memoirs of an Editor.* New York: Charles Scribner's Sons, 1924.

Mix, James B. *The Biter Bit.* Washington, D.C., 1870. Published anonymously.

Moore, Charles. "What Inducements Has Journalism to Offer to Young Men Leaving College?" *Harvard Monthly,* June 1888: 129–35.

Morris, Lloyd. *Incredible New York.* New York: Random House, 1951.

Mott, Frank Luther. *American Journalism.* New York: Macmillan Co., 1947. Originally published in 1941.

———. *A History of American Magazines.* Vol. 4, 1885–1905. Cambridge, Mass.: The Belknap Press of Harvard University Press, 1957.

National Cyclopedia of American Biography, Vol. 1. Ann Arbor, Mich.: University Microfilms, 1967.

Nevins, Allan. *The Emergence of Modern America: 1865–1878.* New York: Macmillan Co., 1927.

———. *The Evening Post: A Century of Journalism.* New York: Boni and Liveright, 1922.

———. *Grover Cleveland.* New York: Dodd, Mead & Co., 1932.

———. *Hamilton Fish.* New York: Dodd, Mead & Co., 1937.

———., ed. *Letters of Grover Cleveland.* Boston: Houghton Mifflin Co., 1933.

Newberry, Lida, ed. *New Jersey: A Guide to Its Present and Past.* (Originally compiled by Federal Writers Project of the Works Progress Administration.) American Guide Series. New York: Hastings House, 1977.

Nind, J. N. "Civil Service Rules in the Newspaper Office." *Writer,* Nov. 1887: 156–57.

Nixon, Raymond B. "Henry W. Grady, Reporter." *Journalism Quarterly,* Dec. 1935: 341–56.

Noyes, Alexander Dana. *The Market Place: Reminiscences of a Financial Editor.* Boston: Little, Brown & Co., 1938.

O'Brien, Frank M. *The Story of the Sun.* New York: George H. Doran Co., 1918.

O'Connor, Richard. *The Scandalous Mr. Bennett.* New York: Doubleday & Co., 1962.

O'Meara, Stephen. "Does It Pay to Be a Reporter?" *Writer,* Apr. 1887: 14–15.

Pakenham, Thomas. *The Boer War.* New York: Random House, 1979.

Parker, George F. *Recollections of Grover Cleveland.* New York: Century Co., 1909.

Parrington, Vernon Louis. *Main Currents in American Thought.* Vol. 3. New York: Harcourt, Brace and Company, 1927.

Parton, James. "Falsehood in the Daily Press." *Harper's Monthly,* July 1874: 269–80.

———. "The Government of the City of New York." *North American Review,* Oct. 1866: 413–65.

———. "Journalism as a Profession for Young Men." *Writer,* May 1888: 103–6.

———. *Life of Horace Greeley.* Boston: J. R. Osgood & Co., 1872.

———. "The New York Herald." *North American Review,* Apr. 1866: 373–419.

Pearson, Edmund, ed. *Trial of Lizzie Borden.* Garden City, N.Y.: Doubleday, Doran & Co., 1937.

Perry, Edwin A. *The Boston Herald and Its History.* Boston, 1878.

Phelps, Henry P. *The Albany Hand-Book.* Albany: Brandow and Barton, 1884.

Pollard, James E. *The Presidents and the Press.* New York: Macmillan Co., 1947.

Poore, Ben: Perley. *Perley's Reminiscences of Sixty Years in the National Metropolis.* Philadelphia: Hubbard Brothers, 1886.

————. "Washington News." *Harper's Monthly*, Jan. 1874: 225–36.

"The Profession of Journalism." *Nation*, July 17, 1873: 37–38.

Ralph, Julian. Publications are listed on pp. 293–94.

Remington, Frederic. "Julian Ralph." *Harper's Weekly*, Feb. 24, 1894: 179.

Rhodes, James Ford. *History of the United States*. Vol. 8. New York: Macmillan Co., 1919.

Rice, Wallace. Review of *An American with Lord Roberts*. *Dial*, May 16, 1901: 341.

Richardson, Francis A. "Recollections of a Washington Correspondent." *Records of the Columbia Historical Society*, vol. 6, 24–42. Washington, D.C., 1903.

Riggs, Edward G. "The American Newspaper. The Newspaper and Politics." *Bookman*, July 1904: 476–95.

————. " 'Boss' Lord." *Harper's Weekly*, Mar. 1, 1913: 20.

Riis, Jacob A. *How the Other Half Lives*. Edited by Sam Bass Warner, Jr. Cambridge, Mass.: Belknap Press of Harvard University Press, 1970.

————. *The Making of an American*. New York: Macmillan Co., 1901.

Rosebault, Charles J. *When Dana Was the Sun*. New York: Robert M. McBride & Co., 1931.

Roseberry, Cecil R. *Capitol Story*. Albany: State of New York, 1964.

Ross, Ishbel. *Ladies of the Press*. New York: Harper & Brothers, 1936.

Rugoff, Milton. *The Beechers*. New York: Harper and Row, 1981.

————. *Prudery and Passion*. New York: G. P. Putnam's Sons, 1971.

Russell, Charles E. *These Shifting Scenes*. New York: Hodder and Stoughton, 1914.

Salisbury, William. *The Career of a Journalist*. New York: B. W. Dodge & Co., 1908.

Samuels, Peggy, and Harold Samuels, *Frederic Remington*. Garden City, N.Y.: Doubleday & Co., 1982.

Schneur and Canfield. *Illustrated and Descriptive Guide Book of Mauch Chunk—The Switzerland of America*. Athens, Pa.: Charles Hinton, 1874.

Schudson, Michael. *Discovering the News: A Social History of American Newspapers*. New York: Basic Books, 1978.

Schuyler, Montgomery. "The Capitol of New-York." *Scribner's Magazine*, Dec. 1879: 161–78.

Shaplen, Robert. *Free Love and Heavenly Sinners*. New York: Alfred A. Knopf, 1954.

Shattuck, H. R. "Reporters' Ethics." *Writer*, Mar. 1889: 57–58.

Sprogle, J. L. "A Reporter's Recollections." *Lippincott's Magazine*, Jan. 1899: 136–42.

Stallman, R. W. *Stephen Crane*. New York: George Braziller, 1968.

Starr, Paul. *The Social Transformation of American Medicine*. New York: Basic Books, 1982.

Steffens, Lincoln. *The Autobiography of Lincoln Steffens*. New York: Harcourt, Brace & Co., 1931.

Stone, Candace. *Dana and the Sun*. New York: Dodd, Mead & Co., 1938.

Swanberg, W. A. *Citizen Hearst*. New York: Charles Scribner's Sons, 1961.

————. *Pulitzer*. New York: Charles Scribner's Sons, 1967.

Thompson, Vance. "The Police Reporter." *Lippincott's Magazine*, Aug. 1898: 283–88.

Townsend, Edward W. "The American Newspaper. The Reporter." *Bookman*, Aug. 1904: 558–72.

Townsend, George Alfred. "An Interviewer Interviewed." *Lippincott's Magazine*, Nov. 1891: 630–38.

U.S. Bureau of the Census. *Historical Statistics of the United States, Colonial Times to 1970.* Washington, D.C.: U.S. Government Printing Office, 1975.

Villard, Oswald Garrison. *Some Newspapers and Newspaper-Men.* New York: Alfred A. Knopf, 1923.

Ware, Louise. *Jacob A. Riis: Police Reporter, Reformer, Useful Citizen.* New York: D. Appleton-Century Co., 1938.

Warren, Samuel D., and Louis D. Brandeis. "The Right to Privacy." *Harvard Law Review*, Dec. 1890: 193–220.

Watrous, A. E. "Some Experiences of a Reporter." *Lippincott's Magazine*, May 1887: 829–34.

Watson, Elmo Scott. "The Indian Wars and the Press, 1866–1891." *Journalism Quarterly*, Dec. 1940: 301–10.

Weisberger, Bernard A. *Reporters for the Union.* Boston: Little, Brown & Co., 1953.

Werstein, Irving. *The Blizzard of '88.* New York: Thomas Y. Crowell Co., 1960.

White, Richard Grant. "Wedding, Interviewing, et. Cetera." *Galaxy*, Dec. 1874: 822–30.

Who's Who in America, 1901–1902. Chicago: A. N. Marquis & Co.

Wilkie, Franc B. *Personal Reminiscences of Thirty-five Years of Journalism.* Chicago: F. J. Schulte & Co., 1891.

Wilson, Angus. *The Strange Ride of Rudyard Kipling.* New York: The Viking Press, 1978.

Wilson, Harold F. *The Jersey Shore.* 2 vols. New York: Lewis Historical Publishing Co., 1953.

Wilson, James Grant. *Memorial History of the City of New York.* Vol. 3. New York: New York History Co., 1893.

Wilson, James H. *Life of Charles A. Dana.* New York: Harper & Brothers, 1907.

Winkler, John K. *Hearst: An American Phenomenon.* London: Jonathan Cape, 1928.

Wisconsin Press Association Proceedings. 1862.

Wood's Illustrated Hand-Book to New York. New York: G. W. Carleton & Co., 1873.

Wright, John Livingston. "Reporters and Oversupply." *Arena*, Nov./Dec. 1898: 614–22.

Young, John P. *Journalism in California.* San Francisco: Chronicle Publishing Co., 1915.

Zachariah Chandler: An Outline Sketch of His Life and Public Services. Detroit: The Post and Tribune Company, 1880.

Index

Gentleman of the Press

was composed in 10.5 on 13 Times Roman
on a Linotron 202 by Keystone Typesetting, Inc., Orwigsburg,
Pennsylvania; printed by sheet-fed offset on 60-pound acid-
free Glatfelter Natural Smooth, Smyth-sewn and bound over
binder's boards in Arrestox B, with dust jackets printed and
laminated by Braun-Brumfield, Inc., Ann Arbor, Michigan;
designed by Kachergis Book Design, Pittsboro,
North Carolina; and published by
Syracuse University Press,
Syracuse, New York 13244-5160